New Proclamation

NEW PROCLAMATION

SERIES A, 1999

EASTER THROUGH PENTECOST

EASTER

ROBIN MATTISON

ROY HARRISVILLE

PENTECOST

THOMAS H. TROEGER

RALPH KLEIN

FORTRESS PRESS

MINNEAPOLIS

NEW PROCLAMATION
Series A, 1999
Easter through Pentecost

Scripture quotations, unless otherwise noted, are from the New Revised Standard Version Bible and are copyright © 1989 by the Division of Christian Education of the National Council of Churches in the United States of America and are used by permission.

Cover and book design: Joseph Bonyata
Illustrations: Tanja Butler, *Graphics for Worship,* copyright © 1996 Augsburg Fortress.

ISBN 0-8006-4240-6

The paper used in this publication meets the minimum requirements of American National Standard for Information Sciences—Permanence of Paper for Printed Library Materials, ANSI Z329.48-1984. ∞™

Manufactured in the U.S.A. AF 1-4240

03   02   01   00   99   1   2   3   4   5   6   7   8   9   10

CONTENTS

The Season of Pentecost
Thomas H. Troeger

PUBLISHER'S FOREWORD

Twenty-five years ago Fortress Press embarked on an ambitious project to produce a lectionary preaching resource that would provide the best in biblical exegetical aids for a variety of lectionary traditions. This resource, *Proclamation,* became both a pioneer and a standard-bearer in its field, sparking a host of similar products from other publishers. Few, however, have become as widely used and well known as *Proclamation.*

Thoroughly ecumenical and built around the three-year lectionary cycle, *Proclamation's* focus has always been on the biblical text first and foremost. Where other resources often have offered reprinted sermons or illustrations for the preacher to use or adapt, *Proclamation's* authors have always asserted the best resource for the preacher is the biblical text itself. *Proclamation* has always been premised on the idea that those who are well equipped to understand a pericope in both its historical and liturgical context will also be well equipped to compose meaningful and engaging sermons. For that reason, *Proclamation* consistently has invited the cream of North American biblical scholars and homileticians to offer their comments because of their commitments to the text.

New Proclamation represents a significant change in Fortress Press's approach to the lectionary resource, but it still retains the best of the hallmarks that have made it so widely used and appreciated. Long-time users of the series will immediately notice the most major change, that is, the switch from eight to two volumes per year. The volume you are holding covers the lectionary texts for approximately the second half of the church year, from Easter through Pentecost, which culminates with the Great Vigil of Easter. By going to this two-volume format, we are able to offer you a larger, workbook-style page size with a lay-flat binding and plenty of white space for taking notes.

Because the Evangelical Lutheran Church in America adopted the Revised Common Lectionary as its recommended lectionary source several years ago, the lectionary from the Lutheran Book of Worship no longer appears in *New Proclamation*. This allows our authors to write more expansively on each of the texts for each of the three lectionary traditions addressed here. When a text appears in less than all three of these lectionaries or is offered as an alternative text, these are clearly marked as follows: RC (Roman Catholic); RCL (Revised Common Lectionary); and BCP (Episcopal, for Book of Common Prayer).

Although they are not usually used as preaching texts, *New Proclamation* offers brief commentary on each assigned psalm (or, as they are listed, the Responsive Reading) for each preaching day so that the preacher can incorporate reflections on these readings as well in a sermon. Call-out quotes in the margins help signal significant themes in the texts for the day.

New Proclamation retains *Proclamation's* emphasis on the biblical text but offers a new focus on how the preacher may apply those texts to contemporary situations. Exegetical work is more concise, and thoughts on how the text addresses today's world and our personal situations take a more prominent role. Throughout most of the book, exegetical comments are addressed under the heading "Interpreting the Text," and the homiletical materials come under the heading "Responding to the Text." Readers will note, however, that sometimes there is not an easy division between exegesis and application; thus in her comments on the Easter texts Robin Mattison instead has organized her material somewhat differently.

Each section of this book is prefaced by a brief introduction that helps situate the liturgical season and its texts within the context of the church year. Unlike *Proclamation,* which was not dated according to its year of publication, this volume of *New Proclamation* is dated specifically for the year 1999 when the texts for Series A next appear. Although preachers may have to work a bit harder to reuse these books in three years' time, they will also find that the books should coordinate better with other dated lectionary materials that they may be using at the same time. When feast or saint's days land on a Sunday (such as St. James on July 25) in 1999, the texts for those days are commented on so that preachers have the option of celebrating those days appropriately. Those traditions that follow the numbering of propers or days in Ordinary Time will find those listed as well.

Other conveniences also appear in *New Proclamation*. Preachers who conduct services at different times on Easter will find Robin Mattison has commented on two different sets of texts that are appropriate for each of those times. Bibliographies and notes accompany most of the sections as well.

For all its changes, *New Proclamation* does not claim to reinvent the preaching lectionary resource. It is, in many ways, a work in progress and readers will see even more helpful changes in future volumes. One thing that has not changed, however, is the commitment to offer preachers access to the ideas of the best biblical scholars and homileticians in North America. Robin Mattison, Roy Harrisville, Thomas H. Troeger, and Ralph Klein have each risen to the occasion to address these texts in fresh ways and to make *New Proclamation* truly new. We are grateful to them for their contributions to this new effort.

THE SEASON OF EASTER

ROBIN MATTISON
ROY HARRISVILLE

"Let us not rest on our laurels," says Mary. "Moreover, let us not rest on...
God's lilies!" I laugh when she switches the plant identified with human
heroics for the plant identified with God's full triumph. Mary is my urban neighbor, but whether she be Mary of suburbia, Mary Magdalene, Mary, the Mother of
our Lord, and whether I, her hearer, be a neighbor, or you be a preacher or a
parishioner, her witness is terribly important. Let us do more than admire the
resurrection!

Mary's proclamation shaped my writing of this lectionary commentary. I
hope you will be encouraged by it to explore how the Easter season lections
instruct believers about their mission and encourage believers to offer the good
news in every time and every place. While still joining the season's exultation of
the power of God to save, I will focus on some less-studied dimensions of the lections. I will describe for you the patterns for coming to faith in these texts and
the models for mission noticeable in them. I shall also explore how these models
might be models that present-day believers might employ and what present-day
believers might expect as responses to their own proclamation.

Such a focus is possible because the Lectionary proposes sequential readings
from Acts during the Easter season. You might first think that these lections are
leaping ahead to the festival of Pentecost. In a way, they are. The lectionary bids
you think of two pilgrimages, "resurrection-to-Pentecost" and "Pentecost-to-
the-ends-of-the-earth" as parallel journeys toward faith and faithfulness made
possible by God's gracious action. The testimony to the resurrection goes forth
from the tomb to disciples on the verge of fully believing, in tandem with the testimony that goes forth from Pentecost to those further from believing.

Frequently, the Old Testament lesson alternatives provide a third pilgrimage, which you can set parallel to the other two pilgrimages. These lessons describe journeys of faith that are also spatially marked—"Egypt to the Promised Land" or "Babylon to Jerusalem." These journeys also show believers coming to confidence in God as the effect of what God has done for them.

Studying the pattern for coming to faith is not a review of what believers have done for themselves. What you will be learning is how these authors perceive that encounters with a persistent God and with God's witnesses create conviction in the unconvinced. They will focus our attention on the three qualities that all believers need to have full confidence in God:[1]

1. Knowledge . . . of the proper way to understand God and God's actions in the world;
2. Ability . . . to respond to God's saving actions;
3. Will . . . to overcome fear and to witness to what God has done.

The Easter season lections testify to their writers' hopes to empower much Gospel-telling. At the same time, the stories and contexts the writers choose to describe tell us that they were specifically concerned that their readers and hearers might not have a proper knowledge of the Divine, or fully effective skills for praising God and for neighboring others, or a firm will to do the Lord's bidding. How each writer portrays the presence of (or lack of) knowledge, will, or ability in various characters in the text will help us identify the patterns for coming to faith in these lessons.[2]

The first readers and hearers of these texts did have some concerns about the meaning of the cross and resurrection in the light of their past understanding of God. They sometimes affirmed that all power was in God's hands, but then concluded that they might rest upon God's lilies. Through this they undervalued the testimony that they had been given to make. They sometimes became frightened before death and too fearful to proclaim. Some of these same concerns are undoubtedly starting points for prayer and proclamation for the readers and hearers you serve.

The writers attend to their worries about their readers'/hearers'[3] understanding by proclaiming the effects that the resurrection and the Spirit's descent had on the earliest believers. Startling meetings with angels and the risen Lord gave those at the tomb and those on the way to Emmaus a changed view about death, scripture, the Messiah, and mission.

The second effect on believers, described in the narratives of the descent of the Holy Spirit, empowers willingness by Jesus' followers to proclaim their changed perspective to all peoples. This second effect—an eagerness to say what one has seen and come to understand—is principally described in the Easter Lessons chosen from Acts and from First Peter.

Along with Mary Magdalene and Mary of suburbia, may you and I not rest on God's lilies. We have been equipped by lily-empowered scripture writers to be persuaded that the power of God in Jesus and in the Holy Spirit will continue to transform listeners from caution born of misunderstanding to boldness born of knowledge and Spirit! They do not offer these narratives and epistles so that we might encourage our congregations to be solely stunned before the resurrection or to be simply admiring of the earliest believers. We are told these narratives and epistles so that you and those to whom you proclaim might observe the earliest believers at the thrilling step of coming to confidence in the word of God, and become persuaded to emulate these first believers' proclamation.

Let us pray that all of us may so re-present the powerful effect of knowledge of the resurrection and the Holy Spirit's powerful effect on the will of believers that some, already rejoicing as believers, might go forth willingly as empowered witnesses to the resurrection. So too may others, on the fringes of faith, rejoice to receive an exhilarating word of invitation and transformation, guidance and comfort from other believers who have already gained confidence in God.

Easter, then, is not a Resting Season, but a Rising Season!

> THE POWER OF GOD IN JESUS AND IN THE HOLY SPIRIT WILL CONTINUE TO TRANSFORM LISTENERS FROM CAUTION BORN OF MISUNDERSTANDING TO BOLDNESS BORN OF KNOWLEDGE AND SPIRIT!

Details, Details

Within the Easter Season, the Revised Common Lectionary (RCL), the Episcopal Book of Common Prayer (BCP), and the Roman Catholic lectionary (RC) are fairly consistent in their choices of Gospel texts. All three lectionaries also posit readings from Acts except Easter Evening in the RCL.

The many lesson options in the Easter lectionary require a structure for drawing the similarities and differences among the lessons. Therefore,

- I shall describe the overall themes for each Sunday or festival.
- I shall give an overview of the pattern of coming to faith. Where such effort would be repetitive, you will be referred back to the earliest pertinent section. I will deal with the Old Testament lessons and Psalms in somewhat less detail. Each day's lessons will be examined in the following order: Gospel(s), Acts, Epistles, the Psalm, and the Old Testament Lesson alternatives.
- I shall identify the reversals[4] in time, space, and characters, in a textual unit from its troubled beginning to its positive conclusion. Such reversals are helpful for your preaching the themes of a lesson when the lectionary unit and the textual unit do not match.
- I shall describe the pattern of coming to faith in the God whom Christ proclaims in the Gospels and Acts and the understandings of blessings and evils where faith has already been achieved. In the other lessons, where the reader

is presumed to have attained faith already, I shall focus on the vocation of believers, and its witness to others.[5]

- I shall provide a selection of ways through which you might integrate a particular pattern of coming to faith into your sermon and the liturgy, noting considerations about metaphorical specificity that might need illuminating or adjusting in your context. These may be issues raised by the text itself or interests of particular communities.

- I shall note, at the end of each section, any places where a preacher may combine interests of particular lections into a united perspective.

Because this way of approaching a text might be new for you, it will be helpful if you take time to try some of these new procedures for yourself. I would suggest that you:

- Read the lections, then reflect on the summary of the day's or festival's concerns in light of your reading of the lections.

- Remember that I am teaching you a new approach with an initially steep learning curve. Once you get the hang of it, say, ten pages from here (according to my lay and clergy pre-readers), the rest will be smooth exegeting. The nice thing about this approach is that you can always turn back to check what I'm doing!

- Be sure to refer to any full narrative mentioned as an example to get the full effect of a text's proposal about coming to faith.

- Keep in mind that in exegeting Gospel or Acts readings, the narrator presents hopeful and problematic faith journeys through different characters or character groups. No one character represents all possibilities, just as your congregants tell different stories of their journeys. Different characters in a story are set in opposition to one another to emphasize these varying perspectives. For example, in each Gospel's encounter at the tomb, the women, the disciples, and the religious authorities express different values. Which values are affirmed and which negated depends on the interface between the actions of each character group.

> KEEP IN MIND THAT IN EXEGETING GOSPEL OR ACTS READINGS, THE NARRATOR PRESENTS HOPEFUL AND PROBLEMATIC FAITH JOURNEYS THROUGH DIFFERENT CHARACTERS OR CHARACTER GROUPS. NO ONE CHARACTER REPRESENTS ALL POSSIBILITIES, JUST AS YOUR CONGREGANTS TELL DIFFERENT STORIES OF THEIR JOURNEYS.

- After your preparatory work, decide what you want to accomplish in a particular sermon as part of your mission plan for the congregation. You will be providing new knowledge. Do you want to strengthen your congregants' will to witness or their ability to witness?

- First and last, pray you might illuminate these texts for the strengthening of your witness in light of the congregation's diversity of life experience and social status. I will be praying for all of you.

THE RESURRECTION OF OUR LORD—EASTER DAY

APRIL 4, 1999

REVISED COMMON	EPISCOPAL (BCP)	ROMAN CATHOLIC
Acts 10:34-43	Acts 10:34-43	Acts 10:34, 37-43
or Jer. 31:1-6	or Exod. 14:10-14, 21–25; 15:20-21	
Ps. 118:1-2, 14-24	Ps. 118:14-29	Ps. 118:1-2, 16-17, 22-23
Col. 3:1-4	Col. 3:1-4	Col. 3:1-4
or Acts 10:34-43	or Acts 10:34-43	1 Cor. 5:6-8
John 20:1-18	John 20:1-10 (11-18)	John 20:1-9
or Matt. 28:1-20	or Matt. 28:1-10	

SUMMARY OF THE THEMES IN THE LESSONS

THE EASTER DAY lections focus on THREE THEMES. Different parts of the liturgy might enhance each of them:

1. The angels and Jesus empowering believers by reporting the great deed God has already done (John and Matthew);
2. Believers empowering those who are not yet full believers through witness to what God has done and is doing (Acts, Colossians);
3. Believers in worship praising God and empowering one another to sustain a faith already ignited by God's action (Psalm and the Old Testament lesson alternatives).

John and Matthew offer different perspectives on what the risen Jesus says to believers at the tomb. The difference is not just in the conversation at the tomb but also in what knowledge is given to the disciples prior to the Passion. John's Gospel contains only scant discussion about Jesus physically rising from the dead. Jesus speaks of his coming hour (2:4; 8:14) and his intent to return to the Father thereafter. He advises the disciples that they will not see him for a little while and then will see him again (16:25). He does speak of himself as the resurrection, but it is not defined as an action that occurs to him after the Passion (11:25). To his opponents, but not to his disciples, Jesus speaks directly of their intent to kill him, and his choice to lay down his life (John 2:21-22; 7:19-20; 8:28-41; 10:15-18). It is John's narrator who advises the reader that when Jesus was raised from the dead, the disciples recalled his figurative language about the temple being destroyed and raised, and realized that he was talking about the raising of his own body (John 2:22). So, the reader knows about the resurrection, and knows the disciples understood afterwards. However, the characters in this lection, Mary Magdalene, Peter, and the Beloved Disciple see the opened tomb as representing a devastating certainty that an unidentified "they" have abducted his dead body (20:9). They fear they will not see him again.

In Matthew's Gospel, Jesus has already presented three predictions to the disciples of his being handed over to death and his rising on the third day (16:21; 17:9, 22; 20:17-19). Therefore, the interchanges with the angels and the risen Jesus at the tomb focus on the women's fear that death has triumphed: that neither the scriptures nor the present revelations of God contained a blessing sufficient to overcome death. Here we have a strong issue of lack of confidence in God, born of anxiety. Has God's "nerve" failed or was Jesus not obedient to his mission? Matthew's Gospel offers relief to those so worried.

This Easter, preachers have a choice of Gospel lessons. I hope you will make your decision according to your perception about the congregation in your care. Do they need once more to have their preconceptions of the divine brought to the light? Do they need to know that God is Spirit and not imperiled by death? To know that Jesus' ascension to his Father permits believers to begin a witness to their firsthand knowledge of the divine? Then John's lection would be a wise choice. Or, are your congregants anxious and afraid despite scripture's witness? Are they not particularly trusting of the goodness of God? Does their witness get lost in fear? Does their witness wither? Then Matthew's lection would provide courage.

> THIS EASTER, PREACHERS HAVE A CHOICE OF GOSPEL LESSONS. I HOPE YOU WILL MAKE YOUR DECISION ACCORDING TO YOUR PERCEPTION ABOUT THE CONGREGATION IN YOUR CARE.

The lections from Acts 10:34-43 and Col. 3:1-4 have differing perspectives of the believer's response to being saved by God. The Acts lesson is focused narrowly on the content of Peter's sermon to Cornelius' household. Your exploration of the values in this text will be greatly strengthened by describing the larger narrative unit of Acts 10:1-48, as will be explained below.

The letter to the Col. 3:1-4 proclaims to its Gentile readers the blessed safety of the way the formerly unknown Lord has chosen to relate to them. Extending the lection to Col. 3:29 will clarify the relation between the private, heavenly blessings of God (3:1-4) and the public earthly witness to exemplary behavior that believers must also embody (3:5-29).

Psalm 118:1-2, 14-24, Jeremiah 31:1-6 (RCL alt.), and Exodus 14:10-14, 21-25; 15:20-21 (BCP alt.) all offer the theme of Israel celebrating its sustaining faith within the assembly of believers. The people proclaim their delight in the active and surprising faithfulness of a God who has insisted on salvation despite recurring oppression and recurring sin. The two Old Testament lections refer to the assembled people singing and dancing in thanksgiving for the power of God to save. Jeremiah rehearses the intent of God to save Jerusalem and Israel from its well-deserved destruction, while the Exodus passage, in truncated segments, covers the intervention of God on Israel's behalf in crossing the Red Sea. This material also includes the Songs of Moses and Miriam. Either of these lessons or the Psalm, presented with a brief introduction and some adjustment for continuity, could be read with gusto as an entrance dialog for Easter worship.

GOSPEL

JOHN 20:1-18

The Overall Pattern of Coming to Faith in John's Gospel

John establishes in the Prologue (1:1-18) the pattern by which persons come to faith in this Gospel. The constant repetition of the pattern throughout the Gospel suggests that the reader/hearer who is becoming a full believer is being equipped to conduct a mission in the same way. We, too, are being instructed to read for typology (modeling) as well as for history. While stated in John 1:9-13 as events that have happened in the past, I shall represent the pattern in the present tense, because that is the time frame in which it is to have an effect on your hearer:

> THE PEOPLE PROCLAIM THEIR DELIGHT IN THE ACTIVE AND SURPRISING FAITHFULNESS OF A GOD WHO HAS INSISTED ON SALVATION DESPITE RECURRING OPPRESSION AND RECURRING SIN.

A. *Coming to faith is initiated by Jesus as word and light on behalf of the Father.* Jesus comes to what is his own: his own home and the world created through him (1:9-11a).

B. *People are somewhat willing and able to respond to Jesus' initiative.* Some have a partial knowledge of God's activity apart from Jesus and are willing to come to Jesus and interact with him. Usually, they ask him open-ended questions about his boundary-breaking behavior and his relation to the Father. For example, John 4:9: "How is it that you, a Jew, ask a drink of me, a woman of Samaria?" Dialog with Jesus results in having one's former knowledge, deeds and true character exposed to the Light (1:5, 9).

C. *There are two responses to interaction with Jesus as Word and Light.*

   1) Some respond to Jesus' knowledge of their former deeds and true character by believing in Jesus, delighted to know that he is the Light, and the unique son and savior of the world (1:14).

   2) Others, after conversation with him, do not accept him as the Light because they do not wish to have their deeds exposed as evil (1:10b, 11b; 3:19-20).

D. *There are two results of the interaction with Jesus as Word and Light.*

1) To those who receive him and believe in his message about earthly and heavenly verities (3:12), Jesus gives the power to become children of God (12b-14). The effect of being begotten by God is gaining a full, grace-filled earthly, heavenly, and eternal life, and the commission to witness to it (1:4, 16-17). Those who are fully believers join Jesus, the unique son, as witnessing sons and daughters of the Father after the resurrection (20:17).

2) Those who do not receive the Light hate the Light. Their deeds are evil and they are condemned already by their own traditions (3:18-20; 5:45).

What then can we observe from this pattern of how Jesus comes to people so we might do the same? We see that people who speak to Jesus about their partial knowledge of the activities of God risk having their perspective corrected even though they might not have been approaching Jesus as the Messiah! Jesus takes seriously that all his earthly questioners have heavenly concerns. For some who tumble into these conversations, the benefits are great. Having one's deeds and character "known" (exposed and corrected) by Jesus is a necessary step toward believing with confidence in Jesus' Father.

> HAVING ONE'S DEEDS AND CHARACTER "KNOWN" (EXPOSED AND CORRECTED) BY JESUS IS A NECESSARY STEP TOWARD BELIEVING WITH CONFIDENCE IN JESUS' FATHER.

Those who are becoming fully known will be granted the presence and protection of the divine through Jesus first and then through the Spirit (1:14,16; 20:22). Such benefits make it possible for believers to be witnesses to the Light among those who have not yet come to the Light, and allow them to "keep shining" freely and creatively among those who do not care to have their deeds exposed to the light (John 3:19-20). They, as witnesses, can also expect to have conversations about heavenly things that begin on an earthly plain, and they can expect that some to whom they witness will be delighted and some will turn away. This pattern of odd but striking encounters initiated by Jesus repeats itself throughout the Gospel.

In John's Gospel, those who are shown to come to the Light are often, but not always, outsiders. But those John worries about most are religious authorities who have lost the freedom that the Light gives. These religious leaders are described as types who have strong convictions about how to interpret scripture, how to worship, and how to make boundaries around the believing community. These convictions lead some of them to commitments that are too rigid. The result is that they misperceive who or what is a threat to God (5:10-11). These religious authorities become limited in their interpretation of scripture, their praise of God, and their view of with whom and through whom God is working. All this happens while they continue to dearly love scripture, worship, and the community!

You, as a religious leader, have undoubtedly experienced how your own or others' commitments to scripture, worship, and clear boundaries about congregational membership and leadership may at times work against the good news that you love, and thus against the believers' freedom in the Light. Over against this, John is aiming to persuade you and those who hear you that unusual encounters with the Divine and with others are a result of being Spirit-led. Those begotten by the Spirit's having breathed into them will be led into unexpected, but truth-producing relationships (3:8).

The Reversals of Time, Space, Characters, and Themes in John 20:1-29

John's Gospel approaches the story at the tomb as a last chance for the disciples to come to a full knowledge of Jesus as one with the Father, and gain the ability and will to receive a vocation as those sent (apostles) and not simply those taught (disciples). The full textual unit, through which John portrays this ultimate opportunity for disciples to be begotten of God, is John 20:1-29. The lesson options, John 20:1-18 are subunits of the full pattern of coming to faith in this chapter. As the preacher, you will need to decide how to pick up the other dimensions of the narrative not covered in the assigned passage. This is particularly important because the "doubting Thomas" lection (20:19-29) is separated by a week from the lections with the other Johannine resurrection appearances.

John 20:1-29 falls into two related subunits, each having two stories marked by overlapping characters, whose actions are in tension with each other. In John 20:1-18, the first subunit of the two stories, Mary Magdalene, shocked at the opened tomb, carries her false message of a stolen body to Peter and the Beloved Disciple. After their tentative visiting and silent departure, Jesus appears to Mary Magdalene and gives her a true message of ascension and family relations for Peter and the Beloved Disciple. Since Peter and the Beloved Disciple deliver no messages at all, Mary Magdalene's speaking about Jesus is in tension with Peter's and the Beloved Disciple's silence about Jesus.

In John 20:19-29, the second subunit of the two stories, Jesus appears to the disciples (minus Thomas) who have received Mary Magdalene's true message. The disciples' interpretation, that they have reason to fear the religious authorities, causes them to gather in silence behind locked doors. This interpretation will confine them. Their later joy, as a response to Jesus' teaching, permits them to move out of a shut room. Thomas, unlike the other disciples, is not silent nor shut away. He

JOHN'S GOSPEL APPROACHES THE STORY AT THE TOMB AS A LAST CHANCE FOR THE DISCIPLES TO COME TO A FULL KNOWLEDGE OF JESUS AS ONE WITH THE FATHER, AND GAIN THE ABILITY AND WILL TO RECEIVE A VOCATION AS THOSE SENT (APOSTLES) AND NOT SIMPLY THOSE TAUGHT (DISCIPLES).

blurts out what he needs for faith—needs that are effectively the same as the other disciples—since it was seeing the risen Jesus that has gladdened them. Because he speaks, Jesus can know and attend to his needs directly. The larger reversal, focused on the value of seeing Jesus' body, will be resolved when Jesus informs Thomas, in the presence of the other disciples, of the now low value of seeing his body (20:29).

By looking at how time and space are used in John 20:1-29, we can confirm that the unit focuses on a set of common themes. John 20:1 begins in the dark, never a positive value in John, on the first day of the week, with the characters having expectations that there will be a stone-closed garden tomb wherein a silent Jesus has been laid in fragrant wrappings. At John 20:18, Jesus is speaking to Mary about his return to the Father, and commanding her to witness to the disciples that his Father and their Father are the same.

In the second subunit, 20:19-29, it is still on the Sabbath, but after sunset, when it is dark again. The disciples are shut in a house out of fear until Jesus breaks into their chosen "tomb," a fear-filled room, and blesses them. Jesus commissions the disciples as witnesses, a task they have not had before, and equips them for this mission by breathing into them the Holy Spirit. They will now find that their forgiving or retaining sins is in tandem with the forgiveness and retention of sins by Jesus and the Father. They will be able to function as Jesus has: identifying those whose deeds are of the light and those whose deeds are of the darkness.

At John 20:26, on the next Sabbath, the risen Jesus appears again unexpectedly in the disciples' house to bless them and to open up Thomas' understanding. He honors Thomas' request to touch him, but ends the need for such future events by blessing those who believe without seeing Jesus in the flesh.

If we gather the temporal and spatial references in relation to the themes they involve in the two subunits, we have the following significant reversals. The first subunit moves from Sabbath darkness, the garden tomb, distress about a body not seen, and wrong or no witness (20:1), to the Light of Jesus, the garden around the tomb, joy at seeing Jesus' body, and a proper witness given by Jesus about the ascension of his body—all still on the Sabbath. The second unit moves from Sabbath darkness, a house in fear, a report of a risen body, and wrong or no witness (20:19) to the Light of Jesus, a house at peace, a confession, and a proper witness about not seeing the body—all still on the Sabbath (20:28). Spatially, the entire unit also inverts "someone opening the tomb where Jesus lies" into "Jesus opening the room where the disciples hide." Further details on John 20:19-33 will be found in the exegesis for the Second Sunday of Easter.

> SPATIALLY, THE ENTIRE UNIT ALSO INVERTS "SOMEONE OPENING THE TOMB WHERE JESUS LIES" INTO "JESUS OPENING THE ROOM WHERE THE DISCIPLES HIDE."

The Pattern of Faith in the Specific Gospel Unit: John 20:1-18

The faith pattern developed in John's Prologue made us aware that during his life, it is Jesus who must come to believers for them to gain a proper interpretation of himself and his Father. At 20:18, it will be Jesus' coming into the disciples' presence to expose and correct their wrong view of him that will give them a proper knowledge of himself, themselves, and of the Father's relationship to them. Once again, those who are willing to come to the Light will be those who are growing toward a witnessing faith.

Mary Magdalene at John 20:1 sees through the gloom an empty tomb and interprets it as a worst-case scenario for those grieving for a man already dead: an abduction of his body. Peter and the Beloved Disciple arrive with that interpretation in mind. How they go about getting to the tomb does not bode well. They do not speak to or support one another or Mary, or acknowledge any grief. Seeing the evidence of the opened tomb and the strewn grave clothes does little to change this interpretation, although they had been with Jesus at Lazarus' resurrection (11:7-8, 15-16).

A wild hope strikes the reader/hearer that the Beloved Disciple might have understood, for he went in, saw, and believed (20:8). But what did he believe? The narrator dashes our hopes by saying that they did not yet know the scripture that he must rise from the dead. What Peter and the Beloved Disciple believe is Mary's wrong witness that the body was stolen. Peter and the Beloved Disciple's silent return to their homes shows their alienation. They do not consult with one another about what Jesus had done, said, or meant to them. At best, they do not appear to spread the story of the break-in and the body snatchers. Seeing an opened tomb is not knowledge enough for belief in a risen Lord.

Mary Magdalene, uncomforted by resurrection predictions, or by the disciples, or by a proper knowledge of scripture, weeps. Her weeping is akin to the weeping that so affected Jesus when Mary of Bethany and the assembled community wept for Lazarus (11:28-44). Grief, a stone, a tomb, grave wrappings, and a resurrection all appear in that text as well. Mary Magdalene, however, is not Mary of Bethany, and she is not shown to know about this prior resurrection. It is left to the reader/hearer to draw the parallels. In both accounts, weeping brings forth compassion from the Divine, from angels, and from the Lord alike.

At the tomb, Mary Magdalene blurts out to both angels that her Lord has been taken away, and she does not know where. In one of the lovely ironies of John's Gospel, her statement confirms what Jesus said to Simon Peter, spokesperson for the Twelve: they would not know where he was going (13:36). But no one can take Jesus away. He lays down his life and takes it up again (10:40), a message given to the Pharisees and the reader/hearer, but not to the disciples.

Mary Magdalene is not a shy person in this encounter, whomever she may imagine the angels or Jesus to be. She would take her Lord away (a second snatching). At this point, seeing isn't even *seeing* for her, let alone believing. She mistakes Jesus for the gardener stripped for work (cf. 21:7). And yet her blurting out her grief and passion for her dear, dead Lord—parallel to the blurted passion of Mary of Bethany in grief for Lazarus—begins her renovated relationship with Jesus. She is willing to bring her partial faith and partial knowledge to his Light. He reveals he knows her by calling her name, and she in turn knows him as her Lord. While she is counseled not to touch him, she has been given enough without it to enable her to witness to his new siblings, the disciples. Her confident witnessing without touching will set up an important feature for the continuation of this unit into the next unit, where Thomas needs to touch Jesus.

Mary Magdalene's witness goes beyond what any believer in John's Gospel has been given until now. She is to witness to her knowledge of Jesus and his power, and to say to the disciples that he said, "I am ascending to my Father, and your Father, my God, and your God" (20:17). This is the first use of any familial language extended to believers by Jesus in John. Through his taking up his life again, believers may be taken up into his family. It is also the first time a believer is charged to repeat an exact message of Jesus to another believer. Begotten of God and beckoned by Jesus, Mary is led into a new space and a new vocation where the Spirit of God would have her (and us!) be.

Mary completes the witnessing task. She reports seeing the Lord, and communicates all that he has told her. In John's Gospel, she is in a position to inherit eternal life, for she has the knowledge, will, and ability to witness in the name of the ascended Jesus under the power of the Spirit of God.

AT THIS POINT, SEEING ISN'T EVEN SEEING FOR MARY MAGDALENE, LET ALONE BELIEVING.

Integrating Johannine Values about Mission into Your Preaching

In addition to the points covered in the above sections, believers would be strengthened to know that:

1. Blurting is a positive value in this pattern of coming to a mature faith. Those who speak what is on their mind and ask questions of Jesus have the possibility of coming to a new perspective of faith. Parishioners need to think of themselves as addressing such questions to God as well as responding to such questions from others. For example, someone may ask a "sociological" question of how you or another came to be a believer. We often reply, "My father was a pastor," or, "We have a friendly church." Preach to encourage the congregants to have the ability and will to express a Johannine missional value this Easter. For example, a believer might say, "Jesus has come to me and knows me, faults and all. He has delighted to teach me about earthly and heavenly things and welcomed me to sow and to reap with him, and to see even greater things than these!" Potential believers are eager to hear such a witness from maturing believers.

2. Being known by God in all our specificity is a relief, although it might first feel like a threat. Being able to say to God, "I am an alcoholic and my life is unmanageable," or, "I was abused as a child, and life is so fearful," is a step toward

receiving the grace of God in that particularity. If Mary Magdalene can start by thinking Jesus is a gardener and yet receive knowledge and comfort, so too can others start with their fears and wrong perceptions and still arrive at proclamation. Fundamentally, believers need to respond to others in the same way that Jesus has responded to them, by hearing their partial knowledge of God, their uncertain ability, and their imperfect will. Then believers can model Jesus' activities of assisting their ability and strengthening their will to proclaim.

3. The relational dyad, father-son, is heavily used by John's Jesus to persuade the characters that the knowledge, ability, and will of God and Jesus are the same, with God having given a unique authority to the Word for his time on earth. First-century readers/hearers would find the father-son dyad a familiar way to think about their context, since 1) a father was understood to be the sole progenitor of children, and 2) the son in the dyad was understood to be the primary heir. Neither of these convictions undergirds most North American believers' thinking on procreation and inheritance, but it is still a perspective of note in many other traditions. Because John's interest is that persons come to a mature faith from whatever their starting point may be, the preacher should feel free to work with any images or dyads that will highlight the values of intimacy, knowledge, continuity, and reliability that undergird John's witness to the Divine. The biggest help here is from the Gospel itself, in which Jesus comes continually into dialog with those not thought to be heirs.

THE EASTER GOSPEL ALTERNATIVE
MATTHEW 28:1-20

The Overall Pattern of Coming to Faith in Matthew's Gospel

This lection is the only witness from Matthew's Gospel for the Easter season, so we can work briefly with its pattern of coming to faith.[6] Moreover, the lectionary unit and the textual unit are the same. The pattern and its repetition highlight what Matthew sees as the way in which people do or do not conform their lives to the will of God. This pattern is quite different from that of John or Luke—Matthew believes you can do the will of God because God has provided the revelations necessary for this to happen. The fundamental evils, then, are: not knowing God's will, and, once knowing it, not wanting to do it. After the first statement of God's initiating action, the pattern describes what believers will see as they witness—in themselves or others.

A. *Coming to faith is initiated by God through divine manifestations in the past in the witness of scripture, especially the Law and the Prophets, but also in the present through the witness of angels, dreams, birth stars, earthquakes, and Jesus' teachings.*

B. *Coming to faith depends on a proper understanding of the past and present revelations of God.*

   1) *Some persons understand the authority and goodness of both past and present revelations of God.*

   2) *Others may have difficulty understanding because they have an incorrect knowledge that needs to be overcome.* Some of those may believe God was only active in the past and are threatened by present revelations. Others of those may believe God would only be present now to announce wrath.

C. *Coming to faith next depends on internalizing the manifestations of God as authoritative and good.*

   1) *Some persons are positively affected by both kinds of revelation.* They internalize God's will by appropriating God's good messages.

   2) *Others will have difficulty internalizing God's will.* Some of those may not recognize one or both kinds of revelation as authoritative or as good. Others of those may fear the revelation of God as wrath. Still others may have conformed their will to another authority they believe they must obey, such as religious or secular laws and rulers.

> MATTHEW BELIEVES YOU CAN DO THE WILL OF GOD BECAUSE GOD HAS PROVIDED THE REVELATIONS NECESSARY FOR THIS TO HAPPEN.

D. *Coming to faith is completed when believers bear much good fruit. Believers are willing and able to give glory to God.*

   1) *Some persons who are coming to faith develop an overabundant righteousness.* They are able to do more than what God's law requires because they also have the present revelation of God as good, especially as a bountiful progenitor. Their deeds enable others to give glory to God.

   2) *Others display a limited righteousness.* They may do only what the law requires. They may meet social expectations of religious involvement but these acts do not cause others to give glory to God. Some of those may do evil deeds out of their fear.

E. *The Father makes heirs of those whose will is conformed to his will.*

   1) *Some persons receive the blessing of God in the present and the inheritance of eternal life. They become God's emissaries.*

   2) *Others will not receive the Father's blessing and will be denied entrance into the Father's realm.* Some of those persist in acting out of fear in ways that deny God's authority and assault God's emissaries.

The Reversals of Time, Space, Characters, and Matthew 28:1-20

The character group's status in relation to religious authority is important for understanding the reversals in this lection.[7] The character group of the high priests and elders understand themselves as religious leaders according to the past revelations of God. The disciples, prior to the Passion, imagine themselves as persons who had the potential to be religious authorities in a "Jesus movement" (20:20-28; 26:30-35). Mary Magdalene and the other Mary, a character group of women, are equivalent to Jewish lay believers at the entrance to this text.

Matthew's tomb story serves as a last chance for these character groups to resolve their anxiety about the past and present revelations of God. If any of the character groups were to acknowledge as *good* the authority behind the angel's and Jesus' speaking, they would be empowered to fully become believers and therefore proper religious authorities: able to make disciples, baptize, and teach (28:20). If they do not overcome their fear that God's revelation is wrathful, they will remain "like dead ones" (28:4) with their wrong view of the revelations of God, and "like dead ones" in their limited righteousness. Matthew explores these problems and possibilities through three subunits.

In the first subunit, Matt. 28:1-11, the actions of two groups of characters are used to reverse its values. The two Marys, who came with uncertain intent to see the well-guarded tomb, end up joyfully empowered with a message to the eleven (28:8-10). Their desire to do God's will has been established. The night guards, formerly secure in their task, tremble and fall like dead men before the earthquake and the angel's power. They have lost their will for their task out of fear that the angel and the earthquake are wrathful manifestations from God.

The second subunit, 28:11-15, concerns some of the guards, who go into the city and report *all* that had happened (28:11). Compelled by the chief priests, elders, and a bit of cash, they deliver a wrong message—that the disciples stole the body—to the Jews in Jerusalem. The effect of the guards' wrong reporting is narrated as something that endures among one specific people "to this day" (28:15). The subunit reverses in a negative direction (things get worse!) with a description of the complicated consequences of observing, but denying, the authority and proclamation of the angel as a *good* witness. Many will be told that God does not come through for Jesus or for us. For Matthew, this is why your congregation's witness is so important.

The third subunit, 28:16-20, focuses on the disciples, who were too frightened to stay by Jesus at the crucifixion and too uncertain to come to the tomb. By the disciples' acceptance of the authority of the women's report, the eleven see and worship Jesus outside Jerusalem. The unit's values are reversed: from disciples who are uncertain even after they worship, *to* the communication of Jesus' doubt-relieving full authority. His authority includes that of the past revelation of scripture and the present revelation of the resurrection. It also includes all authority in the Father's heaven, where Jesus, as the Son, had formerly not had authority, and a new authority that can empower a mission to all nations and all peoples. This third subunit has just the opposite values of those expressed by the difficult conclusion at the end of the second subunit. It will be Jesus and his teaching that are with the disciples to the close of the age, even if the false story of the disciples stealing the body continues. Where the prior unit dealt with a message for urban Jerusalem, this unit that began in Galilee now includes a message for all times and places.

The Place of Matthew 28:1-20 in the Gospel's Pattern of Coming to Faith

As happens commonly in Matthew's Gospel, the actions and encounters of some character groups, such as the women and the disciples, are to be read in opposition to the actions and encounters of other character groups, such as the priests, the elders, and the guards. It is not that these character groups necessarily talk to one another. Instead, their actions and encounters portray different responses to the power of God to save. The problematic encounters of any group are just as instructive to us as the beneficial ones are for understanding Matthew's perspective of the journey to faith.

In Matthew's pattern, Mary Magdalene and the other Mary do not understand Jesus' past teaching about his death and resurrection when they come to the tomb (28:6). They have heard it but not internalized it. The angel's counsel against fear suggests that whatever else the women were expecting it was not a mighty shining angel rolling a tombstone. The angel knows why they came and announces the resurrection by reminding them of what Jesus taught them. The women, by acknowledging the authority of this proclamation, become witnesses to the dismayed disciples. Acknowledging the good authority of the divine does not give them a new ability; it gives them the courage to proclaim. Good news overcomes fear.

The guards model what happens if one is uncertain that a present revelation of God is good, particularly if one then seeks to understand its value from others who are sure it isn't good. The guards report correctly what they experience, but they did not value Jesus' prior teaching, which would have helped them understand the angelic revelation. Instead, they mocked Jesus at the crucifixion. Without Jesus' prior instruction about the eternal Parent's goodness, the guards are subject to agreeing to others' wrong interpretation of their experience. Again, Matthew is stressing the need for believers to make their proper witness in the light of misinterpretations.

The chief priests and elders represent a group that acknowledges past divine revelations. However, from their encounter with the Magi onward (2:1-3), they have not perceived the abundance of God's goodness in Jesus. Their spin doctoring of the guards' report leaves them denying the activity of God in the present and compromises the values of goodness the law does hold for them. They lie.

The disciples have experienced a dark night in which their presuppositions of the ways of God and the ways of religious authority have been violently inverted. Such a change proves a benefit more than a liability! Their confidence—in Jerusalem's leadership, in its endurance, and in the success of their own ministry—has been shattered (20:20-28). That they need the authoritative proclamation of

Mary Magdalene and the other Mary shows how far the disciples have come from Peter's denial that the Messiah would suffer and their boast to stay with him through death (16:22-23; 26:31-35). In the end, their shame and grief are subordinated to God's goodness. How else could the disciples be properly prepared for a proclamation of the abundance of the Father's goodness in and out of adversity unless they have known God's bounty *and* have suffered adversity at the hands of those they considered lawful? They are on the verge of being able to give up their pretensions about being religious leaders. The language of Father, Son, and Holy Spirit makes clear that they will not serve the Gospel by becoming religious fathers as were the men of Matt. 1:1-17. They will remain as adult siblings of the primary heir, Jesus, who shall always remain an obedient adult son to a never-dying father.

Integrating Matthean Values about Mission into Your Preaching

1. Matthew is confident that the revelations of God are apparent to believers and nonbelievers such as the guards. The concern is always the effect of these revelations on those who see and hear them, and the necessity that there be a believer nearby who can speak to their authority and goodness. You! Millennial thinking is built on the supposition that the manifestations of God are wrathful. Matthew would disagree. Divine revelation is suffused with goodness in the past and present. It is people in groups who misread the benefits of God. For Matthew, Mission 2000 would be a mission to name the bounty of God, and counter those who think God comes in wrath.

> THE DISCIPLES ARE ON THE VERGE OF BEING ABLE TO GIVE UP THEIR PRETENSIONS ABOUT BEING RELIGIOUS LEADERS.

2. Anxiety and its partner, fear, are the most serious evils in Matthew's Gospel. Anxiety impedes an abundant life with God and is a matter of a wrong will. Whether originating in daily worries or institutional worries, the defenses against anxiety that one chooses only make one more anxious and less able to perceive the present manifestations of God. That is the experience of the guards and religious authorities in Matt. 28:11-15.

3. Matthew perceives that a variety of lessons and fears occur on the way to faith. These are different depending on whether people are coming toward faith by means of past or present revelations of God. Those who have only a past revelation of God need to have that revelation respected and be assured by present-day believers of the blessing of God's present revelations, even when they appear among non-Christians, as they did when the gentile Magi properly understood the star (2:1-3). In the same way, those who have had an experience of the present revelation of God need to have it valued. However, they also need to be strengthened in the past revelations of God so that they can understand that the bounty or safety of their experience with God is akin to what God has done in

the past. For example, during my intern year, a parishioner expressed delight in God that at a family dinner with unexpected guests, the lima beans did not run out. As a lima bean hater, that wasn't surprising to me. "What new did you learn of God here, that you didn't know before?" I asked. Matthew might have said, "That sounds like the same divine bounty that protects each sparrow and lily," so as to draw the present revelation more closely to the past tradition.

4. Matthew wishes to reduce the fear of witnessing among those who think they are not religious authorities by the example of the women. Their authority to witness rests on having experienced the abundant blessing of God in past and present, in and out of adversity, and being willing to have their speech and actions cause others to give glory to God. The Easter lection is also a caution to us religious authorities not to value our own sense of the past revelation of God too highly, for our presuppositions can impede our seeing the present activity of God.

5. The authority of the heavenly Father[8] in Matthew's Gospel is set most favorably as parallel to the authority of biological parents. This authority is in contradistinction to the patriarchal religious authorities of 28:11-15, whose speech and actions cannot be considered abundant because they do not raise glory to God. In the first century, a human father had various powers of life, inheritance, and death over offspring until his own death. Now, American citizenship supports parental separation at eighteen. What was a natural lifelong parallel between the authority of the divine and human parent in Matthew's world is no longer a presupposition for us. You may find it useful to reflect on the relation between adult children and their parents, because Matthew is not imagining that the offspring of God are other than obedient adults able to witness to the glory of God in their complex personal and work identities.

6. The command to make disciples, baptize, and teach suggests a three-part approach to mission. The act of making disciples—which relates to the revelations of God in the present—precedes baptism, which for Matthew is a commitment to a life fulfilling all righteousness (3:15). Teaching, which interprets God's revelations in the past and in the present (as the angel and Jesus do for the women, and the women for the disciples), empowers believers to proclaim. Proclamation then calls into being more disciples, with more baptisms and more teaching. And so it goes, bountifully, to the end of the age.

ACTS 10:34-43 (RCL, BCP alt.);
ACTS 10:34, 37-43 (RC)

The Pattern of Coming to Faith in the Acts of the Apostles

Luke's pattern of coming to faith presented in the Gospel is intention-ally re-presented in Acts. Once the believing community receives the Holy Spirit at Pentecost, the community's life of faith is parallel to Jesus' life in these areas: proclaiming, freeing from social evil (oppression, healing, forgiveness), and teach-ing, as well as rejoicing. So, one may describe one pattern of coming to faith with examples from both writings. After a statement of God's initiating action, Luke's pattern describes how Jesus comes to people, how believers come to faith, and what actions full believers need to take and what kind of teaching full believers need to do for the proclamation of the Gospel.[9] Out of the patterns we have seen, this one is the most intentional about the mission of believers. Positive and negative responses to God's acts will follow each section.

A. *God acted in the past by 1) freeing people from social evil (slavery), and 2) by giving to believers the Law and sustaining them through the Spirit that rested on the prophets (including Moses and David). God acts in the present by 1) freeing people from social evil (oppression, poverty, demonic possession, sin) through the actions of John the Bap-tist, Jesus, disciples, and others, and 2) by giving believers a proper knowledge of God's actions and desires through the proclamation of John the Baptist, Jesus, the disciples, and others under the power of the Spirit, which the prophets also had.*

B. *Coming to faith depends on being in the time of Jesus, a time that the prophets longed to see (10:24). From Pentecost on is the time of the Holy Spirit resting on the disciples, prophesied by Joel (Acts 2:16-21).*

1) Some people are able to acknowledge Jesus' connection with God or the disciples' connection with the Holy Spirit because they have a preliminary knowledge of God's activities in the past (Elizabeth, Luke 1:41-43; the Ethiopian eunuch, Acts 8:26-40).

2) Others may be in bondage to social evil, and need to be freed before they can acknowledge Jesus (one leper, Luke 17:1-9; the lame man at the gate, Acts 3:1-10). Still others may have a preliminary knowledge without the proper interpretation of the present activities of God (nine lepers, Luke 17:1-9; Paul, Acts 9:1-6).

C. *The potential for persons to come to faith depends on Jesus (in Luke) or the disciples (in Acts) initiating a close relationship with people: travelling through villages proclaiming, healing, forgiving, and teaching.*

1) Some people are willing to come to Jesus. They ask for help and absorb answers.

2) Others whom Jesus approaches are not willing to listen to him (or to the disciples in Acts).

D. *Coming to faith depends on Jesus teaching willing people how to interpret properly what God is doing and the significance of their present context: Jesus' death and resurrection, the forgiveness of sins, and the vocation as believers.*

1) Some people receive this teaching.

2) Others do not know how to interpret what is in front of them, and disbelieve that Moses and the prophets testified to Jesus' coming.

E. *Having been taught by Jesus to have a proper interpretation of God-given things and of the concrete situations before them, some become full believers.*

1) Some persons now have a proper understanding of the law and what loving God and loving neighbor means, so that God is properly praised and the neighbor is freed from social evil.

2) Others, without a proper interpretation, take advantage of the poor and kill those sent by God (John the Baptist, Jesus, James, and Stephen).

F. *The Spirit of Jesus is given by the Father to full believers after Jesus' ascension, so that they may continue the work of Jesus for God.*

1) Some persons become apostles: those sent. In his name, they proclaim, heal, forgive, teach, and baptize. The Spirit continues to fall on those given the proper interpretation of what God is doing and what believers should do.

2) Others resist the Holy Spirit or try to buy it, like Simon Magus (Acts 7:51; 8:18-20).

G. *God grants blessings in the present and the future to those who have the proper interpretation of God's actions and desires (the thief on the cross, Luke 23:40-41).*

1) Full believers who have received the Spirit receive eternal life.

2) Others, not fully believers, are subject to the power of Satan and may lie to the Holy Spirit (Acts 7:51) and lose their lives (Luke 22:3; Acts 1:18; 5:1-11).

The Reversals in Time, Space, and Characters in Acts 10:34-43

Acts 10:34-43 is almost the end of a lengthy unit which began at 10:1 and ends at 10:48. Without the names of any other characters but Peter, the lection is a generalized proclamation that is hard to preach "as is." The lection in its larger context, however, allows the preacher to draw a connection between John's Easter Gospel's emphasis on the nearness of Jesus and Luke's emphasis on the same.

Appreciating the reversals of time and space in the larger unit will help you perceive the smaller reversals in the lection. The smallest subunit that surrounds the lection is 10:34-48, since the time, space, and character referents are the same throughout. However, this subunit leaves out the desires of God behind the arrival of Peter with other believers from Joppa! That impetus is only reflected in 10:34-35, "I truly understand that God shows no partiality, but in every nation anyone who fears him and does what is right is acceptable to him."

The pattern of coming to faith in the larger unit, 10:1-48 informs the lection in the following ways. Cornelius, a devout Italian Centurion who has a proper understanding of what "loving God" and "loving neighbor" mean (10:2) is directed by God to find Peter. Cornelius is without the knowledge of Jesus' death or resurrection and therefore without baptism by water or the Holy Spirit. Peter, staying at Simon's house in Joppa, is without a proper interpretation of how God regards what Peter deems unclean. Peter's dream of the lowered net permits God to help Peter see that the death and resurrection of Jesus has effected acceptable purity and holiness for living beings that Peter had formerly *withheld* himself from. Peter's perplexity about the food vision will remain until he meets Cornelius. Nevertheless, he expresses his love for neighbor by hosting Cornelius' Gentile emissaries. The unit reverses in 10:44-48 when Peter is in Cornelius' house and all there have received the Holy Spirit and are speaking in tongues and praising God. Finally, Peter gains the proper interpretation and says, "Can anyone *withhold* water for baptizing these people who have received the Spirit just as we have?" (10:47). The entire unit effectively portrays the conversion of *Peter* effected by God and Cornelius coming close to him. Peter's conversion to a new interpretation allows him to preach to the Gentiles, and they in turn receive the Holy Spirit by God's action.

The Place of Acts 10:34-43 in Luke's Pattern of Coming to Faith

In no small way, Acts 10:34-43 is a miniaturization of Luke's pattern of coming to faith as noted above. The two characteristics "fearing God (loving God)"[10] and "doing what is right (loving the neighbor)" describe Cornelius prior to the visit of Peter (10:34). Cornelius and his family also appear to have a preliminary knowledge of the word that God sent to Israel preaching good news of peace by Jesus Christ and healing those oppressed by the devil (10:36-38). What they do not seem to have had among themselves as Gentiles are witnesses who can proclaim the proper interpretation of these events, particularly the death, resurrection, and appearances. These witnesses should come from those who remained in a close relationship with Jesus, those who had eaten and drunk with him after the resurrection. At first glance, this looks like it means Peter and the new twelve (1:15-26), but the "we" of the context is also the believers from Joppa, so the eating and drinking is a witness to the breaking of bread, the praise, and the prayers that mark the new community (2:46). The reference to the prophets in 10:43 is therefore a recalling that what the prophets proclaimed in the Spirit is now about to come to pass for the Gentiles.[11]

Integrating Lukan Values about Mission into Your Preaching

1. "What would Jesus do?" According to Luke: mission! Jesus would free persons from social evil, forgive, proclaim, and teach the proper interpretation of

the events before us. But then, one must ask, "What would the believers do?" As far as Luke is concerned, mission: free from social evil, forgive, proclaim, and teach the proper interpretation of the events before us and others. Two things make possible this mission for believers: the gift of the Holy Spirit for courage and proper interpretation, and eating and drinking with Jesus, which maintains that close relation with Jesus and between believers. Luke's sense of the resurrection meal (and the Passion meal) is Jesus' strong and continuing desire to eat with us (Luke 24:30, 41-42). This desire is so strong that Peter will find his conversion to the gentile mission takes place through a food dream! How might you help those you serve to expand their interpretation of the dual thrust of being near to Jesus while speaking in the Spirit?

2. I like to think of Acts 10:1-48 as "First-century Inter*Net.*" It is a strong witness to the interpersonal nature of the proclamation of the gospel. God comes near Cornelius and Peter, making their coming near to each other possible. Neither Peter nor Cornelius would have gone to one another without the impulse of God, because of differing national (i.e., religious) identities. Within the nearness of the witnessing believer lies the possibility of many being baptized.

"WHAT WOULD JESUS DO?" ACCORDING TO LUKE: MISSION! JESUS WOULD FREE PERSONS FROM SOCIAL EVIL, FORGIVE, PROCLAIM, AND TEACH THE PROPER INTERPRETATION OF THE EVENTS BEFORE US.

3. One way to make the power of this text clear in the midst of the powerful Gospels of Easter is to create a community reenACTment from 10:34-48. Around the font, this four-person drama might occur with these actors: a narrator, Cornelius, Peter, and the Jewish-Christians from Joppa played by the congregation. The parts are as follows:

Narrator (setting up the drama): "The gentile Cornelius, gathered with his kin and friends in his own house, said to Peter and his Jewish-Christian companions who have come from Joppa following divine instruction,

Cornelius: "Therefore I sent for you . . . " (v. 33b).

Peter: "I truly understand . . . " (34-39).

Jewish-Christians from Joppa (the congregation): "But God made him manifest . . . " (40-42).

Peter: "All the prophets testify . . . " (v. 43).

Narrator: "While Peter was speaking . . . Gentiles!" (44-45)

Jewish-Christians from Joppa (the congregation): "We hear them speaking . . . " (46a).

Peter (turning to congregation): "Can anyone withhold . . . " (47b).

Jewish-Christian believers from Joppa (the congregation): "No, Not one!"

Cornelius: "We are now your brothers and sisters in Christ" (10:48).

This drama could be an opening rite, with passing of the peace following, or part of a baptismal liturgy, or a form for the reading of the first lesson.

4. Hospitality in Acts is "Gospeltality." Hospitality has the larger goal of allowing persons to be drawn near to the proclamation of the power of God in Jesus once they are freed from social evil or whatever binds them. It also has the goal of the strengthening of those who are already believers. Watching out a hotel window on Thanksgiving morning in San Francisco, I saw and heard, 20 floors below, the energetic choir and clapping members of Glide Memorial Methodist Church. They poured into the street after services for a hymn sing and a meal for any hungry passersby and the homeless. Hospitality and Gospeltality were as one! Think about hospitality in the congregation. How might yours proclaim as well as sustain? And how might it intentionally strengthen believers for witness?

The Second Lesson
COLOSSIANS 3:1-4

The Pattern of Faith and the Development of Values in Colossians

Epistles do not lend themselves—in the way narratives do—to the study of patterns for coming to faith, because they assume that the addressee is already a believer. Still, what can be discerned is the structure of blessings and evils in the past and present that impinge on what mission the receivers of an epistle are being persuaded to conduct. Epistles, like narratives, do have a cast of characters. In an epistle, the units and subunits are most easily identified by locating where there are changes in characters in the author's speech. "I" identifies the author, or supposed author (in pseudonymous material).[12] "You" identifies the receivers. A variety of persons whose actions impinge on the conversation between "I" and "you" are referred to in the third person: "God," "those in Laodicea," "no one," and so on. Time and space issues are read as in narrative. Looking at characters in Colossians 3:1-4, we find that the full unit of "you" references, which includes this subunit 3:1-4, begins at 2:6, "As therefore you . . . " Prior to 2:6, "Paul" was describing the shape of his mission (1:24—2:5). The larger unit ends at 3:17 since 3:18 begins a different term of address and a different subunit. To keep the values of the epistle from escaping from us into the past, I shall preserve the receiver's identifying "you" in what follows.

Significant for the subunit is that, in the larger unit, your life was rooted and built up in Jesus, your head and ruler (2:6-7), when God cancelled the bond that stood against you and triumphed over the principalities and powers (2:14). However, these great blessings of God given in the past (redemption, forgiveness,

> THINK ABOUT HOSPITALITY IN THE CONGREGATION. HOW MIGHT YOURS PROCLAIM AS WELL AS SUSTAIN? AND HOW MIGHT IT INTENTIONALLY STRENGTHEN BELIEVERS FOR WITNESS?

reconciliation, 1:13-14, 20) are endangered in your present by a teaching authority that is evil. You might fall prey to those who speak on behalf of the elemental spirits of the universe (2:8, 16, 18) who serve the power of darkness (1:13) under the appearance of wisdom and discernment (2:23). The evil that faces you is one of wrong teaching opposed to the blessing of right teaching, such as is offered by Paul, Timothy, and Epaphras (1:1, 7). In 2:20-23, the passage immediately preceding this lection, you are endangered if you submit to human regulations around worship and purity, for you have accepted someone's authority over you which is not Christ's authority. In addition, accepting ritual purity regulations may lead you to a second evil. You may submit to the false view that regulations will check your indulgence of the flesh. They won't. Enticing immorality is part of your gentile heritage. Therefore, you will have endangered your baptism (2:11-12) if, when you meet in assembly, you lie, slander, talk foully, or regard each other by your social roles or nationalities (3:8-11). Instead, you can preserve your heavenly blessings through compassion, patience, forgiveness, love, and peace, while you teach one another Christ's wisdom (3:16).

The Pattern of Faith in Colossians 3:1-4

Colossians 3:1-4 sits in the midst of this call to congregational values, most closely linked metaphorically with 2:11, 20-23. In that section, it was proposed that if you died with Christ to the elemental spirits, you should not be continuing to live according to the world. Colossians 3:1 makes a parallel statement. "If you have been raised with Christ, then seek the things that are above where Christ is seated at the right hand of God." There, your hope (1:5), your inheritance (1:12), and your life (3:3) are hidden—protected and secured—with Christ, through whom you were also already raised (3:1). That protection given in the past rests in heaven until you appear in glory with Christ when he comes (3:4).

Colossians' author is convinced that seeking the things that are above is something that you can do. You have the knowledge, will, and ability to do it because you are fully believers. In fact, you appear to hold fast the middle ground of time (the present) by endurance until the last day. That last day will make manifest what God has already done by raising you. You will be able to overcome the evil of wrong teachers and wrong wisdom if you focus on the rule of Christ, which is a rule of reconciliation, and as long as there are Pauls and Timothys and Epaphrases to recall you to the tradition and admonish you.

Integrating Colossians' Values about Mission into Your Preaching

1. The values of Colossians are very different from Easter Sunday's other lections. Not only has the believers' resurrection already happened, but also the congregation does not have an external mission itself; that is left to travelling religious authorities. Contrasted with the confidence that the author Luke had

in a basically safe and just gentile world in which all may proclaim by the power of the Spirit, Colossians' author evinces serious uncertainty about whether the powers of gentile evil are truly on the run. The author teaches to assure gentile converts that they are strong enough to withstand the onslaughts of those powers that formerly held them in bondage without additional but improper teaching. And yet, the author does not appear to see the Old Testament as a better source of teaching or modeling for the Colossians. It is the "mystery that has been hidden throughout the ages and generations that has now been made manifest to the saints" (1:26) which is their strongest ally.

2. That said, Colossians provides a fine proclamation for persons and communities that are in threatened situations. The double whammy of enticing immorality and threatening racism is well met by the proclamation of Colossians. In a hostile world, hostile to the reconciling values of the Lord Jesus, a counsel to be wary of elemental spirits and secular knowledge is a welcome one. Moreover, the counsel for steadfastness, a keeping one's eye on the prize of appearing on the last day with Christ, is a call to maturity. As you do not want your children to always remain babies in the faith, neither does God.

3. Mission in Colossians, then, is not absent so much as it involves a model of religious authority as rescuing folks from the enticing immorality of their former ways through correct teaching. Following the rescue/resurrection of believers, a congregation will model endurance and mutual admonition for those already baptized. While many of our congregations may see themselves as working on the endurance model with a view of the world outside as evil, the effectiveness of this model depends on there being a large class of missionaries outside the local congregations, to effect rescues from the culture and increase the numbers of believers. Endurance by itself is not mission. The question, "Why endure?" demands a joyful answer.

4. The phrase, "power of darkness" (1:12) is ably portrayed in the hit television show, "Buffy the Vampire Slayer." Each week those who appear to be wise authorities (familial, religious, romantic, or educational) turn out to be agents of the elemental spirits of the universe. Those who submit to their authority, or have it forced on them (fangs, usually) become estranged and hostile in mind (1:21). Given the world of teenagers where significant confusion exists over what is a good and bad authority, Colossians might be a resource for sorting out which is which.

The Witness of the Psalm and the Old Testament Lessons Alternatives

The interrupted sections of the Psalm and the Exodus lection, plus the narrowly defined unit of the Jeremiah text advise us that the selection of these texts is done to support the Gospel and Acts lessons for Easter. All three lections entail themes of rescue and rejoicing, although these occurrences reflect wide differences in time and space. In each lection, those deemed chosen by God, whether individuals ("I" references in Psalms) or groups (Israel freed from Egyptian captivity in Exodus and Jerusalem to be freed from captivity in Jeremiah) are reassured of divine affection, admonition, and steadfastness. Also in each lection, those who receive this divine message respond or will respond with praise and rejoicing in temple, wilderness, or exile. Because the New Testament lections mute a corporate rejoicing as the full assembly of believers does not yet know of the resurrection, it is appropriate to borrow a past rejoicing, remembering singing and dancing in victory as also the duty and delight of believers in Israel.

Three lectionaries have chosen Psalm 118 for Easter, Easter Evening, and for the Second Sunday of Easter, although the verse selections vary. All the selections for Easter Day and Easter Evening include 118:17 and 118:22, and all exclude 118:3-12, where the specific context of praise and salvation is explored. Verse 17, "I shall not die, but I shall live and recount the deeds of the Lord," can be used to describe the effect of the resurrection on believers who experience Christ's resurrection as the end of death for them, as Col. 3:1-4 implies, although the original context involves the fear of death rather than actual dying. Psalm 118:22, "the stone that the builders rejected has become the chief cornerstone," employed five times in the New Testament, would support your preaching on either of the lections from Matthew or Acts. Either verse might serve as a refrain for sermon sections or in a call and response pattern between you and the congregation.

The Exodus text is particularly fine for the African American tradition of worship and other traditions for which it is important to say, with Luke, that it is the God who would free from social oppression who wants to raise Jesus from the dead. In this lection, the values concerning the resurrection do not focus so much on a triumph over death as on God's gracious triumph over evil for the sake of the very people who brought that social evil about. If Israel survives the predation of Egypt (and it does), then a message from God to Ethiopians (like the God-fearing eunuch) or to Gentiles (like the God-fearing Cornelius) can go forth in its proper time. Getting out of Egypt is not abandoning that part of the world to nonbelief, for all people need freeing from the bondage of social evil so that they can interpret what God has done for them. Jeremiah 31:1-6 shows this same concern for social evil when it calls for its present believers, now in exile, to remember that the former believers who survived the sword found grace in the wilderness (Jer. 3:2).

Modern worshipers may have doubts about the connection between New and Old Testament lections on Easter—they may think of Israel's history with God as time past and that God attends to personal suffering, or the oppression of death, but not to social oppression in the present. It would be good for your sermon to make clear what kind of gimlet eye God casts on the evils of coercive authority in any age. While some Christians may be uncomfortable with the specifics of the exultation of believers who have found their God effective over armies and enemies, we need to recognize that the triumph of the resurrection is equally a triumph over particular enemies of God's way of engaging the world. That this triumph permits some enemies, like Paul, to become converts does not obviate the fact that God's enemies have not won the day.

These three lections, then, collect God's powerful energy to save in past, present, and future. For Christians on Easter, they serve best as typologies of the resurrection in advance of the resurrection. They link easily with both Matthew's and Luke's conviction that remembering the past interventions of God is necessary to have a proper interpretation of the present activities of God in the witness of Christ and in our own witness. John makes the same point by saying that without knowing the Old Testament scripture about the resurrection, Simon and the Beloved Disciple are at a loss before the tomb (20:9).

As a support to your preaching, it may be helpful to explain to the congregation that the view of God's activity in Matthew, Luke, and John is not based on our own view of history as, a professor of mine said, "one

> THESE THREE LECTIONS, THEN, COLLECT GOD'S POWERFUL ENERGY TO SAVE IN PAST, PRESENT, AND FUTURE.

darn, but unrepeatable, thing after another." Their views think about time as patterns of activity of God claiming us, God distressed with us, and God rescuing us. It is a view that thinks cyclically about the interaction between time and space as well. What is fundamental in this patterned view is that God is effective against evil assuredly and repeatedly. Although we may perceive the resurrection as unique,[13] the will to save is not. Easter worshipers might be well served by singing a hymn such as "Victory Is Mine," closely based on the Exodus text. The hymn has the effect of putting the singer in the position of both the celebrating Israelite and the celebrating Christian. The God who saved then is the God who saves now and the God who brings a salutary conclusion to the end of times.

EASTER EVENING

APRIL 4, 1999

REVISED COMMON	EPISCOPAL (BCP)	ROMAN CATHOLIC
Isa. 25:6–9	Acts 5:29a, 30–32	Acts 10:34, 37–43
	Dan. 12:1-3	
Ps. 114	Pss. 114, 136,	Ps. 118:1-2, 16-17,
	118:14-17, 22-24	22-23
1 Cor. 5:6b-8	1 Cor. 5:6b-8	Col. 3:1-4;
	or Acts 5:29, 30–32	1 Cor. 5:6-8
Luke 24:13-49	Luke 24:13-35	Luke 24:13-35

SUMMARY OF THE THEMES IN THE LESSONS

ISAIAH 25:6-9 AND 1 CORINTHIANS 5:6B-8 focus on the feasting dimensions of festivals of victory. These lessons are thus associated with Luke 24:13-49 on the strength of Luke 24:30, the meal at which Jesus blessed bread, and gave it to the two disciples near Emmaus. First Corinthians 5:6b-8 does provide a caveat for those who would approach the Eucharist cognizant only of its end-time feasting dimensions and not of the sincerity and truth necessary for truly being fed. First Corinthians 5:1-11, the full subunit, points to arrogance as the old leaven that pollutes (desecrates) the feast. Having been offered a meal with Jesus does not obviate that one must participate willingly and appropriately in the kind of feast that has been offered (cf. Luke 14:15-24). No lily resting here!

Luke 24:13-49 provides a different model for the nature of this meal that puts it smack in the middle of the ongoing witness of believers. Like the Pauline text, it will not play to a premature triumphalism. For Luke, the meal does not resemble a victory feast, but rather an intimate supper with an unrecognized Jesus during which those who have been slow to understand scripture have a Leader and Savior revealed to them.[14]

The BCP alternative from Daniel is chosen for its appeal to a resurrection when those who sleep in the dust at the end time will be awakened to everlasting life or everlasting shame and contempt. It is meant to function with Ps. 118, described in the Easter Day discussion. The Daniel text strengthens the rescue/raising connection of Ps. 118:17. Acts 5:29a, 30-32—the alternate second lesson for the BCP—also focuses on the resurrection connection. This lesson can effectively be preached in relation to the Lukan Gospel's concern, once one realizes that the proclamation of Peter (Acts 5:30-32) is identical to that communicated to the disciples by Jesus at Luke 24:46-47: the testimony of past witnesses, the present action of God, and the disciples' commission, empowered by the Holy Spirit, to be witnesses to these things. Psalm 114, Easter Evening's Psalm, focuses on the catastrophic effects of salvation by God even on the earth itself. There is a bucking and bouncing to the universe when God acts to save. The trembling fear of the earth might be thought as parallel to the effect of God's action to destroy Moab in Isa. 25:6-9, and also as parallel to the effect of being raised from the dust to judgment in Dan. 12:1-3.

GOSPEL
LUKE 24:13-49

The Reversals of Time, Space, Characters, and Themes

The full unit, of which Luke 24:13-49 forms a section, is Luke 24:1-53. All the events happen on one Sabbath, although they take a full day to accomplish. The character group formed is "shocked believers waiting." However, the locations do change. These spatially identified subunits are as follows: 24:1-11(12) (tomb in Jerusalem to disciples' location in Jerusalem); 24:13-32 (departure from Jerusalem, Emmaus, return to Jerusalem); 24:33-52 (Jerusalem, Bethany, Jerusalem). The full unit, 24:1-52, reverses *from* a group of believing women who had observed the command to rest on the Sabbath (23:56b), coming to anoint a body they cannot find, *to* a group of male[15] disciples returning to Jerusalem from Bethany in great joy, praising God, having been blessed by the very person whose body could not be found in 24:1.

The first subunit finds its reversal when the women who are perplexed by an absent body have angels come near to them and ask, "Why do you seek the living among the dead? Remember what he told you in Galilee" (24:5b-6). These women *remember* the past message of God's good news, and as simply as that, they return and report it. The disciples do not believe them, for they *do not remember* what Jesus has said and how it relates to scripture.

The second subunit picks up the sadness of the Emmaus travelers (24:17) who have not the proper interpretation of scripture for full confidence in God. Their sadness and their departure from Jerusalem are reversed when the proper interpretation of the past activity of God, of which Jesus reminds them, is conjoined with his coming near to them in a way he has been with them before as a teacher and at meals.

The third subunit begins at the reporting of the Emmaus disciples to the eleven who already know of a resurrection appearance to Simon (24:34). Then the eleven plus two suppose that the one they see is a spirit of Jesus, not Jesus himself. Touching his body and his eating broiled fish prove the type of appearance, but once again it is a proper interpretation of scripture that makes it possible for these disciples to rejoice and bear witness.

The three subunits inform the whole by these three reversals of the effects these events have on believers: 1) the women's perplexity and fear, having forgotten Jesus' words, become joy and an ability to report properly to the disciples; 2) the Emmaus travelers' sadness while they hold an improper understanding of all that the prophets had spoken becomes joy and a proper reporting; 3) the disciples thinking they saw a Spirit becomes rejoicing in the temple and the potential for a proper witness to others, once the promise of the Father has come upon them. Note the two pieces of the pattern that occur in all three units: a drawing near, a willingness to be in dialog, and the giving of a proper interpretation. Interestingly enough, reporting within the community by those instructed by Jesus and angels in the context of scripture can be done before the gift of the Holy Spirit. However, witness outside the community cannot occur until after that gift. The alternative lesson from Acts 5:29b, 30-32 (BCP) portrays why: the ability to speak boldly and face the suffering that comes from it is tied to the Holy Spirit witnessing with them.

> THE ABILITY TO SPEAK BOLDLY AND FACE THE SUFFERING THAT COMES FROM IT IS TIED TO THE HOLY SPIRIT WITNESSING WITH THEM.

The Place of Luke 24:13-49 in Luke's Pattern of Coming to Faith

Luke 24:13-49 provides a full pattern of the disciples coming to faith in the way that Luke sees as fundamental for believers to understand for their own witness. (Pattern details are available under the Acts lesson for Easter Day.) In this lesson, the sad travelers left Jerusalem and the temple, the site of the proper worship of God, for Emmaus. Jesus draws close to them when they are not willing to stay in Jerusalem. They do have a preliminary interpretation of scripture—they value it and Jesus as a prophet (like John) mighty in word and deed—but they do not have a proper understanding of that which has happened among them or how scripture pointed to it. Their eyes are therefore kept from recognizing Jesus due to their own misinterpretation. Still, some things that are proper to do are clear to them. "Doing something for others" leads them to provide overnight housing to this stranger. Their action keeps Jesus safe from a night sleeping on the cold ground and the concomitant evils of first-century travel (banditry). For the reader/hearer, this is especially touching, because we know this is he who was raised from the dead, who spent three days in the tomb! They are also willing to offer their guest the opportunity to thank God for the meal they share. Because the Passover and the Sabbath are over, the meal in which they are intimate with Jesus is a daily evening meal. When they recognize him, they recognize the full dimension of table ministry they shared with him: the teaching meals and the meals with tax collectors and sinners (6:1-5; 7:36-50; 9:10b-17; 10:38-42; 19:1-9), as well as the Passover supper (22:14-20). The reader/hearer will also recall that Jesus said he would not eat a Passover meal again or drink the fruit of the vine until the kingdom of God came (22:16-18). Effectively, the kingdom of God has come near in the resurrection; but believers need to learn its proper interpretation for their ministry—it does not equal the end of time. Were it not for the teaching of scripture, and Jesus' interpretation of it, the two on the way to Emmaus would not have recognized him (24:32).

The second portion of this lesson reinforces Luke's values about intimacy and scripture. Again Jesus draws near to the thirteen disciples where they *are* and becomes a neighbor to them. The Gospel ends with them in the temple praising God.

> EFFECTIVELY, THE KINGDOM OF GOD HAS COME NEAR IN THE RESURRECTION; BUT BELIEVERS NEED TO LEARN ITS PROPER INTERPRETATION FOR THEIR MINISTRY—IT DOES NOT EQUAL THE END OF TIME.

This time, the disciples recognize him, and he asks their help. Because spirits do not need to eat, his eating satisfies his hunger and their surprise. After this meal, the hospitality of mission may begin. Repentance and forgiveness are to be preached by drawing near in his name to all peoples by his scripture-sharing and meal-sharing witnesses. The immediate effect on the disciples is that they are willing and able to be back in the temple praising God and waiting for the promise from on high. Fully taught, fully intimate with Jesus, the disciples are now fully believers ready for mission.

Integrating Lukan Values about Mission into Your Preaching

For Luke, how Jesus acts toward the disciples in their coming to faith is how believers should act toward others coming to faith. Similarly, those who have fallen aside from the faith because of social evils are due the same kind of interested intimacy. One might think of the disciples in Luke 24 as some who have already believed, but have fallen aside due to the assault of the Roman Empire on Jesus. While this is not an exact match for the text, it does allow us to think about how Luke might see us in mission to those who have left our worshiping communities as well as those who have not yet entered them. In any case, Luke has little use in his own Gospel or in our churches for narratives of conversion to belief or narratives of recovery of wholeness, which do not portray the converted or recovered as in mission to others.

1. It is clear from Luke 24 that for our witness to those who might be coming to belief, we need to interpret things about Jesus before the potential believer can recognize him in a eucharistic meal. First, we must draw near to believers with freeing actions and freeing words. Luke, then, would see open communion not as what occurs during the Eucharistic rite, but as that which precedes it: the

mission of the church. Ultimately, the meal with Jesus serves as a confirmation, fulfillment, and extension of this mission for adults committed to their own mission to draw near to others in dialog about the power of God to save. Luke's counsel grows out of his worry that too many folks, including priests and preachers, know the ritual of praise without a living relationship with a God who is active in the present and has mission on the divine mind. This very problem confounds Zechariah in Luke 1, when he knows the ritual of praise but does not trust God's archangel. He is praising God without the proper interpretation of God's acts in the present. In Luke 24, in a fine reversal, Jesus is a free agent for witness, just as a witnessing believer needs to be. For all that God raises Jesus from out of the social evil of crucifixion, Jesus is not in the temple praising God, but is out drawing near to his distressed disciples. With the proper interpretation supplied by Jesus, they too will be able to praise God properly in the temple (24:49).

> LUKE, THEN, WOULD SEE OPEN COMMUNION NOT AS WHAT OCCURS DURING THE EUCHARISTIC RITE, BUT AS THAT WHICH PRECEDES IT: THE MISSION OF THE CHURCH.

2. Jesus' and our drawing near to others is meant to function as an impetus to the relief of the social evil we find. Jesus' and our conversations about God's actions occur after the relief of social evil, and are meant to move others to join us in witness. Each new understanding Jesus offers, and each way he approaches a conversation, is focused on the evil a particular group of believers has experienced. There is no blanket proclamation of the good news by Jesus or by us, Luke would say, just as there is not one meal with Jesus in Luke 24—there are two! Once a believer has drawn near to a person and the person is willing to invest in a conversation or a meal, then teaching may occur through various means. The two meals for two purposes in Luke 24 point to each meal being a cooperative venture between those coming to full belief and their Lord. All meals of believers and seekers are meals with Jesus, as far as Luke is concerned, because they are meals with those who have the spirit of Jesus. Similarly, intimidation and coercion—the model of worldly rulers in Luke—is ruled out as a model for mission; it will not make witnesses out of the detached or the distressed.

3. For those believers who have lost their faith to fear or sadness, Luke assures us that Jesus' spirit will still come near and invite disconsolate believers to participate actively in their own restoration. Those who formerly were full believers may be so mired in fear, despair, or a deep sense of annoyance at the church that they no longer know what loving God entails. In Luke 24, sadness and the inability to worship the Father of the Son are linked. While the disciples have not needed healing from despair up until the Passion, now they do. The Passion has led them to know, through Jesus being executed, that they too are subject to the deconstructive power of social evil, despite the triumph they felt when demons were subject to them in Jesus' name (Luke 10:17). Like Jesus, we are to invite our

distressed former sister or brother into a relationship. That relationship is enhanced for us by knowing that our Lord wants to eat with us and them for the sake of God.

4. In Luke 24, notice that it is not just Jesus who attends to the Gospel ministry, it is also the women to the disciples, and the enlightened travelers to the eleven. Jesus' ministry is, from the beginning, a corporate one in Luke. He calls groups of people, and in turn they need boatloads of fishers to gather a net full of fish (5:1-11) at his behest. It will take 70 to go on a gathering mission, two by two (10:1-20) as the first step to making believers. Here too the activity is corporate and pragmatic, not solitary and hierarchical, for mission is the desire and action of all believers. Where once the two on the way to Emmaus could do no more than offer hospitality to Jesus, a drawing near to him in presumed need, now they will be empowered to offer "Gospeltality" to others.

5. Suffering as the result of proclaiming the good news is a foregone conclusion in Luke. Additional results, however, are rejoicing, and an increase in believers drawing near to those who are captive. Social evil does come upon those who seek to be a neighbor to those in need, and that includes the prophets and God's own son. Suffering occurs in Luke largely because some, usually leaders, do not know what they are doing. Jesus' petition from the cross (23:34a) marks this as a fundamental sin. Still, those acting destructively toward others need from us a proper inter-

SUFFERING AS THE RESULT OF PROCLAIMING THE GOOD NEWS IS A FOREGONE CONCLUSION IN LUKE.

pretation of what loving God and loving others mean, despite consequences. The believer needs to draw near to the destructive one, because to be destructive of another is to be destructive of oneself. Prayer for the self-destructive person needs to include a prayer for us—that we and others might have the spirit to approach them. The bottom line for believers, as shown in Acts 5:29-32, is that it is better to suffer social oppression with and for Jesus than without him.

SECOND SUNDAY OF EASTER

APRIL 11, 1999

REVISED COMMON	EPISCOPAL (BCP)	ROMAN CATHOLIC
Acts 2:14a, 22-32	Acts 2:14a, 22-32 or Gen. 8:6-16, 9:8-16	Acts 2:42-27
Ps. 16	Pss. 111; 118:19-24	Ps. 118:2-4, 13-15, 22-24
1 Peter 1:3-9	1 Peter 1:3-9 or Acts 2:14a, 22-32	1 Peter 1:3-9
John 20:19-31	John 20:19-31	John 20:19-31

THE SUMMARY OF THE THEMES IN THE LESSONS

THE SECOND SUNDAY OF EASTER IN THE RCL provides a cohesive set of themes of salvation typology that should make it possible for you to move easily between lessons. Psalm 16, attributed to David, provides David's testimony that the Lord did not give him up to Sheol, but will show him the path of life (16:10-11). Acts 2:22-32 echoes this witness in a long discussion that points to David as speaking not about himself, but about Jesus, the one crucified and risen.

In a parallel fashion, "Blessed are those who have not seen, yet believed," from John 20:29, is echoed in 1 Peter 1:8, with its "without having seen him, you love him." Together the four lessons point to the issue of a rejoicing faith without sight: 1) David, a prophet, rejoicing, knows the faithful one will not see the pit and 2) he points ahead to Jesus, 3) for whom there was rejoicing when he was raised and was seen, if only for a short time and, 4) people all over the Empire, even Gentiles, became believers and rejoiced without seeing Jesus.

The BCP and the RC lectionary suggest Psalm 118 again for the power of 118:17, "I shall not die but live." The alternate BCP Old Testament lesson reports the story of the rescue of Noah, with the rainbow as a reminder to God of the covenant God has made with the peoples of the earth. This works well thematically with Psalm 111, the BCP alternative, which focuses on the faithful reliability of God. Beyond the thematic connection, of course, each text has its own concerns about creating or sustaining faith. This will be explored below.

GOSPEL

JOHN 20:19-31

The Reversals of Time, Space, Characters, and Themes

John's pattern for coming to faith and the full textual unit of John 20:1-31 was explored under the Easter Day Gospel. Please refer there for more details on themes and characters continuing into this unit. John 20:19-29 has time, space, character, and theme reversals *from* the disciples (although having received a report from Mary Magdalene), hiding in Sabbath darkness (in a shut room out of fear of the religious authorities) without seeing the body, *to* a visible body, a confession by Thomas and Jesus stating the low value of seeing and touching his body for those who will believe.

Within 20:19-29 is a further subunit, 20:19-23. In it, the disciples, shut-in out of fear, are in no position to believe or witness. The subunit reverses *from* fear and shut-in silence to "Peace" (i.e., calm yourselves), and commissioning the disciples as apostles of the Father by the power of the Holy Spirit. Additional reversals in this unit pick up on what has been communicated before to Mary Magdalene about the disciples' new status. Until Jesus' report to Mary Magdalene in 20:17, Jesus' Father was not the disciples' father. So, the shut-in disciples perceive themselves as alienated from their family of origin but do not yet have a new identity. Jesus' sending them as his Father has sent him marks the reversal as completed: the disciples are fully transferred in genealogy and inheritance to be offspring of the heavenly Father, commissioned children of a different *pater familias*.[16]

In the next subunit (20:24-29), Thomas, by getting stuck on Jesus' visibility and corporeality, impedes his receiving a transfer to the family of the Father and a commission from Jesus. The reversal in this subunit occurs when Jesus, knowing Thomas through his blurted comment about touching, is willing to come to Thomas and allow him to do the very thing that Mary Magdalene (20:17) was advised not to do. If in Luke, Jesus goes the extra mile to Emmaus, here in John, Jesus turns up the wattage so Thomas can see better. But this is not all. Jesus' response points to another reversal related to a character group picked up from 20:1-28. Those who have seen Jesus so far have been Israelites from Galilee. Now, those who will be blessed for not seeing, but believing, will be identified not by ethnicity or religious background, but by belief. So, the last reversal points onward to believers that Thomas will never see (20:29).

> THOSE WHO HAVE SEEN JESUS SO FAR HAVE BEEN ISRAELITES FROM GALILEE. NOW THOSE WHO WILL BE BLESSED FOR NOT SEEING, BUT BELIEVING, WILL BE IDENTIFIED NOT BY ETHNICITY OR RELIGIOUS BACKGROUND, BUT BY BELIEF.

The last subunit of the Gospel, John 20:30-31, picks up the same themes of not seeing/seeing and not touching/touching as the unit above. *From* Jesus having done signs (past time) in the presence of the disciples (space) so that they would believe (past time), *to* the author having written signs (space and past time) so that *you* may believe and have life in his name (in the present space and time).

At first, these two verses seem more disconnected than connected with John 20:19-29, because the characters differ. The narrator is speaking, and you (the reader/hearer) are addressed directly. These two verses return the reader/hearer to the values described in the prologue, where the narrator sets up a frame of "they" (nonbelievers) and "we" (believers). The prologue did not say how the reader/hearer, who was not present during Jesus' life, could become part of the "we" who were with Jesus during that time. That is now clear. These signs, which were things that were *seen* during Jesus' life, are now *written* so that *seeing what is written* replaces *seeing the earthly Jesus,* under the aegis of the Holy Spirit. His flesh is now the written word: It is pages and pixels.

John 20:19-31 in the Gospel's Pattern for Coming to Faith

From the beginning of John's Gospel the issue about the knowledgeable response to Jesus' ability to do signs has been wending its way through the text. Jesus' final sign in this chapter is his willingness to be touched by Thomas. Thomas's role as receiver of this action by Jesus is paradigmatic of the experience of the disciples throughout the Gospel. Jesus coming to him to show and teach him allows Thomas to move from amazement at the story of Jesus' resurrection, to belief in Jesus, to finally believing in Jesus' message about future believers. These three stages of believing were necessary for the other disciples before they could become witnesses to the witness that Jesus had made. We might say Jesus uses his last breath to give them the Holy Spirit. They are commissioned, like Jesus, by the power of his Spirit to make the message of the Father known, drawing people to the light by revealing the truth about their knowledge, deeds, and true character. Then, if the hearers are open to being known, the disciples will give them the Spirit and the power to become children of God under the authority of the Father and the Son. If some are not open to the light, the disciples have the power to retain sins, which is, effectively, preserving the condemnation for what has already been done.

We learn from Thomas's story that witnessing to a belief in Jesus as incarnate has preliminary value in drawing others to God. However, it points no further than Jesus' corporeality. Witnessing to Jesus' message about earthly and heavenly things, the time of the Messiah, salvation and judgment, the Spirit and the will of God has enduring value. Others then may also, through the witness of the disciples, make the journey through Jesus to the Father, beginning first with the amazement of signs, moving then to confidence in the doers of such deeds, until finally they reach the new-world ordering values presented in Jesus' witness for the Father.

1. The preacher may find John 20:30-31 a useful summary of how the entire Gospel has been persuading believers toward a mature faith. John 1:14, 16-18 might be read as an introduction to the Gospel reading each week that Johannine texts are used in the Easter Season. John 20:30-31 could be read at the end of the Gospel to inform the parishioners of what the purpose of the public reading of scripture is in John's eyes. Your sermon might focus on how "we the believers whose confidence and proclamation came from seeing Jesus in the flesh" (1:14) have now become "we the believers whose confidence and proclamation come from being begotten of the Father and taught by the Spirit and scripture about our Ascended Lord."

2. You might also focus a sermon on the whole unit of 20:1-31, showing parishioners how what has happened to Peter, the Beloved Disciple, Mary Magdalene, Thomas, and the rest of the disciples in this chapter is *also* what has happened and is happening to them as believers. This would help encourage your parishioners in their necessary private study of scripture as a family album of their own coming to faith and witness.

3. The strong focus at the beginning of John 20 on seeing the physical body of Christ shows that the first readers/hearers were inclined to feel bereft and unsure of their witness without the first generation of believers' experience. The low value placed on Christ's body at the end is John's proposal as to how believers are to regard Jesus' body. Knowing where Jesus' body is and knowing how his body looks or feels turn out to be unrelated to believing that he is the unique son of the Father.[17] The time for seeing Jesus in the flesh is over, according to John's Gospel, and need not be part of our witness. At the same time, John encourages believers to hold a low value about their bodies as well. A proper knowledge of earthly and heavenly things will sustain believers through their own lives, deaths, and resurrections. The Spirit will blow them where it will and may also put them in situations where others may confuse their signs with their witness. They need not to overvalue the signs they do, but point to beliefs in Jesus' words about the Father.

THE FIRST LESSON
ACTS 2:14a, 22-32 (RCL, BCP);
ACTS 2:42-47 (RC)

The Pattern of Coming to Faith in Acts Chapter 2

Luke describes the descent of the Spirit on the disciples, and the beginning of Peter's proclamation to the devout Jews who see and hear it, in two subunits of Acts 2 which all three lectionaries reserve for Pentecost Sunday (2:1-21). The rest of the chapter, in which Luke is greatly interested in your knowing what effect the Spirit's power has on proclamation and mission, is reserved for the *preceding* second through the sixth Sundays of Easter (2:22-47). This may cause you a bit of consternation in organizing your witness—the effects of the Spirit are preached before its descent.

The schema that follows will help you understand how the subunits of Acts 2:1-47 are meant to function in their proper order as the first Acts narrative where the mission and proclamation activities of the disciples parallel the witness of Jesus, the one now raised. I have assigned each subunit of the chapter to the place in Luke's pattern of coming to faith that it represents most completely. You'll find it helpful to compare this schema with the overall pattern described at the first lesson for Easter Day, since the letters of the steps are parallel to that schema. You will also find that the First Lesson for the Second Sunday of Easter (RCL, BCP) is contained in Step D 2-3, which I have lengthened accordingly. The First Lesson (RC) is contained in Step E. The beginning of the First Lesson is actually the completion of the pattern of coming to faith of the disciples begun in Luke's Gospel. The Spirit of Jesus equips the apostles and other believers for proclamation and mission to continue the work of Jesus for God (2:1-4). Acts 2:5ff then begins this pattern again as Jews from everywhere gather in Jerusalem at Pentecost.

A. Those attending the pilgrimage festival in Jerusalem at Pentecost are honoring commitments made at Sinai. What God did for Israel at Sinai, after saving them from physical and social oppression in Egypt, was to tell Israel what they should do for God and others to honor this holy relationship (Deut. 26:1-19; Acts 2:5) and not oppress others now that they were free to worship God.

B. The power of the Holy Spirit resting on the disciples shows through tongues and wonders that the devout Jews at the festival are in the time of the disciples' empowerment by Jesus' Spirit (Acts 2:1-4). These Jews, who already have a preliminary knowledge of God's actions to save people from oppression and a preliminary knowledge of the Law and the proclamatory Spirit of the prophets, perceive correctly that they are hearing testimony to the mighty acts of God (Acts 2:5-12). However, all who hear do not have a proper interpretation of what occasions this testimony (Acts 2:13).

C. Peter, on behalf of the other Spirit-filled believers, initiates a close relationship with the devout Jews by answering their queries to each other about the meaning of these events (Acts 2:14-15).

D. Peter provides the proper interpretation of what they are seeing and hearing. He proclaims how the present activity of God's Spirit relates to the past activity of God's Spirit. His teaching reinterprets three of God's activities that these devout Jews in Jerusalem need reinterpreted if they are to desire the salvation that Peter would offer to them (Acts 2:16-36).

1. They need a proper interpretation of the present time (Acts 2:14-21). It is not the time for drinking but for rejoicing. Peter properly identifies the

time as the last days, and the authority for this proper interpretation is that of the prophet Joel: prophecies and wonders mark the present beginning of the end. Believers prophesying with tongues of spiritual fire, and visions occurring to all kinds of people, are beneficent signs of the drawing near of God, as they were in the past. Other signs of God's drawing near now and in the past are fearsome: blood and fire, and vapor of smoke. All these will occur before the great last day. Still, as Joel prophesied, all persons who call on the Lord, whether their turning to God was initiated by beneficent or fearsome signs, will be saved!

2. They need a proper interpretation of the life and death of Jesus of Nazareth (Acts 2:22-24, 31-36). The signs of the Spirit and words of the nearness of salvation from Joel (2:21) prepare the devout Jews to hear a new interpretation of Jesus' actions. Jesus, a worker of beneficent signs, put to death by those who did not know God's law, acting at the hands of those who did, was raised from the physical and social evil of crucifixion by God. Such commitment by God is parallel to God's saving Israel from physical and social evil in Egypt, and giving them commands and ordinances to follow to praise God and to prevent the oppression of others. Moreover, this event with Jesus is not a deed completed in the past, for Peter and other believers are witnesses to its power in the present by virtue of the promised Holy Spirit. They can all testify that the one the devout Jews caused to be crucified by the hands of the lawless, God has made Lord and Christ. This testimony by unexpected persons (those looking drunk) is a sign of the beginning of the end times.

3. They need a proper interpretation of the prophecy and kingship of David as it relates to Jesus' Lordship before God (Acts 2:25-30, 34). Peter's scriptural testimony is to David as prophet, who rejoices and hopes in the near presence of God to him and the unequivocal guarantee of rescue from Hades. The praise and hope of David parallel the pattern of beneficent nearness of God and the dangerous nearness of God who has power over Hades. Peter, having established David's credentials as a prophet concerned with salvation and the future of Israel, changes the metaphorical value of David from prophet to mortal king. David, to whom the promise of a royal descent was made, is dead and buried; the crucified one is alive by God's own action. Therefore, David is speaking from his vision of the resurrection of Christ, that he was not abandoned to Hades, but raised. In summary, David foresaw the Christ from the past, while Peter proclaims that the Jews at the festival of Pentecost were not properly observant of the Law, "you shall not kill," nor of the power of God in their midst.

E. Many of the devout Jews, showing their willingness to be taught about the present times, and about Jesus and David's life, death, and prophecy, are cut to the heart by the accusation of Peter that they acted lawlessly toward the one God named Lord and Christ. They ask, as once John the Baptist's hearers asked in Luke 3:10, "What shall we do?" Repentance will be necessary, as well as baptism for the forgiveness of sins, because these devout Jews have been identified as assisting in the crucifixion of Jesus, which makes them lawless also, much as the priest and Levite are identified with the lawless bandits in Luke 10:30-36. With God's help, they then can regain a proper understanding of what loving God and neighbor mean, a meaning that re-presents God's past and present actions to save and God's insistence on drawing near to the oppressed and the sinful (Acts 2:37-40).

F. The Holy Spirit promised to be coming upon them after their repentance and baptism permit the Jews at the feast to begin properly praising God and properly relating to one another. They then become a mixed community of Judean, Galilean, and Diasporan Jews who have experienced and taken unto themselves the power of God in Christ through the disciples' witness. Once they receive the Holy Spirit they will be enabled to proclaim to those who are far off in Parthia, Pontus, Phryrgia, and so on. Their mission upon returning home will be "doing something for God" and "doing something for others" by saying to their co-religionists words like these, "Scripture testifies that the one we crucified was raised by God who still draws near to us." "Save yourself from this corrupt generation by repentance and baptism." And, "The promise is . . . for everyone to whom the Lord our God calls" (Acts 2:38, 41-47).

The Reversals of Time, Space, and Characters in Acts 2:1-47

Acts 2:38-40 is a complete discourse unit since the time, space, and some characters are different before and after this chapter. The chapter begins with all the believers (the twelve plus the women, Mary, the Mother of Jesus, and his brothers) waiting for the action of God as announced by Jesus to impel their mission (Luke 24:49; Acts 1:4-5). It ends with many wonders and signs done by the apostles, and the number of believers increased (Acts 2:43-47). Now all three thousand have a common stewardship, a common worship in the temple and at home, and the respect of all the people. Plus, the Lord acts to save more daily.

Several themes for preaching become apparent through these full chapter reversals: those waiting (2:1) *become* those rejoicing (2:46); those following (2:1) *become* those proclaiming and doing wonders (2:14-43, 46); a small number of believers (2:1) *become* a great number of believers (2:41); believers able to "do something for God" (waiting and praising God, 2:1) *become* believers able to "do something for God" and able to "do something for others" (proclaiming the good news, having everything in common, 2:44-47); a few followers together in a private house lacking the approval of the wider community (2:1-2) *become* religious leaders, led by Peter, and believers having the approval of the wider community

(2:47); and, most important, devout Jews gathered for the festival of Pentecost, uncertain of what is happening before them, *become* Jews repentant before God, baptized in Jesus Christ for the forgiveness of sins, and soon-to-be spirit-filled. That is a lot of reversals! So, what connection do these reversals have to the first lesson for the Second Sunday of Easter? (Acts 2:22-32). How does our out-of-order text help effect the change from a meager beginning to an end with such a wealth of new believers?

The Reversals in Time, Space, Characters, and Themes in Acts 2:22-36

First, we need to note that the effective subunit for the First Lesson is Acts 2:22-36. Cutting the unit at 2:22-32 leaves off the final comparison between David and Jesus. Adding these extra lines helps us see that the function of this subunit is for Peter to bring to light the present interpretation the devout Jews have of Jesus (as debased) and David (as exalted) and to offer an alternate interpretation. The structure of the subunit is a "dialog" with Peter presenting both points of view about Jesus and David: that of the devout Jews and that of the spirit-filled believers. The point of this "talking heads" format is not for Peter (or Luke or you or me as readers and hearers) to condemn David as ungodly. Luke wants to offer to the reader a proper interpretation of the activities of God in past and present that will make new sense of Jesus and David to devout Jews. Then they will know how eagerly God is seeking them out with salvation in hand.[18] Acts 2:37 shows us that the persuasion of this subunit is successful, because the devout Jews "were cut to the heart." As a result, the reader/hearer is invited to ponder how he or she, as a Christian coming out of another religious tradition (as everyone did!) might persuade his or her former co-religionists to a new interpretation of the values of certain heroes and certain villains of the tradition.

Gathering the descriptions of the character "Jesus," the reversals in the values associated there are as follows. Jesus, as Peter describes him in 2:22, is recognized as a mighty wonder worker by the devout Jews. And yet they caused him to be crucified by those outside the law (Gentiles and/or the immoral). They therefore understand him as a threat to Judaism and as lawless himself, worthy of debasement. They do not know him as the agent of God. At 2:24, 31-33, 36, we identify the perspective of Peter and the spirit-filled believers. Jesus is exalted as Lord and Christ and has been raised from the dead, all by the action of God who is providing the wonders that surround Peter's speech and had given Joel the spirit to prophesy.

The character "David" begins as one recognized by the devout Jews as having a special relationship to God, both as Israel's Lord and God's anointed (cf. Ps. 2; Acts 2:25). Through that relationship, David, as a spirit-filled prophet, foresees that he will not be abandoned to Hades or into physical corruption (*diaphthora means* "the pit[s]" in Greek!). For the devout Jews, in Ps. 16:8-11, David, then, is testifying about himself. According to the perspective of Peter and the others, David was not foreseeing his own future, because David died (Acts 2:29-31). David was foreseeing the resurrection-rescue of Jesus who is David's Lord, and more exalted than he, for his Lord Jesus has been exalted to God's right hand. It is Jesus who has actively poured out his spirit in the present (2:33). David foresaw Jesus' power, but it is not his to share, since he did not live "in the time of Jesus" (Luke 10:23-24).

In the devout Jews' perspective (according to Peter), the themes of unshakenness, safety from death, and honor are associated with David's character, while the themes of abandonment, endangerment from death, and dishonor are associated with Jesus. In Peter's own perspective unshakenness, safety from death, and honor are associated with Jesus, while abandonment to Hades, endangerment from death, and dishonor (in comparison with Jesus: David is not Lord or Christ) are associated with David. And yet, it is David, whom the devout Jews value, who foresaw what they did not: that the wonder-worker was his Lord and Christ according to the definite plan and foreknowledge of God (2:23).

In effect, the devout Jews in this subunit are presented with the opportunity to experience themselves as dishonored by not properly understanding what God was doing in their present with the law or with Jesus freeing people from oppression. On the other hand, these devout Jews also have the chance to avoid remaining dishonored or abandoned by God, but rather becoming safe from death and honored with the Spirit, if they accept the salvation being offered to them (2:38-40).

Integrating Lukan Values about Mission into Your Preaching

Because all of Acts chapter 2 is one narrative, you might preach (and demonstrate in your preaching) the structure of a mission conversation for Luke. By mission, in this context, I mean a conversation (not a monologue) with someone who is not a Christian about the blessings of our God as experienced by the believer through scripture, and in their own congregation, city, and personal life. This mission focus can dovetail with John 20:30-31, where the concern for scripture, so important to Luke, is reiterated. Acts 2:22-36 will provide a plethora of examples of a movement for mission.

1. "Don't start a mission conversation in the middle!" would be Luke's first mission value. Acts 2:22-36 is the turning point of a conversion narrative, not its beginning or end. The flow of mission conversation for Luke begins with expressing the blessed power of God to save in the past and present of those talking.

2. Those talking can be anyone and everyone, since it is the Spirit that gives the power for these mission dialogs to be rich for both parties involved. However, it is important to note that those talking have some things in common and

some things not in common. Peter, as a devout Jew knowing Christ, was readily able to draw near to other devout Jews. A Christian who was formerly a Muslim is readily able to draw near to a devout Muslim. A Filipino Christian seafarer is readily able to draw near to a Filipino non-Christian seafarer. What is harder for the believer is to know how to approach those whose differences one values negatively. On this issue, even Peter needed some instruction from the Almighty (Acts 10:9-16). So, too, does Ananias (Acts 9:10-17).

3. From there, the conversation would move toward the identification of the evil that is impeding freedom, or rejoicing, or confidence in God, and so on. Note that there is no preset mission conversation: no required question or required answer. That is important to your parishioners who may think the discussion about David is a preset answer to a current Jewish concern about Christianity. It is not. The Spirit and the believer together will find their own way of witnessing. Nevertheless, there is an acknowledgment that we do live in the midst of an evil generation, made hopeless for all who live without the nearness of God.

4. The evil that impedes a proper understanding of God's actions may be external or internal. External evil in Luke is oppression: social, physical, and demonic. Internal evil is a matter of a wrong interpretation of the activity of God or others. It is also clear in Luke that God will act in ways that may appear positive or negative to people. Nevertheless, God will respond to people willing to come near to God whether they are startled into it by beneficent or dangerous divine power. In any human endeavor, as well as in any Lukan text, external and internal evils (sin) interrelate. The subunit before us is a good example. Devout Jews, loyal to God and the Law, had misperceived the activity of God in Jesus. They supported lawlessness, and not lawfulness, a failure for them in relation to a principal they held most dear and contributed to the oppressive death of Jesus.

> GOD WILL RESPOND TO PEOPLE WILLING TO COME NEAR TO GOD WHETHER THEY ARE STARTLED INTO IT BY BENEFICENT OR DANGEROUS DIVINE POWER.

5. The third part of Lukan mission conversation is the desire to learn the proper interpretation of one's actions. One may be oppressing others out of fear for one's own safety. One may have a wrong understanding of the figures of the faith or the opponents of the faith. In our subunit, the devout Jews experienced the guilt of their sin like the cut of a knife and immediately wanted to know how they could repair the oppression and their relationship to God.

6. Mercifully, that was what God desired also, for the last part of any Lukan mission conversation is blessing and rejoicing: the restatement that what God desires is the people's hearts turned to the Lord, and the believers doing something for God and something for others.

THE SECOND LESSON
1 PETER 1:3-9

The Pattern of Faith and the Development of Values in 1 Peter

This is the first of several Sundays that consider 1 Peter, an epistle whose text has concerns for purity similar to those in Hebrews. Nevertheless, the recipients of the letter are Gentiles of the Diaspora, who appear to be new to the Christian faith, having recently turned from their Gentile immorality inherited from their fathers (1:18).

As the recipients of the epistle have already come to faith, the interest of the author is in first strengthening what they already believe and providing a regimen supportive of their faith in the top-down but chaotic world of the empire. Second, 1 Peter has a definite concern for a Christian mission. It occurs as a rationale for the many reminders to honor and obey all authority above the believer (2:12). This counsel is important for these Diaspora believers, but especially wives of non-Christian husbands and slaves of non-Christian masters (2:18—3:7) so that they might have an unblemished chance to make account of the hope that is in them (3:15-17), given that they may suffer for it anyway (1:6; 2:20).

The Reversals of Time, Space, Characters, and Themes in 1 Peter 1:3-9

The effective discourse unit in which 1 Peter 1:3-9 is contained is 1 Peter 1:1-23. For the lectionary, the chapter is split between the Second and Third Sunday of Easter: 1:1-9 and 1:17-23. The preacher might divide the unassigned material in the following way, choosing to preach on 1:1-12 and, subsequently, 1:13-23. This division would allow this Second Sunday's focus to be on that which has been done in Christ "for the sake of the Gentiles." The Third Sunday might then focus on what Gentiles need to do in response to the great treasure of Christ's coming, suffering, death, resurrection, and reign.

Much else can also be done with this rich chapter. The time component of this chapter looks back to Christ who was destined before the foundation of the world (1:20), attested to by the prophets for the Gentiles' sake (1:10), and made manifest at the end of times, also for the Gentiles' sake. Still, because his revelation is accomplished at the end of time, the Gentiles who love him do not see him now (1:8), an echo of John 20:19-31. Space is also an important image in 1 Peter. The readers/hearers are identified as exiles of the dispersion, spatially separated from both earthly homelands and their heavenly home. Their hope rests not on the flimsy but dangerous present world but on the rather substantial heavenly realm, large enough for vast spiritual treasures to be kept there.

The Petrine texts that focus on the importance of mission in spite of suffering are those assigned for the Fourth, Sixth, and Seventh Sundays of Easter. First Peter 1:1-23 can provide you with the themes that will then form the backdrop for these more specific texts. First Peter 1:1-23 does well in answering, "What kind of world is this in which this mission is undertaken?" Several themes repeatedly reverse in this chapter, which aim to describe this world. It is a world quite different from current American democracy, but not all that unlike the recent past of Chile, El Salvador, Guatamala, Bosnia, and the Chechen Republic. Moreover, it is not all that unlike the experience of those believers who live below the poverty line in the South Bronx or Jersey City, New Jersey, or who huddle as illegal aliens on the waterfront in San Francisco. One group of my students at L.T.S.P. found that the experience of the spiritually recovering aliens of 1 Peter made good sense of the experience of prisoners who had become Christians in prison. They rewrote the text of 1 Peter as an exhortation to these Christian prisoners to live a life worthy of their new Parent and not to fall back into the futile ways of their fellow prisoners. Instead, these new Christians needed to respect the authorities they formerly maligned, for the sake of being able to give account of the hope that was now in them. I'm sure you will think of other examples where spiritual values must hold a tempted people together in holiness in the face of chaotic civil conditions when the empire does strike back. First Peter attends to these issues in part by portraying destructive themes followed by hopeful reversals.

1. Under Christ's authority of suffering, perishability (1:7, 18, 23) becomes imperishability (1:4, 20, 23), with the former becoming the latter through believers being sprinkling with Christ's precious blood (1:2, 19).

2. By God the Father's blessing, the inheritance of futile, fleshly ways from gentile fathers (1:18) is replaced by an inheritance of undefiled, heavenly blessing (a living hope) kept for Gentiles until the last time (1:5). This hope is substantiated by other family images: begotten again to a living hope (not *born* to a living hope 1:3, 23); becoming "blood siblings" through Jesus shedding his blood (1:2, 22); becoming obedient children of the judge whom they call "Father" (1:14).

3. By Christ's witness, obedience to the passions of believers' former ignorance (1:13) becomes obedience to Christ (1:2).

4. By faith, believers suffering various trials without respect and purity become believers suffering trials under faith in Christ (1:7, 11; 2:21-25). His similar sufferings simply burnished his glory (1:11) and they will do the same for the believer at the end time.

PSALM AND THE OLD TESTAMENT ALTERNATIVES

PSALM 16 (RCL); PSALM 111 (BCP); PSALM 118:19-24 (BCP); PSALM 118:2-4, 13-15, 22-24 (RC) GENESIS 8:6-16; 9:8-16

Psalm 118:2-4, 13-15, 22-24 (RC) is covered at Easter Evening.

Psalm 16 is the intentional parallel to Acts 2:22-32 for the RCL on this Sunday. The preacher might find it more useful to have the Psalm read twice: once from the perspective of David and once from the perspective of David's foresight of the resurrection and exaltation of Christ. Having it sung (except by solo voices) may not assist the preaching intent. Psalm 16:4 also picks up the repeated image from 1 Peter 1:1-23 of sprinkling with blood. It matters whose blood it is! The holy ones in the land (116:3) are exemplified in Acts 2 and 1 Peter as two New Testament examples of holiness. Because of all these connections, a preacher might wish to preach from the pattern of the relationship between God and David in Psalm 16, moving into its echoes in 1 Peter and its changes in Acts. Note also the language of heritage (16:6) which parallels the language of inheritance in 1 Peter 1:1-23.

Psalm 111 serves as a delightful hymn of praise in a corporate situation celebrating that which for us imbues the Easter season with joy: the steadfast and attentive love of God. No particular connections are made to the other lessons.

Genesis 8:6-16; 9:8-16, the Old Testament alternative for the BCP, evokes images of Noah waiting on the Lord, much as the disciples in Jerusalem waited for the descent of the Spirit. As God's reliable rainbow covenant with Noah followed the waiting for God's sign of the readiness of the land for a faithful witness, so too, understood typologically, might the preacher stress the parallels between the waiting of the disciples for the Spirit and the "covenant" of the Spirit's coming. The advantage of such a proclamation would be the reconnection between the God who has acted for believers before, and the God who acts for believers now in Christ. Water (of flood or baptism) might serve as a common denominator between the texts.

THIRD SUNDAY OF EASTER

REVISED COMMON	EPISCOPAL (BCP)	ROMAN CATHOLIC
Acts 2:14a, 36-41	Acts 2:14a, 36-47	Acts 2:14, 22-28
	or Isa. 43:1-12	
Ps. 116:1-4, 12-19	Ps. 116	Ps. 16:1-2, 5,
	or Ps. 116:10-17	7-8, 9-10, 11
1 Peter 1:17-23	1 Peter 1:17-23	1 Peter 1:17-21
	or Acts 2:14a, 36-47	
Luke 24:13-35	Luke 24:13-35	Luke 24:13-35

FIRST READING
ACTS 2:14a, 36-41 (RCL)

"Pentecost"

The theme of deliverance threads through the texts for the Third Sunday of Easter. In Acts 2:38, Peter summons his audience to repent and be baptized in the name of Christ, "so that your sins may be forgiven." In Psalm 116 the composer speaks of his love for the Lord because "when I was brought low, he saved me," and in the alternate, Psalm 16, announces that "my heart is glad, and my soul rejoices . . . for you do not give me up to Sheol, or let your faithful one see the Pit." In 1 Peter 1:18-21, the author describes his reader's redemption through Christ's blood, and the text in Luke records the initial dismay over Jesus' death in the words of the Emmaus travelers: "We had hoped that he was the one to redeem Israel."

Interpreting the Text

Here Luke introduces Peter's Pentecost speech (reminiscent of Marc Antony's "friends, Romans, countrymen, lend me your ears!"), records the reaction of his audience, and his summons to repent and be baptized. But immediately prior to recording the audience reaction, Luke concludes Peter's sermon with an accusation that has exercised Jewish and Christian interpreters for centuries: "Let the entire house of Israel know with certainty that God has made him both Lord and Messiah, this Jesus *whom you crucified*" (v. 36; cf. v. 23: "this man . . . you crucified and killed by the hands of those outside the law"). Whether or not the

Judeans had authority to levy the death penalty, even to execute by way of cruci-fixion; whether or not differentiation should be made between Judean religious leaders and the average Jewish citizen in the matter of Christ's death—about which scholars have differed, and in fact, more heatedly since the Holocaust—the point of our text is to indicate the possibility of forgiveness for the most heinous of crimes, and at the hands of whomever: the death of the Savior.

The audience acknowledges its need: "Brothers, what should we do?" (v. 37); Peter responds with a resumption of Jesus' summons in the Synoptic Gospels ("repent," cf. Mark 1:15 and parallels), and announces the arrival of what once had been merely a promise: "Repent . . . and you will receive the gift of the Holy Spirit" (cf. the Baptist's word in Luke 3:16). Here the gift or reception of the Spirit is not detached from baptism, precisely because the apostle is on hand at the event. Elsewhere, the absence of an apostle will delay the giving of the Spirit.

This remedy for deliverance is effective, states Peter, because God himself is warrant for it: "The promise is for you, for your children, and for all who are far away, everyone whom the Lord our God calls to him" (v. 39). Here, the text of Isa. 43:12 in BCP has relevance, though the prophet's concentration is almost exclusively on Israel's future, with the barest hint of a future for the foreigners.

The alternate text in Acts 2:22-28 (RC) yields a Christological statement (vv. 22-28) and its support from Psalm 15 in Peter's response to the charge in v. 13, and in Acts 2:42-47 (BCP) describes the behavior of the converted following Pentecost.

THROUGHOUT THE NEW TESTAMENT, THE TERM TRANSLATED "REPENT" DOES NOT DENOTE A MERE CHANGE OF MIND OR ALTERATION OF OPINION BUT A TOTAL TRANSFORMATION OF THE SELF.

Responding to the Text

Throughout the New Testament, the term translated "repent" does not denote a mere change of mind or alteration of opinion but a total transformation of the self. A "crookedness" is assumed (v. 40), a state or condition that has occurred "by accident," thus is alien, foreign to my nature, but which leaves me at the center of my universe, skewing my perception of myself, my world, and everyone else in it. From this I need deliverance! And should I yearn for it, it will have been because God intended it: "For the promise is for . . . everyone whom the Lord our God calls to him."

PSALM 116 (RCL/BCP)

"He Has Heard My Voice": Interpreting the Text

Following the statement of theme in v. 1 ("I love the LORD, because he has heard my voice"), the Psalmist states the vow he makes to God for his deliverance, then describes his plight and cry for help. The structure is crochet-like, with the theme, vow, and description of the Psalmist's distress and deliverance alternating and interwoven. The vow is consistently uttered in the future tense: "I will call on him as long as I live" (v. 2); "I will lift up the cup of salvation . . . I will pay my vows to the LORD" (13-14); "I will offer to you a thanksgiving sacrifice . . . I will pay my vows to the LORD" (17-18), but the Psalmist's description of his plight and cry for help moves from the third to the first person: "The snares of death encompassed me . . . I called on the name of the LORD . . . he saved me" (3-6). "You have delivered my soul from death. . . . You have loosed my bonds" (8, 16). The move is calculated to "entrap" the hearer/reader and render the Psalmist's past contemporary: "I love the LORD, because he has heard my voice . . . I will pay my vows to the LORD in the presence of all his people, in the courts of the house of the LORD, in your midst, O Jerusalem. Praise the LORD!"

Responding to the Text

How can anyone plunged in trial pray this Psalm, with its back turned on suffering and full of praise for relief? How could anyone full of grief in that ancient time, in the Psalmist's own time, join in this song, obviously composed for a host of voices? Couldn't some poor, suffering wretch perceive the infinite distance between his plight and the Psalmist's celebration? Or, did he turn schizoid once he entered the "church"? Not at all! What the Psalmist described as his past, the sufferer saw as his future! For what other reason could this praise be sung by a congregation of the dispossessed and disenfranchised? To miss the eschatological, future-oriented context of this psalm in the life of its choir is to miss its heart. And v. 15—"precious in the sight of the LORD is the death of his faithful ones"—is what preserves it from being, as Karl Marx stated, an "opiate of the people." In the midst of all this praise, all the uttering of vows and oaths to the Lord, all the exchange of future for past is the reality of death: harsh, cruel, filthy. Yet, such a death "of his saints" is precious. And there, right there is the warrant for praise, for interpreting the past as promise. As long as I and my death are that dear to God, this Psalm is mine.

> HOW CAN ANYONE PLUNGED IN TRIAL PRAY THIS PSALM, WITH ITS BACK TURNED ON SUFFERING AND FULL OF PRAISE FOR RELIEF?

SECOND READING

1 PETER 1:17-23 (RC to v. 21)

"Not with Silver or Gold": Interpreting the Text

First Peter is a "round-robin" addressed to a congeries of congregations undergoing "exile," the euphemy for persecution. The text opens with a simple condition ("If you invoke as Father," v. 17a), continues with a relative clause describing the activity of the One invoked as such (v. 17b), and concludes with the summons to "live in reverent fear" (v. 17c).

Verses 18-21 give the reason for the summons, introduced by a participle that I construe concessively ("since, seeing that you know," etc.). These verses furnished Martin Luther with the substance of his explanation of the Second Article of the Apostle's Creed: "Jesus Christ, true God, begotten of his Father from eternity, and also true man, born of the Virgin Mary, is my Lord, who has redeemed me, a lost and condemned creature, bought me and freed me from sin, death, and the power of the devil, not with silver and gold, but with his holy and precious blood, and with his innocent sufferings and death. . . ." The author refers to this deliverance as having been "destined before the foundation of the world"—one more link in the chain of our texts. In Acts 2, Peter declared that Jesus had been "handed over . . . according to the definite plan and foreknowledge of God" (v. 23), that forgiveness and the Spirit were the fulfillment of a promise, and that all who came to faith had been called to it (v. 39).

In 22-23, the content of the conduct referred to in 17 is described as love for the other, the reason for the conduct is reprised, likewise introduced by participles used concessively: "[Since, seeing that] you have purified your souls . . . [since] you have been born anew, not of perishable but of imperishable seed, through the living and enduring word of God" (v. 23).

Responding to the Text

It has often been customary to dissociate doctrine from ethics, justification from sanctification, believing from doing, and, at times, to derive the division from the New Testament. The result has often been to accent the one activity to the disparagement of the other, or to complain about the gulf fixed between. Our text resists such division: "Seeing that you were redeemed . . . love one another." The reason for the absence of division is that the One celebrated for deliverance is also the One who furnishes power for the new conduct of life.

LUKE 24:13-35

"Emmaus": Interpreting the Text

There is no mention of Emmaus, scene of this narrative, in ancient church tradition. Of the two villages later named Emmaus, one lies too close to Jerusalem and the other too far from it, so that it is impossible to be sure of what village the evangelist was thinking. In its form, our text contains the same five "constants" or ingredients as the bulk of the miracle stories in the Gospel, that is, a) the setting of the scene (vv. 3-17); b) the statement of the problem (vv. 18-24: "we had hoped that he was the one"); c) Jesus' "advance" to the problem (vv. 25-27: "beginning with Moses and all the prophets, he interpreted"); d) the dramatic result (v. 31: "their eyes were opened"); and e) ending with the "chorus" (v. 32: "were not our hearts burning within us?").

What is striking in our text is its repeated echoing of the passion predictions in chapters 9 and 18. For example, v. 20 refers to the necessity of Christ's passion by way of a verb (*deomai*) occurring in the first prediction (9:22); vv. 7, 20, 26, and 44 employ a verb (*paradidomi:* "I deliver up") appearing in the second prediction (9:44), and finally, vv. 26 and 44 repeat the substance of the third prediction ("everything that is written about the Son of Man by the prophets will be accomplished," 18:31). Why this recapitulation? The answer is that this chapter, with its obviously liturgical overtones, reflected in the episodes of Christ's prayer at the breaking of bread (24:30), and his request for food (24:41-43), is the theological supplement to the accent on necessity or inevitability in the first prediction. From the third prediction, as well as from Luke's word in 9:51 to the effect that Jesus "set his face to go to Jerusalem," it could have been inferred that such a supplement as the Emmaus incident and Jesus' rebuke of those "slow of heart to believe" (24:25) would inevitably follow. Luke is thus something more than a collector or gatherer of the Jesus tradition. In the narrative of the journey toward Emmaus, he has carried the topic of the inevitability of Christ's death to its theological maximum.

It has often been argued that for Luke the death of Jesus is only one element among others in the salvation-historical plan, that the crucifixion is an interlude, a tragic crime unjustly committed against Jesus by malicious leaders against the will of the Roman authority, even against the better part of the people, but which God, through his glorious intervention, corrects after three days. By means of contrasts such as in Acts 14:10, the argument continues, Jesus' death is something provisional, a low point in the divine plan that belongs to the past. And, since his death

IN THE NARRATIVE OF THE JOURNEY TOWARD EMMAUS, LUKE HAS CARRIED THE TOPIC OF THE INEVITABILITY OF CHRIST'S DEATH TO ITS THEOLOGICAL MAXIMUM.

in Luke is a transition to glory, the evangelist stresses the ethical over the soteriological or saving aspect of that death. The passion is thus the martyrdom of the Righteous One, its paradigmatic, and not its saving character, at the center of Luke's concern.

In reply, though in fact the saving significance of Jesus' death does not occupy center stage in Luke, the evangelist does not regard it as a mere transition. In fact, it is surprising to note the extent to which he describes the life of Jesus as the way of the suffering Christ: he suffers *precisely because he is the Christ;* he is not the Christ simply because he suffers. It is striking to note the degree to which the theme of the divine necessity threads through Luke's narrative (cf. Luke 17:25; 24:7; Acts 2:23; 3:18; 4:28; 13:27 and 29). Nothing in the Old Testament or among the rabbis furnishes an analogy to the prediction that the Messiah "must suffer. . . ." Such language corresponds to Greek usage, in which the term translated as "must" expresses what determines the course of the world as destiny, thus as unalterable. Or again, in our text (24:26-27 and 44-46!) the Risen One himself indicates the importance of early Christian meditation on the importance of his death.

Responding to the Text

The gem set in this text is that third "constant" or ingredient with its portrayal of Jesus as interpreter of scripture. In a review of his life's work, a hero of mine, dead at ninety-two, wrote: "Today I incline to the risky (*gewagten*) thesis that the entire Bible must be read and interpreted Christologically," and it was Luther who wrote to Erasmus, "take Christ from the Scriptures, and what have you left?" For Luke, both with respect to method and content, the way to the creation or to the Spirit leads through Jesus Christ. For Luke, in the words of that old hymn, since "[he] is his own interpreter, he will make it plain."

> TAKE CHRIST FROM THE SCRIPTURES, AND WHAT HAVE YOU LEFT? —*Martin Luther*

FOURTH SUNDAY OF EASTER

APRIL 25, 1999

REVISED COMMON	EPISCOPAL (BCP)	ROMAN CATHOLIC
Acts 2:42-47	Acts 6:1-9; 7:2a, 51-60, or Neh. 9:6-15	Acts 2:14, 36-41
Ps. 23	Ps. 23	Ps. 23, 1-3, 3-4, 5, 6
1 Peter 2:19-25	1 Peter 2:1-9 or Acts 6:1-9; 7:2a, 51-60	1 Peter 2:20-25
John 10:1-10	John 10:1-10	John 10:1-10

FIRST READING

For the texts in Acts 2:42-47, or 2:14, 36-41, See the Third Sunday of Easter

RESPONSIVE READING:

PSALM 23

"The Lord Is My Shepherd": Interpreting the Text

This psalm, lodged in the memory of thousands of Christians, called up in moments of stress or even of death, is threefold in structure. First, it identifies God, the Lord as "my shepherd," vv. 1. Next, in indirect as well as direct speech it describes the activity of this Shepherd ("*he* makes me lie down . . . leads me . . . restores my soul . . . leads me in right paths;" "*you* are with me; your rod and your staff—they comfort me . . . you prepare a table . . . you anoint my head with oil"). Finally, over this cascade of blessings it expresses the Psalmist's assurance of repose, guidance, comfort, abundance, goodness, and mercy all his life long.

Responding to the Text

Oddly, interpreters of Paul's epistles seldom or almost never note the link between the apostle's discussion of God's righteousness and the words of our Psalm, "he leads me in right paths for his name's sake." The phrase, "right paths," a Hebrew construct and earlier translated "paths of righteousness," is hardly synonymous with the Pauline "righteousness" as revealed. On the other hand, whether leading me "in paths of righteousness" or "revealing" righteousness, in either case the activity is performed "for his name's sake" (cf. Rom. 3:26). That is, the person of God, the self of God, whatever it is that makes of God a God—on the ancient view resident in "the name"—is identified with leading me "in right paths," or in the revelation of righteousness. There is a strange and alien side to God, just as there is a strange and alien activity of God; but whatever is truest and most genuine about God, whatever is most "godly" of God, whatever gives definition to God without which God would not be God but some other thing, some other one, is that God leads me "in right paths." In the last analysis, everything said of "my shepherd" in this Psalm is truest to his name, to his self. Small wonder at its being carved in our consciousness!

SECOND READING
ACTS 6:1-9, 7:2a, and 51-60 (BCP)

"The First Martyr": Interpreting the Text

In Acts 6, following a complaint by the Hellenists over the neglect of their widows, the apostles call the disciples together, summoning them to choose seven men to "serve tables" (v. 2). The men are selected from a minority group—they are all Greek—suggesting that representation is the primary factor in their selection.

> WHATEVER IS TRUEST AND MOST GENUINE ABOUT GOD IS THAT GOD LEADS ME "IN RIGHT PATHS."

They are to be "of good repute, full of the Spirit and of wisdom." These qualities are not restricted to the "deacons." In Acts 16:2 and 22:12, the "disciples" Timothy and Ananias are described as "well spoken of"; in addition to Stephen, Barnabas is described in 11:24 as "full of the Holy Spirit." If the intention was to restrict the activity of the Seven (thus of Stephen) to caring for the poor, the intention was never carried out. The Seven exercised a form of ministry allegedly reserved for the Twelve ("it is not right that we should neglect the word of God," v. 2). Stephen preached, not incidentally but customarily, and the content of his witness as well as the account of his death are rivaled only by the narratives of Christ's passion.

Two of the lections assigned for the Third Sunday of Easter (RCL/BCP) give merely the introduction to Peter's Pentecost speech, record only its conclusion, and the hearers' reaction. Similarly, one lection assigned this Sunday (BCP) gives merely the introduction to Stephen's speech, records only its conclusion and the hearers' reaction (vv. 51-60). The result in either instance is that the speech is furnished its frame, absent its content. On the other hand, as is clear from the speaker's indictment of his audience, as well as his hearers' reaction, the two pericopes are sharply contrasted. The indictment, in either scene, is equally brutal. Peter says, "this man, handed over to you . . . you crucified and killed by the hands of those outside the law" (2:23, 36), and Stephen declares, "now you have become his betrayers and murderers" (7:52). Following the first speech, however, Peter's hearers are "cut to the heart," ask "what should we do?" and hear his summons to repent. Following the second, Stephen's hearers are enraged, rush at him, cast him out of the city, and stone him to death. The narrative of the gospel's spread from Jerusalem to Judea, to Samaria and the ends of the earth is marked by an alternation of reception and rejection, faith and unbelief, welcome and martyrdom.

At the conclusion of Stephen's speech, replete with tales of Israel's resistance, ignorance, disobedience, and idolatry (the "credo" of the BCP companion lection in Neh. 9:6-15 furnishing the foil in the story of God's deliverance), the about-to-be-martyr pioneers the now ancient adage about history repeating itself ("you are forever opposing the Holy Spirit, just as your ancestors used to do"), and alludes to that "theological maximum" in Luke regarding the necessity of Christ's death ("your ancestors . . . killed those who foretold the coming of the Righteous One," v. 52). In addition, Stephen's reference to the Law as "ordained by angels" may reflect a peculiarly "Antiochene" or Hellenistic-Christian as opposed to a Jerusalemite or Jewish-Christian attitude, as appears in Paul's argument in Gal. 3:19 (cf. Rom. 10:4).

Finally, it is clear that the narrative of Stephen's death has been patterned after the story of Christ's own passion. "Full of the Holy Spirit" (cf. 6:5)—in contrast to his listeners who always resist the Spirit—and following his vision of Jesus as Son of Man, that is, as apocalyptic world-ruler and judge of the end time, Stephen breathes his last in a reversal of two words from the cross in Luke's passion narrative: "Lord Jesus, receive my spirit" (v. 59; cf. Luke 23:46), and, "Lord, do not hold this sin against them" (v. 60; cf. Luke 23:34).

Responding to the Text

Early in this century, convinced that their theological education had been useless to prepare them for the devastation of the First World War, a group of European pastors declared war on "religion" construed as human thought or human speech about God, in favor of a gospel that accented the word of God apart from and independent of human reflection. They could scarcely have overlooked Stephen's narrative as a judgment on "religiosity" in contrast to a God at an "infinite qualitative" distance from human existence, who had determined that salvation should not come by way of human effort—ever short of its goal ("you are the ones that received the law . . . and yet you have not kept it," v. 53)—but solely through the Word he had announced and made incarnate.

1 PETER 2:19-25 (RCL/RC)

"In His Steps": Interpreting the Text

Here, more clearly than in any other portion of the New Testament, Christian discipleship is construed in terms of "imitation." Our author prefaces his description with a reference to suffering injustice as approved by God, with the proviso that one is mindful or "aware of God" (v. 19). However curious, that phrase does not mean that to be approved for suffering injustice one need merely be aware of God. Being "aware of God" in v. 19 takes its definition from the parallel in v. 20: "*If you endure when you do right and suffer for it,* you have God's approval." Nor does our author leave his readers in the dark concerning what "doing right" might mean. In giving the reason for their suffering, he writes, "so that you should follow in his steps," in the steps of Christ, their prototype, whose life is described in a series of conditional clauses (who "committed no sin . . . when he was abused, he did not return abuse"), and against the background of the Isaian Servant Song (cf. 1 Peter 2:22 with Isa. 53:9; v. 24 with Isa. 53:4 and 12; v. 24e with Isa. 53:5, and v. 25 with Isa. 53:6). This concept of imitation is sanctioned in the earliest account of Christian martyrdom outside scripture:

> HERE, MORE CLEARLY THAN IN ANY OTHER PORTION OF THE NEW TESTAMENT, CHRISTIAN DISCIPLESHIP IS CONSTRUED IN TERMS OF "IMITATION."

> We write to you brethren, the story of the martyrs and of the blessed Polycarp, who put an end to the persecution by his martyrdom as though adding the seal. For one might almost say that all that had gone before happened in order that the Lord might show to us from above a martyrdom in accordance with the Gospel. For he waited to be betrayed as also the Lord had done, that we too might become his imitators.[19]

Yet, however great the accent on imitation, the concept is supplemented if not downright challenged in vv. 24-25. One might, as was Christ, be without guile, refuse to return abuse, suffer without threatening, and trust the one who judges justly; but there is no possibility of imitating that once for all event: "He himself bore our sins in his body on the cross . . . by his wounds you have been healed."

Responding to the Text

When I was young and ill, I read and reread Charles M. Sheldon's, *In His Steps*. It's main theme is that when confronted with an ethical question, one need only inquire what Jesus would do, then proceed to do it. I loved that book, but the increase in years impressed on me the distance between Christ and myself, and taught me to cling to what this text has last to say. The idea of imitation does not deserve abandoning. It is as legitimate as any other portrait of discipleship. Did not Jesus say, "If any want to become my followers, let them deny themselves and take up their cross and follow me" (Mark 8:34 and parallels), insisting on the parallel of master and disciple? Still, there is always something to contradict my assumption of a "level playing field" between the Savior and me, and I take refuge in what I could never have done on my own: "He himself bore our sins. . . ."

1 PETER 2:1-9 (BCP)

"You Who Have Tasted": Interpreting the Text

The structure of this text is threefold. First, it summons its readers to a specific activity ("rid yourselves . . . of all malice, and all guile, etc."), an activity resulting from (or conditional upon) their having "tasted that the Lord is good" (the RSV reads: "for you have tasted," and the NIV: "now that you have tasted"). Next, the text describes the One who acts as warranty for that activity (vv. 4-8), and finally it resumes the initial theme (vv. 9-10), all of it against the background of the three constituent parts of the Old Testament: the Law, the Prophets, and the Writings (cf. Exod. 19:5-6 on v. 9; Isa. 8:14-15 on v. 8; 28:16 on vv. 4 and 6; Hosea 2:23 on v. 10; Ps. 34:8 on v. 3, and 118:22 on vv. 4 and 7).

Responding to the Text

As is clear from our text, goodness does not occur naturally, but results from or is conditional upon having "tasted." The assumption threading throughout the contemporary discussion of morality and ethics is that we know by nature what we ought to do, and that what is required of us is simply to give legs to what we know, to do what we know we ought to do. The New Testament does not share this assumption, birthed by Aristotle, raised to maturity by Immanuel Kant, popularized by John Dewey in this country and become a foundation stone in the American educational system. It is not a disparagement of God's creation to acknowledge that something dire has occurred with it, that an event needs to occur that will not only restore it to its pristine state but also carry it beyond to a point the Creator had intended for it from the very beginning: "But you are a chosen race, a royal priesthood, a holy nation, God's own people. . . ."

> IT IS NOT A DISPARAGEMENT OF GOD'S CREATION TO ACKNOWLEDGE THAT SOMETHING DIRE HAS OCCURRED WITH IT.

GOSPEL

JOHN 10:1-10

"More than Shepherd": Interpreting the Text

Here the shepherd theme, struck in Psalm 23, and 1 Peter 2:25, reaches its apogee in a discourse of Jesus. In a discussion of the relation between the Jesus of history and the Christ of Christian proclamation, more than one scholar has regarded the continuity between them as fixed in the self-designations of Jesus recorded in the Fourth Gospel: "I am the light of the world" (9:5), "I am the resurrection and the life" (11:25), and here: "I am the gate" (v. 9), "I am the good shepherd" (v. 11).

The text contains two "figures" or "metaphors." The first is spoken in the third person: "Anyone who does not enter the sheepfold by the gate . . . the one who enters by the gate . . . he calls his own sheep by name . . . and leads them out." This figure then climaxes in a second, which resumes themes struck in the first but harnesses them to the self-identification: "I am the gate . . . I came that they may have life. . . . I am the good shepherd." In either case, the intention is to contrast the true and authentic with the spurious and false, to mark Jesus apart from any other would-be savior. This one is described in the first metaphor as climbing into the sheepfold "by another way," as a thief and a bandit (v. 1), a stranger whom the sheep will not follow, "because they do not know the voice of strangers" (v. 5). In the second metaphor the number of "competitors" has increased to more than one ("thieves and bandits," v. 8), who have come only to "steal and kill and destroy" (v. 10). The tense of the verb in the phrase "all who came before me are thieves and bandits; but the sheep *did not listen* to them" raises a question. Does this phrase reflect a conflict involving our author's community, which it somehow successfully overcame? And did the contest arise over competing objects of worship, over competing redeemers and lords, or over competing concepts of the one Redeemeer and Lord whom all acknowledged?

The text concludes with the words: "I came that they may have life, and have it abundantly." Ultimately, the figure or metaphor of the shepherd cannot bear the weight, cannot take the stress and strain of the thought which needs saying. At the wedding in Cana, the evangelist writes, Jesus changed six stone jars, each holding twenty or thirty gallons, into wine. That is the force of the adverb "abundantly." Life spells light, spells sight, spells knowledge, spells true, spells reality, spells Jesus Christ, and life "abundantly" spells light in contrast with which any other light, sight, knowledge, truth or reality is dark, sightless, unknowing, untrue, unreal.

In v. 6 the author writes that the disciples did not understand the first figure. Whether or not they understood the second, Jesus' opponents clearly did so, as the author notes: "Again the Jews were divided because of these words. Many of them were saying, 'He has a demon and is out of his mind'" (vv. 19-20).

Responding to the Text

Those words in vv. 19-20, putting the period to the entire discourse, allow of no other alternative: Either this Shepherd is what he declares himself to be, or he has a demon, is out of his mind. In a psychiatric study, Albert Schweitzer once attempted to defend Jesus from the charge of megalomania by suggesting that his detractors had concentrated on the Fourth Gospel with its heady self-designations, to the disparagement of the more temperate Matthew, Mark, and Luke. The summons to "accept no substitutes," however, is not at all restricted to the Fourth Gospel. And while it may be comforting to read what one scholar who held no brief for Christian faith had to say of Jesus after reviewing the saviors of history—

and now, as we stand and gaze with our eyes fixed upon the farther shore, a single figure rises from the flood and straightway fills the whole horizon. There is the Savior; "and the pleasure of the Lord shall prosper in his hand; he shall see of the travail of his soul and shall be satisfied."[20]

the alternative remains:

Either this man was, and is, the Son of God; or else a madman or something worse. . . . Let us not come with any patronizing nonsense about His being a great human teacher. He has not left that open to us. He did not intend to.[21]

He is more than shepherd. He is the door. He is the life. . . .

FIFTH SUNDAY OF EASTER

MAY 2, 1999

REVISED COMMON	EPISCOPAL (BCP)	ROMAN CATHOLIC
Acts 7:55-60	Acts 17:1-15	Acts 6:1-7
	or Deut. 6:20-25	
Ps. 31:1-5	Ps. 66:1-11	Ps. 33:1-2, 4-5, 18-19
	or Ps. 66:1-8	
1 Peter 2:2-10	1 Peter 2:1-10	1 Peter 2:4-9
	or Acts 17:1-5	
John 14:1-14	John 14:1-14	John 14:1-12

FIRST READING

ACTS 17:1-15 (BCP)

"Division, Polarity": Interpretation of the Text

For Acts 7:55-60 and 6:1-7, see the Fourth Sunday of Easter.

The bipolarity or alternation of faith and unbelief, reception and rejection characterizing the story of the gospel's spread in Luke's second volume is reflected in the incidents at Thessalonica and Beroea. Our text thus consists of two scenes, the first described in vv. 1-9, the second in vv. 10-15. In "Act One, Scene One," Paul and Silas are in the midst of their second missionary journey (cf. Acts 15:36—18:22). Traveling on the so-called "Egnatian Way" from Philippi through the Macedonian towns of Amphipolis and Apollonia, at the head of that great peninsula called Greece, Paul arrives in Thessalonica, situated on what is now called the Gulf of Salonika.

In "Act One, Scene Two," Paul (and, presumably Silas, because he is included as being joined by those who are "persuaded" v. 4) enters the synagogue to preach, "explaining and proving that it was necessary for the Messiah to suffer" (v. 3), and once more, and for the fifth time in our series of texts, we encounter that "theological maximum" threading through Luke's two-volume work. On the road to Emmaus, Jesus the interpreter remarks: "Was it not necessary that the Messiah should suffer these things and then enter into his glory?" (Luke 24:26). Later, appearing to the eleven in Jerusalem, he says, "These are my words that I spoke to you while I was still with you—that everything written about me in the law of Moses, the prophets, and the psalms must be fulfilled" (Luke 24:44). In

Acts 2:23 Peter declares that Jesus was "handed over . . . according to the definite plan and foreknowledge of God"; and in 6:52 Stephen speaks of the coming of the Righteous One as "announced beforehand."

In "Act One, Scene Three," Paul's hearers are divided. Some—Greeks and leading women of the city—are "persuaded," the pale translation of a verb that denotes a lot falling to someone's share by divine decree (v. 4). Others, Jews, are jealous, incite a gang of brawlers to set the city in an uproar, break and enter the house of Jason, a sympathizer, charging his friends with criminal action before the city authorities which, after setting bail, release the sympathizer "on his own recognizance" (vv. 5-9). Here again, just as in the story of Stephen, the narrative is calculated to call up associations with the history of the passion. The charge against Jason and company that "they are all acting against the decrees of Caesar" reprises the accusation once hurled at Jesus: "We found this man perverting our nation, forbidding us to pay taxes to the emperor" (Luke 23:2). And if we note the actual meaning of that term "persuaded" in v. 4, yet another division is added to that of Greeks and Jews, "joiners" and "jealous," rabble and brothers, that is, of those falling to the apostle's share by divine decree and thus, at least in the eyes of their opponents, of refusing obedience to imperial decree.

In "Act Two, Scene One," Paul and Silas are rescued and sent on to Beroea, another Macedonian town, a day's journey from the Aegean.

In "Act Two, Scene Two," the missionaries once more enter the synagogue to preach. This time their word is heard "very eagerly," not merely by the elite among the Greeks (v. 12), as if the polarity between Thessalonicans and Beroeans were a matter of ethnicity, a division between Judeans and Greeks. The word is eagerly heard by Jews who were "more receptive" (v. 11; in the RSV poorly translated "were more noble"), a set of mind that Luke anchors in their scripture search (the participial construction in the Greek of v. 11c is to be construed causally or concessively, "more receptive for," or "seeing that they examined the scriptures every day to see whether these things were so"; cf. the RSV, which locates the cause in their reception of the word).

In "Scene Three," reminiscent of the "truth squads" and "plumbers" of the 1960s, the Thessalonian Judeans give legs to their "jealousy" by saddling up for and making the fifty-mile trek from their city to Beroea, for the sole purpose of initiating a bedlam. Shades of Saul, "riding, riding, riding" from Jerusalem to Damascus!

And again, in "Scene Four," the "brethren" hustle Paul off, this time to the sea, to the Aegean. His companions, Silas and Timothy (not mentioned after 16:3) remain behind. Paul in the meantime has arrived at Athens, where he delivers one of the longest speeches recorded in Acts (vv. 14-15).

Responding to the Text

How to explain the division or polarity marking the gospel's spread in Luke's second volume if not in the "call to discipleship"? In the Gospel, Jesus announces the inevitability that his own fate should be paralleled in the life of his follower:

> If any want to become my followers, let them deny themselves and take up their cross daily and follow me (Luke 9:23). Whoever does not carry the cross and follow me cannot be my disciple (Luke 14:27).

All the Gospels, John included, promise the irreconcilability of opposing positions deaf to compromise that results from Jesus' "call." And while I cannot call "my cross" whatever pain "historical accident" may assign to me, or whatever consequence may result from my own stupidity, whether from within or without, no matter, I am destined for conflict once I have come to follow him. One line from that hymn in Charles M. Sheldon's otherwise troubling little novel, *In His Steps,* still lingers: "Jesus, I my cross have taken; all to leave, and follow thee," except, that I need not hunt about for any cross to take; it will surely find me. . . ."[22]

> AND WHILE I CANNOT CALL "MY CROSS" WHATEVER PAIN "HISTORICAL ACCIDENT" MAY ASSIGN TO ME, I AM DESTINED FOR CONFLICT ONCE I HAVE COME TO FOLLOW HIM.

DEUTERONOMY 6:20-25 (BCP)

"Credo": Interpreting the Text

Years ago, in an essay entitled "The Form-Critical Problem of the Hexateuch," Gerhard von Rad attempted to demonstrate that the general content of the first six books of the Old Testament footed on a "historical credo" or rehearsal of the saving deeds of God. He believed that Israel's confession, elicited by these mighty deeds, was most clearly reflected in such portions as Deut. 26:5b-9, which he described as the oldest "creed" known to us. Such a creed or confession, von Rad continued, assumed the rehearsal of God's saving deeds in the cultus, in Israel's worship. He located similar credal deposits in Joshua 24 and in Deuteronomy 6:

> We were Pharaoh's slaves in Egypt, but the LORD brought us out of Egypt with a mighty hand. The LORD displayed before our eyes great and awesome signs and wonders against Egypt, against Pharaoh and all his household. He brought us out from there in order to bring us in, to give us the land that he promised on earth to our ancestors. . . . vv. 21b-23).

Our scholar insisted that this great recitation, birthed in Israel's worship, reflected what was fundamental in Old Testament faith, a recitation that might undergo innumerable variations, but beyond whose basic form the Hexateuch (Genesis-Joshua) would never go.

Responding to the Text

What if the reason for my inability to dredge up pure, unadulterated fact from the Bible and to cleanly set it off from interpretation, what if the reason for that irritating mix of historical event and comment, thumbing its nose at my attempts to say "*here* we have fact; *there* we have interpretation," is not so much to be explained from its higgeldy-piggeldy character, stretching over centuries, but finally, from its having been birthed in worship? Every Sunday I recite a confession in which fact and interpretation are so interwoven that I am unable to tell where the one leaves off and the other begins: "Jesus," well and good, but "Christ"? and to the point where the two have become a single, proper name? Worship, cultus: Is that where it all began, that interweaving that gives the sober historian a headache? Is that where it was first discovered and asserted that the facts can never be "bare," without interpretation, and that the interpretation can never be loosed from the facts, without becoming a myth? At any rate, this curious mixture allows me only the possibility of being a believer or unbeliever. I am content with that, since I had rather be one or the other, rather than some unidentifiable thing in between.

RESPONSIVE READING

PSALM 31:1-5 (RCL); PSALM 33:1-2, 4-5, 18-19 (RC); PSALM 66:1-11 (BCP)

"And Credo": Interpreting the Text

With the exception of the lament Ps. 31:1-5 (RCL), more appropriately assigned the Fourth Sunday of Easter, due to its echo in Stephen's final prayer (cf. v. 5 with Acts 7:59), Psalms 66:1-8 (-11 BCP), and 33 (RC), with their hymning of Israel's deliverance, belong to that category of "credal deposits" reflected in Deuteronomy 6:

> He turned the sea into dry land; they passed through the river on foot . . .
> we went through fire and through water; yet you have brought us out to a
> spacious place (66:6, 12). The Lord brings the counsel of the nations to
> nothing; he frustrates the plans of the peoples. . . . A king is not saved by
> his great army; a warrior is not delivered by his great strength (33:10, 16).

For the Second Reading in 1 Peter 2:(1)2-10 (RCL/BCP/RC: 2:4-9), or Acts 17:1-5 (BCP), see the Fourth Sunday of Easter.

GOSPEL

JOHN 14:1-14

"The Way, the Truth, and the Life": Interpreting the Text

These words, set within the context of Jesus' farewell address to his disciples (chs. 13–17), are as familiar to the Christian as any other portion of John's Gospel, to say nothing of the entire New Testament: "Do not let your hearts be troubled. Believe in God, believe also in me." And, Christian or not, anyone who has ever attended a Christian funeral will have heard these lines: "In my Father's house there are many dwelling places. . . ."

The text is composed of an alternation of declaration, demurrer, and remonstrance. The first declaration occurs in vv. 1-4, opening with the words: "Do not let your hearts be troubled," and ending with "and you know the way to the place where I am going." Then follows the first demurrer, voiced by Thomas in v. 5: "Lord, we do not know where you are going. How can we know the way?" followed by the first remonstrance in vv. 6 and 7: "I am the way, and the truth, and the life. No one comes to the Father except through me. If you know me, you will know my Father also." The next demurrer occurs in v. 8, this time voiced by Philip: "Lord, show us the Father, and we will be satisfied," followed by a second remonstrance commencing with "have I been with you all this time, Philip, and you still do not know me?" and ending with "believe me that I am in the Father and the Father is in me" (vv. 9-11), and so on. The "dialogue" is then rounded off with a final declaration: "The one who believes in me will also do the works that I do and, in fact, will do greater works than these" (v. 12), concluding with the promise that "I will do whatever you ask in my name" (v. 13), repeated in v. 14.

This "dialogue" is as clear an echo of the Gospel's prologue as any other portion of the work. In the prologue, the author wrote that nothing, neither light nor life, had come into being without the Word which became flesh (1:3, 4, 9). Here, in one of those sovereign self-designations, Jesus lays exclusive claim to being "the way, and the truth, and the life." In the prologue, the author asserted that no one had ever seen God, but that "the only Son, who is close to the Father's heart" had made him known (1:18). Here, Jesus responds to Philips' "demurrer" with the word that "whoever has seen me has seen the Father." Once more, we encounter that portrait of Christ as revealer, a portrait peculiar to the Fourth Evangelist, and not merely by virtue of its continual repetition. And once more, the "light" that the prologue describes as coming into the world and enlightening everyone (1:9), is or should be immediately perceptible to the senses: "Whoever has seen me has seen the Father. How can you say, 'Show us the Father'?" (v. 10).

Finally, in verse 11 we encounter the "pragmatic" aspect attaching to Jesus' utterances in the Fourth Gospel: "Believe me that I am in the Father and the Father is in me; but if you do not, then believe me because of the works themselves." Earlier, in 10:37-38, Jesus had said: "If I am not doing the works of my Father, then do not believe me. But if I do them, even though you do not believe me, believe the works, so that you may know and understand that the Father is in me and I am in the Father." And again, underlying this "pragmatism," this assertion of truth as the movement from hypothesis ("if I do them") to experimentation ("believe the works"), is the idea of faith as linked to perception.

Responding to the Text

Years ago, one of the greatest interpreters of the early twentieth century lost all patience with a colleague whom he believed had cut the knot between knowing and believing to the point where the one had no relation to the other. He insisted that such a view, rooted in idealistic philosophy, robbed the creature of any possibility of perceiving the Creator through the things that have been made (cf. Rom. 1:19), that it was content with defining human knowledge as totally blighted by sin. The quarrel would come to a head toward the end of this century, culminating in a prodigious production of argument and commentary rivaled only by the Reformation. When I confess that "I cannot by my own reason or strength believe in Jesus Christ, my Lord, or come to him," does this mean that prior to this faith I am absolutely blind to God, that there is no continuity, say, between Matthew sitting at the seat of custom and Matthew the disciple, between Saul, persecutor of "the church of God," and Paul, "least of the apostles"? And if there is none, is not creation divorced from redemption, and everything apart from Christ consigned to a sphere outside the care and love of God? Surely, there must be some perception of God through "my own reason or strength." How else would I recognize that Christ's claim to be "the way, and the truth, and the life" is as legitimate and binding as all the other claims made upon my existence? Or, how else could I sing at Christmas, "The hopes and fears of all the years are met in thee tonight"?

UNDERLYING THIS "PRAGMATISM," THIS ASSERTION OF TRUTH AS THE MOVEMENT FROM HYPOTHESIS ("IF I DO WORKS") TO EXPERIMENTATION ("BELIEVE THE WORKS"), IS THE IDEA OF FAITH AS LINKED TO PERCEPTION.

SIXTH SUNDAY OF EASTER

MAY 9, 1999

REVISED COMMON	EPISCOPAL (BCP)	ROMAN CATHOLIC
Acts 17:22-31	Acts 17:22-31	Acts 8:5-8, 14-17
	or Isa. 41:17-20	
Ps. 66:8-20	Ps. 148	Ps. 66:1-3,
	or 148:7-14	4-5, 6-7, 16, 20
1 Peter 3:13-22	1 Peter 3:8-18	1 Peter 3:15-18,
	or Acts 17:22-31	
John 14:15-21	John 15:1-8	John 14:15-21

FIRST READING
ACTS 17:22-31 (RCL/BCP)

"Mars Hill": Interpreting the Text

Affirmation of the possibility of recognizing the Christian claim apart from faith, while in the condition of unbelief, may have its most eloquent support in this text of Acts 17. Paul, in Athens following his retreat from Thessalonica and Beroea, enters the synagogue to argue with Jews and gentile proselytes to Judaism called "God-fearers" (in the RSV and NRSV loosely translated "devout persons" v. 17a). Provoked at its idolatry, he next takes up position at Athens' "Speaker's Corner," at the marketplace, engaging any and all in debate and argument (v. 17b). Among the passersby are Epicureans and Stoics, who proceed to collar Paul, apparently without evil intent (as, for example, in 16:19), leading him to the Areopagus or Mars' Hill. This was located at or near the ancient Pnyx or "throat," where Socrates contended with his accusers; vv. 18-19.

The Epicureans would have applauded the distance between faith and understanding, because they believed the gods dwelt in an eternal bliss, inaccessible to reason, and denied the existence of life beyond the grave. Stoics, on the other hand, conceived of an eternal, rational principle penetrating the universe like ether and manifest in humans as soul. One's duty in life was thus to live in harmony with the rational, which ultimately meant subjection to fate, and the conquest of passion. What linked these two otherwise so different "schools" was their sharp attack on popular religion, the religion of the "man on the street."

Curiosity about Paul's preaching links the members of the two ancient "persuasions": "Some said, 'What does this babbler want to say?' Others said, 'He seems to be a proclaimer of foreign divinities' " (v. 18). Four hundred years earlier, Socrates had been charged with introducing "strange gods." Once on the Areopagus the inquirers repeat their question: "May we know what this new teaching is that you are presenting?" (vv. 19b-20) and in a scarcely complimentary aside, Luke describes them all as spending their time "in nothing" but telling or hearing "something new" (v. 21).

Paul rushes to make the point of contact between whatever his interlocutors conceive as god and the God of Christian proclamation. In what a classicist would call a *captatio benevolentiae,* a move calculated to ingratiate himself with his hearers, Paul swallows his initial disgust and addresses them as "extremely religious," in the argot of the track, as "covering their bets" by erecting an altar "to an unknown god" (vv. 22-23). Next, Paul proceeds to the identification of this unknown deity with the Lord of heaven and earth by giving a nod to the Epicurean notion of the inaccessibility of the divine: "The God who made the world . . . does not live in shrines made by human hands, nor is he served by human hands" (vv. 24c-25a). In the end, however, he gives greater place to the Stoic notion of the divine principle manifest in every human:

> From one ancestor he made all nations to inhabit the whole earth, and he allotted the times of their existence and the boundaries of the places where they would live, so that they would search for God and perhaps grope for him and find him—though indeed he is not far from each one of us (vv. 26-27).

Then, in support of his argument, the apostle cites a verse from the didactic poem of a third-century Greek poet named Aratus, a favorite with the Romans. In that work, the opening invocation to Zeus reads just as Paul quotes it: "In him we live and have our being . . . for we too are his offspring" (v. 28ac).

The purpose behind this attempt at establishing a point of contact between himself and his pagan hearers is to summon them to repentance and faith: "Since, in the words of that Cilician wordsmith, 'we are his offspring,' we should not conceive God as the construct of human art or imagination. This God overlooked 'the times of human ignorance. . . .'" With that little clause the apostle has taken back with the left everything he gave with the right just minutes ago; has put the question mark to whatever continuity he had urged as existing between himself and his hearers just minutes ago. In that bit of dangling participle he has assigned all that searching and hoping to find that One in whom "we live and move and have our being" to an era of groping and "ignorance" that needed forgiving. "This Deity," Paul concludes, "this Creator, this God has summoned the whole race to repent, because he has fixed a day for earth's judgment by the Man 'of his own choosing,' having gone surety for it by raising him from the dead" (vv. 30-31).

Responding to the Text

More than one interpreter has insisted that at Athens Paul "sold the farm," that he injured the integrity of his message with the attempt to establish continuity with his hearers, that he never again repeated the performance but restricted himself to the announcement of Jesus Christ, dead and risen (cf. 1 Cor. 2:2). This point of view depends on whether Luke shares it, or is merely furnishing us with the example of a tactic that Paul repeated.

When Christian missionaries arrived in Madagascar, they adopted the name for the deity then making the rounds, declaring that this deity, "Zanahary," had now sent his Son to redeem. The trouble was that "Zanahary" conjured up visions of ancestral ghosts. The God of Jesus Christ had to be named by another name: Andria Manitra, "Prince of Sweetness."[23] The point, however, is that those missionaries began where their hearers were, introduced them to the dilemma, and invited them to the change of name. Those early preachers had taken a leaf from Paul at Mars Hill. And so might we. When I engage in conversation about my faith, the scene requires setting in a language and conceptuality intelligible to my neighbor. Ultimately, my neighbor's idea of God may require correction, even cancellation, but not until the point of contact has been made. And in that witness to what God has done in the Man "he has appointed," it may be that my own language, my own "mental furniture" may have to be done to death—or at least suited to the time and place. Paul wrote to his Corinthians, "I decided to know nothing *among you* except Jesus Christ, and him crucified."

RESPONSIVE READING
PSALM 66:8-20 (RCL)

"And Credo Yet Again": Interpreting the Text

As noted earlier (see the responsive reading for the Fifth Sunday of Easter, BCP), this Psalm shares that "credal" character assigned the various portions of the "Hexateuch." Verses 8-20 consist of a recitation of God's mighty deeds on behalf of the people as a whole, then on behalf of the psalmist himself, the two recitations separated by a vow. The author first summons the people, presumably the company of worshipers, to join him in blessing God (v. 8), and in indirect and direct speech recites the divine activity on their behalf as alternating between good and evil and ending in good (vv. 9-12a). Following his vow (vv. 13-15), the Psalmist summons the congregation to hear while he recites the divine activity on his own behalf (vv. 16-17, 19) and concludes with a reprise of v. 8 in v. 20. Verses 17b-18, however, make it appear that the divine deliverance was conditional upon the Psalmist's behavior, and that his vows would not have been paid if his "integrity" had not been acknowledged (v. 14).

What seems to be merely seems to be. True enough, the Psalmist would not have been heard had he not clung to God in the midst of his suffering, but the *reason,* the efficient cause for his being heard, lay in what he confessed his God had not removed, "his steadfast love"!

PSALM 148 (BCP)

"Earth and All Stars!": Interpreting the Text

In a graduating scale, beginning with astral and inanimate and concluding with animate nature, this song calls the entire cosmos to praise. The reason for praise is twofold. First, God has created stability. He has commanded sun, moon, and stars, and "fixed their bounds, which cannot be passed" (v. 6). Not even those creatures suggestive of a universe liable to sudden change, producing anxiety in any "landlubber" Israelite, are outside his command (vv. 7b-8).

The second reason for praise—and make no mistake, the "scale" of the Psalm is graduated, the fixing of the limits of the heights or the restraint of

WHAT SEEMS TO BE MERELY SEEMS TO BE.

the deeps cannot compare with it—is that God has redeemed his people, in that ancient metaphor, "raised up a horn for his people" (v. 14).

A friend of mine has put this Psalm to verse in a way that makes me want to shout. Its first stanza reads:

> Earth and all stars! Loud rushing planets! Sing to the Lord a new song! Oh, victory! Loud shouting army! Sing to the Lord a new song! He has done marvelous things, I too will praise him with a new song![24]

SECOND READING
1 PETER 3:13-22 (RCL/RC: 3:15-18)

"Rescue": Interpreting the Text

Just as its companion, this text refers to the eventuality of the readers' suffering (vv. 13, 14, 16b-17), urges them to make defense of their faith, calls them to "keep their conscience clear"(vv. 15-16a), and cites the example of Christ, the "righteous" sufferer, in the words of what might have been an ancient Christian hymn:

> For Christ also died for sins once for all, the righteous for the unrighteous, in order to bring you to God. He was put to death in the flesh, but made alive in the spirit, in which also he went and made a proclamation to the spirits in prison (v. 19).

For centuries, the phrase "in which he went and made a proclamation . . . " has served as "seat of doctrine" for the confession of Christ's descent into hell. Did it have a "life" in Christian thought and worship before taking its place here? The apocryphal Gospel of Peter lists Christ's preaching to those who have "fallen asleep" among the miracles occurring at his crucifixion, and in the Middle Ages, the "harrowing of hell" was a common theme. Traditionally, the phrase has been interpreted as the initial stage in Christ's exaltation, that is, as his announcement to the once disobedient souls now imprisoned in hell of his mastery over death and the grave. The phrase is one of the oddest and most disturbing in all the New Testament. In an attempt to negotiate the interpretive hurdle, one body of Christians has set an asterisk at the relevant spot in the Apostle's Creed, and at the bottom of the page of its hymnal has interpreted "he descended into hell" to read, "continued in the state of death for three days."

The text, however, does have its parallel, perhaps even its twin, in chapter 4:

> [The Gentiles] will have to give an accounting to him who stands ready to judge the living and the dead. For this is the reason the gospel was proclaimed even to the dead, so that, though they had been judged in the flesh as everyone is judged, they might live in the spirit as God does (vv. 5-6).

Further, in the great Christ-hymn that Paul recites in his Philippians letter, the concluding strophe reads,

> that at the name of Jesus every knee should bend, in heaven and on earth and under the earth (2:10).

The reference to every knee "under the earth" may not be to the dark, demonic powers of the netherworld, but to the disobedient "spirits," whether of Noah's or the author's day. If so, then a parallel exists in this great old hymn as well, suggesting that in one variation or another the concept of Christ's descent reaches back to the earliest beginnings of Christian thought and reflection.

Finally, by way of association with the story of Noah, our text moves to a discussion of baptism and its significance, "not as a removal of dirt from the body, but as an appeal to God for a good conscience" (v. 21). The term translated "appeal" may simply be translated "question" or "inquiry," but a majority, assuming the reference is to water baptism, translates the term "prayer" or "pledge." But what if the term "baptism" embraces all the activity described in v. 13 onward? What if it refers to persecution (just as in Mark 10:38-39), not merely to an antitype of Noah's ark, and in this sense to an obligation or pledge or promise to God?

The Episcopal lection for this Sunday prefaces the text with a table of duties (vv. 8-12), rounded out by five verses of Psalm 34 (vv. 12-16), all of which may reflect early Christian catechetical instruction.

Whether the term "baptism" in our text refers to our sacrament of baptism (which comes closest to mind), or is a metaphor of the suffering of persecution, in either case its mere "performance," its merely having been done or endured does not guarantee deliverance. Was it the flood that saved Noah? Or, was the water the means or instrument *through* which (the little preposition with its noun in the genitive then denoting means or agency) God delivered him? Or again, what does it mean to say that baptism does not remove dirt from the body ("flesh" in the original), but that it is a pledge toward God? Can it mean anything else but that apart from the divine activity, apart from faith, baptism, water or no, is not a baptism? Rescue, deliverance from God, by means of water (or it may be through suffering), and the pledge toward God, the faith that holds to the God who is active through these means or makes his way in the world through those who are his in the shape of a cross. Any other view invites superstition.

GOSPEL

JOHN 14:15-21 (RCL/RC)

"I Believe in the Holy Spirit": Interpreting the Text

The text continues that portion of Jesus' farewell address begun at 14:1, and consists of an alternation of conditions, promises, contrasts.

The discourse opens with a *condition*: "*If* you love me, you will keep my commandments." That little particle translated "if" in v. 15 introduces what the old grammarians used to call "the more probable future condition," which when linked to a verb in the subjunctive mood implies uncertainty: Thus: "If you should ever love me," such and such will occur. Then follows the *promise*: "I will ask the Father, and he will give you another Advocate. . . . This is the Spirit of truth" (v. 16). Attached to the promise is a *contrast*, a device that in one way or another threads throughout the entire Fourth Gospel: "This is the Spirit of truth, whom the world cannot receive, because it neither sees him nor knows him," *but* "you know him, because he abides with you," trailed by the *promise* that "he will be in you" (v. 17). Verse 18 continues with a *promise*, "I will not leave you orphaned; I am coming to you," this time given shape in the *contrast* of v. 19: "the world will no longer see me, but you will see me; because I live, you also will live." In v. 20 the *promise* that "you will see" is altered to "you will know," and in the following verse, the *condition* expressed at the outset in v. 15 is repeated, "They who have my commandments and keep them are those who love me" (v. 21). Finally, the receiving (v. 16), knowing (v. 17), and seeing (v. 19) achieve their maximum in the *promise* that "on that day you will know that I am in my

Father, and you in me, and I in you," that "those who love me will be loved by my Father, and I will love them and reveal myself to them."

Our text reflects that corollary to the Fourth Evangelist's accent on the manifest identity of the Revealer, that is, his concept of "eternal life" as a present possession. The final judgment, which ancient apocalyptic tradition associated with God's dramatic destruction and transformation of the world, is here transposed into the idea of the end as having already occurred, as having become present in faith, or, as our text puts it, in love. "That day" referred to in v. 20, is thus not the day of the Last Judgment, but the "day" of the "Advocate's" arrival. The advent of the Spirit and the Second Coming are the same event. In an attempt to secure John's accent on eternal life as a present possession, many have relegated whatever in the Gospel appears to contradict it to the work of a later hand. So, for example, Jesus' words in 5:25 ("the hour is coming . . . when the dead will hear the voice of the Son of God, and those who hear will live") are set down as a gloss, perhaps after the example of at least one ancient copyist who drew their teeth with appending the words "and now is" (NRSV, "and is now here") to "the hour is coming."

> THE FINAL JUDGMENT, WHICH ANCIENT APOCALYPTIC TRADITION ASSOCIATED WITH GOD'S DRAMATIC DESTRUCTION AND TRANSFORMATION OF THE WORLD, IS HERE TRANSPOSED INTO THE IDEA OF THE END AS HAVING ALREADY OCCURRED, AS HAVING BECOME PRESENT IN FAITH, OR, AS OUR TEXT PUTS IT, IN LOVE.

Responding to the Text

Every Sunday in a creed that took shape in the fifth century, and which we call the "Apostles' Creed," we confess "I believe in the Holy Spirit." Every Sunday on which we take the Lord's Supper, we say with the confessors of old Nicea or Constantinople: "I believe in the Holy Spirit, the Lord, the Giver of life, who proceeds from the Father and the Son. With the Father and the Son he is worshiped and glorified. He has spoken through the prophets." And it may be that on a Trinity Sunday we will confess our faith in the creed to which the name of Athanasius somehow got attached, which describes the Holy Spirit as "uncreated," "infinite," "eternal," "unlimited," "almighty," as God, as Lord. "God" is an idea we can manage. We believe we know what we are doing when we think of God, pray to God, or use his name in vain. The same is true of Christ. But who is the Holy Spirit? When I was a preschooler, my father once found me sprawled on the floor, scrawling some indistinguishable stuff on a scrap of paper. When he asked what I was doing, I replied that I was drawing a picture of the "Holy Ghost"—all scribbles and squiggles, lines without connections. Some are content with leaving the Spirit to the elusive and indistinguishable. William Wordsworth wrote this of the Spirit:

I have felt a presence that disturbs me with the joy
Of elevated thoughts; a sense sublime
Of something far more deeply interfused,
Whose dwelling is the light of setting suns
. . . and in the mind of man:
A motion and a spirit that impels
All thinking things. . . .[25]

It is curious that whenever "Spirit" is left undefined, you and I are somehow turned into God: "A presence . . . whose dwelling is . . . in the mind of man: A motion and a spirit, that impels all thinking things." If some are content with leaving "spirit" there, others are not. And the proof is in the hundreds of cathedrals, on whose stained-glass windows appears that over-sized dove, its beak turned downward, above the head of Christ perhaps, or over a chalice or font.

Where to turn for an understanding of the Spirit? In the Fourth Gospel, wherever Christ is, wherever there is love for Christ, *there* is the Spirit. To know the Spirit, to be possessed by the Spirit, to be alive with the Spirit, filled with the Spirit—such can only occur through love for Christ and the knowledge of him. Only where Christ is, is there Spirit. It may well be that the apostle Paul pioneered this orientation of Spirit to the person and work of Christ, but the insistence upon the Spirit as the presence of the crucified and glorified One is present also in John.

WHEN I WAS A PRESCHOOLER, MY FATHER ONCE FOUND ME SPRAWLED ON THE FLOOR, SCRAWLING SOME INDISTINGUISHABLE STUFF ON A SCRAP OF PAPER. WHEN HE ASKED WHAT I WAS DOING, I REPLIED THAT I WAS DRAWING A PICTURE OF THE "HOLY GHOST."

GOSPEL
JOHN 15:1-8 (B C P)

"Vine and Branches": Interpreting the Text

In this portion of his farewell address, Jesus uses the metaphor of vine and branches to illustrate the relation between him and his disciples. Verse 5, with its expansion of vv. 1 and 3, constitutes the heart of the text: "I am the vine, you are the branches. Those who abide in me and I in them bear much fruit." What precedes or follows is in the nature of a condition or a summons. So, for example, in that alternation of participial and conditional phrase noted in the text above, v. 2 reads, "He removes every branch in me that bears no fruit. Every branch that bears fruit he prunes to make it bear more fruit," and in v. 6, Jesus says, "whoever does not abide in me is thrown away . . . if you abide in me, and my words abide in you, ask for whatever you wish. . . ." Set among these declarative (vv. 1, 3, 5) and conditional sentences (2, 6, 7a) is the summons in v. 4 to "abide in me." Finally, the discourse is cut off at the promise in 7a–8: "Ask for whatever you wish, and it will be done for you. My Father is glorified by this."

In midst of all is that everlasting, "Johannine" contrast between the one and the other: "He removes every branch in me *that bears no fruit*. Every branch *that bears fruit* he prunes (v. 2); "*whoever does not abide* in me is thrown away . . . (v. 6) . . . *if you abide* . . . ask whatever you will" (v. 7). The greatest contrast, however, is not between the fruit-bearing branch and the branch that bears nothing at all, but between the vine and the branches, which requires that the branch "abide," the requirement that determines the contrast between bearing and not bearing, and all in the service of that exclusive claim: "Apart from me you can do nothing."

Responding to the Text

"Ask for whatever you wish, and it will be done for you." That the sentence opens with a "more probable future," implying uncertainty, has nothing to do with its conclusion. The uncertainty has to do with the asking ("if you should ever wish"), not with the receiving. So the problem remains: "ask for whatever you wish, and it will be done for you." Or is the problem reduced by limiting that "whatever," by paring it down, by assuming that there are "whatevers" that cannot reckon on being "done," and that I am invited to make *this* "whatever" (whatever *it* is!) the object of my prayer? Nothing in the text comes close to such an expedient. The problem remains, *this problem*, that I have asked, begged, prayed, petitioned, and pleaded for a thousand things that I have never received. But before I call him a liar for defaulting on his pledge, I need to throw against my disappointment the truth that he loves me, that I am his branch—*this* is better than getting "whatever" I ask. In fact, without *this* whatever, "whatever" would be a poor surrogate.

THE ASCENSION OF OUR LORD

MAY 13, 1999

REVISED COMMON	EPISCOPAL (BCP)	ROMAN CATHOLIC
Acts 1:1-11	Acts 1:1-11	Acts 1:1-11
	or Dan. 7:9-14	
Ps. 47 or Ps. 93	Ps. 47 or Ps. 110:1-5	Ps. 47:2-3, 6-7, 8-9
Eph. 1:15-23	Eph. 1:15-23	Eph. 1:17-23
	or Acts 1:1-11	
Luke 24:44-53	Luke 24:49-53	Matt. 28:16-2
	or Mark 16:9-15, 19-20	

FIRST READING

ACTS 1:1-11

"He Ascended into Heaven": Interpreting the Text

This narrative is unique to Luke-Acts. In Mark's Gospel there is no narrative of the ascension; in Matthew there is no narrative of the descent of the Spirit, and in John the events of resurrection, ascension, and the coming of the Spirit comprise a single event. Luke clearly distinguishes all three events, narrating the resurrection and Jesus' appearances in the Gospel's final chapter, setting the narrative of the ascension here, in Acts 1, and the narrative of the coming of the Spirit in the chapter to follow.

The author prefaces his narrative with a bibliographical reference, reminding his eminent reader, Theophilus, and, obviously, through him his audience, of the scope of his first volume ("in the first book . . . I wrote about all that Jesus did and taught from the beginning until the day when he was taken up to heaven," vv. 1-2a). The preface also includes a summary of Jesus' activity during the forty days between his resurrection and ascension, commencing at v. 2b ("after giving instructions . . .") and concluding at v. 4 ("while staying with them, he ordered them not to leave Jerusalem, but to wait there for the promise of the Father").

The narrative proper begins at v. 6, at which point the disciples put to Jesus the question concerning the restoration of Israel's kingdom: "Lord, is this the time when you will restore . . . ?" The question is neither idle nor irrelevant.

Many years ago, one famous opponent of Christian faith wrote that Jesus heralded the coming of an earthly kingdom, that his goal was nakedly political, but that it suffered shipwreck at his death. The disciples, loathe to abandon their habit of "eating off the fat of the land," reinterpreted his goal in terms of a spiritual redemption from sin and death.

Jesus' answer to the disciples' question has nothing in common with his reply to Pilate's question in the Gospel of John ("Are you the King of the Judeans?"): "My kingdom is not from this world. If my kingdom were from this world, my followers would be fighting to keep me from being handed over to the Judeans. But as it is, my kingdom is not from here" (John 18:36). Here he replies: "It is not for you to know times or periods that the Father has set by his own authority" (v. 7), one more variation on that theme of necessity constantly accented in Luke. To return to the disciples' question, Jesus' answer does not deny a "restoration" of sorts, and of Israel's kingdom. It could not, since Acts is the narrative of a "restoration" in terms of the gospel's spread, though a "restoration" vaster and infinitely more extensive than any mere ordinary return to power.

Verses 9-11 record the ascension proper, ending with the promise of the two men in white standing by: "This Jesus, who has been taken up from you into heaven, will come in the same way as you saw him go into heaven." John may telescope the events of resurrection, ascension, and return, but the fire of expectation of Christ's imminent return for judgment and salvation has not yet been banked in Luke.

Everything said of the text so far has been peripheral, auxiliary, secondary to its central thought: "But you will receive power when the Holy Spirit has come upon you; and you will be my witnesses" and so on (v. 8). In one short, deft stroke, our author has summed up what will occupy all of the space in his second volume: witness, proclamation, sampled, varied, with or without success, commencing halfway in chapter 2, and ending in the last verse of the last chapter with the word of Paul's "preaching the kingdom of God."

Responding to the Text

At bottom, communism was a Christian heresy, taking its text from Acts 2:44-45: "All who believed were together and had all things in common; they would sell their possessions and goods and distribute the proceeds to all, as any had need." What rendered it Christian was that it aimed at matching goods or possessions to need. What rendered it heretical was that it attempted to turn a particular and contingent event in Jerusalem into an international program, and thus to realize here and now what God has reserved for the future. For, the author of Luke-Acts does not construe the kingdom of God as purely "spiritual." In Jesus' reply to the disciples' question there is no spurning of the earthly or mundane, but only the response, "it is not for you to know times or periods that the Father has set by his own authority." Luke would never have quarreled with the thesis that corporeality is the end of the ways of God. It is only that *this* life, which ends in death and martyrdom, awaits the coming of the "new heaven and earth."

DANIEL 7:9-14 (BCP)

"The Son of Man": Interpreting the Text

If we could summarize Jewish national hopes in the word "kingdom," a future world or "aeon" in contrast to this world or "aeon" would eventually make its appearance. Jewish apocalyptic, however, was not content with this contrast. It inquired into the "why" of it all, and began to conceive the course of the world as an inner unity, in other words, to develop a view of history. While earlier times were concerned with the riddle as to how the suffering of the righteous squared with God's righteousness, now it was believed that this entire world was evil, and that the coming aeon would bring the solution. According to this scheme, then, God would appear in judgment over this world and all the powers prevailing in it. From this point on, talk of "the great judgment" or "the last day" dominates Jewish apocalyptic literature. And from this point appears the "Son of Man," world ruler and judge, sitting upon his throne and surrounded by his court of "ten thousand times ten thousand."

Daniel 7 describes a vision and a voice. In the vision the seer sees a great sea from which four fantastic beasts appear (lion, bear, panther, unearthly beast with iron teeth and claws, vv. 4-7). These creatures symbolize empires or epochs of world history (although perhaps not in sequence) which culminate in the end of time and the enthronement of the Son of Man. According to Daniel, what gives this history its unity despite all the variety is its opposition to God's lordship—an opposition to be overcome, not by forces imminent in history, but by an act of God alone: "I saw one like a human being (or, as in the RSV, "one like a son of man") coming with the clouds of heaven. . . . To him was given dominion and glory and kingship, that all peoples, nations, and languages should serve him" (vv. 13-14).

Efforts to construe Jesus' favorite self-designation in the Gospels as "Son of Man" purely in terms of a circumlocution for the first person singular ("I") have not succeeded in dissuading all Bible interpreters from their conviction that, by naming himself such, Jesus conceived himself as the coming world-ruler and judge about to be revealed, but whose revelation would have to wait for his appearing a second time.

Responsive Reading

PSALM 47 (47:2-3, 6-7, 8-9), or PSALM 93 (RCL) or 110:1-5 (BCP)

"Gone Up with a Shout": Interpreting the Text

This cluster of Psalms is part of an association of ideas within the mind of the primitive Christian community. From the first two Psalms in this little collection, that community appears to have gotten "grist" for the mill of its narrative of Jesus' ascension:

> God has gone up with a shout. . . . God sits on his holy throne . . . he is highly exalted! (Ps. 47:5, 8, 9). The LORD is king; he is robed in majesty; the LORD is robed, he is girded with strength (Ps. 93:1).

Perhaps not only for the earliest community, but also for Luke, these words called up associations with the ascension. It was Luke, after all, who described Stephen's vision of the Son of Man as "standing at the right hand of God" (Acts 7:56), in other words, as "highly exalted."

More important, the third Psalm in this cluster, Psalm 110, has influenced the form and perhaps even the substance of more than one narrative in the New Testament. In Mark 12:36 and parallels (Matt. 22:44; Luke 20:42-43) it furnishes the bulk of Jesus' debate with the scribes over the Christ as David's son or as David's Lord. In Mark 14:62 and parallels (Matt. 26:64; Luke 22:69) it is the essence of Jesus' reply to the question of the high priest: "Are you the Messiah, the Son of the Blessed One? . . . I am; and 'you will see the Son of Man seated at the right hand of the Power. . . .'" In Acts 2:34, Peter takes up the Psalm in his proclamation of Jesus' resurrection while denying its relevance to David. First Corinthians 15:25; Ephesians 1:20; and Colossians 3:1 all echo this little Psalm; but no other portion of the New Testament cites it as often as Hebrews (cf. 1:3, 13; 10:12-13; 12:2), all of which yields sufficient evidence of its sovereign place in early Christian proclamation of Jesus' "session" at God's right hand.

Responding to the Text

What does it mean to confess that Jesus is "at God's right hand," or is "highly exalted?" Is this a feat to be set down as occurring solely for his benefit, and "bully for him," but without relevance to my existence? First of all, Jesus' ascension, no more than his death or resurrection, is an event that involves him alone. For the author of Acts it guarantees the fulfillment of promise in the sending of the Spirit and power for witness "in Jerusalem and in all Judea and Samaria and to the ends of the earth." For the writer of Hebrews, Christ's session at God's right hand is the conclusion to his sojourn through the arena of conflict and death, for which reason he is able to draw us through it to the "city which is to come" (Heb. 13:14). Second, "God has gone up with a shout," this time not merely for the sake of "the pride of Jacob whom he loves," or for his "house" (Ps. 47:4; 93:5), but for all the earth. Thus for me! something the singer could scarcely see, and yet caught a glimpse of when he wrote that "the shields *of the earth* belong to God" (Ps. 47:9). One exclusivity (that of Israel's) has been exchanged for another (that of Christ's), to end all exclusivity.

SECOND READING
EPHESIANS 1:15-23 (1:17-23)

"God Is God Forever": Interpreting the Text

The list of interpreters contending for Paul's authorship of the Epistle to the Ephesians grows smaller and smaller with time. Among the many differences that scholars note between it and the "genuine" Pauline letters is its assigning to the present what Paul projects into the future. One example, is its description of those who are alive with Christ as "seated with him in the heavenly places" (Eph. 2:6).

The text consists of a prayer on behalf of the Ephesians, ending in the author's throwing one great, cosmic loop for the divine activity centered in Christ's session at God's right hand, "far above all rule and authority and power and dominion."

Our author first cites the stimulus for his prayer ("I have heard of your faith in the Lord Jesus and your love toward all the saints," v. 15), refers to its constancy ("I do not cease, etc." v. 16), and then, in one of the longest and most unrelieved sentences in the entire New Testament, cites its content. The author prays that his readers might know the "hope" to which God has called them (v. 18a), the riches of their inheritance (v. 18b), and the immeasurable greatness of God's power (v. 19), then ends his petition with a relative clause defining that power as accomplished in the resurrection of Christ (v. 20), whom "the Father of glory" (v. 17) made *"head over all things for the church, which is his body, the fullness of him who fills all in all"* (vv. 22-23).

Responding to the Text

We may be at the end of a long chain, the first link of which was forged when the Christian community began to let go the engine of its faith, the expectation that Christ would soon return, and exchanged it for the idea of an institution, a Church that could gradually and continuously penetrate the inhabited world. And once that idea took root, it was not long until things once said only of God or of Christ could also be said of the church. There is contrast between these lines:

> God also highly exalted *him* and gave *him* the name that is above every name (Phil. 2:9)

and these lines:

> He destined *us* for adoption as his children through Jesus Christ . . . In him *we* have redemption. . . . He has made known to *us* the mystery of his will (Eph. 1:5ff.),

or these lines in our prayer:

> The church, which is his body, the fullness of him who fills all in all.

And because what was earlier confessed of Christ could now be confessed of the Church, it required no great effort to move from an understanding of the gospel as the justification of the godless to an understanding of the gospel as a summons to membership in a society or fellowship.

There is no denying that the change had to occur. Christ had delayed his coming, but the price for that change was high. The price was order, domestication. In an essay on speaking in tongues, Goethe likened the first rush of the Spirit at Pentecost to a brook, then wrote:

> If you look for it, you will not find it. It has run out into the swamps, avoided by all well-dressed persons. Here and there it waters a heather in secret; thank God for that in quiet. For our theological cameralists endorse the principle that one should dam up all traces of it; pave streets and lay sidewalks on it.[26]

But for all this, we are still near the fire. The Bible remains a subversive book, and there is no doctrine, no dogma that can finally spare us the turbulence it promises. With all we have done to tame him, Scripture still yields the figure of that awful Engineer of chaos, to whom not everything is subject yet, but who warps and twists the present to his future in those who come near him, believe him, love him, those for whom life or death, poverty or plenty, status or statelessness, salvation or damnation are nothing beside his name, his kingdom and his will; who spread his chaos, roaring with Bach, that great beast of the musical jungle: "He that reigns will rend my chains: Earth may vanish, heaven may sever, God is God forever!"

BUT FOR ALL THIS, WE ARE STILL NEAR THE FIRE. THE BIBLE REMAINS A SUBVERSIVE BOOK, AND THERE IS NO DOCTRINE, NO DOGMA THAT CAN FINALLY SPARE US THE TURBULENCE IT PROMISES.

LUKE 24:44-53; MARK 16:9-15, 19-20; MATTHEW 28:16-20

For Luke 24:44-53 and Matthew 28:16-20, see the text for Easter Evening (RCL) and Easter Day (RCL)

A Note on Mark 16:9-15

Four endings have been appended to Mark's Gospel, ranging from the fifth to the ninth centuries. The first consists of one verse, the second (from which the companion text to Luke 24:49-53 is drawn) of twelve verses; the third of an addition to v. 14 of this text, and the last consists of a Latin text preserved by Jerome. Our text here is a summary of the resurrection appearances in Matthew and Luke, but also supplies a number of additions to the synoptic narratives. In v. 9 Jesus appears to Mary Magdalene, out of whom he cast "seven demons"; in v. 12 Jesus appears to the two disciples "in another form" (cf. the Emmaus narrative in Luke 24). Verses 17-18 contain the promise of the signs and wonders to be performed by the disciples, and v. 19 refers to Jesus as seated at God's right hand.

SEVENTH SUNDAY OF EASTER

MAY 16, 1999

REVISED COMMON	EPISCOPAL (BCP)	ROMAN CATHOLIC
Acts 1:6-14	Acts 1:(1-7) 8-14 or Ezek. 39:21-29	Acts 1:12-14
Ps. 68:1-10, 32-35	Ps. 68:1-20 or Ps. 47	Ps. 27:1, 4, 7-8
1 Peter 4:12-14 or 1 Peter 5:6-11	1 Peter 4:12-19 or Acts 1:(1-7) 8-14	1 Peter 4:13-16
John 17:1-11	John 17:1-11	John 17:1-11

FIRST READING
ACTS 1:12-14

"Waiting for God"

(For the major portion of the texts in Acts 1:6-14, see readings for Ascension Day)

Interpreting the Text

These verses conclude the ascension narrative, with vv. 12–13a furnishing the setting. The disciples return from the Mount of Olives to Jerusalem, to the upper room, their move consisting of a "sabbath day's journey." As the crow flies, the distance travelled would approximate two thousand, five hundred feet. Regulation of this journey originated in a prohibition against the Israelites' breaking camp on the Sabbath (cf. Exod. 16:29).

Following the setting, v. 13b gives the names of the Twelve minus one (Judas), identical to the list in the Gospel (Luke 6:14-16). Through the casting of lots (vv. 24-26), Matthias will restore the original number, and according to the criterion stated in vv. 21-22:

> One of the men who have accompanied us during all the time that the Lord Jesus went in and out among us . . . one of these must become a witness with us to his resurrection.

In Matt. 10:2-4 and Mark 3:16-19, Thaddeus appears in place of Judas, son of James, and Simon is described as a Cananean, whereas here in Acts and in Luke

6, he is described as "the Zealot." Did Jesus include agitators against Rome in his intimate circle of followers, which, in part at least, suggested a similarity between his movement and the rebellions of later years? What, for example, induced Gamaliel to draw a parallel between the "Jesus movement" and the insurrections of Theudas and Judas the Galilean? (Acts 5:36-37).

The text concludes with the reference to the disciples and the women together with Jesus' mother and "his brothers" as devoting themselves in prayer, in expectation of the fulfillment of the promise of the Spirit. The expedient of interpreting "brothers" to mean persons further down on the family tree, thus as "cousins," or in Lutheran fashion, of referring to Mary as "ever virgin," is challenged here as well as in Mark's Gospel (cf. 3:31 and 6:3).

Responding to the Text

Waiting, waiting, and more waiting seems to be the obverse side, the inevitable consequence of the sovereignty of God. In Acts 1:4 Jesus summons the disciples to "wait for the promise of the Father," and in v. 7 gives to that waiting inevitability in the statement that it is not for them to know "the times or periods that the Father has set." There is an aria for contralto in Mendelssohn's "Elijah," its text dependent on a now-obsolete version of Psalm 37, once sung by one of the greatest voices this country has ever produced: Marian Anderson. Throughout life refused admittance to concert halls and hotels due to the color of her skin, toward the end of her career, in an act followed years later by a black leader who would never be her equal, she sang her heart out from the steps of the Lincoln monument. The life, but also the faith of this wonderful human being had its summing up in that aria which begins: "O, rest in the Lord, wait patiently for him, and he will give thee thy heart's desire." Waiting, waiting. . . .

> WAITING, WAITING, AND MORE WAITING SEEMS TO BE THE OBVERSE SIDE, THE INEVITABLE CONSEQUENCE OF THE SOVEREIGNTY OF GOD.

RESPONSIVE READING

PSALM 68:1-10 (11-20), 32-35

"Captivity Captive": Interpreting the Text

The context of this piece is Israel's deliverance from Egypt, its wilderness wandering, the Sinai theophany, the conquest of the land, and all of it culminating in the temple with its cultus. From all this past redemptive activity the Psalmist derives the "cheek" to summon God to arise and scatter his enemies (vv. 1-2), to make "the rebellious dwell in a parched land" (v. 6). "They flee," "the kings of the armies, they flee!" the singer revels, announcing that God will "shatter the heads of his enemies" (v. 21), will bring them back from Bashan, Og's country with its sixty high-walled cities, so that Israel may bathe in their blood (v. 22). At the conclusion of the Psalm, the singer once more summons God to show his might (v. 28) and trample those who lust after tribute and delight in war (v. 30).

But if God is summoned to act, so are his people summoned to praise the Lord who leads the prisoners out to prosperity (v. 6), who "daily bears us up," is our salvation (v. 19), who has "done for us" (v. 28), and whose majesty is over Israel, "his people," to whom he gives power and strength (vv. 34-35).

And the place of praise is the temple, that "high mount" where God once made ascent with mighty chariotry from Sinai, the "holy place" where he led captives and received tribute, as announced in a verse (v. 18) whose life is extended into the New Testament to describe Christ's ascension (see Eph. 4:7-8).

For the second Responsive Reading in Psalm 47 (BCP), see the Psalm text for Ascension Day.

A Note on the Third Responsive Reading Psalm 27:1, 4, 7-8 (RC)

Though not included in the lection, the conclusion to this Psalm seems more applicable to the day: "Wait for the Lord; be strong, and let your heart take courage; wait for the Lord!" (v. 14).

In Acts 1, Jesus takes the Psalmist's part ("he ordered them . . . to wait there for the promise of the Father," v. 4), and the Twelve, together with the women, with Mary and "his brothers," in fact carry out what remained a possibility with the Psalmist, "wait for the Lord." Whatever the more informed Christians and their leaders may think of occurrences at Garden Grove, California, to hear the Metropolitan's Sherrill Milnes sing "The Lord is my Light, and my Salvation" in its "Crystal Cathedral," and put his soul into it, is remuneration enough for contending with the traffic and confusion involved in arriving at that towering thing of steel and glass, and enduring whatever else may fall under the rubric of hype there.

The Second Reading

1 PETER 4:12-14 (15-19);
or 1 PETER 5:6-11 (RCL)

"No Surprises": Interpretation of the Text

Here once more, as in the texts assigned the Third, Fourth, and Sixth Sundays of Easter (1 Peter 1:17-23; 2:19-25; 3:13-22), the author of 1 Peter takes up the motif of suffering for the sake of Christ, enjoining his readers to await it. In the original language of this piece an imperative (a) is followed by a condi-

tional clause (b) which trails an imperative (c) and a purpose or result clause (d).
Thus, (a) "do not be surprised at the fiery ordeal that is taking place among you
. . . as though something strange were happening to you (v. 12), but (b) "but . . .
insofar as you share Christ's sufferings, (c) rejoice, (d) so that you may also be glad
and shout for joy when his glory is revealed" (v. 13). In v. 14 the condition or
proviso precedes ("if you are reviled for the name of Christ"), a declarative statement is substituted for the imperative ("you are blessed"), followed by a causal
clause ("because the spirit of glory, which is the Spirit of God is resting on you").
In vv. 15–17 the imperative is expressed in the negative: ("Let none of you suffer
as a murderer") followed by the proviso ("if any of you suffers as a Christian")
trailing two imperatives ("do not be consider it a disgrace . . . glorify God"), and
concluding with a causal clause ("for the time has come for judgment to begin
with the household of God"). At the end of v. 17 the author makes use of an
ancient Jewish rhetorical device, the move "from the easy to the hard" to contrast
the lot of his readers and those disobedient to the gospel: "If [the judgment]
begins with us, what will be the end for those who do not obey?" The device
recurs in v. 18, in the quotation from Proverbs: "If the righteous are repaid on
earth, how much more the wicked and the sinner!" (11:31). In v. 19, the author
then concludes with a final summons to his hearers: "Let those suffering in accordance with God's will entrust themselves to a faithful Creator, while continuing
to do good."

Responding to the Text

One note struck in our text is virtually ignored in contemporary Christian reflection and proclamation: The "not yet" as counterweight to the "now
already" of salvation. To that "not yet"
belongs what our author calls "judgment
with the household of God," and which
Paul identified with appearing "before the
judgment seat of Christ" (2 Cor. 5:10).
Whether with Peter or Paul, the outcome

ONE NOTE STRUCK IN OUR TEXT IS VIRTUALLY
IGNORED IN CONTEMPORARY CHRISTIAN REFLECTION
AND PROCLAMATION: THE "NOT YET" AS COUNTER-
WEIGHT TO THE "NOW ALREADY" OF SALVATION.

of that judgment may not be altogether in doubt, but will perhaps have been
"only as through fire" (1 Cor. 3:15), for "if the righteous are repaid . . . ?" The
conviction that we move toward a "time" in which, in the parlance of the
accountant, all the "books" are "opened," and we are held to account, is never
absent from the New Testament. In the words of one great interpreter, apocalyptic, that posture or stance with its centuries-old treasury of figures and images
portraying the Great Assize, is the first and oldest variation on the Good News.
And here, however muted, it makes its appearance once more.

THE GOSPEL

JOHN 17:1-11

"The Hour": Interpreting the Text

To the concept of the Revealer's lack of disguise and its corollary in the accent on eternal life as present possession, the passion narrative of John's Gospel, prefaced by Jesus'"high priestly prayer," provides the contradiction. It is the quite concrete cross and death at which the highest peak of the revelation in John is reached. In light of the cross, the Revealer becomes the "Lamb of God" (1:19). In its light unbelief and blood-lust go hand in hand (8:40, 45). And, the evangelist's striking substitution of the narrative of the foot-washing for the Last Supper in chapter 13 conjures up associations with the servant motif that the primitive Christian community so intimately linked to the message of the cross.

In this prayer, Jesus' death is the event by which the Father gives to the Son and the Son to the Father what is his: the glory. In this event God will be God. The hour of the Son's return to the Father, the hour of Jesus' passion and death, is thus in the principal sense the hour of his glorification. To this extent, the death of Jesus is at the center of gravity in this otherwise so remarkably odd Gospel.

Responding to the Text

Confusion abounds over that little line in v. 11, "so that they may be one." Did Jesus pray for uniformity among his followers? Is the existence of a pluriformity of confessions among believers a scandal? The years have seen the gathering of councils, the convening of conferences, the establishing of departments and committees, the construction of programs, and the publication of thousands of monographs, pamphlets, and reviews designed to obliterate diversity in teaching or structure among Christians around the world. No doubt, the Christian confession must be concrete, tangible, palpable. But Jesus' prayer is that the disciples' unity be made analogous to his relationship to the Father: "Protect them in your name . . . *so that they may be one, as we are one."* Where is the concrete, the tangible in such oneness, since it cannot be seen, but can only be believed (cf. 1:12), more, believed by those to whom the power to believe is given (v. 2)? It is in light of the cross, that place where both Son and Father receive their due, that the keeping and the oneness are achieved.

1. Daniel Patte, *Structural Exegesis for New Testament Critics* (Minneapolis: Fortress Press, 1990), 41–45.

2. The reader will do well to remember that this is only one of several possible approaches to these texts: it is a partial witness that will be extended and changed by your preaching and the congregation's proclamation. This caveat is important because any short commentary format encourages the writer to be terse: to describe things in the third person objective witness rather than the first person partial witness. The former tends to obscure the writer's own subjectivity.

3. While we might think the believers who first received the witness of the Old Testament and the Gospels were readers, the level of literacy was low among any but high-status men. The Gospel that persuaded those who believed before us was proclaimed aloud. We are in a similar situation today. Much mission goes forth still with the energy of the oral, despite a higher level of literacy. The doubled reference, reader/hearer keeps this before us.

4. Formally, in structural exegesis, these changes are called "inverted parallelisms." In this context, the common term seems more useful. See Daniel Patte, *Structural Exegesis for New Testament Critics*, 16–17.

5. Because the purpose of this commentary is to focus on the pattern of coming to faith in various lections, I shall do what I can to reduce the historically limited language of "Israelite," "Jew," and "Christian" by talking about "those believing," and "those coming to belief" wherever possible.

6. Daniel Patte, "The Main Characteristics of Matthew's Faith" (Department of Religion, Vanderbilt University, 1989, photocopy), 12–13.

7. For more detail than is possible here, see Daniel Patte, *The Gospel of Matthew* (Philadelphia: Fortress Press, 1987), 394–402.

8. This is Matthew's perspective, rather than that of Judaism. The language of the deity as Father is increasing in frequency in Judaism in the first century and at the same time was the prime metaphor for Zeus. It was not unique to Christianity. Robin Mattison, *To Beget or Not to Beget* (Ph.D. diss., Vanderbilt University, 1995), 133–65.

9. Adapted from Daniel Patte, *Structural Exegesis for New Testament Critics,* 113–18.

10. Fearing God is a positive activity in Luke, shorthand for an awesome though close relationship. This is not true in Matthew, where fear was related to anxiety.

11. Luke is thinking of adult baptism, for one needs to be taught to interpret properly to receive the Holy Spirit.

12. The authorship of Colossians by Paul is disputed, due to its assumption that the resurrection of believers is already past, the paucity of its Old Testament material, the implication that believers can do the will of God, a Christ who is already ruling before the last day, and the ordering of family structure according to Hellenistic household code. However, the lack of certainty about its Pauline authorship does not imply that its vision is not without value for reflection and proclamation.

13. The uniqueness of the resurrection is qualified by the resurrection of Jairus' daughter in the triple tradition (Mark 5:21-33 and par.), as well as the resurrection of Lazarus in John and the resurrection of Tabitha in Acts 9:36.

14. Interactive initiation to structural exegesis using Luke 24:1-53 as a sample text is available in *Computer-Assisted Lessons* (Durham: Duke University Press, 1989).

15. Luke assumes that the disciples are male because the others are "the women."

16. John has been tipping his hand on this one to the reader for a while, yet it is not until here in the text where the identification of the Jews is qualified by opposition to the disciples having a different Father. Being in fear of those you consider of the same lineage as yourself is ameliorated when you are begotten into a family whose primary heir, Jesus,

is greater than those who have witnessed and died, like Father Abraham and Father Moses (1:16-18).

17. Not the *only* Son of the Father, given that believers are begotten of God (1:12-13) and are siblings to Jesus after the resurrection (20:17).

18. We shall see Luke showing Paul employing the same model when he draws on the Greek poets for his speech on the Areopagus (Acts 17:22-31).

19. *Loeb Classical Library, The Apostolic Fathers,* trans. Kirsopp Lake (New York: Heinemann, 1930), II 313.

20. Arnold Toynbee, *A Study of History,* Abridgement of Volumes I-VI. (New York: Oxford University Press, 1946), 547.

21. C. S. Lewis, *Mere Christianity* (New York: Macmillan, 1960), p. 56.

22. Charles M. Sheldon, *In His Steps* (Philadelphia: Judson Press, 1935).

23. From a conversation with the Rev. Roald Carlson, son of missionaries to Madagascar.

24. *Lutheran Book of Worship* (Minneapolis: Augsburg Publishing House, 1978), No. 558.

25. William Wordsworth, "Tintern Abbey," *The Standard Book of British and American Verse* (New York: Garden City Publishing Company, 1932), 258.

26. *Goethes Sämmtliche Werke* (Stuttgart: J. G. Cotta, 1868), VII, 190.

FOR FURTHER READING

Brown, Raymond E. A *Once-and-Coming Spirit at Pentecost.* Collegeville, Minn.: The Liturgical Press, 1994.

Johnson, Luke Timothy. *The Gospel of Luke.* Collegeville, Minn.: The Liturgical Press, 1991.

Neyrey, Jerome H., ed. *The Social World of Luke-Acts.* Peabody, Mass.: Hendrickson, 1991.

Patte, Daniel. *Discipleship According to the Sermon on the Mount.* Valley Forge, Pa.: Trinity Press International, 1996.

Patte, Daniel. *Structural Exegesis for New Testament Critics.* Minneapolis: Fortress Press, 1990.

Patte, Daniel. *The Gospel of Matthew.* Philadelphia: Fortress Press, 1987.

Reimer, Ivoni Richter. *Women in the Acts of the Apostles.* Minneapolis: Fortress Press, 1995.

Shelton, James. *Mighty in Word and Deed: The Role of the Holy Spirit in Luke-Acts.* Peabody, Mass.: Hendrickson, 1991.

THE SEASON OF PENTECOST

THOMAS H. TROEGER
RALPH KLEIN

T HE CHURCH IS ON FIRE! The church is on fire! How do we respond to these words? If the building where we worship is going up in flames, we respond with panic. But if it is the Spirit that came as fire and wind to the early church, our heart rejoices.

Fire and wind. They are ambiguous images. There is the fire of hatred and the fire of love. There is the ill wind of revenge and the refreshing wind of new ideas.

Fire and wind. Acts 2 presents these elemental realities as the expression of the Spirit rushing upon the church; and we, therefore, assume that fire and wind are safe: They are the manifestation of the animating energies of God, the vitalizing force of all that lives and of the church's ministry to the world.

But just how safe is the Spirit, the fire and wind of God? If we want to remain in our own constricted communities of meaning and custom, then the fire and wind of God are not safe. The Spirit will break down barriers so we can no longer be satisfied with our inherited biases, our fears of those who differ from us. If we want to think of the church as a shelter from the storm, then the wind and fire of God are not safe. We will have to bend before the gale and flame of the One who has packed every atom and sun in the universe with energy and who now pours the transformative power of Christ into our hearts with the same cosmic extravagance.

> FIRE AND WIND ARE THE MANIFESTATION OF THE ANIMATING ENERGIES OF GOD, THE VITALIZING FORCE OF ALL THAT LIVES AND OF THE CHURCH'S MINISTRY TO THE WORLD.

The church is on fire! The church is on fire! Will our preaching express panic or joy? That is the great question of Pentecost and the season that follows.

THE DAY OF PENTECOST

MAY 23, 1999

REVISED COMMON	EPISCOPAL (BCP)	ROMAN CATHOLIC
Acts 2:1-21	Acts 2:1-11	Acts 2:1-11
or Num. 11:24-30	or Ezek. 11:17-20	
Ps. 104:24-34, 35b	Pss. 104:25-37	Ps. 104:1, 24, 29-30,
	or 104:25-32	31, 34
	or 33:12-15, 18-22	
1 Cor. 12:3b-13	1 Cor. 12:4-13	1 Cor. 12:3-7, 12-13
or Acts 2:1-21	or Acts 2:1-11	
John 20:19-23	John 20:19-23	John 20:19-23
or John 7:37-39	or John 14:8-17	

As BREATH MOVES IN AND OUT OF OUR LUNGS, so the Spirit of God pervades the readings for this day. The Spirit rests upon the elders in Numbers. The Spirit gives breath to creatures in the Psalm. The Spirit activates the gifts of the church in Corinth. The Spirit brings understanding across divisions of language and culture in Acts. The Spirit flows like a river and empowers the ministry of the church in John. The living Spirit of God is to the church what our breath is to our bodies. No breath, no life. No Spirit, no ministry.

FIRST READING
ACTS 2:1-21 (2d Reading alt.: RCL/BCP)

Interpreting the Text

Luke addresses the Book of Acts to "Theophilus," which means "lover of God" (Acts 1:1-2; compare Luke 1:1-4). The name may refer to a real person or it may stand for anyone who has a heart open to God. When we read the story of Pentecost in Acts 2 we learn what a "lover of God" needs to know about the Spirit of God. Luke does not begin, "When each believer was on his or her own private spiritual quest." Instead he writes, "When the day of Pentecost had come, they were *all together* in *one place*" (2:1).

Luke's description of Pentecost is more than a video replay of a dramatic experience. It is a sermon on the importance of the church. It is in the gathered community of faith that the Spirit helps us understand one another, even when we speak different languages (2:7-11). Lovers of God who experience the Spirit do not form an exclusive clique, but reach out to others who are "amazed and perplexed" by the reconciling work of holy wind and fire (2:12).

Responding to the Text

Two great concerns of our own age find illumination in the story of Pentecost: the hunger for spiritual experience and the need for understanding between different ethnic groups and cultures. If we think of religion as a private matter between God and the individual, then our spiritual quest may isolate us from this world of teeming differences. But in Luke's account of Pentecost, the spiritual and the societal are not split apart. The Spirit enables a community of diverse people ("Parthians, Medes, Elamites . . .") to understand one another in their "own native language" (2:8, 9).

A language is far more than a collection of words organized by certain grammatical principles. A language is a way of perceiving and processing reality, and something is always lost in translation. We discover this when we learn a foreign tongue, or when we converse with someone who works in a different field or comes from a different background. As we often say: "We speak different languages."

> IF WE THINK OF RELIGION AS A PRIVATE MATTER BETWEEN GOD AND THE INDIVIDUAL, THEN OUR SPIRITUAL QUEST MAY ISOLATE US FROM THIS WORLD OF TEEMING DIFFERENCES.

Pentecost celebrates a time when the breakdowns in communication are overcome by the presence of the Spirit. Luke's Spirit-filled church offers a model of mutual understanding to a world that does not know how to live with differences.

I recall attending an international meeting of Christians from Asia, Europe, India, Africa, and North America. Translators helped us understand one another in conversation, but the moments of deepest communion were when we shared the Lord's supper and prayed the Lord's prayer, each in our own tongue. Pentecost was not only a past event but a living reality. Although we were often baffled by our differences, the Spirit held us together.

NUMBERS 11:24-30 (alt.)

Interpreting the Text

The two titles given to this biblical book are helpful in understanding today's alternate reading. In Greek the book was titled "Numbers" while in the original Hebrew it was called "In the Wilderness." Both titles are accurate, given the book's repeated use of lists and its depiction of the Hebrews in the wilderness. Both themes are alive in today's reading.

The seventy elders gather because caring for "six hundred thousand people" in the wilderness has become more than Moses can bear (11:14, 21). Because Numbers was produced long after the exodus, the book's authors and editors may have been appealing to the example of Moses to explain to a later generation why spiritual leadership needs to be spread among many in the community of faith. Leaders are not to be jealous of their prerogatives, but to rejoice as Moses did whenever the Spirit is present in other members of the community (11:27-28). The hope in a great leader's heart is that all the Lord's people would be prophets filled with the Spirit (11:29).

Responding to the Text

Once when I was taking a course in leadership in the church, the instructor during the first session placed before us a typical organizational chart: at the top is a box for the chief officer, then there are lines that move down and out to other boxes, which in turn are connected to still lower boxes. Such charts give an overview of the whole organization, indicating who is responsible to whom. Only in this particular chart every single box had the name Moses!

The instructor explained that this was the pattern of organization that exhausted Moses in the wilderness so that he cried out to God: "I am not able to carry all this people alone, for they are too heavy for me" (11:14). The "Moses chart" is typical of the way many churches have run in the past. Either the pastor or a lay leader takes on total responsibility for the church or for a significant group within the church.

It may be that when the book of Numbers was written the community of faith was facing its own problems of organization and leadership. They drew on the ancient story of Moses and the seventy elders to remind their generation that the Spirit of God is not the exclusive possession of one leader, that the Spirit can be shared among many. And in that story they prefigured what the church would discover on Pentecost and what the church discovers anew in every age: the Spirit provides gifts of leadership not to one but to many in the community of faith.

RESPONSIVE READING
PSALM 104:24-34, 35b

Interpreting the Text

"Bless the LORD, O my soul, Praise the LORD!" (104:35b). The words are a liturgical formula, a pattern common to the worshiping community in the temple and common to the church. Such ritualized words are essential to drawing a congregation into a state of corporate prayer. But the very repetition that makes them beloved also can empty them of their spiritual force. By preceding them with acute observations of animals of every kind (104:1-30), the psalmist helps the familiar words burst forth with renewed vigor.

Responding to the Text

Astonished by the natural world, the psalmist reflects upon how all living things give witness to the Spirit. The psalmist observes that the earth is full of God's creatures (104:24), and sees them not merely as biophysical phenomena, but as evidence of the creator's ceaseless giving. Breath by breath, pulse by pulse, cell by cell every living thing is utterly and absolutely dependent upon God's vitalizing energies: "These all look to you to give them their food in due season . . . when you take away their breath they die" (104:27, 29). The Spirit that blazed and blew upon the church is manifest in all that lives.

SECOND READING
1 CORINTHIANS 12:3b-13

Interpreting the Text

Paul is writing to a congregation in a thriving, cosmopolitan city. Corinth offered a range of religious beliefs. It was a setting for public competitions in athletics and oratory, for drama, and for the swinging life that went along with being a major port as well as the home of many shrines to various deities.

Paul describes his vision of what the church can be at its best in a letter that is filled with observations about the church at its worst. The Corinthian Christians were a squabbling, fractious congregation with various groups each claiming spiritual superiority. Their values and way of relating to each other reflect more the ethos of Corinth than the gospel of Christ.

Paul tries to bring order out of this chaos by more than conflict management. His starting point is a theological principle: "no one can say 'Jesus is Lord' except by the Holy Spirit" (12:3b). Having appealed to the church's earliest creed, "Jesus is Lord," Paul draws out its implications for congregational life. The same Spirit that blesses the Corinthians with the faith to say the creed also blesses them with a variety of spiritual gifts for the sake of "the common good" (12:7). Paul calls for the Corinthians to embody the meaning of what they profess, not an easy thing to do in their city with all its competing perspectives and values.

Responding to the Text

An avid downhill skier, I have long been drawn to those pages in newspapers and magazines that feature an expert on the sport describing how to master a particular technique. There are similar articles on golf and tennis as the seasons change. They feature line drawings or stop-action photographs of the expert with written commentary on how to coordinate feet, legs, hips, arms, and shoulders. It looks effortless on the page, and the instructions only reinforce the apparent simplicity of mastering the sport. But translating the written instructions into the movement of the body is another matter.

Paul's letters to Corinth reveal a similar difficulty: it is one thing to describe the church as the body of Christ whose various members are gifted to work in harmony with one another, and it is altogether something else to live that way. Evidently, the Corinthians knew at least some of the basics about being part of the body of Christ. They were familiar with the church's early creed, "Jesus is Lord." But when it came to living out the meaning of that creed in the corporate body of Christ, the Corinthians were no more graceful than amateur athletes trying to master what they read on the page.

Like us, the Corinthians had difficulty grasping that the church's creed has implications not only for the individual Christian, but for Christians working and ministering together. In much of American Christianity we add a personal pronoun to the creed of the early church, "Jesus is *my* Lord." This distorts faith by suggesting that each of us relates to Jesus only on our own whereas the church's formulation, "Jesus is Lord," reminds us that Jesus is more than any of our personal versions of him.

We are most faithful to Jesus when we bring together our gifts as a body, and we honor the contribution of every member to the group's life and ministry. This was not an easy task in Corinth, and it is not an easy task in our culture, but it is a way of witnessing to the world how the grace of God redeems groups as well as individuals.

GOSPEL
JOHN 20:19-23

Interpreting the Text

The Muratorian Fragment, an early listing of books that were coming to be considered canonical, tells us that the Gospel of John was written near the end of the first century with assistance from members of the church to which the author belonged. Not an eyewitness account of the life and ministry of Jesus, the Gospel reflects the community's understanding of Christ as it developed through their telling the stories

WE ARE MOST FAITHFUL TO JESUS WHEN WE BRING TOGETHER OUR GIFTS AS A BODY, AND WE HONOR THE CONTRIBUTION OF EVERY MEMBER TO THE GROUP'S LIFE AND MINISTRY.

of his ministry, through their life of worship and support, and through the conflicts they had with religious authorities. John's language is resonant with the
experience, the worship, and faith of his community.

This understanding of the communal context that produced John helps us
appreciate in deeper ways the Gospel reading for Pentecost. We are dealing with
more than the events of the first evening following Easter (20:19). Many details
in the narrative express the continuing experience of the community that produced the Gospel. "Fear of the Judeans" (20:19) reflects the church's conflict with
religious authorities, and must not be preached to reinforce the anti-Semitism
that has characterized much of Christian history. "Peace be with you" (20:19 and
21) may echo the practice of passing the peace as part of worship. The instructions about receiving the Spirit and forgiving and retaining sins may express the
language and practice of church discipline, the declaration of pardon and judgment among members.

These observations help us understand the ongoing presence and meaning of
Christ to the church. Upon reading John's account of the story, the members of
his community would realize anew that the giving of the Spirit and being sent
forth were not simply things that had taken place some sixty years earlier. They
were happening here and now in the life of their community.

Responding to the Text

Every generation seems to have its code words, a lingo that captures
something of its particular ethos and compelling concerns. In the 1960s the code
words were "relevance" and "the establishment." These gave way to the "me generation," and nowadays we hear again and again the term "dysfunctional."

The word comes from a number of social science disciplines that seek to
understand how behavior is more than a function of the individual. What people
do and say arises from a complex network of relationships that shape and instigate
their behavior. Thus, for example, a problem student in school may be acting out
the dysfunction of his or her family in which he or she is abused or ignored.

The concept of dysfunction provides a helpful way for us to understand the
forces that shaped the Gospel of John and particularly our reading for today. By
the time this Gospel was written the church faced a number of crises that shook
its confidence as a social system. First and foremost was that Jesus had not
returned as the church had expected he would. When year after year passed
without his bringing in the full and complete reign of God on earth, it was
inevitable that doubts arose, such as those expressed by Thomas in the passage that
follows the reading for today. The community probably began to lose its firm
grasp on the teachings of Christ, including the importance of offering one
another the solace of pardon and the bracing word of ethical judgment (20:23).
The church's sense of urgent mission may also have waned. The cumulative effect

of such doubts and failures was probably to threaten the church with dysfunction so that it was on the verge of becoming a community lacking the grace and conviction that once made it vital.

John and all those who helped him in the writing of the Gospel faced this crisis head-on. They recalled stories of Jesus, shaping them in light of their worship and communal life. They realized that when they passed the peace to each other, when they had a sense of Christ's presence among themselves, then they were being empowered anew, even as their grandparents and great-grandparents in the faith had been empowered following the resurrection. In other words, the community of John handled the threat of becoming dysfunctional by recalling the stories of Jesus and by courageously telling those stories in ways that could vitalize their own witness and ministry. When the church in any age starts becoming dysfunctional, it could not practice a better strategy than that of John and his community.

JOHN 7:37-39 (alt.)

Interpreting the Text

By the time John and his community were writing their Gospel, hardly anyone was left who had known Jesus in his earthly ministry. Some people were falling away from the faith while others were growing nostalgic for earlier times. They may have pined: "If only we had been alive when Jesus walked this earth." Such a perspective creates a romanticized version of the past that debilitates the capacity of believers to deal adequately with the present.

John corrects this distorted use of the past by developing a strong theology of the Spirit. He places today's reading in the context of the Israelite festival of booths, a harvest celebration that also commemorated how God protected the wandering Hebrews in the wilderness, providing them food and water. But instead of dwelling upon what God did in the past, John portrays how God through Jesus provides water that flows not only in the wilderness but in the believer's heart: "Let anyone who is thirsty come to me, and let the one who believes in me drink. . . . Out of the believer's heart shall flow rivers of living water" (7:38). There is no need to long for the past when the Spirit is flowing here and now.

> THERE IS NO NEED TO LONG FOR THE PAST WHEN THE SPIRIT IS FLOWING HERE AND NOW.

Almost as if John fears the reader will not get the point, he affirms that members of his community are in a more enviable position than those who knew Jesus in the flesh: "as yet there was no Spirit, because Jesus was not yet glorified" (7:39). It is best not to build a full theology of the Spirit from this single verse but to understand that it is part of John's polemical sermon to his community: Do not be mournfully wishing for the past, but receive the riches of the Spirit that are available in the present moment.

Responding to the Text

A child of one of my parishioners once asked his mother while he was eating a sandwich if he could taste God in the bread and peanut butter. He was serious about the question. He had learned that God is everywhere, and he wondered, therefore, if he could taste God in what he ate.

Like many stories about young children, the little boy's question reveals in an unguarded way a need that never leaves us, even after we become adults and think at more sophisticated levels. As creatures with a spiritual hunger, we want more than principles or doctrines about the nature of God. We thirst to taste, to experience, to know God.

Our age gives evidence that people are famished for the Spirit. An astounding variety of gurus and spiritualists lecture, write books, and appear on television. Although it is easy to dismiss some of this as shallow or self-serving, the mere phenomenon is significant. It reveals how broad and deep the thirst for an authentic encounter with the Spirit is.

One standard Christian response to this spiritual seeking is to point people to the Bible, but such a strategy is not adequate on its own because the spiritual struggles that helped to produce the Bible are not always self-apparent from the text. The Gospel of John is a case in point. If it is used as a straightforward narrative about Jesus, then its verses often get quoted out of context, and Jesus becomes an imperialistic savior: either accept him or God has no interest in you. Many seekers rightly find such an attitude repulsive, not at all extending the grace and hospitality of Christ to them.

It is at this point that biblical scholarship becomes helpful to the task of evangelism. For the close study of John reveals that the Gospel is a much more complex work than it appears upon a first reading. The book arose out of a time of spiritual struggle for the church, and thus the historical circumstances of its writing provide a connection to our current age of spiritual struggle. Like many seekers today, members of John's community were filled with fear (20:19) and

> JOHN'S GOSPEL AROSE OUT OF A TIME OF SPIRITUAL STRUGGLE FOR THE CHURCH, AND THUS THE HISTORICAL CIRCUMSTANCES OF ITS WRITING PROVIDE A CONNECTION TO OUR CURRENT AGE OF SPIRITUAL STRUGGLE.

doubt (20:24-29), while others wanted to hang on to what they had once known (20:16-17). When we read the Gospel with this historical understanding, we are able to receive afresh the assurance that John offered to his own anxious community: "Out of the believer's heart shall flow rivers of living water" (7:38). The vitalizing power that rises from the depths of God is available to any open heart that turns in trust to Christ.

HOLY TRINITY SUNDAY

MAY 30, 1999

REVISED COMMON	EPISCOPAL (BCP)	ROMAN CATHOLIC
Gen. 1:1—2:4a	Gen. 1:1—2:3	Exod. 34:4-6, 8-9
Ps. 8	Ps. 150	Dan. 3:52, 53, 54, 55, 56
2 Cor. 13:11-13	2 Cor. 13:(5-10), 11-14	2 Cor. 13:11-13
Matt. 28:16-20	Matt. 28:16-20	John 3:16-18

EVERYONE BRINGS PRESUPPOSITIONS TO interpreting the Bible, but this is especially apparent on Trinity Sunday—a thoroughly developed doctrine of the Trinity emerged only after the biblical books were written. Therefore, Trinity Sunday can be a day for bold theological thought in the pulpit, a day for asking: If the early church dared to formulate the doctrine of the Trinity from the interaction of scripture with more philosophical forms of thought, then what fresh theological understandings is God calling us to develop in our own age? Such an approach affirms that tradition is not dead, but alive and evolving.

FIRST READING
GENESIS 1:1—2:4a

Interpreting the Text

Although chapter one of Genesis opens "In the beginning . . ." it is not the earliest written of the scriptures. This beautiful poetical account of creation was probably written in the sixth century B.C.E. by someone whom scholars call the Priestly writer, P for short.

The Israelite readers and hearers of this story would have brought to it a long, rich, tumultuous history that included their ancestors' escape out of Egypt, the tribal league they formed for mutual defense in the Promised Land, the establishment of the kingdom, its rocky years of domestic injustice and foreign threat, and finally the destruction of Jerusalem and exile in Babylon.

If we read the text with these turbulent memories in mind, then it becomes more than an account of creation, as magnificent as that is. The opening of Genesis is a testimony to God's original intention for creation and human life. As a people devastated by the failures of their past, the dissolution of their society, and their degradation at the hands of captors, it would be easy for the Israelites to lose all sense of human worth and value. But this account calls them back to the fundamental realities of existence. It reminds them that they are part of a splendid creation, that they bear the creator's image in their very being (1:26-27). Furthermore, they can reclaim these values in their lives by maintaining the religious discipline that has given them a special identity: the keeping of the Sabbath, which was instituted by the One who made everything (2:1-3).

Genesis 1:1—2:4a is, then, not only about the creation of the heavens and the earth, but also about creating a sense of purpose and value in human beings, even after centuries of tragedy and failure.

Responding to the Text

The text is so familiar that we assume we know what comes next, and as we read, we miss some of the most telling details. Here is a way to slow down and linger over the nuances of this magnificent vision of God at work.

Imagine God as an artist painting a canvas. You are looking over God's shoulder the way curious observers will watch a landscape painter at work. Take delight in what God is doing by stopping after each addition to the picture. Hear the painter say with deep satisfaction, "That's good." Look at how much of the canvass is still empty. Imagine what the artist will paint next.

Note how God sometimes modifies an initial effort. For example, God first "paints" light and darkness as great contrasting swaths (1:3-4), next proceeds to water, land, and sky, then returns to the painting of light. God refines the original effort by painting the moon and the sun that now provide greater and lesser light (1:14-19).

You observe all of this from behind the artist, never looking at the painter face-to-face. Now you hear the artist saying, "Let us make humankind in our image, according to our likeness" (1:26a). You stand on tiptoe to see what these new additions will look like, hoping to gain from them some idea of the artist's own likeness. And as these new figures take shape, you attempt to figure out their effect upon the total picture. You study them more closely and realize they look like you! And then it becomes clear: The impact of these new beings upon creation depends on you, how you understand yourself in relation to the artist and all that the artist has created.

RESPONSIVE READING
PSALM 8

Interpreting the Text

In the ancient Mediterranean world it was customary for kings to set up statues of themselves in the territories they controlled, a reminder of whose law and rule were to be obeyed.

The psalmist draws upon this ancient understanding of sovereignty in describing the relationship between the Lord and humanity. God's "glory above heavens" (8:1) finds a parallel in the "glory and honor" of human beings (8:5). Like the statues of the kings, we bear the image of the One who is sovereign.

Responding to the Text

The Psalm lends itself to two very different theological emphases. One reading, drawing upon the kingship patterns of ancient times, stresses the sovereignty of God and the hierarchical relationship between humanity and the Lord. The problem with this reading is that it tends to reinforce a top-down perspective that can nurture various forms of authoritarianism, including sexism.

Another reading would focus on the graciousness of God who is willing to share "glory and honor" with humanity, God who entrusts creation (8:6-8) to our mortal care. In this reading, the psalm's final acclamation of praise is offered by human beings who have learned from God's own example that power is to be shared and used responsibly.

SECOND READING
2 CORINTHIANS 13:11-13

Interpreting the Text

We distort the final verse if we read into it a trinitarian understanding that was to be developed many centuries after Paul wrote his letters. A more accurate interpretation gathers the force of Paul's benediction by considering the entire last chapter and the stern admonition that it carries: "I warned those who sinned previously and all the others, and I warn them now while absent, as I did when present on my second visit, that if I come again, I will not be lenient" (13:2). The tone is like a telephoning parent who threatens discipline upon arriving home. But this is moderated by an appeal to the children's best understanding of who they are and how they are to act: "Examine yourselves to see whether you are living in the faith. Test yourselves. Do you not realize that Jesus Christ is in you?" (13:5a).

The prelude, then, to Paul's seemingly trinitarian blessing is a pastoral appeal that oscillates between threat and supplication. How better to move from this taxing confrontation than to call upon the language of worship that reminds both the Corinthians and Paul of the holy things that they share in common?

In the final three verses Paul employs language that resonates with the worship of the early church: "brothers and sisters," "peace," "holy kiss." And to sum it all up, there is a benediction that concisely expresses some of the multiple ways that we are blessed by God: "The grace of the Lord Jesus Christ, the love of God, and the communion of the Holy Spirit be with all of you" (13:13).

Responding to the Text

When we are locked in conflict with other Christians, it is helpful to remember the bonds of shared religious belief and practice that keep us connected to one another despite our differences. I think of times when I have been alienated from someone, but then during a service of worship we have passed the peace of Christ to one another or we have knelt at the same altar. That common act of worship reminded us of a communion deeper than our immediate differences so that each of us appeared more human and less demonized.

From talking with other worshipers, I know my experience is not unique. Corporate prayer has often been for them a way of ritually enacting what they have not yet been able to realize in their relationship to one another. They are not being hypocritical when they pass the peace to someone with whom they are struggling. The liturgical action is a way of initiating that openness of spirit that may in time lead to reconciliation.

At the conclusion of 2 Corinthians, the apostle Paul appears to draw upon a similar understanding of the power of worship. This epistle has been pieced together from a number of different letters by Paul. As a result it is not the most coherent book in the New Testament, but among the clear recurring themes of this varied correspondence is Paul's anger at the behavior of church members, including the unwarranted attacks of some people upon his pastoral authority. It is a nasty church conflict, and Paul fights back as hard as any of his opponents. But that is not where he leaves the matter. At the end he draws upon the language of worship to remind the Corinthians and himself of the larger and more generous values they share as believers in Christ.

The word from God that emerges through Paul's tangled correspondence is this: no matter how hard we fight with each other, we need to remember the holy dreams and gracious actions we have shared in worship.

GOSPEL
MATTHEW 28:16-20

Interpreting the Text

Verse seventeen recapitulates two motifs from earlier in the gospel: worship and doubt.

It is the magi who first realize that Jesus is to be worshiped. Even before they find the infant, they acknowledge they are coming "to worship him," or as the NRSV translates the Greek, "to pay him homage" (2:1b). As the magi worshiped the newborn Christ, so Matthew's community now worships the risen Christ. The gospel begins and ends with worship, and the language of worship marks Christ's final words: "baptizing them in the name of the Father and of the Son and of the Holy Spirit" (28:19b).

The final act of adoration, however, is not unanimous: "but some doubted" (28:17b; see 14:31). Matthew's closing scene is likely a description of the varied responses to the resurrection that characterized the early church's membership: some worshiped the risen Christ and some, who evidently were students of his teaching, doubted his resurrection.

It is this mixture of believers and doubters who gather as one body (28:16), and together receive the Great Commission (28:18-20). Matthew does not picture Jesus entrusting the ministry to the worshipers alone, but to the doubters as well! This is rather astounding when you consider how Matthew treats doubt in earlier passages such as Matt. 14:31. Perhaps the final verses of Matthew are a sermon to his community about its mission: the church is not to wait until every last member has overcome doubt before it carries the gospel into the world.

> MATTHEW DOES NOT PICTURE JESUS ENTRUSTING THE MINISTRY TO THE WORSHIPERS ALONE, BUT TO THE DOUBTERS AS WELL!

It is no surprise that the concluding verses announce the necessity of carrying on the teaching ministry of Christ. The training of disciples for the reign of God is a dominant theme throughout Matthew's Gospel. Like "The Sermon on the Mount" (5:1—7:27), the last scene also takes place on a mountain (28:16), as if Matthew wants to emphasize the connection between the original teaching of Jesus and his final instructions to pass it on to "all nations" (28:19).

Though not in the text, it is reasonable to wonder whether Matthew realized that when those who doubted the resurrection told others about Christ *the teacher* they would sense his unwavering presence with them (28:20b) and through their witness come to know and worship Christ *the risen Lord*.

Have you ever thought about all the different ways that people picture God? A walk through any cathedral, especially one that was built over several centuries, will show you an amazing range in statues, carvings, and stained glass, and the variety increases when you leave the cathedral to consider artwork from around the world.

If in a similar fashion you peruse the cathedral of your own heart, starting with your childhood, then continuing through youth up to your adult years, and if you stop to examine those places where you knelt in joy or grief, you may be astonished at the variety of your images and understandings of God.

Some of this variety represents the process of maturation. Our modes of thought, especially our ability to think conceptually and metaphorically, become more sophisticated as we grow up. A greater range of experience and responsibility draws us into more complex reflection upon the nature of God.

The cathedral of stone and glass, the cathedral of the heart, and the relationship of each to the other provide a way of thinking about church doctrine and its relationship to the faith of believers. Just as our own lives are marked by a process of development in our understanding of God, so too the life of the church reveals an increasing theological

> IF IN A SIMILAR FASHION YOU PERUSE THE CATHEDRAL OF YOUR OWN HEART, STARTING WITH YOUR CHILD-HOOD, THEN CONTINUING THROUGH YOUTH UP TO YOUR ADULT YEARS, AND IF YOU STOP TO EXAMINE THOSE PLACES WHERE YOU KNELT IN JOY OR GRIEF, YOU MAY BE ASTONISHED AT THE VARIETY OF YOUR IMAGES AND UNDERSTANDINGS OF GOD.

sophistication that resulted from Christ's command to the disciples to "make disciples of all nations" (28:19). Different nations have different thought forms and different cultures and languages, and such differences inevitably led to historical variations and developments in the expression of the Christian faith.

By the time Matthew wrote his Gospel (fifty to sixty years after Jesus' earthly ministry), the church had already begun to develop some of its distinctive practices of worship. Inheritors of rich traditions from temple and synagogue, the early Christians modified and developed these ancient practices in light of the Gospel. Matthew employs some of the language characteristic of this worship in his closing verses, especially the words, "baptizing them in the name of the Father and of the Son and of the Holy Spirit." At this point in the church's history, the words did not carry all the elaborate theological meanings that they now have for us.

When the church began to spread the gospel around the Mediterranean basin, however, it encountered peoples whose ways of thinking and talking about God included philosophical forms of thought. They wanted to understand more precisely the relationship of Father, Son, and Holy Spirit, and so they formulated doctrines of the Trinity that went far beyond the original meaning of Matthew's language. To return to our earlier analogy, they added to the cathedral in the heart new and more intricate images of God, new ways of reflecting upon the divine reality that created us and that lies at the center of our faith and hope.

There are two ways of thinking about these developments in the doctrine of God. One is that the process has ended, that the cathedral of belief is now a finished building. But the other is that the cathedral is still under construction, that the story of the development of the Trinity is a parable illuminating our need to continue reflecting upon God in light of the novel ways that human thought and culture are always evolving and changing. We honor what past theological builders did by taking their process seriously enough to continue it in our own day. And in doing that we do something even greater: We honor the living God who is greater than all of our human formulations and church doctrines.

SECOND SUNDAY AFTER PENTECOST

JUNE 6, 1999 / PROPER 5

REVISED COMMON	EPISCOPAL (BCP)	ROMAN CATHOLIC
Gen. 12:1-9	Hosea 5:15—6:6	Hosea 6:3-6
or Hosea 5:15—6:6		
Ps. 33:1-12, 50:7-15	Ps. 50:7-15 or 50	Ps. 50:1, 8, 12-13, 14-15
Rom. 4:13-25	Rom. 4:13-18	Rom. 4:18-25
Matt. 9:9-13, 18-26	Matt. 9:9-13	Matt. 9:9-13

IN LAST WEEK'S GOSPEL, Christ commands his followers: "Go therefore and make disciples of all nations" (Matt. 28:19a). In this week's first reading, God commands Abram: "Go from your country . . . to a land that I will show you" (Gen. 12:1). What energy is condensed in that simple verb! Its repetition in the first two weeks after Pentecost serves as a reminder that the Spirit does not come to us only to gladden our hearts and strengthen our fellowship. The Spirit comes to send us into the world as a witness to God. Go!

FIRST READING
GENESIS 12:1-9

Interpreting the Text

The stories preceding this passage amplify its theological force. The editors of Genesis have strategically placed it after the narratives of creation, the garden, Cain and Abel, Noah and the flood, and the Tower of Babel. The human family has consistently frustrated heaven's high hopes for earth. Now God intervenes, not taking control but providing an opportunity for faith as a way out of the human muddle.

Faith means a willingness to leave behind a known world "your country and your kindred and your father's house" for territory not yet in view, "the land that I will show you" (12:1). Abram's and Sarai's response is unlike the response of the characters who have appeared before them. When Abram and Sarai leave their home as God instructs them, they model a different pattern of behavior from Adam, Eve, Cain, and the tower builders, all of whom in their own way tried to grasp the power that belongs to God alone. Abram and Sarai act trusting that God has in mind for them a greater reality than what they immediately see.

Responding to the Text

Many families have stories that they tell again and again, especially at Christmas and Thanksgiving or at weddings and funerals. The story does more than surface a memory. It releases certain qualities and values in the heart of the teller and the listeners. It reminds people of who they are as a family, what special events and values have shaped their character and their identity.

The sagas of the early chapters of Genesis are among the oldest and most repeated stories in the family of faith. They recount the worst deeds of some ancestors; but they also remind us of our great forebears, who inspire us, who give us courage to respond faithfully to the call of God.

When we retell the story of Abram and Sarai setting out for an unknown land, we realize that we are not the first who are commanded to leave our familiar securities. They are the pioneers whose adventurous faith is an example to all the generations that follow them. Young adults leaving home, exiles from their native land, people whose spiritual experience leads them beyond their childhood belief, philosophers realizing the inadequacy of conventional thought, explorers starting out for unmapped regions, scientists testing theories that challenge the prevailing accounts of matter and energy, artists creating forms of expression that break new imaginative ground, social reformers who work for a society of greater justice—all of these in their own way give witness to the meaning of faith, to trusting the God who commands us, "Go from what is familiar and comfortable. There are realities greater than you now know and I will lead you there."

> THE STORY DOES MORE THAN SURFACE A MEMORY. IT RELEASES CERTAIN QUALITIES AND VALUES IN THE HEART OF THE TELLER AND THE LISTENERS. IT REMINDS PEOPLE OF WHO THEY ARE AS A FAMILY, WHAT SPECIAL EVENTS AND VALUES HAVE SHAPED THEIR CHARACTER AND THEIR IDENTITY.

HOSEA 5:15—6:6 (alt.)

Interpreting the Text

The Northern Kingdom of Israel was in turmoil when Hosea was prophesying during the latter half of the eighth century B.C.E. Assyria, the military superpower of the day, threatened it from without. Meanwhile, Israel's government suffered from a constant change of leadership. In one twenty-nine year period there were seven different kings! On top of all this was a longstanding theological propensity for this region to be drawn away from the worship of the Lord to the worship of fertility gods, particularly Baal.

The instability of the times made it easy for the people to justify themselves, not to acknowledge their own responsibility for their plight as a nation. They had a diminished version of what the life of faith requires.

Hosea deals with these distortions by presenting a dialogue between God and the people. God speaks first, naming their need for repentance (5:15). Then the people respond, modifying the divine request to suit their less-strenuous faith (6:1-3). But God, persistent as ever, states yet again the case against Israel and the true demands of faith (6:4-6).

Responding to the Text

How easily we reshape words to suit our purpose, especially words that demand something of us. Ask any parent who has told a child to do something only to discover the most important part of the task left undone. And it is not just children who keep fudging what is asked. The legal system and our everyday lives are filled with disagreements over what was asked and what was done.

During the eighth century B.C.E. Israel tried to reshape the word of God, to soften its demanding nature. Although some of the people's problems were beyond their control, they could at least maintain their faithfulness to God and the moral life that flows from such belief.

Through Hosea's prophetic imagination God has a conversation with them about their behavior. God is clear about their need to repent: "I will return again to my place until they acknowledge their guilt" (5:15a). God will retreat to heaven until they confess their wrongdoing.

The people respond by modifying what God asks. They agree that they need to return to God, but they offer not one word of contrition. They simply assert that "God will come to us like the showers, like the spring rains that water the earth" (6:3).

God picks up on their weather imagery, turning it around to show how fickle their faith is: "Your love is like a morning cloud, like the dew that goes away early" (6:4). God insists that a facile religiosity, the performance of piety without the embodiment of "steadfast love," is not acceptable. The word that calls us to a just and loving life is not open to modification.

RESPONSIVE READING
PSALM 33:1-12

Interpreting the Text

The attention to musical details in the first three verses is striking, especially the command, "Make melody to him with the harp of ten strings . . . play skillfully." This encouragement to musical artistry on the part of the worshiper leads to a posture of awe before the master creator: "For he spoke, and it came to be" (33:9).

Responding to the Text

Churches debating the place of music and the arts in their mission have reason to reflect on this psalm. It reveals a sophisticated understanding of the interrelationship of music and art to the social dimensions of faith. The artisan who crafts "the harp of ten strings" and the musician who plays it "skillfully" are feeding an appreciation for the master creator who "loves righteousness and justice" (33:5), and who puts worldly power in perspective: "The Lord brings the counsel of the nations to nothing" (33:10).

PSALM 50:7-15

Interpreting the Text

This psalm might have been part of a covenant renewal ceremony. In the ancient Mediterranean world, it was common for people to have a formal understanding with the suzerain or lord who ruled over them, and the terms of that covenant might periodically be renewed through ritual. In these verses the Lord God of Israel reminds the people what lies at the heart of their covenant.

Responding to the Text

A spiritual booby trap for any group of worshipers is to think that their ritual controls God. It is not that their offerings are offensive in themselves (50:8). The problem is the worshipers' presumption, reversing the proper understanding of their relationship to God. Worship is not magic, it is not the control of the divine by human artifice. Worship is instead a "sacrifice of thanksgiving" to the one who owns "the world and all that is in it" (50:12). The psalm calls us to an honest reckoning with the spirit in which we worship.

SECOND READING
ROMANS 4:13-25

Interpreting the Text

Although Romans is a densely packed letter, there are moments in Paul's complex thought when he makes a statement of belief that shines like a lighthouse along a shrouded coast: we gain our bearings and the other features of the land begin to make sense.

One of Paul's lighthouse statements occurs in today's reading when he describes the character of God "who gives life to the dead and calls into existence the things that do not exist" (4:17c). How do humans relate to a God this great? Paul turns to the example of Abraham, one of the heroes of Jewish tradition. Paul reminds us that Abraham's faith did not waver in the face of God's seemingly impossible promise (4:18-21). For Paul the meaning of the story of Abraham comes down to this: even the proper use of a good and holy gift (the law) is not what ultimately puts right our relationship with God. Only faith can do that. And because faith is a response that anyone can make, faith allows room for the diverse religious backgrounds present in the church of Rome, those who keep the law and those who do not (4:16). Both alike can live by faith. Paul's insistence on the primacy of faith thus provides a theological basis for an inclusive church.

Responding to the Text

Here is a parable designed to help listeners who find Paul's thought thick and perplexing. The parable is a door to understanding, not a full exposition of the reading.

A group of travelers undertook a wilderness tour, which promised adventure, an opportunity to live on the edge but with an experienced guide.

One day they were traveling deeper and deeper into the wild. Their adrenaline was pumping with the excitement of seeing fierce creatures, spectacular geophysical features and plant life unlike anything that grew in their native lands. In the severe heat of the mid-afternoon, they stopped beneath a large tree for shade. A severe wind came up suddenly and the tree toppled over the front of their vehicle killing the driver and guide but leaving the rest unscathed.

The vehicle was inoperable, and even if the survivors could have driven it, none of them had the slightest idea which direction they ought to head. They all had been preoccupied with taking pictures.

Now in desperation they rummaged through the first aid locker to find a book entitled, *How to Survive in the Wilderness.* Taking the book with them, they started out. But after several days many were on the brink of collapse, even though they had followed the commandments to the letter. Most were ready to give up. But one traveler, Abe Constance, kept hoping against hope that they would survive. He was not an expert on such matters, but he recognized the name of the author of the book as someone to be trusted. Abraham's trust kept the group together and eventually they found their way to safety.

Many generations later a man named Paul wrote an interpretive essay about this much-beloved story, and he sent his interpretation to a group made up of Abe's descendants and people who were in no way connected to him by blood.

Some of Abe's descendants who had passed on the book that Abe used believed that it was the book's directions that had kept him and the other travelers alive. But Paul insisted that what really saved Abe Constance was not the commandments themselves, but his faith in the one who wrote them.

GOSPEL
MATTHEW 9:9-13, 18-26

Interpreting the Text

The suddenness and brevity of the call of Matthew is breathtaking. Jesus says, "Follow me," and Matthew does not hem and haw or ask whether it fits with his career or self-image. Instead, "he got up and followed him" (9:9).

One helpful approach to such a compacted scene is to examine how the verb "follow" returns again and again in the Gospel. Jesus says to Peter and Andrew, "*Follow* me and I will make you fish for people" (4:19). He says to a disciple who hesitates in order to bury his father, "*Follow* me and let the dead bury their own dead" (8:22). He teaches in a later discourse, "whoever does not take up the cross and *follow* me is not worthy of me" (10:38). He tells the rich young man, "If you wish to be perfect, go, sell your possessions, and give the money to the poor, and you will have treasure in heaven; then come, *follow* me" (19:21). And he evidently said the same to "many women" because at the crucifixion they "were also there, looking on from a distance; they had *followed* Jesus from Galilee and had provided for him" (27:55).

Putting the call of Matthew in the context of these other passages, we come to see that the writer of the Gospel is like a preacher who has a favorite theme that keeps returning again and again in his sermons: "Follow Jesus." The list is strikingly inclusive of many classes and kinds of people, as if to say, "Whoever you are, whatever your station in life, follow Jesus."

Of course, not everyone does. The rich young man "went away grieving" (19:22), a striking contrast to Matthew who "got up and followed him" (9:9). Matthew as a tax collector was probably well-off himself, but as an agent of the occupying Roman army, his wealth came at a high cost: the ostracism and hatred of his community.

If we have missed the point of Jesus' openness to those the community rejects, the writer of the Gospel expands on the theme in the next verse, which pictures Jesus eating with "many tax collectors and sinners" (9:10).

Jesus continues breaking the circle of social exclusion in the second half of the reading. He praises a bleeding woman who, contrary to the law (see Leviticus 15:19-30), dares to touch him, and he risks polluting himself by taking the hand of a girl who is presumed dead (9:25).

Responding to the Text

A large part of growing up in any family or community is learning who is in and who is out. The parent instructs the child: "No, Honey, we do not make friends with them. They are not our kind of people." Children absorb these messages quickly and thoroughly. By the time they are old enough to attend school, they apply the principles of acceptance and exclusion in their own way. Remember your own years as a child on the school playground or observe children during recess outside: some are choosing teams and playing in circles, some are off alone in the corners looking longingly toward the others.

We repeat the pattern when we grow up, on the job and in our communities. Some people are in, some are out, and breaking the social circle is risky business. Worthy candidates for promotion are passed over because management considers them too friendly to the support staff. Neighbors at the block party cannot understand why a certain family was invited to attend. Church boards and academic councils have silent understandings about certain members who are not to be asked to serve on prestigious committees. Clubs and civic organizations have unspoken agreements that it would not be proper to admit persons of a particular racial or ethnic or religious background.

Part of what makes Jesus so attractive is his willingness to risk censure in challenging the exclusion of people from the circle of God's hospitality. It is also what makes him perplexing and threatening to those whose sense of self-worth is built on keeping themselves separate from those they deem unworthy.

The writer of Matthew portrays the Pharisees as just such a group. This may not be historically accurate—the Pharisees did not emerge as a significant power until about thirty years after Jesus' earthly ministry. Without joining Matthew's attack upon the Pharisees, we can still affirm his essential revelation: Jesus breaks the barriers of human exclusion by inviting a tax collector to follow him and eating with many others of that hated fraternity (9:10).

The graciousness of Jesus that disturbs some people is inviting and assuring to others. The woman "who had been suffering from hemorrhages for twelve years" (9:20) must have gotten wind of Jesus' hospitality to the outcast. His willingness to reach out to people like Matthew, to eat with him and other tax collectors, probably traveled through the grapevine that grows up in any of community of untouchables. It took courage for the woman to break a taboo as strong as the prohibition of contact between a bleeding woman and a man. Perhaps having heard of Jesus' initiative toward other outcasts, she reasoned he would not reject her touch.

And perhaps in a similar fashion her courage in reaching for him strengthened Jesus in reaching for the dead girl (9:25). The text does not tell us any of this for

> PART OF WHAT MAKES JESUS SO ATTRACTIVE IS HIS WILLINGNESS TO RISK CENSURE IN CHALLENGING THE EXCLUSION OF PEOPLE FROM THE CIRCLE OF GOD'S HOSPITALITY.

sure. But Matthew's arrangement of the stories, the breaking of one social taboo after another, suggests that graciousness has a snowballing effect: Jesus' willingness to reach for the outcast tax collector encourages the outcast bleeding woman to reach for him that in turn strengthens his willingness to reach to the dead girl. Hospitality begets hospitality, acceptance begets acceptance. This is the pattern we see in today's reading, the pattern we pray for in our own life and ministry. If we reach to one outcast and the word gets around, there is no telling how quickly and widely grace will spread.

THIRD SUNDAY AFTER PENTECOST

JUNE 13, 1999 / PROPER 6

REVISED COMMON	EPISCOPAL (BCP)	ROMAN CATHOLIC
Gen. 18:1-15 (21:1-7) or Exod. 19:2-8a	Exod. 19:2-8a	Exod. 19:2-6
Pss. 116:1-2, 12-19; 100	Ps. 100	Ps. 100:1-2, 3, 5
Rom. 5:1-8	Rom. 5:6-11	Rom. 5:6-11
Matt. 9:35—10:8 (9-23)	Matt. 9:35—10:8 (9-15)	Matt. 9:36—10:8

G OD IS ACTIVE AND DYNAMIC, reaching out to us in many different ways. In Genesis God visits Abraham and Sarah through three mysterious guests and promises the birth of a child to the elderly couple. In Romans God's love is poured into our hearts by the Holy Spirit, and in Matthew God's reign comes close to people through the disciples whom Jesus sends out on a mission of healing and exorcism. The readings give us a sense of God's persistence, the way that God again and again breaks into human life.

FIRST READING
GENESIS 18:1-15; (21:1-7)

Interpreting the Text

The text sometimes speaks of God alone: "The Lord appeared to Abraham by the oaks of Mamre" (18:1), "The Lord said" (18:13), and "He said" (18:15). But these verses are interwoven with references to "three men" (18:2) to whom Abraham shows hospitality, inviting them to rest and refresh themselves (18:4-5) and standing by them to meet any other needs as they eat (18:8). A deity accompanied by attendants was common to many ancient religions, and could be reflected here. But alternating between three and one might also be the author's way of expressing God's elusive nature. The oscillation between plurality and singularity keeps us from putting God into our neat categories.

We cannot control this enigmatic God who promises that despite their age Sarah and Abraham will have a child. Sarah greets this with understandable laughter (18:12), but nothing is "too wonderful" (18:14) for the God whose visitation awakens not comprehension but worship (18:2) and hospitality (18:4-8).

Responding to the Text

Nations take themselves too seriously. It is amazing how quickly the fortune of any great power can shift and decline. One empire gives way to another. But as long as a nation is at its zenith, it will often build monuments and make illusory claims of lasting forever.

Imagine, then, naming one of a country's founding fathers "Laughter." What a name to have in the lexicon of honored ancestors for it would be a way of puncturing a country's pretensions. A country might build "The George Washington Monument" or "The Lincoln Memorial." But who would build "The Laughter Monument"? Yet "Laughter" was to be the name of Sarah's and Abraham's son. When God promised them in their old age that they were going to have a child, each of them laughed (Gen. 17:17; 18:12), and so their son was named "Isaac," which means in Hebrew, "He laughs."

Every time the Israelites told the story of their forebears and they came to the name of Isaac, they would remember that Sarah and Abraham, two of their most honored ancestors, had laughed at God and the preposterousness of what God promised. The name would remind them that their welfare lay not in claims of superiority and group pride, but in God who from the start did laughably impossible things for their founders. Hearing laughter in their sacred chronicles, they could laugh at themselves and give honor to the one who had given them whatever they possessed as a people, the one whose intention is never deterred simply because human beings find it to be laughable.

EXODUS 19:2-8a (alt.)

Interpreting the Text

This is the first of many sections of the Sinai revelation. The author sets the scene with keen attention to the spatial relationships among the mountain, Moses, God, and the people. These details help us understand the character of the divine encounter between God and the liberated Hebrews. The people are camped "in *front* of the mountain" (19:2). "Moses went *up* to God; the Lord called to him *from* the mountain" (19:3). Then Moses summoned the elders and "set *before* them all these words that the Lord had commanded him" (19:7).

The precision of the description makes one think of the way an architect for a sanctuary might describe a building plan or a liturgist a ritual. Moses is an intermediary between God and the people. He ascends the mountain alone, listens to God, and then returns to give the message to the people. Moses acts as a priest, but the message he brings back makes it clear that the priestly vocation is not his alone. It belongs to them all: "You shall be for me a priestly kingdom and a holy nation" (19:6).

Responding to the Text

Many times when I have been visiting someone in the hospital and have offered a prayer, the patient in the next bed has asked, "Will you put in a good word for me with the man upstairs?" Although there are any number of ways we might criticize the theological inadequacy of this statement, I have no intention of doing so. I always take the request seriously for I believe it reveals something that many human beings fervently desire: an intermediary who is willing to approach the divine on their behalf.

We can also see the desire for an intermediary in purely secular relationships. We sometimes ask someone who is better placed in an organization: "Would you please speak to the president about this? I do not feel I have the standing to do it."

But sometimes the need for an intermediary awakens our resentment. We question the hierarchy of power that seems to make it necessary. And yet it does not appear possible to eliminate all hierarchies. Therefore, the question becomes: when there is a hierarchy, particularly a religious one, how should it function?

Exodus 19 provides a profound answer to this question. Moses fills the role of intermediary. He is priest to the people, but his priesthood is in the service of making them "a priestly kingdom." This passage is not an eyewitness account but rather is shaped by centuries of worship and tradition. It probably served to remind priests and people alike that the holy calling of the clergy is to help the whole community fill its calling to be holy.

RESPONSIVE READING
PSALM 116:1-2, 12-19

Interpreting the Text

The psalmist is bursting with unrestrained gratitude because God "has heard my voice and supplications" (116:1). Joy finds expression in an extravagant promise, "I will call on him as long as I live" (116:2). But even that is not thanks enough. The psalmist pledges to make a public witness before the congregation which will include participation in a ritual libation (116:13).

Responding to the Text

Think of the best thing that ever happened to you: you met your closest friend, a surgery saved your life, you gave birth to a child that you had long wanted, you had an overwhelming sense of God's love and care for you. In return you wanted to send a thousand long-stem red roses, present a check for a billion dollars, write a hundred sonnets as beautiful as Shakespeare's.

But because you cannot do these things, do what the psalmist does: love God and call on God as long as you live.

PSALM 100 (alt.)

Interpreting the Text

The first verse calls "all the earth" to worship, while the fourth invites people into the temple: "Enter his gates with thanksgiving." It appears from the development of the psalm that the joyful noise of the earth belongs in the temple. The sacred space does not shut out but welcomes in the worship that happens beyond its walls.

Responding to the Text

Noise pollution has become a major problem in our lives. Jets intrude on the wilderness. Junk music and announcements assault us in waiting rooms, elevators, malls, and stores.

The psalm exhorts us to something entirely different: a joyful noise with a holy purpose. If we join in this noise, then perhaps we will find the wisdom to reduce the intrusive noise that pollutes our environment. We will no longer be afraid of silence because our songs of praise will have taught us that even when our voice is stilled, God's "steadfast love endures forever" (100:5).

SECOND READING
ROMANS 5:1-8

Interpreting the Text

The reading begins with "Therefore," an indicator that Paul is about to trace the implications and consequences of what he has already written. The opening verse summarizes the essence of Paul's argument. His first phrase, "since we are justified by faith," recounts what he has finished demonstrating in the fourth chapter: how it is by faith that our relationship to God is put right. The second phrase, "we have peace with God through our Lord Jesus Christ," tells us what follows from our renewed relationship.

Notice the order of things. It is not that we find peace in ourselves and from that peaceful center build the right relationship to God. Instead, peace flows from our having been justified through the death and resurrection of Christ (4:25). If we fail to keep clear the order of the process, then we may misread Paul's subsequent statement that "suffering produces endurance and endurance produces character, and character produces hope" (5:3-4). Paul is *not* laying out a system for building character through suffering. He is not telling victims of abuse to bear passively their pain. Instead, he is describing how, when we have been restored by

Christ, hope unfurls in our hearts as we live through the suffering that inevitably comes to all of us.

All of this is a gift from God whose gracious character is self-evident in the way that Christ died for us while we were anything but good or worthy (5:6-8).

Responding to the Text

I was standing in line at the airport for a taxi when a bus with a platform elevator drove up to the curb. A bus passenger wheeled herself onto the elevator which then descended to the ground. The woman wheeled off the platform onto the sidewalk and headed up a ramp into the terminal. What years ago had been a major obstacle course was now an accessible path.

If we have walked all our life and then find ourselves using crutches or a wheel chair, we instantly appreciate how important access is. We are grateful for the ramp instead of the stairs and for the button that opens the door automatically.

Access. It is a concept as real for our spirits as our bodies. We are never more desperate than when we feel there is no way for us to gain entrance to the presence of God, when we sense that we are confined to a world that is strewn with the insurmountable obstacles of doubt, fear, and sin. We spend our energies trying to find a spiritual peace that eludes us. We have no access to hope, peace, or grace.

Sometimes our quest is not explicitly religious. It takes shape as an obsession. We are always wanting to rise higher, own more, become who we are not. What provides access to the peace for which we hunger?

Paul writes that "we have peace with God through our Lord Jesus Christ, through whom we have obtained *access* to this grace in which we stand" (5:1-2). This peace is not an illusory world in which everything works perfectly and we are forever free of suffering. The peace to which Christ provides access is a new way of being that sets off a transformative process: "suffering produces endurance, and endurance produces character, and character produces hope" (5:3-4). This is not something that happens automatically by our willing it. We sadly know that suffering often produces defeat and defeat produces dysfunction and dysfunction produces despair. What makes the difference between these two processes is Jesus Christ, the one who gives us access to the grace of God, the grace that does not abrogate suffering but transforms it into hope.

Gospel
MATTHEW 9:35—10:8 (9-23)

Interpreting the Text

The reading first focuses on Jesus and his ministry (9:35-36), and then shifts to the disciples and their commissioning (10:1-8).

A detailed recapitulation of themes occurs between the first and second parts of the reading: Jesus is pictured "proclaiming the good news of the kingdom" (9:35), then instructs the disciples they are to "proclaim the good news, 'the kingdom of heaven has come near'" (10:7). Jesus goes about "curing every disease and every sickness" (9:35), then gives the disciples authority "to cure every disease and every sickness" (10:1). Jesus views the crowds that gather about him as "sheep without a shepherd" (9:36), then sends the disciples "to the lost sheep of the house of Israel" (9:6).

Although these verbal repetitions may reflect the oral form in which the earliest traditions about Jesus were passed on, their accumulative effect is to suggest how the ministry of Jesus was passed from him to the disciples. If the text stopped at 9:36, then we would be left with an attractive picture of the compassionate Jesus tending to a people "harassed and helpless." We would be impressed with Jesus, but we might conclude: although what Jesus did was wonderful, it ended with him. Instead, the story continues and shows Jesus giving authority to the disciples to do the very things they have seen him doing.

Matthew interrupts the commissioning of the twelve disciples with the list of their names, making revealing asides about the kind of people they are: "Matthew, the tax collector . . . Judas Iscariot, the one who betrayed him" (10:3). Matthew achieves two things by placing the list here and adding his small but telling observations. First of all, he makes it clear that Jesus shared his ministry with others, and second, they were not all exemplary characters. Two of them were traitors: Matthew would be considered a traitor to the Judeans because he worked for the Roman tax system and Judas became a traitor to the cause of the gospel.

Because Matthew is writing his Gospel between 80 and 90 C.E., he may be recalling these details as a way of telling his own community not to be discouraged in their current ministries. Disappointed with one another, facing persecution, and often questioning how they can carry on, Matthew reminds them that when Jesus commissioned the first disciples fifty years ago they were an imperfect and motley crew.

Responding to the Text

It is a scene to awaken our deepest feelings of piety and reverence, an image worthy of a stained glass window: Jesus having "compassion" for the crowds because "they were harassed and helpless, like sheep without a shepherd" (9:36). If we are feeling "harassed and helpless," we may well picture ourselves among that needy crowd, awestruck by the wonderful things that Jesus does.

But just as we settle into the role of grateful admirers, Jesus turns to us who are his disciples and tells us, "The harvest is plentiful, but the laborers are few; therefore ask the Lord of the harvest to send out laborers into his harvest" (9:37-38).

Although we are "harassed and helpless," prayer does not seem an impossible task. We at least have enough energy to ask God for the laborers Jesus needs to spread his ministry of healing and teaching. And so we begin to pray as fervently as we can that God will raise up people to carry on the strenuous work that Jesus has begun.

But when the prayer is over we realize that we, the very disciples whom Christ instructs to pray, are the laborers for whom we were praying! Intentionally or not, Matthew has drawn a scene that rings true to any faithful disciple: Praying for someone to do something, we discover that God has chosen us for the task.

We may be amazed that Jesus would risk giving us the authority to carry on his ministry, but Matthew reminds us of the characters Jesus initially chose. They included a tax collector who had colluded with the Romans, and Judas, whose name would become synonymous with traitor. Matthew is reshaping the early traditions about Jesus to deny us any excuse we might offer for not carrying on the ministry of Jesus. Matthew says in effect:

"So you are busy praying for people to carry on the ministry of Jesus? Well, you are the answer to your prayer. Jesus wants you."

"So you admire what Jesus did but you cannot picture yourself continuing his work? Well, look at how Jesus commissions those first disciples: he gives them authority to do the exact same things that he has been doing.

"So you feel unworthy, not holy enough for ministry? Well, consider that list of first disciples. It is not a collection of names you would find in *Who's Who* or the glamorous types that make the cover of *People*."

Matthew gives us his version of Jesus' instructions to the disciples. Even if the directions make no literal sense today, they hold implications for ministry in any age. There is a sense of urgency about Jesus' instructions, of moving out quickly and unencumbered: "Take no gold, or silver, or copper in your belts, no bag for your journey, or two tunics, or sandals, or a staff; for laborers deserve their food" (10:9)

PART OF WHAT JESUS MODELS FOR US IN HIS MINISTRY IS A FREEDOM FROM PREOCCUPATION WITH HIMSELF AND HIS OWN NEEDS. HE TRAVELS LIGHT, AND HE URGES US TO DO THE SAME.

We need to travel light. If we are overburdened we will not have the energy and attentiveness that are required to minister to others. Part of what Jesus models for us in his ministry is a freedom from preoccupation with himself and his own needs. He travels light, and he urges us to do the same.

Among the burdens Jesus removes is the unrealistic expectation that everyone will respond favorably to our ministry. The gospel is not something that we can force upon those who are unreceptive (10:13-14). But the "harassed and helpless" who welcome our ministries will be blessed with peace. They will give thanks to the shepherd who sent us to make clear by word and deed that "The kingdom of heaven has come near."

FOURTH SUNDAY AFTER PENTECOST

JUNE 20, 1999 / PROPER 7

REVISED COMMON	EPISCOPAL (BCP)	ROMAN CATHOLIC
Gen. 21:8–21	Jer. 20:7–13	Jer. 20:10–13
or Jer. 20:7–13		
Pss. 86:1–10, 16–17 or	Ps. 69:1–18;	Ps. 69:8–10
69:7–10 (11–15), 16–18	or 69:7–10, 16–18	
Rom. 6:1b–11	Rom. 5:15b–19	Rom. 5:12–15
Matt. 10:24–39	Matt. 10:(16–23), 24–33	Matt. 10:26–33

TO WHOM DO WE BELONG? The question runs like a deep current in a river through the readings for today. When Hagar and her son Ishmael are banished from Abraham's and Sarah's household, they discover in the wilderness that they still belong to God. The psalmist acknowledges "You are my God; be gracious to me, O Lord" (Ps. 86:2). Paul reminds us we are united with Christ through our baptisms and are, therefore, no longer enslaved to sin. Jesus tells us that our allegiance to him exceeds even the bonds of family membership. To whom do we belong? God.

FIRST READING
GENESIS 21:8–21

Interpreting the Text

It was Sarah's idea in the first place that Abraham have sexual intercourse with her slave woman Hagar in hopes of obtaining heirs (Gen. 16:2). But now, having born a son of her own, Sarah wants the woman gone (21:10).

The conflict began as soon as Hagar realized that she was pregnant by Abraham (16:4-16). The sight of Ishmael playing is the last straw for Sarah (21:9). A pun in the Hebrew text suggests that Sarah is afraid Hagar's child will usurp her own son, Isaac.

When Sarah tells Abraham to throw Hagar and Ishmael out he is very distressed "on account of his son" (21:11), but he does not stand up for the defenseless woman. It may be that a later editor, wanting to defend Abraham's reputation, adduces the patriarch's behavior to the intervention of God (21:12-13). But the explanation is not very convincing, because all Abraham provides Hagar and the child is bread and a canteen of water (21:14).

The patterns of the story—an unfairly treated slave, expulsion, wandering in the wilderness, divine intervention—suggest that the writer is prefiguring the revelation of God's compassion in the Israelites' exodus from Egypt.

Responding to the Text

A child's hollow eyes look out and convey a bleakness in the heart as severe as the surrounding desert. He clings to a mother whose face is set like stone to admit no more reality than what it takes to place one foot in front of the other. That is how I picture Hagar and Ishmael wandering in the wilderness of Beer-sheba (21:14).

As she wanders, Hagar reviews all that led to her expulsion. Sarah had been willing to have Hagar bear her husband a son when she herself was barren, but once Sarah had born Isaac, everything changed. Hagar and Ishmael became disposable. Hagar's role as surrogate mother counted for nothing. She was a slave and therefore on the bottom rung of the ladder of power.

Listen to Hagar's lament, "Do not let me look on the death of the child" (21:16), and hear in her weeping the realism of the biblical writer about the cruel and tangled past of the community of faith.

But that is not the whole story. There is something more: "God heard the voice of the boy; and the angel of God called to Hagar from heaven" (21:17). The failure of people whom we have most honored and admired, people like Abraham and Sarah, cannot defeat the compassion of God who intervenes to rescue and uphold us.

God emerges from the story as the one whose purposes transcend our family feuds and jealousies, the one who shows compassion for the very people we want out of the way.

JEREMIAH 20:7-13 (alt.)

Interpreting the Text

Jeremiah charges that God has "enticed" and "overpowered" him (20:7). The words may accurately be translated "seduced" and "raped." I am hesitant to include these translations because they sound so blasphemous. But an accurate understanding of the language does not obligate us to accept the theology that it implies.

The violence of Jeremiah's experience of God feeds in him a hope of violence against his enemies. Like God, they seek to "entice" him (20:7 and 10). The prophet prays that his violent God will pay back his violent enemies with violence: "let me see your retribution upon them" (20:12).

Fortunately, a mature understanding of God is never derived from a single passage of scripture. We consider each reading in light of the larger patterns of the biblical writer and the canon as a whole. When we grant this grace to Jeremiah, then we realize the vastness of the opposition to his speaking the truth, and we realize a feeling any less intense than his would not have sustained him in his hard calling.

Responding to the Text

Some passages of scripture make us wonder: Why is this in the Bible? Our reading from Jeremiah is just such a passage. I find myself tempted to tone down its blasphemy, particularly the charge that God has seduced and raped the prophet! If we skipped these troubling words, we could focus on what is more palatable. Verse 9 is a favorite of many preachers because the image of fire in the bones captures the irrepressible nature of God's word.

Or we can face the prophet's blasphemy head-on, remembering that God does not require us to accept every word of the Bible as true for our life and faith. Instead, we are called to think through how it clarifies what we do believe and how we are to live.

Using this last strategy, I find Jeremiah's words bracing: they bring me to terms with the violence that religious people often ascribe to God and the way such images of deity may reinforce the human tendency to vengeance, as in this passage.

> JEREMIAH 20:9 IS A FAVORITE OF MANY PREACHERS BECAUSE THE IMAGE OF FIRE IN THE BONES CAPTURES THE IRREPRESSIBLE NATURE OF GOD'S WORD.

Jeremiah's words are a word of judgment upon us in a way the prophet never intended: they call us to confess how we, like him, have appealed to a violent God to justify our desire for violence and revenge. This judgment leaves me hungering for the more gracious understanding of God that impelled this same furious prophet to write the exiles in Babylon that they should pray for the welfare of their captors (29:7).

Perhaps, then, Jeremiah upsets us because the wide range of his humanity reminds us that we, too, are an astounding mixture of fury, blasphemy, and grace.

RESPONSIVE READING
PSALM 86:1-10, 16-17

Interpreting the Text

A complementary contrast exists in the psalm between the state of the supplicant and the character of God. The psalmist is "poor and needy" (86:1) while God is "abounding in steadfast love to all who call on you" (86:5). In desperate straits (86:2), the psalmist maintains confidence in the power of God for deliverance (86:7).

123

FOURTH SUNDAY
AFTER PENTECOST

JUNE 20

Responding to the Text

Computerized phone answering services have added to our sense of a depersonalized world. "Welcome and thank you for calling. Please listen to the following menu and make your selection at any time."

I believe our dissatisfaction with such service goes deeper than our immediate frustrations. It springs from a fundamental need to know that we are heard and understood. Even if we cannot reverse the spread of electronic voices, we can rejoice with the psalmist at the responsiveness of God: "In the day of my trouble I call on you, for you will answer me" (86:7).

PSALM 69:7-10; (11-15), 16-18 (alt.)

Interpreting the Text

The psalmist's passion for God, which includes a desire to rebuild the temple (69:9), has brought him "reproach" (69:7) and made him an "alien" in his family of origin (69:8). The psalmist experiences his rejection and persecution as "sinking in the mire" (69:13). His fear culminates in the vision of a terrifying death (69:15) and a plea for rescue (69:16-18).

Responding to the Text

Frantic, the psalmist prays to God: "Do not let the flood sweep over me, or the deep swallow me up, or the Pit close its mouth over me" (69:15). We associate this imagery with nightmares, with dreams that wake a child in the middle of the night, with the terror in our own souls. The psalm gives witness to a great spiritual truth: authentic prayer is not always reverent and dignified. The psalm reminds us that God is ready to listen to our profoundest fear expressed in the bluntest language.

SECOND READING
ROMANS 6:1b-11

Interpreting the Text

The passage begins with Paul imagining a question that might be brought against his theological argument (6:1). He offers a rebuttal and a further set of questions (6:2-3), which in turn develop into a reflection upon the meaning of baptism (6:4-11). The technical name for this style of writing is "diatribe," a word that in modern usage has come to mean a contentious harangue, but which in the ancient world was considered a powerful means of persuasion.

Baptism for Paul is a transformative act that initiates in us a replication of the pattern of Christ's death and resurrection (6:4-6). Notice the important shift in tenses "we *have been* buried" with Christ (9:4), but "we *will* be united with him in a resurrection like his" (9:5).

Although the process is yet to be finished, it already has an impact upon our lives: we do not "go on living" in sin (6:2) but instead "walk in newness of life" (6:4). "Walk" is an expression for the moral character of one's entire life.

Notably absent in this passage is the imperative voice. Paul does not command us to walk in newness of life. He does not tell us what we ought to do, or must do. Christ's death and resurrection and our baptism into them are such powerful realties that the possibility of a transformed life inevitably flows out of them.

Responding to the Text

People sometimes say of themselves that they followed in the footsteps of a parent or a teacher or an individual who gave them their first break in life. Whether or not we personally have followed in someone else's footsteps, growing up for all of us involves trying out different patterns, modeling ourselves after those we admire.

There is a long-standing debate about the respective roles of environment and genetics in deciding the course of our lives. Do we choose those whom we emulate or does some innate disposition lead us to follow them? There is no conclusive argument one way or the other.

Today's reading invites us to consider the spiritual dimensions that shape people's lives in ways that transcend the dichotomies of environment and genetics. Paul describes how people who have been baptized are initiated into the pattern of Christ's death and resurrection. The death that comes through baptism is a radical break from being controlled by the forces that fracture life and that lead us from the intention of God, forces that Paul gathers together under the word "sin." Having died with Christ through baptism, we are freed from sin (6:6). Of course, being human we still fail to be what God calls us to be, but Paul does not dwell on our weakness in this passage. Instead, he focuses on the glorious potential that is opened up by our baptism, by our identification with the pattern of Christ's death and resurrection: it is now possible for us to walk in newness of life, to live in a manner that shows forth the same grace, justice, and compassion that were embodied in Christ.

So the next time we look back over the pattern of our lives or we think what direction our lives ought to take, let us remember our baptisms. Let us remember that we have already started on the path that Christ took, and that no matter what happens in our other life choices, we are being drawn toward resurrection, toward a fulfillment greater than any finite human accomplishment.

MATTHEW 10:24-39

Interpreting the Text

Upon first reading, it is difficult to discern a coherent thread to the passage. But if we place these verses in the context of Matthew's community, which, some two generations after Jesus' ministry, is experiencing conflict with the established authorities and conflict among its members, then we can hear these words through the ears of a struggling church.

Matthew reminds those who are discouraged by vicious name-calling that Jesus "the master of the house" was called "Beelzebul," and, therefore, as his disciples it is only reasonable to expect that they will also be maligned (10:25).

For those who are afraid for their lives Matthew recalls how Jesus taught a serene confidence in God: "even the hairs on your head are all counted" (10:30). Jesus' teachings about trust in God must have been a favorite of Matthew's; they figure prominently in the Sermon on the Mount as they do here. Compare 10:26-31 with 6:25-34.

To those who are thinking of leaving the church, Matthew calls up the final judgment: "but whoever denies me before others, I also will deny before my Father in heaven" (10:32). And to those who are discouraged because of the conflict that has resulted when family members have responded in very different ways to the gospel, Matthew recounts how Jesus said: "Do not think that I have come to bring peace to the earth; I have not come to bring peace, but a sword" (10:34).

Putting all of these varied concerns together, Matthew emerges from the reading as a pastor dealing with a church in turmoil from without and within. Typical of any conflicted organization, Matthew's community threatens to come apart as people's fears drive them to consider dropping out or to complain that they never knew that being a member would involve them in this much difficulty. Anyone who has ever been in a position of leadership in such a community will have sympathy for Matthew's apparent leaping from one teaching of Jesus to another to answer all the complaints and fears.

The reading concludes with Matthew reaffirming the central principle of Jesus' teaching, the high and noble vision that had first fired believers' hearts and gave the community birth: taking up the cross and living for others (10:38-39).

Responding to the Text

"I have not come to bring peace, but a sword. For I have come to set a man against his father, and a daughter against her mother. . . . Whoever loves father or mother more than me is not worthy of me" (10:34-37). These verses are troubling to anyone who believes that the gospel is about family values, that faith in Jesus Christ will nurture and reinforce family relationships. Following Jesus can have a divisive impact upon our most intimate associations. However, a close examination of the passage reveals that the divisive power of the gospel can be the starting point for healthier and more enduring family relationships.

By the time Matthew writes this version of Jesus' teaching, acrimony is growing between those who have joined the church and those who have decided that the Jesus movement is disrupting the established community's beliefs and traditions. Matthew is describing what has already happened: Following Jesus has touched off conflict between people who were once close.

Although Matthew's historical circumstances help us to understand this troubling passage, they do not clear away all the tensions. The followers of Jesus in any time and place often find themselves at odds with people they love. We know this from our own experience. If we see someone we love acting destructively, and if we confront them about their behavior, the reaction may be hostile and angry. That is why we often decide not to speak even though their behavior is contrary to everything Christ teaches us. We keep silent because we "want to keep the peace" or because somebody else counsels us "just let it be." But the peace our silence buys is not an authentic peace. It is a simmering volcano: the landscape looks the same as before, but there are tremors underneath, and we are frightened for the day all of these things come to a head and our shaky world blows up.

Jesus calls us to a responsible relationship with one another. He refuses to offer us a cheap peace that corrodes affection and genuine care for one another. Jesus teaches us it is not true that we must keep quiet "to keep the family together." Of course, there are mistakes and failures and personality quirks that we overlook in one another. That is part of living a life of grace. But as people of faith we are to hold each other accountable when our behavior is contrary to the purposes of God. Christ brings a "sword" to such behavior, a word of clear judgment against it.

> JESUS CALLS US TO A RESPONSIBLE RELATIONSHIP WITH ONE ANOTHER. HE REFUSES TO OFFER US A CHEAP PEACE THAT CORRODES AFFECTION AND GENUINE CARE FOR ONE ANOTHER.

Think of the number of families, offices, social organizations, neighborhoods, and churches that are in a state of constant covert tension because no one dares to risk the "peace" of the status quo even though that peace is depleting the energies and corroding everyone's commitment. Everybody tiptoes around the problem that no one will mention: the drug dependency, the abuse, the cheating, the injustice, the self-promotion at the expense of the community.

Notice the Gospel principle that guides a Christlike confrontation. We do not make our judgment with arrogance or self-righteousness. We make it understanding the pain of judgment, the pain of taking up the cross (10:38). We do it because we are willing to lose our lives for the sake of Christ (10:39). If we embody these spiritual principles, then the word that divides parent and child, in-law and in-law, can clear the way for the family values that matter most: integrity, justice, mutual respect, and a love that has the courage to face the truth about how each of us live.

FIFTH SUNDAY
AFTER PENTECOST

JUNE 27, 1999 / PROPER 8

REVISED COMMON	EPISCOPAL (BCP)	ROMAN CATHOLIC
Gen. 22:1-14	Isa. 2:10-17	2 Kings 4:8-11, 14-16
or Jer. 28:5-9		
Pss. 13; 89:1-4, 15-18	Ps. 89:1-18	Ps. 89:2-3, 16-17, 18-19
Rom. 6:12-23	Rom. 6:3-11	Rom. 6:3-4, 8-11
Matt. 10:40-42	Matt. 10:34-42	Matt. 10:37-42

WHAT A RANGE OF HUMAN RESPONSES to God these readings present! In Genesis, Abraham demonstrates unquestioning obedience to God, and in Romans, Paul makes a plea that we give ourselves with a similar absolute devotion to God. But Psalm 13 is utterly different: not obedient or subservient, the psalmist cries out to God. The gospel reads as a counterbalance to these intense dramas. Answering God means giving a "cup of cold water" to a little one. Where are your people this week: tested like Abraham, lamenting like the psalmist, needing to remember simple acts of charity?

FIRST READING
GENESIS 22:1-14

Interpreting the Text

No amount of scholarly research will eliminate the terror that this passage can strike in children: a father who is willing to sacrifice his own child because God commands him to do it.

There are, however, details in the text suggesting that the story functioned to liberate ancient people from the practice of child sacrifice. The story opens: "God *tested* Abraham" (22:1). The verb alerts us that the story is part of the recurring theme of faith. Also, notice that when Isaac asks about the burnt offering, Abraham replies "God himself will provide the lamb for a burnt offering, my son" (22:8). This exchange between father and son reads like a catechism. It is the language of a sophisticated cultic life that developed centuries after Abraham lived. Compare a similar question and answer form in Deut. 6:20-25. Thus, although the story horrifies us, it may in fact be a way of reassuring a child that in the worship of Yahweh, God will provide the offering and it will *not* be the child!

Responding to the Text

Is it good or bad to obey orders? If it means obeying the doctor's orders, it is good. But if obeying orders means implementing an immoral policy simply because it came down from management, then it is bad.

What about obeying God? People have killed and tortured, claiming God commanded them to do it. On the other hand, people have done extraordinary acts of kindness out of obedience to God.

What about Abraham? Should he have obeyed God's call to sacrifice Isaac? If we read the story without any historical background of the ancient world, then the answer is clearly "No, Abraham should not have obeyed God!" If we fail to say this, we will have no grounds to challenge all of the ways God's name is used to justify destructive behavior.

But if we consider the story from the perspective of ancient society, then we may be freed to glimpse its redemptive meaning. The story rejects the sacrifice of children. In the middle of the story, Abraham says that God will provide a lamb for the offering, and God later instructs Abraham "Do not lay your hand on the boy or do anything to him" (22:12). Abraham sums up the story by a pun in Hebrew (22:14) which is lost in the English translation, "The Lord will provide" (22:14). The pun suggests the story is about the generous God who appears to the pilgrims worshiping in Jerusalem.

Should we obey God? Yes, we should obey the loving God who wants us never to harm our children and provides what we need for faithful worship and service.

JEREMIAH 28:5-9 (alt.)

Interpreting the Text

We must consider the whole chapter to understand the context of the reading. Jeremiah 28:1-4 places the confrontation between Hananiah and Jeremiah after the first exiles and the vessels from the temple were hauled off to Babylon in 597 B.C.E., a decade prior to the total destruction of the temple and final deportation.

Hauling away sacred objects represented far more than looting in the ancient world. The conquerors did this to make a theological point: "Your god is not powerful enough to protect you from our power." The loss of the temple vessels would have created a crisis of faith among people. How could the Lord allow this to happen to Israel? Hananiah's prophecy that God will restore both vessels and exiles within two years (28:3-4) assures people that God is as powerful as they believe.

Jeremiah initially hopes that Hananiah's prophecy is true (28:6), but with his typical realism about the terrors of history, Jeremiah also reminds Hananiah, the priests, and the congregation (28:5) that the test of a prophet's word is what actually comes to be (28:9).

Responding to the Text

Jeremiah 28 is a dramatic confrontation between different understandings of how God is acting in the affairs of Israel.

On one side is Hananiah, who holds to a highly traditional understanding of God: God is the protector of Israel and will restore all that the nation has lost to Babylon. On the other side is Jeremiah, who wishes Hananiah's prophecy were true but who reminds the entire congregation (28:5) not to assume a vision is true simply because they wish it were so.

Hananiah answers Jeremiah's challenge by engaging in a prophetic action, breaking the wooden yoke that Jeremiah wears to represent the yoke of Babylon's power.

"Sometime after" (28:12) their confrontation Jeremiah receives a word from God that brings a radically new understanding of God: God is not simply the protector of Israel. God is sovereign over all peoples, including Nebuchadnezzar of Babylon, to whom God has given all the conquered nations and even "the wild animals" (28:14). Jeremiah tells his new vision to Hananiah, and in the name of God tells the man "the Lord has not sent you, and you made this people trust in a lie" (28:15).

Hananiah was not an evil person. He was declaring what he genuinely believed to be the word of God. Jeremiah was not a man without faults, but he was the one who saw more accurately who God was and how God was acting. The new truth about God was not apparent to Hananiah and the others, and their story is a reminder that our heartfelt beliefs about God may be every bit as false as the prophecy that Hananiah delivered with such conviction.

RESPONSIVE READING

PSALM 13

Interpreting the Text

The psalm is a lament, a quarrel with God for ignoring the supplicant's prayer. The final affirmation of trust (13:5-6) rings true because of the struggle that dominates the first four verses. Such a psalm is significant for the pastoral care of people because it removes the burden of believing that all prayer must be upbeat and filled with praise and thanksgiving.

Responding to the Text

I once visited a woman who was facing her eleventh or twelfth operation to correct a chronic problem. Although she was a lifelong church member, she had given up praying for herself since God never answered. I asked if I might read a few verses from the Bible. She said, "Yes, but make it brief." I read her Psalm 13:1-2. She responded, "That's in the Bible?" The next morning when I returned before she went to surgery, she said: "I have been praying that psalm all night." The psalmist's lament had liberated her lament.

PSALM 89:1-4, 15-18

Interpreting the Text

The affirmation that the Davidic covenant is "forever" (89:4) makes for a revealing dialogue between the royal theology of Jerusalem and the realities announced in Jeremiah 28. Perhaps it was singing hymns like this psalm that reinforced the erroneous creed that God would never allow Jerusalem to crumble. However, vv. 5-14 may be a self-contained corrective to the psalmist's initial rhapsody about David's line: for They remind us that God is the only eternal ruler of all.

Responding to the Text

No government lasts forever. Yet those in power in any age make grand claims for their enduring existence. The psalmist captures the extravagance of such belief in vv. 3 and 4. But at the same time, the psalmist is wise enough to hold up a vision of God's reign that inevitably throws into question all passing politicians, including David and his heirs.

SECOND READING
ROMANS 6:12-23

Interpreting the Text

Paul himself names a principle for interpreting today's reading: "I am speaking in human terms because of your natural limitations" (6:19). As late twentieth-century readers, we now see that those "human terms" are conditioned by the world in which Paul lived: a world where slavery was a social institution and its patterns of power were commonly understood. But nowadays Paul's talk of slavery and obedience may sound antiquated. Furthermore, it may be hard for people who have suffered from the misuse of power to receive Paul's message, especially if their oppressors have appealed to Paul's language to justify their behavior.

The apostle anticipates these potential difficulties. He reminds us he is "speaking in human terms," and he imagines the arguments brought against his position: "What then? Should we sin because we are not under law but under grace?" (6:15).

Having drawn upon analogies of slavery and obedience, Paul drives to a level of human transformation profounder than the social institutions of his age: "[You] have become obedient from the heart to the form of teaching to which you were entrusted" (6:17). This obedience is not something imposed and enforced from above: it is "from the heart." And we obey not an order or a command, but "a form of *teaching*." When we entrust ourselves to that teaching, then we find our lives turned around, redirected from sin to righteousness, from brokenness to integrity (6:12-14, 20-23).

Responding to the Text

A couple once told me how after their son's graduation from high school, they informed him he would no longer have a curfew. He was going away to college in the fall, and they wanted him to adjust to his new responsibility.

The first night after they told him of his new freedom, he stayed out until two a.m. Neither parent slept until they heard him come through the door, but they did not say a word as he walked down the hall, nor the next morning at breakfast. They had given their word: he was free from his former restrictions.

The next night he stayed out until four a.m. The parents became very concerned and considered calling around to the young man's friends, but they did not.

The third night it was six a.m. before he arrived home. That morning at breakfast—the son had a summer job that started at eight—the young man looked nearly as exhausted as his parents from his late nights. But not a word was said.

Finally, on the fourth night the young man came straight home from work and after supper went directly to bed. Thereafter, he kept reasonable hours, except on weekends, when he would stay out later. Even then he'd call his parents if he were going to be out past midnight.

What does it mean to be free in life? That young man initially construed freedom to be complete liberty from his former restraints, and he tested his parents to the limit to see if they meant what they said. But in testing them, he found himself bound to something else: the limits of the human body and its inability to continue functioning in the absence of sleep. He learned that absolute freedom is an illusion. We are never absolutely free, we are always beholden to certain limits, certain powers and forces that determine how we shall live.

The apostle Paul realized this, and wrote about it in terms that may jar our contemporary understandings: He spoke of slavery and obedience. His original readers would have grasped the analogy because they were familiar with the institution of slavery. There were people who gave orders and people who obeyed. Paul drew upon this common knowledge of his listeners to lead them into a deeper understanding of what it is to be a human creature. He told them that whatever they gave themselves to, whatever held "dominion" over their "mortal bodies" would end up taking control of them, directing their "passions" and behavior (6:12-13).

We may no longer have first-hand knowledge of the institution of slavery, but Paul's insight remains true for us. We can often see it at work in others even when we fail to see how it is operating in us. We describe people as "passionately committed" to a career or their family or a hobby or a cause or a group, and their passion controls their lives. What they buy, how they spend their time, how they organize their priorities, whom they associate with, the choices they make at key points in their lives—all of these are shaped, even controlled by their commitments.

> WE ARE NEVER ABSOLUTELY FREE, WE ARE ALWAYS BEHOLDEN TO CERTAIN LIMITS, CERTAIN POWERS AND FORCES THAT DETERMINE HOW WE SHALL LIVE. THE APOSTLE PAUL REALIZED THIS, AND WROTE ABOUT IT IN TERMS THAT MAY JAR OUR CONTEMPORARY UNDERSTANDINGS.

For Paul an elemental choice is at the heart of life; none of us can avoid it (6:13-14). True freedom is not the absence of commitment and constraint. True freedom is giving ourselves to God so that our passions may be directed toward ends that are holy and good and eternal. We have to choose where our ultimate commitment lies: "No longer present your members to sin as instruments of wickedness, but present yourselves to God as those who have been brought from death to life" (Romans 6:13).

GOSPEL
MATTHEW 10:40-42

Interpreting the Text

Do not be fooled by the brevity and apparent simplicity of the reading. These verses capture at least three layers or stages in the development of the gospel of Christ during the first century C.E.

The first layer, never to be entirely recovered by scholarship, is that of Jesus' preaching. All three synoptics give witness to an urgency, a passion to see that God's approaching reign is declared to a weary world. No matter how we interpret this eschatological proclamation today, it figured prominently in Jesus' sermons. Otherwise it would not have sounded so clearly in all of the Synoptic Gospels.

The second level of history that shaped today's reading flowed from the generations following Jesus' earthly ministry, from those traditions that were first passed on orally, then later written down to serve as one of Matthew's basic sources for the creation of his Gospel.

The final level of development behind the reading is marked by the needs and understanding of Matthew's own community, by people who, two generations after Jesus, continued to carry on his itinerant ministry. By this time many were skeptical of the church's efforts. Because the reign of God had not materialized and Jesus had not returned, they wondered why they ought to show hospitality to the church's wandering evangelists, whom Matthew, using a term of endearment, calls the "little ones" (10:42).

Reading the passage through this three-layered perspective, it becomes a revealing study of how the church continues the traditions of Jesus while reinterpreting them for a later age. If Matthew were a literalist, he might be content to reassert the original teaching of Jesus, at least to the extent that he had access to it. Or if Matthew were a purely innovative theologian he might try to formulate the proclamation of the gospel in terms of the immediate concerns of his community with nothing more than a formal nod to the historical Jesus. But Matthew is much more sophisticated than either of these simplistic extremes, and thus we get in today's reading an attempt to draw on the urgency of Jesus' original proclamation while reframing it for the peculiar needs of the evangelist's readers and listeners. Matthew assures them that the acceptance of a prophet, of one who preaches the gospel, brings with it the blessing of God, or as Matthew puts it, "the reward of the righteous" (10:41).

Responding to the Text

I recall from many years ago a line of greeting cards that featured pictures of infants out of whose mouths came a cartoon balloon filled with a saying from the adult world. There was always a startling juxtaposition between the image of the baby and the language. For instance, an infant with furrowed brow and stern eyes featured a cartoon balloon saying: "Never forget who's the boss around here." Inside, the card read: "Good luck in your new job."

Another card featured an infant in diapers looking out with an astonished face and a balloon caption: "Have I really got this right?" Opening the card, one read: "Happy fortieth birthday!"

I remember sending and receiving several of these cards. The reason for their popularity was deeper than cuteness. Those infants disarmed the assumed values of the grown-up world, making the readers of the cards laugh at the presumption and self-importance we often acquire over the years.

In a similar fashion, today's Gospel gives us a caption to juxtapose with scenes of religious conflict, a caption that puts all of our theological warfare to shame: "Whoever gives even a cup of cold water to one of these little ones in the name of a disciple—truly I tell you, none of these will lose their reward" (10:42).

Imagine Matthew's community trying to continue the urgent, passionate preaching ministry of Jesus. There are many naysayers who would be glad if the more fervent souls among them would cool their zeal. Intense and elaborate debates break out among them, but above them all appears this simple saying about a drink of cold water, reminding the community that greater than their divisions is the need to meet the elemental needs of those who thirst.

Imagine the reforms of the sixteenth century and the horrifying religious wars that followed, people on every side being disemboweled or burned at the stake. Juxtapose the bloodcurdling scenes with this simple saying from Matthew: "Whoever gives even a cup of cold water to one of these little ones in the name of a disciple—truly I tell you, none of these will lose their reward."

Imagine a cartoon balloon with this saying floating over pictures of our current religious divisions.

What seems such a simple and naïve statement is in fact filled with wisdom and grace, the wisdom and grace of remembering that our bitterness, our theological wars, our claims to have the truth while our opponents do not—all of these evaporate before the more fundamental human needs that Christ calls us to fill: Give a glass of cold water to the thirsty. This is not theological reductionism. This is the profound revelation of the Spirit that calls us never to lose our basic human compassion under the guise of being dogmatically correct.

What would happen if for the next two thousand years, we gave up our theological debates and generation after generation simply offered hospitality and a drink of cold water to the thirsty? Maybe Matthew has a profounder insight in these simple words than he knew when he wrote them. The best way to find the unity and community to which God calls us in Christ is not to work out a formal statement of our common belief. It is rather to welcome and sustain one another with the elemental needs of life. If we do that, then the unity that has so long eluded us may flow as richly as the grace that has redeemed us.

SIXTH SUNDAY AFTER PENTECOST

JULY 4, 1999 / PROPER 9

REVISED COMMON	EPISCOPAL (BCP)	ROMAN CATHOLIC
Gen. 24:34-38, 42-49, 58-67; Zech. 9:9-12	Zech. 9:9-12	Zech. 9:9-10
Ps. 45:1-17; Song of Sol. 2:8-13; Ps. 145:8-14	Ps. 145	Ps. 145:1-2, 8-9, 10-11, 13-14
Rom. 7:15-25a	Rom. 7:21—8:6	Rom. 8:9, 11-13
Matt. 11:16-19, 25-30	Matt. 11:25-30	Matt. 11:25-30

L OVE AND WAR DOMINATE TODAY'S READINGS and give us a sense of how close the Bible is to perennial human concerns. But we are simultaneously struck by the great gulf between the Bible and our own age. Abraham's sending a servant to find his son a suitable bride, a psalm that celebrates a royal wedding with the disturbing assumption of the bride's subservience, an epistle that describes complex warfare between our best desires and sin—all speak of human life in ways remote from our common idiom. But these very differences are a resource for looking at love and war with fresh eyes.

FIRST READING
GENESIS 24:34-38, 42-49, 58-67

Interpreting the Text

The way the lectionary breaks up the text signals the difficulty modern listeners have in attending to a story that features multiple repetitions, a trait characteristic of the oral culture from which it comes.

Before you get lost in the details, return to Gen. 12:1-9, a reading for Second Sunday after Pentecost (see above) that marks the beginning of the cycle of stories about Abraham. Abraham leaving his family and Rebekah leaving hers to marry Isaac are an antiphonal chorus echoing a primary theme of faith: doing what God says. Abraham is commanded, "*Go* from your country." (12:1), and Rebekah, when asked, "Will you *go* with this man?" answers: "I will" (24:58). God promises Abraham: "in you all the families of the earth shall be blessed"

(12:3), and Rebekah's family blesses her by praying: "May you, our sister, become thousands of myriads" (24:60).

Today's reading reveals that the fulfillment of God's purpose required more than Abraham's faithfulness. It also took the faith of a woman, Rebekah, who shows as much courage as Abraham in responding to God's promised blessing.

Responding to the Text

I have long been intrigued by the late nineteenth- and early twentieth-century photographs my wife has of her extended family. These are posed pictures in which the children stand in front, teenagers in the next line, and adults behind them, the grand patriarchs and matriarchs toward the center, and more distant relatives toward the periphery.

These century-old photographs tell us something essential about the way families remember their past: There are those whose stories dominate the family memories and those whose names may even be forgotten.

Although ancient Israel did not have photographs, its oral traditions preserved a similar distinction between the central and lesser characters in its period of formation. Given that it was a patriarchal culture, Abraham and Isaac figured prominently in the family's memory. But in today's story the male domination of the early traditions gives way to a focus on Rebekah, a woman who shows no less courage and faith than Abraham.

There is a telling detail in the story that may have been embroidered by generations of raconteurs but that strikes me as preserving something of the ancient woman's boldness. Rebekah's brother and mother try to gain her some extra time to consider the proposal that is brought by Abraham's servant (24:55); but having done this, they consult with Rebekah, who then agrees to leave at once.

The story is not a model of how all women ought to respond to marriage proposals! It is rather a testimony to what is required when we sense that God is calling us: No delay, go immediately.

ZECHARIAH 9:9-12

Interpreting the Text

Chapter 9 begins by describing how God will subdue Israel's enemies so that "no oppressor shall again overrun them" (9:8). How comforting these words must have sounded to people who had been hauled into exile and whose defenseless little country had been shattered by the superpower Babylon.

Zechariah does not provide a political platform to reassure his listeners. Instead, he depends upon symbolic action: "Lo, your king comes to you: triumphant and victorious is he, humble and riding on a donkey" (9:9). The first two adjectives suggest everything that the world expects of a powerful leader:

"Triumphant and victorious." But no sooner are the words out of the prophet's mouth than they are radically modified: The leader will be "humble and riding on a donkey." Israel's tragic history revealed to the prophet that permanent peace will be achieved by a leader who gives up the war horse for a donkey, or in our modern terms, who surrenders tanks and missiles for an identification with the lowest and least powerful.

Responding to the Text

I was born as World War II was ending, but I recall as a child hearing my parents and relatives talk at length about that horrible conflict. And once we had purchased our first television, we watched programs that featured black and white movies of the war. I remember how moved the adults were by scenes of victorious allies marching into a town or city. People waved flags, soldiers and citizens embraced, kissed, danced, and toasted one another with smiles on their faces.

> IN A WAY HE NEVER INTENDED, ZECHARIAH SUPPLIED MATTHEW AND JOHN WITH THE IMAGE THEY NEEDED TO DESCRIBE THAT GRACIOUS LEADER WHO BRINGS TO FULFILLMENT THE AGELESS DREAM OF PEACE.

There must have been a similar euphoria among the Israelites in exile when Babylon collapsed, and Cyrus, king of Persia, the ascendant superpower of the age, issued an edict allowing the Judahites to return home and rebuild their temple. It probably seemed to them in their joy as if God's reign would at long last be established, not only in Zion (9:9), but "to the ends of the earth" (9:10).

And who of us would not hope and believe the same? Release from any great oppression brings with it a surge of hope in the human heart: this time surely the dominion of peace shall be "from sea to sea" (9:10). But after Persia came Greece and after Greece, Rome . . . after World War II came Korea and after Korea, Vietnam and after Vietnam, Bosnia . . . when does the cycle of terror end?

It ends when we follow the one who comes "humble and riding on a colt" (9:9). In a way he never intended, Zechariah supplied Matthew and John with the image they needed to describe that gracious leader who brings to fulfillment the ageless dream of peace.

RESPONSIVE READING
PSALM 45:1-17

Interpreting the Text

The psalm celebrates the wedding of a king. These are not merely decorative verses but are intended to make clear the relationship between God's sovereignty and the governance of the realm (45:4-7). The wedding brings with it the hope for sons that presumably will continue the king's just rule so that his name will be praised by future generations (45:16-17).

Responding to the Text

Because a royal wedding has implications for the whole nation of Israel, it is an occasion for reaffirming principles that lie at the heart of Israel's governance. Whatever power the king possesses, that power is a gift from God who has anointed him (45:7); and he is, therefore, obligated to use it as God intends.

The model of a king ruling over his subjects may be antiquated; but the principle of a moral life arising from a relationship to God still holds, whether or not we are royalty.

SONG OF SOLOMON 2:8-13

Interpreting the Text

There is a fusion of nature and erotic passion in the passage. The two lovers draw upon the exuberance and fecundity of nature to give expression to their desire for one another. She describes her lover as "a gazelle or a young stag" (2:9), and he entices her with images of flowers and vines in blossom and fragrance upon the air (2:12-13).

Responding to the Text

One of the saddest distortions of biblical faith is to think that it eschews sexual desire and pleasure. The Song of Solomon is a happy reminder of the holy gifts of desire, courtship, and bodily passion.

The church has often had difficulty with this book being in the canon. Interpreters have put an allegorical slant on the work, seeing in it a symbolic expression of the love between Christ and the church. That is a charming, pious conceit, but it draws us away from the celebration of our sexuality as a gift from God.

PSALM 145:8-14

Interpreting the Text

Unlike many deities of the ancient world, God is not fickle or unpredictably temperamental but steadfast in love and compassion (145:8-9). Because of these qualities the praise of God is not a burden, not something added on to the chores of existence. Praise arises naturally out of a creation that is filled with gratitude for this utterly reliable God (145:10-11).

Responding to the Text

The psalm reminds us that our worship is an expression of a process that is built into creation. God is by nature "gracious and merciful" (9:8) and God's "compassion is over all he has made" (9:9) so that all of God's works give thanks (9:10). When we worship we are harmonizing our lives with a gratitude that radiates from every dancing atom that has been given existence by God; we are joining the river of wonder and praise that flows unceasingly from creation to creator.

SECOND READING
ROMANS 7:15-25a

Interpreting the Text

The NRSV subtitles this section, "The Inner Conflict." Although the title makes sense, it is laden with difficulties. Most of us have certain presuppositions about the nature of inner conflicts. We often characterize them as the battle between good and evil, right and wrong, falsehood and truth. We view them as polarized conflicts. But Paul is not describing someone who is irreligious or wrestling with evil intentions. Quite to the contrary, Paul is discussing someone whose commitments are in the right place: "For I delight in the law of God in my inmost self" (7:22), and, as he acknowledges earlier in the chapter, "the law is holy, and the commandment is holy and just and good" (7:12).

Paul, then, is describing someone who is committed to what is holy, who has the highest ideals, who is in the best sense of the word "religious." It is this person who discovers that all the right creeds and rituals, all the best intentions and practices of the religious life, all that is embraced by the word "law" does not enable him to embody the good that God intends: "I can will what is right, but I cannot do it" (7:18).

The failure of his religious efforts drives him to a point of desperation: "Wretched man that I am! Who will deliver me from this body of death? Thanks be to God through Jesus Christ our Lord" (7:24-25).

Responding to the Text

Every Bible and church ought to come with a label that reads: "Warning! Religion may be hazardous to your health." We usually think of religion as being health-giving, not health-destroying. Otherwise, we would not go to church or pray or draw upon God's word to illumine our lives or seek to follow Jesus Christ. We believe and practice our religious belief because it brings health and wholeness, not just to ourselves, but to those whose lives we touch. If we were to summarize all these positive qualities of religion with the biblical term, "the law," we would be close to the spirit of what Paul is describing in today's reading from Romans.

Although there is nothing inherently wrong with "the law," its observance always holds the potential for self-deceit and arrogance. Delighted with what we accomplish by our religious practices, impressed with our idealism, we act in a manner that pulls us away from the grace of God, and religion then becomes hazardous to our spiritual health and to the health of those around us.

These are difficult things to see in ourselves, although they are easy to spot and to spoof in others. The character "Church Lady" on the television show "Saturday Night Live" presents a caricature of the problem as she keeps repeating "Aren't we special?!" Her religiosity is her downfall.

To understand the issue in a less satirical fashion, consider the various ways that people have shown concern for you. There is a kind of care that you avoid because it comes with an air of condescension or self-righteousness. It is anything but healing. And then there is the concern of someone who is genuinely gracious to you: there is no self-promotion, no seeking after adulation, but a pure and simple desire to help that expects no future repayment. When you encounter that kind of grace you experience it as spiritual liberation. Paul encountered it in Jesus Christ, and when he did he broke into a doxology of gratitude (7:25). To experience and live this grace represents the deepest spiritual health, a wholeness that comes as a gift and transforms hazardous religion into redemptive, faithful living.

> ALTHOUGH THERE IS NOTHING INHERENTLY WRONG WITH "THE LAW," ITS OBSERVANCE ALWAYS HOLDS THE POTENTIAL FOR SELF-DECEIT AND ARROGANCE.

GOSPEL
MATTHEW 11:16-19, 25-30

Interpreting the Text

Multiple expectations about both John the Baptist and Jesus were in the air during their ministries and continued to be a source of confusion to Matthew's church. Today's reading is part of Matthew's effort to clarify these misunderstandings. The process begins a few verses before the lection. Jesus asks the people about their expectations of John the Baptist: "What then did you go out into the wilderness to look at?" (11:7). A series of questions leads to the typically Matthean device of quoting from the scriptures, in this case Malachi 3:1, to show that John is not the messiah but the one announcing the messiah's coming.

All of this sets the stage for today's reading, especially 11:16-19, in which Jesus and John turn out to be far different from the people's expectations. Matthew

142

THE SEASON
OF PENTECOST
─────────────
THOMAS H.
TROEGER

uses the illustration of contrasting kinds of music: dancing to the flute at a wedding, and wailing in lament at a funeral. Jesus is not in tune with the expectations that people have of him, and the same is true for John the Baptist. The result is that rather than accepting the new reality that John announces and that Jesus brings in, people dismiss the two of them, claiming John "has a demon" (11:18) and Jesus is "a glutton and a drunkard, a friend of tax collectors and sinners" (11:19). Drawing on conventional religious thought, the people miss the creative power of divine wisdom (see Proverbs 8-9) that is working through Jesus.

The second portion of today's reading (11:25-30) continues the opening themes by affirming that God works in ways that do not conform to the established patterns of wisdom and intelligence. What is hidden from adults is revealed to "infants" (11:25). Infants here may mean not only babies, but all believers who have accepted Jesus in simple trust.

Although the final two verses (11:28-30) are often quoted as a source of pastoral comfort during grief and crisis, the context suggests that the "heavy burdens" are the weighty expectations and theological understandings that make it impossible to receive the wisdom of God that is revealed in Jesus. If people want to know who Jesus is, they need to put down their heavy theology and take up his "yoke" (11:29-30), a common image among rabbis for obeying the Torah.

Responding to the Text

I once heard of a minister who said that on the day of final judgment he believes each of us will see God as the person we would least expect to find in heaven. Something like that is happening in today's lesson, only the encounter happens on earth, not in heaven. People carry peculiar expectations of the way the messiah will look and act, and these assumptions become the basis for their response to Jesus.

Rather than allowing themselves to become receptive to the novelty of God's wisdom appearing in unexpected ways, they dismiss it out of hand. The first charge is that Jesus does not move to their beat, does not harmonize with their music: "We played the flute for you, and you did not dance; we wailed, and you did not mourn" (11:17). The image raises a pointed question about human receptivity to the work of God: Who calls the tune, God or humanity? Is God to step to our music or we to God's?

We may fail to recognize the wisdom of God breaking in upon our lives not only because God's music is not the same as ours, but also because the appearance of God does not mesh with what we expect to see: "The Son of Man came eating and drinking, and they say, 'Look a glutton and a drunkard, a friend of tax collectors and sinners.' Yet wisdom is vindicated by her deeds" (11:19). Although this description of Jesus is a caricature provided by his detractors, it is clear from all four gospels that the man was not like John, an ascetic who "came neither eating nor drinking" (11:18). There is a gutsy earthiness about Jesus that does not square with the prim piety of the religious establishment.

Yet the deeds that mark his life are nothing less than the deeds of wisdom. The word "wisdom" is a theological term, referring to the feminine creative power of God, described at length in the Book of Proverbs. Wisdom embraces those who are left out, "tax collectors and sinners" (11:19), because they do not fit the conventional assumptions of the religious establishment.

Jesus does not step to our music, Jesus does not fulfill our pious expectations, and Jesus interprets himself in terms of the feminine manifestation of God. Before we judge those who failed to recognize God acting in Jesus, we ought to stop and consider all the ways we may be failing to see God's wisdom appearing in our own lives because we, like Jesus' initial detractors, hold assumptions and expectations that are completely at odds with the eating, drinking messiah who identifies with the divine feminine.

The way to become receptive to the wisdom of God, to the messiah among us, is to lay down the "heavy burdens" of our pious preconceptions about how God will appear in life. If we lay down the burden of insisting that God dance to our music, then we will be free to dance to God's music. If we lay down the burden of insisting that God associate with our closed circle of believers, then we will be free to join the meal Jesus is sharing with the outcasts. If we lay down the burden of always seeing God as male, then we will be able to welcome divine wisdom into our lives. No longer crushed by heavy theology, we will be free to eat and dance with the wisdom who comes among us in the most joyfully unconventional ways.

SEVENTH SUNDAY AFTER PENTECOST

JULY 11, 1999 / PROPER 10

REVISED COMMON	EPISCOPAL (BCP)	ROMAN CATHOLIC
Gen. 25:19-34	Isa. 55:1-5, 10-13	Isa. 55:10-11
or Isa. 55:10-13		
Pss. 119:105-112	Ps. 65	Ps. 65:10, 11, 12-13, 14
or 65(1-8), 9-13		
Rom. 8:1-11	Rom. 8:9-17	Rom. 8:18-23
Matt. 13:1-9, 18-23	Matt. 13:1-9, 18-23	Matt. 13:1-23

"THE RIVER OF GOD IS FULL OF WATER" (Psalm 65:9). The river is a common mythic symbol in literature from the ancient near east. It represents the life-giving powers of the divine. In today's readings the vitalizing energies of God do not flow through paradise, but through the world we know, the world where brothers vie for their parents' affection and blessings (Genesis 25), where people need assurance that God's word is reliable (Isaiah 55), where life is a struggle between flesh and spirit (Romans 8), where the seeds of faith do not always take root (Matthew 13). We can face these realities because "The river of God is full of water."

FIRST READING
GENESIS 25:19-34 (alt.)

Interpreting the Text

The story of Esau and Jacob reveals multiple layers of tradition and history. The tale explains historical rivalries: "Two nations are in your womb, and two peoples born of you shall be delivered" (25:22).

The story continues a recurring theme in Genesis: God does not necessarily follow the sacred traditions of the culture. Primogeniture is the law (Deut. 21:15-17) so the reversal of how things ought to be is the vehicle of an ironic and sophisticated theology: The purposes of God do not proceed in a straightforward way, but through the convolutions of human greed, favoritism, and fakery.

The story also picks up the earlier motif of the struggle between agrarian and hunting cultures (Gen. 4:1-16), a conflict that haunted ancient peoples in the process of fashioning a civilization.

Finally, there is the family's actual life. Although embroidered by interpretation, the saga rings true to what we know of human relations. Verse 28 echoes the experience of parents and siblings who are honest enough to acknowledge the favoritism and rivalry that are part of family life.

Responding to the Text

The story of Jacob and Esau will either sadden you or fill you with hope. If you turn to the Bible to find the meaning of life clearly and simply laid out, this is a depressing story. It would make a good documentary on dysfunctional families. Watching it, you would shake your head in discouragement about how conflicted and devious human families are.

But if you want to see how God never gives up working through our lives, even when we are behaving our worst, then this is a story for you. The reading begins: "These are the descendants of Isaac, Abraham's son" (25:19). That opening phrase alerts us that the story continues the earlier narratives of God's promise to give Abraham heirs as numerous as the stars (Gen. 15:5-6). From the readings of recent weeks we know that this promise seemed ludicrous. But here it is returning again. This time the threat to God's purpose is not the advanced age of Sarah and Abraham (Gen. 18:9-15), and it is not that God will demand the sacrifice of a child (Gen. 22:1-14). This time it comes down to the acrimony between Isaac's two sons, a conflict that starts even before they are born: "The children struggled together within her" (25:22). The struggle continues from the womb to the day they are born—"his brother came out with his hand gripping Esau's heel" (25:26). Their differences stalk the deal they strike over a bowl of porridge (25:29-34), and will haunt their lives in years to come. But through all these human contortions, the promises of God are still fulfilled.

ISAIAH 55:10-13

Interpreting the Text

The various plants that appear in these verses are significant to understanding the prophet's vision. The cycle of rain and snow that feeds the wheat (55:10) is an analogy for the reliability and efficacy of God's word. Observation of a normal natural process illuminates a theological reality.

However, all the other plants in the passage represent God's radical new work: bringing the Israelites back from exile. The trees of the field, like worshipers in the temple, will "clap their hands" (55:12). The thorn, a weed that is of no life-sustaining use, "shall come up the cypress" (55:13), a tree is valued for its aromatic wood and its use in the construction of buildings. In a parallel fashion, "instead of the briar shall come up the myrtle" (55:13), an evergreen whose uses include: decorating booths during the Feast of Tabernacles, making perfume, and symbolizing peace and justice.

When God acts to bring the exiles home even nature joins in the reconstruction of the nation. Noxious plants give way to those that make possible rebuilding and celebration.

Responding to the Text

"For as the rain and the snow come down from heaven . . . so shall be my word that goes out from my mouth . . . it shall accomplish that which I purpose, and succeed in the thing for which I sent it" (55:10-11). Many of the prophet's listeners must have received this promise with skeptical hearts. After more than two generations of Exile, it had to be difficult for them to trust words spoken in the name of God. They had heard so many predictions from so many prophets that never materialized. But Isaiah affirms a principle that lies deeper than foretelling the future. It is a principle about the nature of God that holds true even when prophets fail: God's word is as unstoppable as the cycle of sowing, growth, and harvest.

I have experienced this again and again in my own life. Like all preachers, I say some foolish things in the name of God, yet sometimes my words will touch off meanings in a listener that I did not intend nor could have imagined. Years later I receive a letter in the mail telling how a sermon I wish I had never preached was an occasion for the rebirth of faith or the undertaking of an arduous but worthy course of action. I am always astounded by these letters; but then I realize that the letter is not about me and what I said. It is about the word of God released in another's soul and succeeding "in the thing for which [God] sent it" (55:11). And when I read such a letter, even the trees clap their hands! (55:12).

RESPONSIVE READING
PSALM 119:105-112

Interpreting the Text

One of the greatest distortions of Christian preaching is to pit law and grace against each other as diametrical opposites. The law was a gracious reality for the Israelites. Instead of being at the mercy of a mercurial deity, they knew what the Lord expected and thus the precepts of God were not an onerous burden but rather "the joy of my heart" (119:111).

Responding to the Text

Sometimes life is more like wandering beneath a clouded midnight sky than walking a sunny path at noon. I recall a camping trip where I spent the night on an island with not a star in the sky and my flashlight batteries ran out. I tripped on roots and stones every time I left the tent. How happy I was when someone else loaned me a flashlight. My joy was like the psalmist who exclaims "Your word is a lamp to my feet and a light to my path" (119:105).

PSALM 65:9-13 (alt.)

Interpreting the Text

The psalm leaps from the season of planting (65:10) to the season of harvest (65:11) without any of the anxious worries that all of us who garden and farm know: Is there too much rain, too much sun? The psalmist is at ease trusting in the gardener who begins the season (65:9) and who ends it (65:12).

Responding to the Text

I sometimes despair of conveying the meaning of a psalm like this to people who have been born and raised in the city. I think of a boy in a summer camp where I was a counselor. We went to a cattle show, and upon watching a cow being milked for the first time, he asked: "Is that milk? In the city we get it from cartons." How do we interpret to someone like him the psalmist's wonder at how God provides us with food? It is worth a sermon.

SECOND READING
ROMANS 8:1-11

Interpreting the Text

"There is therefore now no condemnation for those who are in Christ Jesus" (8:11). Although there are dangers in interpreting Paul through the lens of our subjective experience, we may get closer to the nerve of Paul if we read this particular text in light of our fears and anxieties rather than reach for a purely objective understanding. Pastors deal constantly with people who feel condemned within their hearts, and Paul, himself a pastor, was no stranger to the torment of the overburdened soul.

Nearly every verse in the lesson is as rich as the first one. Paul announces in tightly compressed language a resolution to the tangles of human existence that he has been tracing since chapter one of Romans.

Exegetes should mark not only the tone of release and joy that fills the reading, but also the precision with which Paul announces what Christ has done. Christ has accomplished "what the law, *weakened by the flesh,* could not do" (8:3). The emphasized words warn us against unjustly stigmatizing the law. The law is not the problem (see remarks on Psalm 119 above), but instead the way human beings orient their lives to "the flesh" rather than "the Spirit" (8:5ff.).

"Flesh" for Paul means not the body, but the sum total of what it is to exist as an imperfect human creature. "Flesh" includes emotion, reason, lust, fear, and violence as well as muscle and bone, pulse and breath.

Responding to the Text

I have known people who were biologically alive, yet felt like the walking dead. Their pulse and blood pressure were fine, their breathing normal, all the vital signs in order. Their finances were sound, they lived in a good neighborhood, had a nice house, drove a fine car. But inside they felt condemned, empty, dead.

They had given themselves to behavior that destroyed their gifts or the people they loved. In some cases they were raising a family they loved, but career goals ate away their time with spouse and children. In other cases they held a set of high ideals, but they sold out to get the big promotion. They had dreams of serving others, but they got caught up in serving only themselves. Whatever the details of the situation, the dissonance between their ideals and the reality of their behavior deadened their vitality. They may have possessed all the accoutrements of success, but inside each felt like a corpse. To use Paul's words, they were entirely oriented to the "flesh," and they sadly learned that "To set the mind on the flesh is death" (8:6). It was a walking death that they hid behind what they owned and a conviviality that they conjured up for social occasions.

> PASTORS DEAL CONSTANTLY WITH PEOPLE WHO FEEL CONDEMNED WITHIN THEIR HEARTS, AND PAUL, HIMSELF A PASTOR, WAS NO STRANGER TO THE TORMENT OF THE OVERBURDENED SOUL.

But the Spirit working through people who were close to them did not give up on them. Through the concern of others Christ began to redirect their energies. By the grace of the tenacity of Christ, they saw that their life was not what they intended, and more important, not what God intended for them to be and do. They reoriented their entire way of living and began to become what God willed them to be. Then they finally understood, even if they would not have used his words, what Paul writes: "But if Christ is in you, though the body is dead because of sin, the Spirit of him who raised Jesus from the dead dwells in you" (8:10).

Perhaps you feel dead, and the story of transformation that I have told is not your story. But by the grace of Christ it could become your story!

MATTHEW 13:1-9, 18-23

Interpreting the Text

Matthew places this familiar parable after two chapters that feature an increasingly hostile reaction to Jesus. The organization of the material suggests that Matthew has in mind, as he often does, an instructional goal for members of his community. By now they have faced their share of rejection, and furthermore, people who were initially enthusiastic have fallen away from the church. On top of all this, Jesus has not returned, so the temptation to follow in the steps of those who have already given up is very high. It would probably not be an exaggeration to say that Matthew and his community are facing a pastoral crisis in their ministry: Is it really worth all the effort they are expending to plant the seeds of the gospel when so much of their work turns out in the long run to be futile?

Just in case his listeners fail to take from the parable the message that he intends for them to get, Matthew includes Mark's allegorical interpretation (13:18-23). This consists of a point-by-point explanation that explicates each image of the narrative.

Although it is understandable why Matthew is so anxious to make everything crystal clear, the allegorical explanation probably did not accompany the parable in its original form. Unfortunately, the explanation tends to strangle and limit the multiple ways the Spirit might seek to use the parable to illuminate the different needs of other congregations. One of the glories of the parables is their poetic ambiguity that allows them to engage a wide range of human situations. Therefore, it may be a helpful preparatory exercise for preachers to drop Matthew's (Mark's) interpretation, to describe what is happening in their own congregations, and then to reflect and pray for the Spirit to clarify the meaning of the parable for this time and place. What seed are you sowing that often fails long before achieving its purpose: youth ministry, feeding the hungry, working for peace? And what is it like when your efforts really take off? (13:8).

The problem with what I have just suggested is that it still stays with an allegorical interpretation: each element of the story still stands for something else. What insights might break forth if we did not insist on interpreting each detail and simply focused on the extravagance of the sower who throws seed out with such abandon that it lands all over creation?

Responding to the Text
"Get real!"

With two words we throw up a barrier to anyone who seems overly idealistic. Or if we are in a classroom or workshop trying out a new skill and it is not going well, we dismiss the challenge by saying, "This is not the real world."

Both responses assume that we know what reality is, and those definitions are usually built upon assumptions that are drawn from the limits of our personal experience. Our assumptions stand as entrance guards at the gates to our mind, and these guards are very strict about what ideas they allow in and which ones they keep out. Jesus employs parables to send the entrance guards away so that new truth can enter the mind and our assumptions about what is real and not real can be challenged and changed.

In today's parable a sower goes out and throws seed so that it lands all over the place: on a path, on rocky soil, on shallow soil, among thorns, and on good soil. This part of the story, though foreign to our modern agricultural practice, would not have seemed strange to the first listeners—what Jesus describes was the way crops were planted in ancient Palestine.

If the story originally ended with the statement, "Let anyone with ears listen" (13:9), then that is the point at which the parable would have challenged Jesus' listeners. Why was Jesus describing this common scene and telling them to listen to it? Were they supposed to think about the extravagance and persistence of the sower? About how many different kinds of soil there are? About the possibilities for growth? About the precariousness of new life? About the stubbornness and abundance of new life?

Or perhaps Jesus wants his listeners to think about all of these together and thereby achieve a mature vision of the life of faith, one that does not succumb to despair or feed the deception of unqualified optimism. Reality includes more than the seed that fails and more than the seed that takes deep root and produces an amazing harvest. It includes them both. To despair because of failure is to be blind to the seeds that produce. To expect total success is to be blind to the failure that will be part of any ministry. So if somebody gives you a stop action photograph of reality and announces "This is the way things are," remember the parable and tell them you want to see the entire video, the whole process with its multiple outcomes: seeds that never sprout, plants that wither, abundant harvests.

Jesus told the parable and let it stand on its own. He was more interested in chasing away the entrance guards at our minds than substituting new ones for those we already have. But by the time Matthew recorded the parable of the sower, Jesus' open-ended, ambiguous story had taken on a particular meaning. Matthew's church had faced disappointments: People were leaving who had once been enthusiastic followers of Christ. And some of the remaining church members were probably beginning to respond to the call to spread the gospel with a shrug of the shoulders. In effect they were saying: "Get real!" Folks get excited for a while and then abandon the gospel as quickly as they took it up.

Faced with a discouraged church, Matthew found in Jesus' ambiguous parable an unambiguous meaning: Yes, a lot of our efforts fail; but when they take root, then the results multiply in astounding ways, making it worth all of our efforts to spread the gospel. Get real!

EIGHTH SUNDAY AFTER PENTECOST

JULY 18, 1999 / PROPER 11

REVISED COMMON	EPISCOPAL (BCP)	ROMAN CATHOLIC
Gen. 28:10-19a	Wis. 12-13, 16-19	Wis. 12-13, 16-19
Wis. 12-13, 16-19	or Isa. 44:6-8	
or Isa. 44:6-8		
Pss. 139:1-12, 23-24	Ps. 86:11-17	Ps. 86:5-6, 9-10, 15-16
86:11-17		
Rom. 8:12-25	Rom. 8:18-25	Rom. 8:26-27
Matt. 13:24-30, 36-43	Matt. 13:24-30, 36-43	Matt. 13:24-43

EVERY READING DEALS WITH THE CHARACTER of God. A ladder of angels tells us God communicates with us (Genesis 28). God exercises sovereign power with restraint (Wisdom 12). God is the only God, but not to be feared (Isaiah 44). God is inescapable (Psalm 139). God abounds in love and mercy (Psalm 86). God's spirit prays with us (Romans 8). God is the ultimate judge of all things (Matthew 13). Reading these passages one after another awakens a state of holy wonder. This would be a good day to arrange all the lections and the sermon around a single question: who is God?

FIRST READING
GENESIS 28:10-19a

Interpreting the Text

The text hints that the story of Jacob's dream explains the importance of the shrine at Bethel. We often picture the angels ascending and descending a "ladder" of rungs (28:12), but the word could just as easily mean the "ramp" or "stairway" a worshiper climbs to an altar to offer a supplication or a sacrifice. Parents probably repeated the story to their children to explain the sacred origins of the shrine and to assure them that Bethel was a place where God communicates with the community.

Jacob's dream is, then, more than an individual's personal religious experience. It is a sign of what happens when people pray at the shrine: Angels ascend and descend; God hears and answers them.

Responding to the Text

One of the most difficult things for many people to talk about is why a place or service of worship means so much to them, why it moves them in the depths of their being. Making matters even more complex is that so much of our language is technological and denotative, while our faith points to matters of soul that cannot be reduced to transistors and circuitry.

Jacob's dream at Bethel, for all its apparent simplicity and naïveté, is in fact a sophisticated story about a holy place where generations of faithful ancestors worshiped. The story gives us a vision and a language for expressing what seems too mysterious to articulate in words. To be in such a place is to find that God communicates with us: Angels ascend and descend (28:12). And the result is that our perceptual capacities are expanded to see what we failed to see before: "Surely the Lord is in this place—and I did not know it" (28:16). God opens Jacob and us to dimensions of reality we would otherwise never see.

WISDOM 12:13, 16-19

Interpreting the Text

The Wisdom of Solomon reveals how a religious faith that originates in one culture may adapt itself to a new setting. Probably written in the cosmopolitan city of Alexandria, Egypt, sometime after 30 B.C.E., the book presents the faith of Israel in a way that simultaneously honors that tradition while boldly speaking in terms that will make sense to the more philosophical Hellenistic culture that prevails in Alexandria.

The blending of Jewish and Hellenistic theologies is apparent in today's reading. God is, as Jewish tradition maintains, the only God, "neither is there any god besides you," but God's care "is for all people" (12:13). God is not exclusively the God of the Jews, but exercises "sovereignty over all" (12:16).

Responding to the Text

How people use whatever power they possess has consequences for everyone around them. If parents batter their offspring, the children may spend their adult lives searching for love and understanding. If a boss uses her or his position to take things out on people lower down the organizational ladder, there may be retaliation in the form of decreased productivity or the subversion of policy. And if a government fails to use its power fairly, the population may grow cynical or even revolt.

These power issues were alive in the ancient world as empires rose and fell. The author of today's lesson pictures how God uses divine power: "Although you are sovereign in strength, you judge with mildness, and with great forbearance you govern us" (12:18). God models for us how we are to employ any power granted to us. God's use of power instructs us in the morality of power: "Through such works you have taught your people that the righteous must be kind" (12:19). The sacred goal of power is not domination but kindness.

ISAIAH 44:6-8 (alt.)

Interpreting the Text

These verses are part of a series of courtroom trials (43:9 and 26) between heaven and earth in which God seeks vindication for what has happened to Israel. The trials also aim to settle who is to be worshiped and served: The idols of the nations (44:9ff.) or the Lord, who alone can claim, "I am the first and I am the last; besides me there is no god" (44:6).

As the trials proceed, there is a shift in the role of the Israelites. At the start of the proceedings they stand among those who have wronged God (43:22-28), but in today's lesson they are called as God's witnesses (44:8), and have nothing to fear from the Lord.

Responding to the Text

As a child I used to love building sandcastles on the beach. Now and then I thought that if I could just pack the sand hard enough it would survive the returning tide and breakers, but of course no sandcastle ever did.

As adults we continue to build sandcastles, and we still have the illusory hope that they will withstand the tides of time. We jog, we work out in the health club, we eat a high-fiber diet determined that we will be paragons of healthy youthfulness. But we discover that even the best exercised and rightly dieted body is a sandcastle.

We start a career or a business and for a while it looks like the ticket to success. Then the fashion changes, the market shifts, and we find ourselves sending out dossiers.

Whenever a sandcastle collapses it can bring on a crisis, as it did when Israel fell to Babylon and was hauled into exile. Only then did the people begin to realize that there "is no other rock" than God, "not one" (44:8).

Responsive Reading
PSALM 139:1-12, 23-24

Interpreting the Text

The psalm is filled with balanced antitheses: "sit down" and "rise up" (139:2), "path" [which implies walking] and "my lying down" (139:3), "heaven" and "Sheol" (139:8), "darkness" and "light" (139:11, 12). The cumulative effect of these contrasts is to portray the utter impossibility of escaping God. No corner of reality is secure from the presence of the Lord.

Responding to the Text

This psalm is an antidote to any spirituality that assumes the experience of God is something people automatically desire. The psalmist is possessed by an overwhelming sense of God's presence throughout reality, a God who comprehends what is beyond mortal calculation (139:6).

In a computerized age that makes exaggerated claims for its accomplishments, the psalm reminds us of our finite limits. No computer program will ever answer the psalmist's profound supplication: "Search me, O God, and know my heart . . . and lead me in the way everlasting" (139:23, 24).

PSALM 86:11-17

Interpreting the Text

A progression of thought is expressed through the image of the "heart." The reading begins with a prayer for "an undivided heart" (86:11), and the next verse reads, "I give thanks to you, O Lord my God, with my whole heart" (86:12). The psalmist needs a wholehearted devotion to survive threats of destruction (86:14).

Responding to the Text

The life of faith often oscillates between a divided heart and a whole-hearted devotion to God. It is difficult not to have a divided heart, especially when the world is a threatening place, as it is for the psalmist facing a "band of ruffians [that] seeks my life" (86:14). The psalmist finally discovers the basis of a wholehearted devotion to God not in the psalmist's own efforts, but in the nature of God's heart, which is "slow to anger and abounding in steadfast love and faithfulness" (86:15).

Second Reading
ROMANS 8:12-25

Interpreting the Text

The apostle squarely faces how hard life is in the present age. It is marked by suffering (8:17, 18), "futility" (8:20), "bondage to decay" (8:21), and "groaning in labor pains" (8:22).

But Paul interweaves these observations about the mortal world with images of hope. We are "joint heirs with Christ" (8:17). Although heirs have not yet inherited their fortune, they are assured that it will be theirs in the future.

The pattern of thought—present suffering and future glory—continues throughout the reading. What we are going through now is nothing compared to "the glory about to be revealed to us" (8:18). We "groan inwardly while we wait for adoption, the redemption of our bodies" (8:23).

Perhaps to correct the false belief that the reign of God has fully arrived, Paul stresses in these verses the need to wait "with patience" (8:25) for the redemption of creation and life.

Paul, however, does not conclude that the present age is without any comfort other than the promise of the future. During this period of waiting, the Spirit of God comes to us in the act of prayer (8:14-17). The language of prayer used here appears to be drawn from corporate worship: "When we cry, 'Abba! Father!' it is that very Spirit bearing witness with our spirit that we are children of God" (8:15, 16). We "groan" through this period of waiting, not on our own, but in community.

Responding to the Text

I recall a get-well card with a greeting that has never left my mind: "We are pulling with you all the way." The cover featured a line drawing of three people rowing a boat together into the oncoming waves.

Something in the human soul cries out in times of pain to know that we are not alone, that others are pulling with us. I think of the hours spent in hospital waiting rooms with families and friends of people undergoing surgery. Their conversation and silence contain a palpable sense that their hearts are focused on a single goal: the hope of healing and restoration. Holding hands in prayer, we are "pulling" for the one we love.

Paul tells us God is pulling for us, that the Spirit prays with us as we pray (8:15, 16). This same Paul is very realistic about how difficult life can be. He knows it is filled with suffering and decay.

Media images of perpetual youth and health represent something that has always been a temptation for human beings: to romanticize creation in ways that hide the suffering and decay that is the lot of mortal life. We sometimes come to believe these illusions, and are then unable to pull for one another as God pulls for us. Frightened by pain and death, we do not visit the person who needs us because their condition reminds us of our own mortality, an awareness that we have repressed. We forget that we have received the Spirit of God, and so in Paul's terms, we act as though we have received a "spirit of slavery to fall back into fear" (8:15).

Instead of repressing or ignoring the pain of mortal life, Paul points to the presence of the Spirit who is pulling for us, interweaving hope with realism. This hope in "what we do not see" (8:25) gives us strength to travel through "the suf-ferings of this present time" trusting that they "are not worth comparing with the glory about to be revealed to us" (8:18).

GOSPEL

MATTHEW 13:24-30, 36-43

Interpreting the Text

The pattern of today's reading is the same as last week's gospel lesson: a parable and then an allegorical interpretation by Matthew of what the parable means.

These are not mutually exclusive strategies. Nevertheless, it is helpful to keep them distinctly in mind because it is easy for Matthew's interpretation to over-take our reading of the parable.

Every element of the story holds multiple possibilities beyond those chosen by Matthew. Therefore, in what follows, I concentrate on the parable, not Matthew's allegorical explanation.

INSTEAD OF REPRESSING OR IGNORING THE PAIN OF MORTAL LIFE, PAUL POINTS TO THE PRESENCE OF THE SPIRIT WHO IS PULLING FOR US, INTERWEAVING HOPE WITH REALISM.

The parable does not identify the "someone" who sows good seed. Although it might be the "Son of Man" (13:37), nothing intrinsic to the parable makes this the only possibility. "Some-one" might mean anyone who has sown good seed.

The "seed" might include "the children of the kingdom" (13:38), but we have no reason to limit it to them. The seed might be any act of justice, any word of love, any witness to the gospel of Christ.

Likewise, nothing in the parable says "the field" can refer only to "the world" (13:38). It might equally well be the church, the family, the neighborhood, the human heart. And the "enemy" might not simply be "the devil" (13:39), it might be doubt or fear or something that is not purely evil but that nevertheless com-petes with the "good seed."

Finally, Matthew focuses most of his interpretation on the concluding two verses of the parable, from which he develops a vivid scene of the last judgment (13:41-43). But he ignores the middle section of the parable: the grain that the good seed is bearing (13:26), the slaves who are puzzled by the origin of the weeds (13:27), the necessity of learning to live in a world where good and evil exist side by side (13:28). Matthew illuminates one interpretation brilliantly while leaving many rich possibilities untouched.

A reader is faced with at least three possible interpretive strategies. (1) Focus on the parable itself (13:24–30) to allow for multiple implications, including those that Matthew's allegorical approach eliminates. (2) Focus on how Matthew applies the parable to his own community (13:36–43). (3) Move back and forth between strategies one and two to start a conversation between the parable and the contemporary situation of your listeners.

There are times in life when Matthew's vision of the final judgment speaks to our frustrated hearts. We are involved in a good cause, an outstanding program with positive benefits for our children or our community, when some group or individual becomes involved whose entire way of behaving is at odds with the ideals that we dreamed would be realized. We find that instead of unalloyed good, there are now results and features of the program that are less than desirable. All of a sudden there is a refreshing appeal to Matthew's clear distinction between the evil and the righteous (13:42, 43).

The turmoil in Matthew's community fuels his zeal for judgment. The evangelist knows a high level of frustration from trying to guide a church in which discipline and faith keep breaking down: people tangling over internal disputes, disciples who are unwilling to forgive each other, debates about the relationship of the law to the teaching and person of Jesus, and external threats from the authorities. All of this pushes Matthew to his wit's end so that he takes this parable of Jesus with its abbreviated vision of final judgment (13:30), and amplifies the punishment from simply being "burned" to being thrown into "the furnace of fire, where there will be weeping and gnashing of teeth" (13:42).

If we are honest, we will acknowledge that we are tempted to the same desire for judgment. We are eager for God to act decisively against "all causes of sin and all evildoers" (13:41). But Jesus' parable, with its more restrained last judgment, and its fuller exploration of how we live between seed time and harvest is much closer to the wisdom that we need for here and now.

Life is not perfect. Even planting good seed in one's own field (13:24) does not guarantee an ideal crop. The weeds will still come. No matter how much good we start with, no matter how noble and godly our intentions, no matter how fine the soil and the weather, the outcome is not totally within our control. Evil will spring up with good.

The mixture of the two will often baffle us as it does the householder's workers (13:27), for evil sneaks in when we are sleeping (13:25), and none of us can go without sleep. Eternal vigilance is not a possibility for mortal flesh.

The temptation will be to root out evil, to go on a crusade, to make life pure as we understand purity. But this is not possible because "gathering the weeds you would uproot the wheat along with them" (13:29). It is helpful in reading the verse to remember an earlier teaching of Jesus in this same Gospel: "Why do you see the speck in your neighbor's eye, but do not notice the log in your own eye?" (7:3). Perhaps, it is not only the intermingled roots that would lead us to tear up the wheat along with the weeds. It may be that our vision is far from perfect in attempting to distinguish weeds from grain.

No matter how gratifying we find Matthew's picture of the final judgment, especially if we are convinced that we are "the children of the kingdom" (13:38) and others are the "evildoers" (13:41), ultimate vindication lies in the future, not in the present. We live between seed time and harvest, between the planting and the triumph of what is good. We are to leave the final judgment to God, and to live as faithfully as we can in a world filled with both grain and weeds.

NINTH SUNDAY AFTER PENTECOST

July 25, 1999 / Proper 12

Revised Common	Episcopal (BCP)	Roman Catholic
Gen. 29:15-28	1 Kings 3:5-12	1 Kings 3:5, 7-12
1 Kings 3:5-12		
Pss. 105:1-11, 45b	Ps. 119:121-136	Ps. 119:57, 72, 76-77,
or 128; 119:129-136	or 119:129-136	127-28, 129-30
Rom. 8:26-39	Rom. 8:26-34	Rom. 8:28-30
Matt. 13:31-33, 44-52	Matt. 13:31-33, 44-49a	Matt. 13:44-52

KING SOLOMON ASKS FOR "an understanding mind to govern your people, able to discern between good and evil" (1 Kings 3:9). The spirit of Solomon's prayer illumines several of today's readings. An understanding mind requires spiritual discipline. The psalmist seeks understanding in the study and keeping of the law: "The unfolding of your words gives light" (119:130). For Paul such understanding is never possible on our own, but requires the Spirit that "helps us in our weakness" (8:26). And for Matthew's community the development of an understanding mind requires reflection on Jesus' varied parables of the kingdom.

FIRST READING
GENESIS 29:15-28

Interpreting the Text

Families often replicate their dysfunctional behavior, so it is not unreasonable to suppose that Laban was in fact every bit as much a trickster as Jacob. Nevertheless, it seems likely that the story has been augmented by legend and literary invention because of the large number of parallels between Laban tricking Jacob, and Jacob tricking his father, Isaac (Genesis 27). Isaac is blind so that he mistakes Jacob for Esau (27:1) while Jacob's own vision is probably not the best on his wedding night because he has been drinking at a feast (29:22) and Leah is brought to him by dark (29:23). Jacob violates the law of primogeniture in stealing his older brother's blessing (27:35), and now in an ironic reversal he gets caught in the marriage law of Laban's country (29:26). Jacob's mother helps him in his deception (27:6 ff.), while Leah's father helps his daughter in hers. In the most ironic twist of all, Jacob plays the role his father played earlier; he is the deceived instead of the deceiver.

Responding to the Text

There is something irresistible about making echoes. We look down a well and call out our name to hear it return with greater resonance. The echoes disclose nuances and overtones that usually elude us.

The book of Genesis is an echo chamber. One character behaves in a particular fashion, and the action sets off a train of events that reverberate again and again through the evolving family saga. Consider, for example, Jacob's words when he discovers that Laban has presented him with Leah for his wife instead of Rachel: "What is this you have done to me" (29:25)? This is not the first time we have heard this question. Abimelech uses the same words when he confronts Abraham for lying to him about Sarah (20:9), and Isaac follows in his father's footsteps, repeating the same lie about his own wife that Abraham did about his (compare 20:2 and 26:7). Although Isaac never gets to ask Jacob, "What is this you have done to me?" he is no less deceived by his younger son, who in turn is deceived by Laban.

The cycle goes on and on: lie, lie, lie; deception, deception, deception. They echo again and again in the sagas of Genesis. It is not the kind of thing that most of us like to tell about our ancestors. We may speak of "the ghost in the family closet," but we usually relate it to one nefarious character. In Genesis, however, deception is a family constant! It is a reminder that God, not the unreliable human family, will bring the divine promises to fulfillment.

1 KINGS 3:5-12

Interpreting the Text

The opening verses of the chapter portray Solomon as a significant player in international politics, and under his reign Israel's economy is booming. He makes a marriage alliance with the Pharaoh of Egypt, and he oversees several major building projects, including his palace, the city fortifications, and the temple (3:1). Given these signs of fame, fortune, and power, it would be tempting for him to pray for the continuance of his success, a temptation that God identifies in his response to the king: you "have not asked for yourself long life or riches, or for the life of your enemies" (3:11).

Whether or not an actual dream lies behind the passage, the editor shapes the exchange between Solomon and God to conform to Deuteronomic theology:

God will bless the country if it seeks not wealth and power but to do the will of God as revealed in the law. Solomon's dream and prayer are more than the private religious experience of a the monarch. They are a model for the spiritual posture of the whole country.

Responding to the Text

We sometimes say of people who are balanced and perspicacious in their judgments that they are "as wise as Solomon." This ancient king of Israel who lived some nine hundred and fifty years before the time of Christ has long been identified as a paragon of wisdom. Like most heroes, his actual performance falls short of the ideal. Solomon overextended the political economy, and the high taxes needed for his extensive building program fed the schism of the country that followed his reign.

Whatever Solomon's limitations, today's lesson pictures the king as a model of spiritual discernment worthy of everyone's emulation. None of us is perfect, so there is no reason why we cannot learn from Solomon at his best.

God appears to the king in a dream, saying, "Ask what I should give you" (3:5). It is difficult to hear the question today without thinking of all the jokes and commercials for state lotteries that begin from the premise: If you could have whatever you want, what would it be?

Solomon answers: "An understanding mind to govern your people, able to discern between good and evil" (3:9). The phrase "understanding mind" means literally in Hebrew "listening heart." Because the heart was thought to be the location of both intelligence and perception, Solomon is requesting the ability to see and to act with wisdom.

The author who is recounting this story intends it to be a model for the country. When the economy is booming, the country is an international power, and everything looks secure and prosperous; it is above all then that the entire society needs a listening heart.

RESPONSIVE READING
PSALM 105:1-11, 45b

Interpreting the Text

Each of the first five verses begins with a command to the congregation: "O give thanks," "Sing," "glory in," "seek," and "remember." The subsequent verses tell who God is and what God does, and they thus make clear the basis of the commands.

Responding to the Text

There is a revealing contrast between vv. 5 and 8. We human creatures require an exhortation to "remember" what God has done, but God "is mindful of his covenant forever." We forget—God remembers. There is both judgment and comfort in the difference between us: judgment against how easily God fades from our minds, yet comfort that God never forgets us.

PSALM 128 (alt.)

Interpreting the Text

It may be that this psalm was given as a blessing to families that made a pilgrimage to Jerusalem (128:5). Or perhaps the psalmist is simply making a connection between the sacred space of the temple and the family circle (128:3).

Responding to the Text

What a contrast between the psalm and the story of Laban's deception of Jacob! (See above on Genesis 29.) The psalm paints a Norman Rockwell portrait of the faithful family, and the patriarchal saga presents a soap opera, exposing the deceit and intrigue of family life. Between the two emerges the truth of most families: They are a blend of love and deception.

PSALM 119:129-136 (alt.)

Interpreting the Text

The psalmist's passionate desire for God's law may baffle us unless we remember that the Israelites found the law to be liberating. Unlike many ancient deities, the Lord was not a fickle, unpredictable God, but one whose law made clear the divine will.

Responding to the Text

"The unfolding of your words gives light" (119:130). Words often puzzle us. We may understand the grammatical, dictionary sense, but the meaning still eludes us. The truth is hidden in the creases of the words. The psalmist realizes that the "unfolding" of God's words is not something that comes with a cursory reading, but with a passionate pursuit of their meaning.

ROMANS 8:26-39

Interpreting the Text

This is one of the most comforting passages in the Bible. It is as if Paul hears the fundamental anxieties of the human heart bubbling to the surface of life and calling out in exclamations of fear. The apostle answers each of them by affirming the power of the Spirit and the love of God in Christ Jesus.

We do not know how to pray! "The Spirit helps us in our weakness," interceding "with sighs too deep for words" (8:26). We are overcome by the circumstances of life! "All things work together for good for those who love God" (8:28). Notice: it does *not* say that all things are good. We fear we are condemned by God! "If God is for us, who is against us? He who did not withhold his own Son, but gave him up for all of us, will he not with him also give us everything else" (8:31-32)? We are being done in by the world! "No, in all these things we are more than conquerors through him who loves us" (8:36). Death will end our relationship to God! "Neither death nor life . . . nor anything else in all creation will be able to separate us from the love of God in Christ Jesus our Lord" (8:37, 39).

The seemingly bottomless pit of human neediness meets in these verses the measureless depths of the wonder of God.

Responding to the Text

Language is a net with a lot of gaping holes, and no matter how skillfully we cast it into the sea of existence, the net never brings up more than a small catch of reality.

But there is always the temptation to tell a big fish story, to claim that we caught something much larger than we in truth did. The temptation is especially alluring to those who are religious. We think we have caught God in our ritual speech and theological formulations.

It would seem that if anyone might give in to this temptation it would be Paul the apostle. His letter to the Romans is one of the densest and most complex writings in the history of the Christian faith. It has spawned enough sermons, tomes, essays, and commentaries to fill a university library. Yet today we find Paul acknowledging that the yearning of the heart and the work of the Spirit exceed the capacity of language: "The Spirit helps us

> WE ARE CONNECTED TO GOD BY SOMETHING GREATER THAN THE HOLE-FILLED NET OF LANGUAGE. WE ARE CONNECTED BY THE "SIGHS" OF THE SPIRIT.

in our weakness; for we do not know how to pray as we ought, but that very Spirit intercedes with sighs too deep for words" (8:26). We are connected to God by something greater than the hole-filled net of language. We are connected by the "sighs" of the Spirit.

Think of the things we sigh about: the child whom we love but whose behavior is beyond our comprehension and influence, the remembrance of someone who died long ago but whose face and voice are still precious to us, the hatred of one group of people for another.

A sigh is the expressive sound of breath giving voice to the meaning that cannot be subdivided into words. And it is something even greater than this: it is the Spirit praying in us and through us and reminding us that at the heart of our faith breathes a reality greater than mortal tongue can adequately name.

What would happen to our theological wars if we began with the sighs of the Spirit instead of always appealing to the word of God? We and our enemies might embrace and weep.

GOSPEL

MATTHEW 13:31-33, 44-52

Interpreting the Text

The first two parables involve the same contrast: something tiny produces great abundance. The mustard seed, "smallest of all the seeds" becomes the "greatest of shrubs" (13:32), and a small quantity of yeast leavens "three measures of flour," about fifty pounds or a hundred loaves' worth (13:33).

The second set of parables also features a parallel pattern: selling all to buy what one values most, be it treasure in a field (13:44) or an incomparable pearl (13:45).

The one who finds the treasure in the field does not appear to have been looking for it, while the merchant is "in search of fine pearls" (13:45). The method of discovery is less important than the fact that once found, the kingdom is worth more than anything else one owns.

The final parable about good and bad fish (13:47-50) parallels last week's reading about the wheat and the weeds and Matthew's allegorical interpretation (13:24-30, 36-43). He even repeats the exact details of the last judgment when the angels throw the evil ones "into the furnace of fire, where there will be weeping and gnashing of teeth" (13:42 and 50).

Given the care with which Matthew has organized this chapter, it appears that the evangelist is pointing to himself in 13:51-52. When he asks, "Have you understood all this?" he may be referring not only to the parables but to the way he has arranged and interpreted them.

Matthew has been modeling the words he now gives to Jesus to pronounce: "Therefore every scribe who has been trained for the kingdom of heaven is like the master of a household who brings out of his treasure what is new and what is old" (13:52).

Beginning with the parable of the sower (13:3 ff.), Matthew has been bringing out of his treasure the "old," the parables of Jesus, and he has also been bringing out "what is new," the interpretations that will make the parables live afresh in his community.

Matthew's description of a "scribe who has been trained for the kingdom" identifies a principle of discipleship that is more enduring than his peculiar readings of Jesus' parables: it is not enough simply to repeat what Jesus taught. The faithful disciple, "the scribe who has been trained for the kingdom," is the one who dares to offer what is new in understanding the old.

Responding to the Text

"The kingdom of God is like a Bible study." No, Jesus does not say this. "The kingdom of God is like a prayer fellowship." No, Jesus does not say this. "The kingdom of God is like a church at worship." No, Jesus does not say this.

As a matter of fact, in all of the parables that Matthew has collected in today's reading there is not a single reference to anything religious or devotional. "The kingdom of heaven is like a mustard seed . . . like yeast . . . like treasure hidden in a field . . . like a merchant in search of fine pearls . . . like a net thrown into the sea." The similes of the kingdom range from the farm to the kitchen to surprising discovery to the market to the sea. They embrace the fullness of common human labor and commerce. The way to understand the reign of God is not to immerse ourselves in religiosity, but in being attentive to the experience of everyday life.

The reign of God is not a mass popular movement. We will not find it in *People* magazine or on "The Lives of the Rich and Famous." It is like a seed that becomes a tree, like the yeast that raises a loaf of bread. Tiny things. But from each springs a new world.

How easy it is to miss the wonder of what is happening. That was probably true in Matthew's community when he gathered these parables. His listeners already knew the parables because they had been passed on by word of mouth and recorded by scribes of the movement that Jesus started. But with constant repetition the words began to lose their startling strangeness. Furthermore, the church was facing its own internal conflicts and persecution from religious and political authorities. Roman

> THE REIGN OF GOD IS LIKE A SEED THAT BECOMES A TREE, LIKE THE YEAST THAT RAISES A LOAF OF BREAD. TINY THINGS. BUT FROM EACH SPRINGS A NEW WORLD.

politics captured the evening headlines, not the small things, not the word of forgiveness to an estranged friend, not the meal shared with a stranger, not the prayer offered for the sick. All those would have seemed too insignificant. But Matthew knew that these were the very acts that sustain the community of faith, that they are how we taste the reign of God even in the midst of a brutal world.

According to Matthew, it is not adequate for us as disciples to limit ourselves to "what is old," to the parables we have received. We need also to bring out "what is new," parables that expand upon what Jesus taught us so that we can see afresh the reign of God. We are not faithful to the gospel unless, tending to the same Spirit that inspired Jesus and Matthew, we risk creating new parables. So here goes!

The kingdom of God is like Isaac Newton being struck by a falling apple. A tiny event: then physics.

The kingdom of God is like a black woman named Rosa Parks refusing to give up her seat on a segregated bus. A tiny act: then a civil rights movement.

The kingdom of God is like Dr. Fleming noticing an unusual growth in a Petri dish. A tiny observation: then penicillin and antibiotics.

The kingdom of God is like the adult neighbor who when you were a child gave you lemonade on her porch and told you that you could become whatever you wanted to be. A tiny kindness: then a fulfilling life.

The kingdom of God is like one more infant among all the billions that have been born, only this one in a manger at midnight. A tiny new life: then the salvation of the world.

*Readings for Celebrating Saint James on the
Ninth Sunday after Pentecost*
FIRST READING

JEREMIAH 45:1-5

Jeremiah had the thankless task of prophesying the collapse of his country—not because he was unpatriotic, but because he saw into the heart of current events. He faithfully reported what he heard God saying through the upheaval of his era: "I am going to break down what I have built, and pluck up what I have planted—that is, the whole land" (45:4). Not exactly words to endear a religious leader to people who want their country to survive and prosper!

Baruch, son of Neriah, recorded this unpopular prophet's unpopular message. It was a dangerous job that would earn him no accolades, but at least he would be spared his life, a blessing that was not to be granted to James whom we remember this day (Acts 12:1, 2).

ACTS 11:27—12:3

James is decapitated by King Herod (12:2) in a passage that pictures opposition to the church moving beyond religious authorities to include those with political power.

As James stands before his executioner, do the scenes of his discipleship flash before him? Perhaps he remembers the great catch of fish that his brother John, Simon Peter, and he made when Jesus first called them at the lake shore (Luke 5:1-11). All of them "left everything" to follow Jesus, and now James is to lose his life because of his allegiance to Jesus.

Or perhaps as the sword is lifted, James remembers how he and his brother once asked if they ought to invoke violence upon people who did not receive Jesus, and Jesus rebuked them for their question (Luke 9:51-55). Maybe now James understands Jesus' response as never before. Perhaps James' last thought is to pray for the end to all violence, the violence that was once in his own heart and the violence that now brings his death.

GOSPEL

MATTHEW 20:20-28

What a revealing contrast there is between the gospel lesson and our pious expectations of those that the church has deemed "saints." Here is James' mother, long before her son is known as Saint James, pleading with Jesus to give him and his brother, John, a special place in the kingdom. There does not seem to be much promise of sainthood here.

And yet James ends up drinking the same cup of suffering and death as Jesus (20:22). A man whose desire for a place of privilege once infuriated his fellow disciples (20:24) ends up dying for the cause of Christ. Unsaintly James becomes Saint James.

Maybe there is hope for us.

TENTH SUNDAY AFTER PENTECOST

AUGUST 1, 1999 / PROPER 13

REVISED COMMON	EPISCOPAL (BCP)	ROMAN CATHOLIC
Gen. 32:22-31	Neh. 9:16-20	Isa. 55:1-3
Isa. 55:1-5		
Pss. 105:1-11, 45b	Ps. 78:1-29	Ps. 145:8-9, 15-16, 17-18
or 128; 145:8-9, 14-21		
Rom. 9:1-5	Rom. 8:35-39	Rom. 8:35, 37-39
Matt. 14:13-21	Matt. 14:13-21	Matt. 14:13-21

WHEN JACOB WRESTLES AT THE RIVER Jabbok, he tells his adversary, "I will not let you go, unless you bless me" (Gen. 32:26). The words are more than the demand of a single individual. They represent the prayer of the community of faith through the ages: Bless us! God answers that prayer again and again in today's readings. We are blessed with abundant life (Isa. 55), blessed with an open hand (Psalm 145), blessed with the rich traditions of the Israelites (Romans 9), and blessed with a meal served by Jesus (Matthew 14). God's response to our prayer is extravagant.

FIRST READING
GENESIS 32:22-31

Interpreting the Text

The story is a complex amalgamation of myth, family memories, and theological interpretation. The location, the river Jabbok, resonates with ancient beliefs about deities who manifest themselves at streams. The darkness evokes associations with the unknown, the world of dreams and night spirits.

Added to these mythic elements is how the story fits in the larger narrative. Jacob is returning to face his brother Esau, whom he cheated so many years ago. Does he wrestle with the lie he perpetuated, or with fears for his life at his brother's hands, or both?

Then there is the mysterious stranger who wrestles with Jacob all night. Only at the conclusion is the stranger identified as God (32:30), and this seems a later addition, a way of explaining the place name Peniel. The story's reserve in using the name of God heightens the sense of mystery about the encounter.

Finally the name change from Jacob to Israel (32:28) suggests that the story is about far more than an individual. It is about the nation and its experience of wrestling with God and humanity.

Responding to the Text

Jacob was a fighter from the start. He wrestled with his twin brother in their mother's womb (Gen. 25:22), and the day he was born he came out "with his hand gripping Esau's heel" (25:26). He wrestled the birthright away from Esau, first by driving a hard bargain when his brother was famished (25:29-34), then by deceiving his father (27:18-38). Later he contended with Laban who tricked him into marrying his older daughter before giving him the hand of Rachel, the woman Jacob really loved (29:21-28). True to his tenacious character, Jacob evened the score by increasing his own flocks at Laban's expense until he "grew exceedingly rich" (30:43).

It seems that Jacob had it made. A life spent wrestling for position, power, and wealth had gained him everything he sought. But on the night before he faces the brother he defrauded years ago, Jacob sends his family and "everything that he had" (32:23) across the river. Everything!

Did he send them ahead hoping to placate Esau? Whatever the reason, Jacob is now alone with himself, free for a night from all that he has fought so hard to attain.

Reflecting the ancient belief that rivers mark not only territorial boundaries but also the domain of deities and spirits, Jacob finds himself wrestling with a mysterious adversary. The stranger blends in one figure the multiple conflicts and yearnings of Jacob's life, and yet the stranger is far more than this: He is the one with whom the whole people of Israel wrestles as it strives to be faithful to its holy calling.

ISAIAH 55:1-5

Interpreting the Text

Just as the inauguration of a president is accompanied by sumptuous state dinners, so in the ancient world monarchs ushered in their reign with feasts. This celebratory practice is apparent in the invitation that the Lord issues through the prophet. There is to be a feast with no charge for admission: "Come, buy wine and milk without money and without price" (55:1).

With each succeeding verse the meaning of the feast is deepened and expanded. There is a contrast between bread and labor that do "not satisfy" and the "rich food" offered by God, representing the difference between the foolish and the faithful life (55:2).

Next comes the promise of "an everlasting covenant," modeled after the covenant with David (55:3, 4). Finally, other countries will be attracted as well because of how God has "glorified" Israel (55:5).

Reading this passage is like receiving a gilt-embossed invitation to a great event to which you never expected to be invited. The further you read the more astonished you are at the lavish intentions of the host.

Responding to the Text

There used to be a TV commercial that featured close up the profile of a man in a business suit climbing steep stairs. The background was pure white so that all the viewer saw was the outline of the stairs as a bold black line and the lone figure panting with exertion. Then the camera pulled back to reveal that the stairs were in fact the pattern of a sales graph recording upward trends. Other men and women were also climbing up the graph, all of them weary but determined.

By now the original man was carrying his suit coat. With his tie loosened and his sleeves rolled up, he kept overtaking the other climbers in their business suits. Finally, he made it to the top of the sales graph and stood there alone, perusing the vastness about him. A voice-over exclaimed: "You have worked hard to make it to the top, and you deserve the best."

There followed a sales pitch for some product that I have forgotten, except that I remember thinking: He did all that work climbing, left all the others behind, and arrived at the top just to buy some product!

"Why do you spend your money for that which is not bread, and your labor for that which does not satisfy" (55:2)?

The assumptions and values behind the television commercial are at least as old as the ancient Israelites, who like us, were tempted to settle for bread "which is not bread" (55:2). God offers them and us an alternative: "Ho, everyone who thirsts, come to the waters" (55:1).

Psalm 105:1-11, 45b and Psalm 128 (see last week)

PSALM 145:8-9, 14-21

Interpreting the Text

The psalm combines the Mosaic covenantal traditions (compare 145:8 and Exod. 34:6) with an affirmation of God's love for the whole creation: "His compassion is over all that he has made" (145:9).

The poetry flows so smoothly between history and nature that it awakens an awareness of how animals and humans share a mutual dependency upon God.

God satisfies "the desire of every living thing" 145:16) and attends to all those who "who call on him in truth" (145:18).

Responding to the Text

For many people who have grown up in an urban environment a vast gulf exists between their daily routine and the natural processes that sustain all of life. The psalmist helps us to overcome this estrangement by depicting the utter dependence of all creatures upon the one who has made them and who meets all their needs. Without this awareness, we risk taking breath and bread for granted and abusing our relationship to the creator and creation.

To sustain a healthy relationship to the environment requires as well a sense of our covenant with God. If God is only a nature deity we will lose the moral commitment that comes with the psalmist's blending of nature and covenant.

SECOND READING
ROMANS 9:1-5

Interpreting the Text

Upon first reading, there seems to be a gap between the affirmations with which Romans 8 concludes and today's text. Paul becomes intensely personal, using passionate language: "I could wish that I myself were accursed and cut off from Christ for the sake of my own people, my kindred according to the flesh" (9:3). The apostle has just finished declaring that nothing can separate us "from the love of God in Christ Jesus our Lord" (8:37-39) yet here he is willing to be separated from that love for the sake of his own people.

Despite the contrast between chapters 8 and 9, they fit coherently together. Paul has been dealing all along with the reliability of God and the human response of faith. He has traced faith back to Abraham and explored how faith is illumined, deepened, and extended through Christ and the Spirit.

But Paul's argument will collapse if the work of Christ abnegates what God has revealed through the "Israelites" (9:4), the name for his people that Paul now uses to remind us of their long and rich history. The traditions of the Israelites (9:4, 5) are an essential witness to the reliability of God, which Paul believes has been affirmed anew through Christ. Pained by their failure to share his belief, Paul begins an elaborate effort (Romans 9–11) to understand theologically why his people have not accepted Jesus as the messiah.

Responding to the Text

The meaning born by some biblical texts includes subsequent events that their authors never foresaw. I find this to be especially true of passages in the New Testament that deal with the Jews and their relationship to the gospel of Jesus Christ. I read these texts and I see emaciated human figures in broad striped uniforms looking out with haunted eyes from their barbed wire enclosures. I sense their eyes tracing the words with me: "They are Israelites, and to them belong the adoption, the glory, the covenants, the giving of the law, the worship, and the promises; to them belong the patriarchs, and from them, according to the flesh, comes the Messiah, who is over all, God blessed forever, Amen" (9:4, 5).

Here there is not a single word of condemnation against the Jews. Paul truly is in personal agony that his people do not believe in Christ as he does (9:1-3), but that does not remove his profound affection and respect for them. Even more important, it does not alter his central affirmation of God's revelation in and through the Israelites.

Paul's words bring to mind the editor of a university press who oversaw the publication of my Christian hymn texts. A superb critic, she knew when my work was at its best and when it was below standard. But always I felt her support and encouragement. I had assumed that she was Christian because of her theological acumen, yet I discovered after publishing two books under her guidance that she was a Jew. When I asked how she could be so supportive of my Christian poetry, she told me that she could see we were both ultimately interested in the same thing: a witness to the God of justice, and a commitment that human beings would no longer destroy each other. I felt at that moment as deep a religious connection to her as I have ever felt with any Christian. We were bound by the same spirit that moved through the ancient Israelites and for me, though not for her, through Jesus Christ. I am sure that God rejoiced that day.

GOSPEL

MATTHEW 14:13-21

Interpreting the Text

Jesus has just learned that John the Baptist has been beheaded and buried (14:10-12). His immediate response is to take a boat to a deserted place (14:13). But there is no escaping the crowds who "followed him on foot from the towns" (14:13). Instead of getting in the boat and trying to find another place where he really can be alone, Jesus shows compassion and heals the sick (14:14).

Whether or not Matthew has recorded accurately all the historical details, the scene is touching. It conveys the intensity of Jesus' commitment: Needing time and space for himself to absorb the terrible news about John, he sacrifices his own desires to serve the people who are desperate for his ministry.

Matthew's portrait of the disciples highlights Jesus' perseverance: "When it was evening, the disciples came to him and said 'This is a deserted place, and the hour is now late; send the crowds away so that they may go into the villages and buy food for themselves'" (14:15). It nearly sounds as if the disciples are as eager to get rid of all those people as they are for them to have something to eat. It is not unreasonable to speculate that the disciples would like some time alone with Jesus to discuss the beheading of John the Baptist, to consider what it portends for their ministry, to assess the dangers they now face, to share the fears in their hearts.

Matthew may be telling this story to his own community some two generations later as a way of addressing believers who are wary of continuing the church's mission in light of increasing persecution. Matthew is reminding them that when Jesus and the original disciples faced similar dangers, Jesus reached beyond his own desires to meet the needs of the people.

Jesus met those needs not only by healing them but also by feeding them. The language that Matthew uses for the preparation of the meal is resonant with the eucharistic practice of the early church: "he looked up to heaven, and blessed and broke the loaves, and gave them to the disciples" (14:19; compare 26:26). By using eucharistic language, Matthew reminds his community that Jesus not only fed people way back then, he continues to feed his followers today when they gather to bless and break bread in his name.

Responding to the Text

You have just heard some profoundly upsetting news: an unexpected death, a divorce of a couple you thought had the ideal marriage, the sudden cross-country move of your closest friend and confidant, a betrayal by someone you had always trusted. . . . Whatever it is, you are shaken to the bone. Reeling. Disoriented. You do not want to see anybody. You want to be alone so you can catch your breath and find your bearings. If only the phone would not ring, if only your students this day would just work at their desks, if only your patients would all rest quietly, if only your children would play contentedly in their rooms, but, of course, that is not the way it is. When you most need to be alone is the very moment you will be most needed.

Jesus had received terrible news. John the Baptist had been beheaded and buried. The preacher who had baptized him: executed! Did Jesus remember the vision and excitement of rising wet from the waters of the Jordan River, the descending dove, the clarity of God's approval, the period of temptation that immediately followed his baptism? (3:16—4:1). Did Jesus now wonder if his call had all been illusory, did he fear for his own safety? Whatever his interior state,

Jesus withdrew in a boat "to a deserted place by himself" (14:13). He did not even collect the disciples to join him. He sought to be entirely alone.

Crowds who must have seen him from the shore circled around the lake, bringing their sick to his place of retreat. Still absorbing the news of John's death, aching for silence and solitude, Jesus faced massive numbers of people who needed him. It would be understandable if he had leapt in the boat and prayed for a wind to carry him quickly away but instead "he had compassion for them and cured their sick" (14:14).

When the day was wearing on, the disciples suggested that Jesus send the crowds away for something to eat. But he was in the thick of it now. The chance to be alone had vanished like the sun that was setting behind the hills. Taking the five loaves "he looked up to heaven, and blessed and broke the loaves, and gave them to the disciples, and the disciples gave them to the crowds" (14:19). In that precise description of looking up, blessing, breaking, giving, and distributing, Matthew is doing two things.

First of all, he is repeating words and actions that his community knows by heart from their regularly sharing the ritual meal of the church and, in the case of many people, ritual meals familiar from their Jewish upbringing.

But by placing the liturgical words and actions in the context of this story, Matthew does something more. He shows how the ritual meal is a source of strength when the demands of ministry fall upon us at the worst possible time. Jesus was not able to be alone when he most needed to be, but he was able to look "up to heaven," to remember that reality was greater than his grief and fear. He was able to invoke a blessing, to ask for power beyond mortal capacities. He was able to break and give bread, to share whatever resources were available. And through all of these things flowed the energies of grace so that Jesus could minister to others even when his own heart was heavily burdened.

Break bread with Jesus and discover the same is true for you.

ELEVENTH SUNDAY AFTER PENTECOST

AUGUST 8, 1999 / PROPER 14

REVISED COMMON	EPISCOPAL (BCP)	ROMAN CATHOLIC
Gen. 37:1-4, 12-28	Jonah 2:1-9	1 Kings 19:9, 11-13
Ps. 105:1-6, 16-22, 45b	Ps. 78:1-29	Ps. 85:9, 10, 11-12, 13-14
Rom. 10:5-15	Rom. 9:1-5	Rom. 9:1-5
Matt. 14:22-33	Matt. 14:22-33	Matt. 14:22-33

ANCIENT WORSHIPERS BELIEVED that when they retold the stories of faith something greater happened than the simple recall of the past. The power of the events that initiated belief was released anew among them. This pattern is apparent in the relationship between today's Genesis reading and the psalm, and between the gospel and epistle. The story of Joseph that begins in Genesis 37 is liturgically recited in Psalm 105. Christ saves Peter from drowning (Matt. 14:30), and he also saves worshipers who confess him as Lord (Rom. 10:9-10). In worship the stories of God's salvation become our stories.

FIRST READING
GENESIS 37:1-4, 12-28

Interpreting the Text

Jacob's sons include six by Leah, four by Bilhah and Zilpah, and two by Rachel: Joseph and Benjamin. Having children by surrogate mothers, concubines, and multiple wives was part of the ancient Hebrew culture, and the resulting relationships provided rich soil for power struggles, conflict, favoritism, and jealousy.

Jacob loves Joseph "more than any of his other children" and provides him with a special garment (37:3). When Joseph is wandering in search of his brothers (37:15-16) they spot him from a distance (37:18), probably because they would recognize his robe anywhere. The first thing they do when he arrives is strip him of that symbol of his privileged status in the family (37:23).

The author, however, has far more than a psychological interest in the story. He carefully constructs the narrative, giving us hints that this is more than the tale of a family breaking down. For example, he describes Joseph as "shepherding the flock with his brothers" (37:2). A shepherd of flocks who becomes the shepherd of the country is a recurring theme in the history of Israel. It is true of Moses (Exod. 3:1) and David (1 Sam. 16:11), as well as Joseph. From the opening verses, then, the author alerts us that "the story of the family of Jacob" (37:2) is about the Lord who is at work amid a very human and imperfect family.

Responding to the Text

The author does not begin "This is the story of Joseph," but rather "This is the story of the *family* of Jacob" (37:2). If we focus on Joseph alone, then we will miss the entanglements, and we may end up making Joseph appear more heroic than he is.

We know in our own society how difficult it can be to maintain healthy relationships in mixed families. Consider then the impact of Jacob's preferential treatment of Joseph in a family that included twelve sons by four mothers! Although family arrangements vary with culture and history, favoritism and jealousy are perennial, and the family of Jacob is torn apart by these forces.

Joseph is the first son of his father's most beloved wife, Rachel. Her favored status must already be cause for jealousy and conflict. But now Jacob increases the family stress by his preferential treatment of Joseph. Everywhere the teenager goes, his special attire reminds the others: "I am Dad's favorite. Don't you forget it."

Joseph is no saint himself. He squeals on the sons of Bilhah and Zilpah (37:2), two of Jacob's slaves who have born him four sons and who already have to deal with their inferior status to Leah and the beloved Rachel.

Adding to the interpersonal pressures is the patriarchal society where honoring the father of the household is a rigidly held value. No matter how furious his sons are with Jacob, they will not violate the taboo against attacking the grand patriarch. But Joseph is another matter. He is one of them, a brother, and a younger brother at that—not someone very high in the pecking order of a culture that practices primogeniture. How gratifying it must be to strip him of his coat, throw him in a pit, and then sell him into slavery.

THIS STORY IS A WITNESS TO HOW GOD BRINGS REDEMPTION THROUGH IMPERFECT HUMAN RELATIONSHIPS, WHICH IS GOOD NEWS IF ANY OF US HAPPEN TO LIVE IN IMPERFECT FAMILIES.

Nowadays we would call this the story of a dysfunctional family system, and it is in part exactly that. But only in part. It is also something more. It is a witness to how God brings redemption through imperfect human relationships, which is good news if any of us happen to live in imperfect families.

PSALM 105

Interpreting the Text

The psalm provides an abbreviated narrative of the way God keeps faith with Israel through the centuries. After a general call to thanksgiving, the psalmist provides a poetic account of the covenant with Abraham and the great events that followed. These include the story of Joseph, which is presented here as a sign of God's providential care (105:17).

Portions of the psalm appear in 1 Chron. 16:7 giving us a sense of how it functioned in ancient worship.

Responding to the Text

If we are under the illusion that the language of prayer, especially the liturgical prayer of the ancient Israelites, was only high-toned and spiritual, then we ought to read this psalm: Joseph "was sold as a slave. His feet were hurt with fetters, his neck was put in a collar of iron" (105:17, 18). What a graphic description of Joseph's degradation and pain! And this occurs in the context of a poem about the faithfulness of God. It appears that the poet wants to make clear that we are not to confuse God's faithfulness with times of prosperity and pleasure. God is with us even through the most trying experiences and most anguished memories of the community's life.

SECOND READING

ROMANS 10:5-15

Interpreting the Text

Paul interprets the meaning of Christ through a famous passage about the law (Deut. 30:11-14). He eliminates the word "it" (referring to the law) from the original question, "Who will go up to heaven for us, and get it . . . ?" (Deut. 30:12), and he employs an Aramaic paraphrase of the Hebrew text that substitutes "abyss" for "sea" (Deut. 30:13).

These alterations to the tradition and the argument that Paul builds upon them are typical of the exegetical methods common to his age. His parenthetical interpretations of the modified text draw out its meaning in light of God's revelation in Christ. Paul is honoring what for him is more central than the literal meaning of any text: the reliability of God and our need to respond in faith.

Paul draws on another Jewish theological principle in stating that "one believes with the heart and so is justified, and one confesses with the mouth and so is saved" (10:10). Words for Paul's tradition are not casual utterance but the expression of the deepest reality. The fusion of being and word enables him to assert, "if you confess with your lips that Jesus is Lord and believe in your heart that God raised him from the dead, you will be saved" (10:9).

Paul's exegesis and his witness to the power of confessing Christ culminate in a joyful affirmation of those who bring the good news (10:15).

Responding to the Text

My wife's mother tells how her father struck a deal with a builder when he needed a new barn. The two shook hands, each giving his word to fulfill his part of their mutual understanding. No paper passed between them, no contract in triplicate, no indelible ink on vellum, no legal witnesses—just each other's spoken word and a handshake. It was all they needed because each knew that the other's word was the complete guarantee of keeping the terms. Each person's word was one with his character and intention.

I compare that to the last time I bought a house. Signing the paperwork took over forty-five minutes, and my hand nearly fell off from the number of disclosures and guarantees I had to sign in full or initial. The agent at the signing was apologetic but explained that there had been so much fraud in recent years, that all the different parties to a mortgage are wary of leaving a single item uncovered by legal paper work.

From a handshake to a mountain of paper: I am not a romanticist about a simpler bygone era, I appreciate the need for law and contracts; but even the agent at the signing acknowledged that the amount of paper had grown "astronomically" in recent years.

I find in this expanding mass of legal entanglement a parable that gives us a glimpse and a taste of what Paul had discovered about the difference between "the righteousness that comes from the law" and "the righteousness that comes from faith" (10:5, 6). The former keeps proliferating understandings and interpretations, the volume of religious legalism in the heart keeps expanding, but "the righteousness that comes from faith" is direct and simple: The lips confess what the heart believes, and the utterly reliable God accepts our response of trust. The insecurities of wondering if we are worthy of God's love, if we are saved, if God will catch something that we missed and hold it against us—all of these give way to joy and gratitude for the word of Christ that is, as Paul tells us, "near you, on your lips and in your heart" (10:8).

MATTHEW 14:22-33

Interpreting the Text

The reading opens with a transitional sentence. After healing and feeding the crowds, Jesus finally gets rid of everyone so that he can at long last be alone (14:22; compare 14:13). Matthew stresses Jesus' solitude by mentioning it twice: Jesus went "by himself to pray" and he "was there alone" (14:23).

The storm comes up in the evening, at the same time that Jesus is praying on the mountain. But Jesus does *not* go to the rescue, even though the boat is already "battered by the waves" (14:24). It is not until "early in the morning he came walking toward them on the sea" (14:25). Jesus leaves them—to be storm-tossed all night long—to pray. In last week's lesson, Jesus sacrificed his need to be alone to meet the crowd's needs. But not in this week's lesson. This time Jesus prays until dawn.

The "early in the morning" scene of walking on the sea, the way the disciples are "terrified" and mistake Jesus for a "ghost" as well as the concluding affirmation of faith (14:33) suggest that the story may be shaped by the resurrection faith of Matthew's community.

The passage is an Easter sermon to a church caught in violent seas. The boat is a symbol for the church that Matthew has used earlier in the Gospel: "And when he got into the boat, his disciples followed him" (8:23). The disciples of Jesus are those who join him in the boat/church and sail dangerous seas.

Afraid they may be swamped by the persecution of the authorities, Matthew's community wonders where Jesus is, what he is doing when they are so desperate. Matthew answers their pastoral concerns by reshaping a story that he has received from the traditions before him. He suggests that Jesus is praying and that at the right time he will come to them, only they may be surprised at his appearance, and reacting out of fear, think him to be a ghost. Then, like Peter, they may finally be emboldened to walk on the sea, to risk a life of faith in a threatening society, and to find Jesus reaching out his hand to save them when their doubts overtake them (14:29-31). When this happens, they will know anew the faith they celebrate in worship: "Truly you are the son of God" (14:33).

Responding to the Text

The wind had come up the evening before. Jesus had sent off the disciples in their boat and then started up the mountain on his own. Probably the last thing they had seen as they pulled away from shore was his figure growing fainter and smaller in the descending dark. By the time Jesus had disappeared to spend the night alone in prayer, "the boat, battered by the waves, was far from the land, for the wind was against them" (14:24).

The precision of the description has the ring of someone who knows about boats and the terror of being caught in a storm, unable to get to land. The storm started in the evening and was still raging early in the morning (14:25), which means the disciples spent the whole night fighting the wind and waves, reefing sails, struggling at the helm, bailing, and, as the gale shifted, redistributing their weight to help the boat take the swells without capsizing.

The story was the perfect metaphor for Matthew's community as their faith wavered when Jesus failed to return and establish the full reign of God. Matthew's listeners could easily have identified with the disciples in the boat. Weary and afraid of death, like sailors who have fought a storm all night, Matthew's community may have begun to lose their ability to identify Christ coming to them. Perhaps their savior was approaching them through people and ideas that they found as terrifying as a ghost walking upon a raging sea (14:26).

When Jesus calls to the disciples, "Take heart, it is I; do not be afraid" (14:27), Matthew's community may have found in Peter's response an echo of their own skepticism: "Lord, *if* it is you, command me to come to you on the water" (14:28). Peter does not automatically grant that the figure on the sea is Jesus and not a ghost. Peter wants a sign, a clear word from Jesus that will settle the matter with finality. Surely, that is something that Matthew's community would also like, and if we are candid, something we have often sought when the storms of life have risen to frightening intensity.

Jesus answers Peter's request with a simple command: "Come" (14:29). The word must have pierced the hearts of Matthew's community. Here is Jesus answering Peter's prayer with all the directness that they wish in response to their own prayers.

But when Peter "noticed the strong wind, he became frightened, and beginning to sink, he cried out, 'Lord, save me'" (14:30). Peter, having walked on the water, still had doubts that would have drowned him if it were not for the hand of Jesus. Matthew appears to be using the story to tell his community: even if they receive from Jesus what they ask, they will be like Peter. They will find that the wind is still blowing and they still have doubts.

Yet there is something greater than the wind, greater than the raging sea, greater than the doubt that Peter or Matthew's community or we ourselves have: It is the hand that will save us even when we doubt. We are not saved by our human skills, by our ability to keep the boat upright and afloat through the stormy night. We are not saved by some superhuman act, by walking on water. We are saved by the hand of one who is praying for us through the night and who comes to us across the deep and catches us just when we fear we are sinking into eternal nothingness.

TWELFTH SUNDAY AFTER PENTECOST

AUGUST 15, 1999 / PROPER 15

REVISED COMMON	EPISCOPAL (BCP)	ROMAN CATHOLIC
Gen. 45:1-15	Isa. 56:1, 6-8	Isa. 56:1, 6-7
or Isa. 56:1, 6-8		
Pss. 133, 67	Ps. 67	Ps. 67:2-3, 5, 6, 8
Rom. 11:1-2a, 29-32	Rom. 11:13-15, 29-32	Rom. 11:13-15, 29-32
		or 1 Cor. 15:20-26
Matt. 15:(10-20), 21-28	Matt. 15:21-28	Matt. 15:21-28

HUMAN BARRIERS COME DOWN. Relationships are mended. Joseph is reunited with his brothers (Genesis 45). God declares that the temple shall be a house of prayer for all peoples (Isaiah 56). One psalmist celebrates the joy of unity (Psalm 133), another prays that all peoples may revere God (Psalm 67). Paul affirms that Israel is not cut off from God (Romans 11), and a Canaanite woman reaches across a gap between cultures to receive healing for her daughter (Matthew 15). Today's readings offer a vision of the reconciliation that God intends for all members of the human family.

FIRST READING
GENESIS 45:1-15

Interpreting the Text

There is an enormous leap between last week's reading (37:1-4, 12-28) and today's. Preachers need to decide which details they want to summarize from the intervening chapters to interpret today's lesson.

We recall that this is not the brothers' first encounter with Joseph as a high official in Pharaoh's administration. Each previous appearance (Genesis 42–44) increases the narrative tension. Joseph puts his brothers to the test, while they have no idea they are dealing with the very one they sold into slavery. All of this helps to explain their stunned silence when Joseph at long last reveals his identity (45:3).

Their reconciliation becomes the occasion for the narrator to reflect on the workings of God: "And now do not be distressed, or angry with yourselves, because you sold me here; for God sent me before you to preserve life" (45:5).

The words are a small sermon about God's providential care. See Gen. 50:20 for a summary verse of this two-leveled theology: the brothers' evil and God's good intention.

Responding to the Text

We often misspeak when we say, "It was the will of God." How easily that phrase becomes a way of excusing human evil or denying unspeakable tragedy.

If we confined our consideration of today's reading only to the assigned verses, we might conclude that the narrator comes dangerously close to holding such a facile theology. It seems that Joseph excuses his brothers from their culpability (45:5).

But when we consider the reading as one more episode in the larger story of God's promise that Abraham's descendants would be as numerous as the stars, we understand that the narrator is focusing on God's dependability. God keeps faith even though it requires working in a world where people do things as rotten as Joseph's brothers did—stripping him, throwing him into a pit, and selling him into slavery. No ethically responsible theology would deny the moral depravity of their action.

The book of Genesis names their action as evil. In the last chapter, Joseph tells them in a single verse: "As for you, you meant evil against me; but God meant it for good, to bring it about that many people should be kept alive, as they are today" (50:20, RSV, not the NRSV).

Note three things about this tightly compacted statement. One, it follows immediately upon the brothers' repentance (50:17, 18). Two, Joseph speaks these words, not his brothers. He offers them grace, not an excuse for their immoral behavior. Finally, these words affirm that the guiding purpose of God is the preservation of life. God's promises survive human evil.

ISAIAH 56:1, 6-8 (alt.)

Interpreting the Text

Given what Israel has been through at the hands of the Babylonians, this is not a time when they are eager to accept people different from themselves. Instead, they are feeling a need to define what makes them unique, what sustains their self-worth after the loss of Jerusalem and the temple, after defeat and exile. They want to shore up their identity with a wholehearted allegiance to *their* God, observance of the Sabbath, and keeping the covenant. All of these help to draw about them a circle of religious identity that provides a sense of value and security in a hostile world.

But God intervenes through the prophet to remind the Israelites that God is equally pleased with foreigners who live by these same theological and moral principles. God welcomes all "who join themselves to the Lord . . . all who keep the Sabbath . . . and hold fast my covenant" (56:6).

God tells the exiles who are returning home to rebuild the temple "my house shall be called a house of prayer for all peoples" (56:7).

Responding to the Text

Here is a story that I have heard from so many pastors that I think of it as prototypical; it recurs in church after church.

An outside group requests to use the church building for a worthy community cause. This touches off a debate: Some say that the building is for the congregation, "not for outsiders." Others say the purpose of the outside group matches the congregation's mission statement, that the church exists to serve the community.

Isaiah, I believe, would understand the debate every time the story repeats itself. In his day there must have been those who grumbled against his words, "My house shall be called a house of prayer for all peoples" (56:7). Spiritually beaten and discouraged by the exile, many of the Judahites would have asked why God was not more sensitive to their need to draw into themselves after all they had suffered. Why put out the welcome mat to foreigners when it was foreigners who had done them in? The temple ought to be for Judahites, not for outsiders. But God was not only willing to admit the foreigners. God wanted them to be "joyful in my house of prayer" (56:7).

> THE PURPOSE OF THE CHURCH'S DEEPEST VALUES IS NOT TO EXCLUDE BUT TO INVITE ALL PEOPLE TO A LIFE OF FAITH AND LOVE.

God has no interest in a temple or a church that is little more than a religious clubhouse whose membership misconstrues the principles and practices of faith as exclusionary rules. Doing justice, observing the Sabbath, and keeping the covenant delight God, and God welcomes "all" who live this way (56:6). The purpose of the church's deepest values is not to exclude but to invite all people to a life of faith and love.

RESPONSIVE READING
PSALM 133

Interpreting the Text

This psalm might have been sung by pilgrims on their way to Jerusalem. Scholars are not certain, but the superscription, "A Song of Ascents," possibly refers to a journey up to the temple. If this is the case, then the psalm reveals that temple worship provided clan and kindred a common center of meaning that helped them live together (133:1).

Responding to the Text

When people live in a hot, arid climate, images of moisture and coolness powerfully express the deep yearning of their hearts. The psalmist pictures the extravagant use of refreshing ointment upon a guest: not a few stingy drops but enough to run down the beard and "over the collar" (133:2). And as if this were not enough, the psalmist invokes the vision of the highest mountain in the land covered with "dew" (133:3). That is how wonderful it is when families live together: Arid human existence becomes refreshing and cool.

PSALM 67 (BCP)

Interpreting the Text

The psalm complements Isaiah 56:1, 6-8; like the prophet, the psalmist holds up a vision of God's concern for the whole world. God watches over both the political and natural realms. God judges and guides the peoples (67:4), and God "has blessed us" through the earth that "has yielded its increase" (67:6).

Responding to the Text

There are times when the distance between ourselves and our ancient forebears seems so great that we wonder what they have to tell us scientifically enlightened people. Although they never saw earth from outer space as we have, still the Spirit moving through their poets lifted up a vision that can help sustain our pursuit of international environmental cooperation. The creator's concern for countries and nature (67:4-6) is the basis for an appeal to all people to praise God (67:3); and praise is empty if it ignores good stewardship of the earth.

Second Reading
ROMANS 11:1-2a, 29-32

Interpreting the Text

Paul brings to a climax his argument that starts in Rom. 9:1. He is trying to make coherent sense of three realities whose interrelationship puzzles him: (1) his identity as "an Israelite, a descendant of Abraham, a member of the tribe of Benjamin" who has accepted the revelation of God's grace in Christ Jesus (11:1); (2) that the Gentiles have accepted the gospel while most of his own people have not; and (3) his belief that "the gifts and calling of God" to the Israelites are "irrevocable" (11:29).

Paul believes God is working through these different elements in such a way that one complements the other. He writes an extended sentence in which the first phrase is balanced by a second phrase that is nearly its mirror-reversed image: "Just as you were once *disobedient* but have now received *mercy* so they now have been *disobedient* in order that, by the *mercy* shown to you, they too may now receive *mercy*" (11:30–31). Paul's rhetorical precision reveals that Gentiles and Jews share in common a fundamental pattern of existence: human disobedience met by the mercy of God.

Paul's complex argument does not end where the reading does. He concludes with a magnificent doxology to the wonder of God, thus indicating that even his most strenuous thought bends before the mystery of the One whose ways he has sought to understand (11:33–36).

Responding to the Text

More than once in my ministry people have told me they resent how Paul the apostle messed up the simple message of Jesus. Many of us may respond that way to the epistle for today because of its dense and elaborate argument.

From our perspective in history, Judaism and Christianity are two distinctly different religions. But Paul has no knowledge of the history that was to follow him. It is only some fifteen to twenty years after the earthly ministry of Jesus when he writes to the Romans; and although the apostle has been transformed by the grace of Christ, he is still keenly aware and appreciative of his deep Jewish roots. As a matter of fact, he depends upon that tradition to interpret to himself and others what Christ means for human life.

Aware of the multitude of religious traditions on this planet and the long history of anti-Semitism, it may be that every detail of Paul's argument does not make as much sense to us as it did to him. Nevertheless, there are three great truths to which Paul's argument gives witness that are essential to the Christian faith.

The first is Paul's absolute and unshakable conviction about the merciful, reliable character of God. No matter how tied up Paul appears to be in his arguments, he never loses sight of the wonderful God who intends to "be merciful to all" (11:32). Think of what it would mean if in the midst of all our theological differences, we too never forgot this central affirmation.

Second, even if Paul's questions are not our questions, his writing is a witness to the importance of wrestling theologically with the great entanglements of belief and experience. Part of being faithful to God is being willing to struggle with what baffles us.

And finally, after Paul has done everything he can to understand faith and experience, he acknowledges that even his best thought is inadequate to the full comprehension of the ways of the divine, so he breaks into the unrestrained praise of God (11:33–36).

Mercy. Theology. Doxology. They animate Paul's writing and make him a powerful witness to Jesus.

GOSPEL

MATTHEW 15:(10-20), 21-28

Interpreting the Text

In the Bible a place is never just a place. Because of ancient beliefs about the connection between group identity and geographic location, it is always significant when a writer calls attention to the setting of a story. "Jesus left that place and went away to the district of Tyre and Sidon" (15:21). It is not certain what "that place" refers to, though it appears to be Gennesaret (14:34), a town on the northwestern shore of the Sea of Galilee, which is the last place name Matthew mentions before Tyre and Sidon.

Jesus is leaving behind his home territory in Galilee for a region that belongs to the Gentiles. It is a journey not only through space but also across cultures: He is approaching the turf of the alien, the stranger, those who stand outside the circle "of the house of Israel" (15:24).

The mere mention of the setting of the story must have had a powerful impact in Matthew's community. It was difficult for many of them to accept that the Gospel was intended not only for Israel but for the Gentiles as well. Jesus' crossing the geographic/cultural boundary would have awakened in them resistance and fear.

As portrayed in the story, Jesus himself turns out to have difficulty with the idea of extending his mission to the Gentiles. Whether this was historically true or whether Matthew projects his own community's struggle on Jesus is not something we can solve by the consideration of this text alone.

Taking the story on its own terms, we are struck by the way the Canaanite woman addresses Jesus: "Lord, Son of David" (15:22). Whereas the religious authorities of his own people are shown repeatedly discounting Jesus, this gentile woman recognizes his authority with the same title that the admiring crowds will use on Palm Sunday, "Hosanna to the Son of David" (21:9).

Jesus' first response is to turn down the woman's request. Jesus explains that his ministry is limited to the Israelites (15:24). But the woman is desperate about her disturbed daughter (15:22) and she persists, kneeling before Jesus. Still refusing, he equates her people with "dogs" (15:26). When the woman makes a swift and witty retort (15:27), Jesus finally relents and grants her petition (15:28). The woman's persistence and faith have opened Jesus (and/or Matthew's community) to reach beyond the old boundaries of prejudice and exclusion.

Responding to the Text

"I do not want you associating with them. They're not our kind. Wrong neighborhood, wrong people."

"What's wrong with them? I just want to go to and play with them."

"You belong here. Now I don't want you going over there."

"But you always say, 'Be nice to everybody.'"

"Yes. And you can be nice to them in school or if you meet them on the street. But they're not our kind. We live here, they live there. Wrong neighborhood, wrong people. You have plenty of friends right around this block. Go play with them."

"But why?"

"I've told you why! Wrong neighborhood, wrong people."

Is there any of us who never heard words like these? If so, we still picked up the message. It came in a myriad of forms, from how we dressed to where we lived to what we celebrated.

Something deep in the human soul draws boundaries and makes distinctions. We believe that God loves all people and that we ought to do the same; but in practice we leave universal love to God and concentrate on the group to which we belong, be it family or church or company or social clique or neighborhood.

There is much to affirm about these allegiances. If we tried to embrace the whole world in love, we might end up loving no one at all. None of us is as universal as we fancy ourselves. People are not all alike. Culture, upbringing, values, and beliefs differ enormously among the multitude of human communities. The command to love our neighbor as ourselves is a reminder that love is not a generalized sentiment toward the whole human race. Love for Jesus is a form of behavior, showing compassion and care for particular people.

But the circles of affiliation that provide us with our identity and teach us what it means to care for one another run the danger of making us suspicious of those who are beyond their bounds. Matthew was familiar with this danger. His own community needed to offer the gospel to the larger world, to groups whom they had been taught were not their kind.

Matthew was a realist about how hard it is to reach across deeply ingrained differences, and so he retold a powerful story about a time when Jesus left his home turf to travel to Tyre and Sidon—wrong neighborhood, wrong people.

One of those people, a Canaanite woman, desperate to have her disturbed daughter healed, confronts Jesus. And Jesus, whom we picture as always compassionate, always caring and responsive to human need, turns her down. Wrong neighborhood, wrong people. But the woman will not be deterred. Although as a Gentile she would have been raised with as much prejudice against the Israelites as they had against her, she has learned to enter their culture on their terms. Instead of using a Canaanite form of address in speaking to Jesus, she calls to him in terms honored by his culture: "Lord, Son of David" (15:22). She enters his world that he might enter hers and heal her daughter. She does not give up, but persists until he says "Let it be done for you as you wish" and it is (15:28).

If Jesus had the wisdom to learn from that persistent woman, and if we are his followers, then we can learn from her too. Yes, we may have our differences; but for God working through us, there is no wrong neighborhood, no wrong people.

Readings for Celebrating St. Mary on the
Twelfth Sunday after Pentecost
FIRST READING

ISAIAH 61:10-11

Although it would be historically inaccurate to treat the reading as a prediction of Mary's bearing Jesus, a close examination of its poetry may be useful in finding language appropriate to a homily about her. The passage is filled with images of rich attire that are often associated with Mary through devotional literature and iconography: "garments, "robe," "garland," "jewels." The prophet gathers these to the climactic announcement: "The Lord God will cause righteousness and praise to spring up before all the nations" (61:11). A similar extravagance of language will echo again in Mary's Magnificat (Luke 1:46-55).

Revelation 11:19; 12:1-6, 10 (RC)

The image of the woman draws upon elements of Hellenistic myth as well as Christian and Jewish belief. It is impossible to disentangle all of these and make a precise logical statement about the meaning of the image.

Nevertheless, the poetry makes it clear that the woman is a figure of cosmic power. She is "clothed with the sun, with the moon under her feet, and on her head a crown of twelve stars" (12:1). Her son is the messiah (12:5), so it appears that the poet is presenting a vision of Mary amplified and ornamented with images associated with ancient goddesses, including Artemis, Hekate, and Isis.

The fusion of so many elements in one rhapsodic vision suggests a sermon that celebrates how faith draws upon multiple sources and breaks into poetic language at the wonder of who Mary is and what she has done.

SECOND READING

GALATIANS 4:4-7

The passage places the birth of Jesus in the sweep of history and points out how he knew the same conditions of human finitude as the rest of us: He was "born of a woman . . . in order to redeem us" (4:4-5). Redemption requires a woman. Although preachers must avoid sexist reductionism that constricts the role of women to motherhood, it is not wrong to acknowledge that if Mary had not given birth to Jesus "the fullness of time" (4:4) would have culminated in emptiness instead of redemption.

1 CORINTHIANS 15:20-26 (RC)

Paul's vision of the future resurrection is built completely upon what has already happened through Christ. In a single verse Paul traces the story of salvation from Adam to Christ, using parallel structure and repetition to bring out how God's purposes are achieved through human agency: "Since death *came* through a *human being*, the resurrection of the dead *has also come* through a *human being*" (15:21).

Although there is no allusion here to Mary as there is in Gal. 4:4, the salvation of human beings by a human being would never have been accomplished without her.

GOSPEL
LUKE 1:39-56

It is not uncommon to interpret the *Magnificat* (1:46-55) as Mary's response to the announcement from Gabriel that she will bear Jesus (1:26-38). But if we study the text, we discover that she does not immediately praise God upon hearing from the angel. A touching story lies between Gabriel's announcement and Mary's song. She visits Elizabeth who confirms the meaning of Mary's pregnancy and the child that she will bear (1:42-45).

Only after Elizabeth's affirmation does Mary break into praise (1:46). Whether or not it was Luke's intention, the effect of this narrative order is to suggest that Mary's "spirit rejoices in God" (1:47), not only because of Gabriel's announcement, but also because of the wisdom and graciousness of Elizabeth. She speaks as one pregnant woman to another; and her words, therefore, probably carry as much weight as that of the angel's. The significance of Elizabeth's acceptance and support finds confirmation in the verse that follows Mary's song. She stays with her three months (1:56).

These observations would be helpful in formulating a sermon about Mary that did not focus on her in isolation. The Magnificat arises from Gabriel's announcement or Mary's private musings upon it, and from the relationship of two pregnant women supporting each other and celebrating God working through them.

THIRTEENTH SUNDAY AFTER PENTECOST

AUGUST 22, 1999 / PROPER 16

REVISED COMMON	EPISCOPAL (BCP)	ROMAN CATHOLIC
Exod. 1:8—2:10	Isa. 51:1-6	Isa. 22:15, 19-23
or Isa. 51:1-6		
Pss. 124; 138	Ps. 138	Ps. 138:1-3, 6, 8
Rom. 12:1-8	Rom. 12:1-8	Rom. 12:1-8
Matt. 16:13-20	Matt. 16:13-20	Matt. 16:13-20

"IF IT HAD NOT BEEN THE LORD who was on our side . . . (Psalm 124:1). Consider each of today's readings in light of the Psalmist's intriguing "If." If pharaoh's daughter had not befriended the infant Moses (Exodus 2). . . . If each of us heeded Paul's advice "not to think of yourself more highly than you ought to think" (Rom. 12:3). . . . If we consistently lived up to Peter's profession of faith, "You are the Messiah" (Matt. 16:16). Do the "ifs" of our lives lead us to the same affirmation as the Psalmist's? (124:8).

FIRST READING
EXODUS 1:8—2:10

Interpreting the Text

The opening chapter of Exodus repeatedly emphasizes how prolific the Israelites are (1:7, 8, 12, 20). This theme first appeared in God's command, "Be fruitful and multiply" (Gen. 1:28), which was later repeated to Noah and his sons (Gen. 9:1) and then confirmed by God's promise to Abraham (17:6). Exodus 1 uses the theme to dramatize the confrontation between the policies of Pharaoh and the purposes of God.

Shiphrah and Puah stand against mass murder and offer an ingenious excuse to cover their actions (1:19). While the midwives are mentioned by name, the writer never provides the Pharaoh such distinction. He is the prototypical oppressor whose cruelty displaces his individual humanity so that his name, a precious thing in Israelite culture, is withheld.

The nameless tyrant, frustrated by the courage and shrewdness of Shiphrah and Puah, now commands "all his people" to participate in the genocide (1:22).

Although this time the terror is carried out, once again it is women, Moses' mother and sister and the daughter of Pharaoh, who become the agents of God's enduring purpose.

Responding to the Text

Either the Pharaoh was a frightened man or he was playing up to the jingoism of the rabid patriots, or perhaps both. He had gone on public record that the growing number of resident aliens was a political threat: "Look, the Israelite people are more numerous and more powerful than we" (1:8).

Completely forgotten was Joseph (1:8), a resident alien who had rescued from famine not only his own family but the Pharaoh's ancestors and the whole nation of Egypt. The Pharaoh does not appear to be someone who studied the past to gain what wisdom it might offer him in understanding the present.

When he suggested "They will increase and, in the event of war, join our enemies and fight against us and escape from the land" (1:9), it was not a totally logical position if you consider the last phrase: if they escaped, they would be gone! But the Pharaoh appears to be no more attentive to logic than he is to history.

There were surely many who cheered on the chief of state for attacking the resident aliens. Any two-penny dictator knows that if you focus the frustration on the aliens you will have a lot less pressure on yourself.

But what the Pharaoh could not control, what dictators can never command, is the heart that fears God (1:17). And so this nameless tyrant, playing to all the worst in his own people, was to find his pogrom derailed by Shiphrah and Puah, two courageous, faithful midwives who kept alive not only Israelite infants but also the work of God.

ISAIAH 51:1-6 (alt.)

Interpreting the Text

The repeated phrase, "Listen to me" (51:1, 4, 7), signals that the prophet has a word from God. Judah has been through a long night of destruction and exile, and now an age of light is about to dawn.

Having had the ground ripped from under their feet by the Babylonians, the Judahites may find it difficult to believe the good news Isaiah announces. So the prophet uses a metaphor of solidness to stabilize their shaky spirits: "Look to the rock from which you were hewn" (51:1). Abraham and Sarah are the rock (51:2). As God "blessed" their forebears with a child when they were long past the age of parenting so now God "will comfort Zion" (51:3).

There follow a number of astounding metaphors for the "deliverance" God will bring: the wilderness will become "like Eden" (51:3), the heavens will "vanish" and earth "wear out" (51:6). The images of a restored garden and a worn-out earth are not logically consistent. They are rather the rhapsodic extravagance of a prophet trying to convey the wonder of God's "salvation" (51:5).

Responding to the Text

Because the building of a medieval cathedral took so long, the masons and workers who quarried and laid the giant foundation stones never got to see the splendid edifice that their labor made possible. It took faith for them to commence building a cathedral that their mortal eyes would never behold. It must have been like the faith of Abraham and Sarah who left for a land unknown and who trusted that from a single child, born in their old age, would come a great nation (51:2).

I have wondered if those who were privileged to lay the capstone on the cathedral's spire had some sense of the builders, now dead and gone, whose work made possible their final achievement. Did they look down from that dizzying height and give thanks to God for the workers in stone who so many generations before them had quarried and transported and laid the foundations on which everything else depended?

It is easy to forget those who have preceded us because we are consumed by our own immediate past and the present reality into which it has thrown us. This happened to the Judahites. They had been through hell: the destruction of their country and exile in a foreign land. To restore their sense of identity and their trust in God's power to deliver them, the prophet reminds them of the historic foundations of their faith: "Look to the rock from which you were hewn, and to the quarry from which you were dug. Look to Abraham your father and to Sarah who bore you" (51:1, 2).

RESPONSIVE READING

PSALM 124

Interpreting the Text

The psalm is filled with one terrifying image after another: an enemy attack, being swallowed up alive, drowned by a flood, eaten as prey, snared like fowl (124:2-7). But none of these things has happened! Our worst nightmares did not come true because God was with us. "Our help is in the name of the Lord, who made heaven and earth" (124:8).

Responding to the Text

The doctor reports: "It's not as serious as we initially thought. You'll be fine." Your child phones an hour after curfew: "We're okay. We just ran out of gas, but we'll be home soon." Away on a trip, you call home because the weather station says your region was hit by a bad storm, but the report is "No damage."

What is your immediate response when any of these things happen?

"Thank God, thank God, thank God!"

You will never come closer to understanding this psalm than in that moment of boundless gratitude.

PSALM 138

Interpreting the Text

The psalmist remembers Jerusalem from afar: "I bow down *toward* your holy temple" (138:2). Scribes and interpreters have often had difficulty with the phrase "Before the gods I sing your praise" (138:1). But if the psalmist is in a foreign land, the verse may be an affirmation of continuing loyalty to Yahweh in the face of other religions.

Responding to the Text

The aunt who raised my mother used to say, "Don't ever forget where home is." There was more in that little saying than the hope that my mother would come back for visits after she had married and moved away. "Home" represented the values and relationships that were at the center of my mother's childhood. To remember home was to remember those treasured realities, to keep them alive even when she was far away.

The psalmist remembers where home is. He bows toward the temple and recalls God's "steadfast love" (138:2).

Second Reading
ROMANS 12:1-8

Interpreting the Text

The first eleven chapters of Romans have demonstrated how God has acted in Jesus Christ to put right the contorted nature of human existence. Now Paul changes his approach and exhorts his readers to live in a manner that is congruent with what God has done in Christ. Without an awareness of this shift from grace to exhortation, we may misread Paul and turn the gospel back into the human striving for religious perfection that Paul has spent the first half of the book refuting.

We are to present our "bodies" (12:1). The word in Greek is not "thoughts" or "souls," but literally "bodies." Good Hebraic thinker that he is, Paul is interested in the whole human being. He does not spiritualize our existence, but insists that we bring to God the totality of who we are as material creatures.

Although we generally make a distinction between "body and soul," we preserve something of Paul's perspective in the common English idiom, "Put your body on the line," a phrase that reminds us it is easy to think noble thoughts, but noble action requires placing ourselves physically behind what we claim to believe.

There is a coherent flow to Paul's exhortation: Once we have presented our bodies as a "living sacrifice" (12:1) then we are lest apt to think of ourselves "more highly" than we ought (12:3), and hence we can realize more perfectly the life of the corporate body (12:4-8).

Responding to the Text

Human resolutions to change how we behave are notoriously short-lived. Old habits quickly reassert themselves, and our best-willed intentions swiftly vanish. So when Paul exhorts us "to present [our] bodies as a living sacrifice, holy and acceptable to God" (12:1), the best desire of our hearts may briefly awaken to the challenge; but soon we find ourselves falling into patterns of speech and action that do not measure up to that high ideal.

Paul's exhortation to a life worthy of the faith we profess comes only after he has described how the grace of Christ Jesus has transformed our relationship with God. Yet so many of our best intentions fail precisely because of this: We act as though their fulfillment were entirely within our own capacity. Paul has shown throughout Romans how this attitude breeds self-presumption and alienation from God on whom we are utterly dependent.

It may be helpful here to consider an analogy from the common experience of growing up to adulthood. We know that simply telling children to treat others with respect and consideration does not lead to good behavior. Children must themselves receive respect and consideration or they have no idea of how to put the words into action.

I recall a sampler I once saw in a home: "A child who lives with hate grows up to hate. A child who lives with love grows up to love." This does not mean that the child who lives with love will never require reprimand and instruction. All the love in the world does not negate the necessity of exhorting children to live out the meaning of the affection they have received. The most loving parents end up saying a thousand thousand times: "Share." "Say 'Thank you.'" "Help clean up." But the command only makes sense if the child has experienced sharing, gratitude, and help. It is the combination of formative experience and clear instruction that results in treating others graciously.

And so it is that Paul's exhortations make sense to us because God in Christ Jesus has already treated us with the sacrificial, discerning grace that the apostle now asks of us.

GOSPEL

195

THIRTEENTH
SUNDAY
AFTER PENTECOST

AUGUST 22

MATTHEW 16:13-20

Interpreting the Text

Caesarea Philippi forms a dramatic setting for Peter's profession of faith. A shrine to Pan, the nature God of the Greeks and Romans, was located there. Philip, the son of Herod the Great, rebuilt and renamed the city to honor both the emperor (the Caesar of Caesarea) and himself (the Philip of Philippi). Since the emperor was thought to possess godlike attributes, the location provides theological tension between the world's understanding of divinity and Peter's confession: "You are the messiah, the Son of the living God" (16:16).

Matthew has rewritten Mark's version of the story. In Mark, Jesus asks, "Who do people say that *I* am?" (8:27), while in Matthew he asks, "Who do people say *the Son of Man* is?" (16:13). The title "the Son of Man" has various meanings in the gospels. It sometimes refers to Jesus in his present earthly ministry. Other times it serves as a way of speaking about the risen Christ, and still other times as the judge who is to come at the end of time. Matthew uses the title here to suggest that his community, unlike Mark's thick-headed disciples, already knows something of who Jesus is.

When Jesus turns from asking about others (16:13) to the disciples themselves, the question becomes more personal: "But who do *you* say that *I* am" (16:15)?

The language that Matthew employs suggests that he may be reading a resurrection story back into the narrative of Jesus' earthly ministry, and then using this to instruct his community about the nature of Christ and the church that follows him. There is a catechetical tone to the way the story unfolds: It moves from a general question about what people are saying (16:13) to Jesus' more intensely personal question (16:15) to Peter's confession (16:16) to a statement about the theological basis of the church and its authority (16:17-19).

The "keys of the kingdom" is a powerful image of authority since in Jesus' time the steward of a household held the keys as a way of determining who was permitted or denied admittance to the master. That Jesus grants this authority in Caesarea Philippi, a city that memorializes imperial power, underlines the audacity of what is claimed for the church (16:19). This is not a passage that would sit well with Caesar!

Responding to the Text

Built like a rock. Rock hard. Rock solid. Rock is one of those images that is so primordial that it reaches across cultures and centuries. Jesus calls "Simon son of Jonah" (16:17) by the name "Peter," which in Greek is the word for "rock." Because the name "Peter" has taken on a holy patina from so many centuries of devotional use, I will for now refer to him as "Rock" in order to convey the liveliness of the nickname bestowed by Jesus.

"Rock" appears to earn his name in this passage. Rock is the one who first professes: "You are the Messiah, the Son of the living God" (16:16). While other people are speculating that Jesus is John the Baptist or Elijah or Jeremiah or another of the prophets (16:14), and while the rest of the disciples offer no clear response to Jesus' question, Rock blurts out the truth of the matter without hesitation or reservation.

But how solid is Rock? How likely is his faith to crumble and erode under the onslaught of the world's doubt and persecution? Is Rock dependable enough to bear the authority that Jesus grants him?

Jesus says he will build the church on Rock, and he gives Rock the keys of the kingdom and says that what Rock binds and loosens on earth will be bound and loosened in heaven. Surely, Jesus would not entrust this kind of power to Rock unless Rock were utterly dependable.

But in truth Rock is not like granite, he is much more like sandstone or shale. We have already seen Rock's faith falter in the storm (14:30); and shortly Rock will rebuke Jesus for talking about his suffering and death (16:21, 22). And after the arrest, Rock will deny Jesus three times and break down in bitter tears at his unfaithfulness (26:69-75). Rock is not rock solid!

Why then would Jesus call him Rock, and why would Matthew report it and show Rock at his worst as well as his best? One possible interpretation is that Matthew wants to remind his community of the high hopes that Jesus has not only for Rock, but for all of us who, like Rock, profess to Jesus: "You are the Messiah, the Son of the living God" (16:16). Like Rock, we may often fail to live up to the faith that we claim, but then more than ever we need to remember the faith that Christ has in us.

At the same time, we need never to lose sight of our fallibility. We have often failed Jesus as thoroughly as Rock did; and the remembrance of it is enough to humble our judgments when we are binding and loosening on earth, when we are making decisions about what is right and wrong, when we are defining the belief and practice of the church.

The name Rock reminds us that we are most solid when what we do and say points to the central truth of our lives: "You are the Messiah, the Son of the living God." But simultaneously the name Rock reminds us that we are sandstone and shale, that we often crumble and fail under the pressures of the world.

Like Matthew's community we need to fill the role that Jesus has entrusted to the church. We need to make judgments in Caesarea Philippi, in the world of imperial arrogance, that will serve to correct the distorted values of our society. But we need to make those judgments humbled by the awareness of how often we follow in Rock's faltering footsteps.

FOURTEENTH SUNDAY AFTER PENTECOST

AUGUST 29, 1999 / PROPER 17

REVISED COMMON	EPISCOPAL (BCP)	ROMAN CATHOLIC
Exod. 3:1-15	Jer. 15:15-21	Jer. 20:7-9
Jer. 15:15-21		
Pss. 105:1-6, 23-26,	Ps. 26	Ps. 63:2, 3-4, 5-6, 8-9
45c; 26		
Rom. 12:9-21	Rom. 12:1-8	Rom. 12:1-2
Matt. 16:21-28	Matt. 16:21-27	Matt. 16:21-27

ALTHOUGH POPULAR PIETY OFTEN ASSUMES that to receive a clear word from God would be a wonderful spiritual experience, today's lessons reveal the burden and challenge of God's word. Moses doubts his ability to confront Pharaoh (Exodus 3). Jeremiah finds himself ostracized by the community to whom he speaks the word of God (Jeremiah 15). And when Jesus makes it plain that he will suffer and die, Peter does not want to hear of it (Matthew 16). A clear word from God is *not* always welcome for it often requires that we face the sadness of life and undertake difficult tasks.

> A CLEAR WORD FROM GOD IS *not* ALWAYS WELCOME FOR IT OFTEN REQUIRES THAT WE FACE THE SADNESS OF LIFE AND UNDERTAKE DIFFICULT TASKS.

FIRST READING
EXODUS 3:1-15

Interpreting the Text

Moses does not immediately identify that the burning bush is a manifestation of God (3:4). The repetition of Moses' name, the directions to remove his sandals, and God's words of self-identification gather into an overwhelming awareness of being in the presence of the divine (3:5, 6). Moses then hides his face, reflecting the belief that it is death to look directly into the face of God (3:6).

The mysterious character of God that dominates the opening verses is followed by a revelation of God's compassion for the people (3:7, 8). The God to whom Moses listens is a God who listens to the slaves.

Still all of this is not enough to assure Moses that he is up to the task of confronting Pharaoh or convincing the Israelites that God has sent him (3:11, 13). God answers Moses' reservations with a promise (3:12) and a deeper revelation of the divine character: "I AM WHO I AM" (3:14), a name that expresses the commanding autonomy of the One Moses has encountered.

Responding to the Text

Moses is a shepherd tending his father-in-law's flock when God calls him to lead the Israelites to freedom (3:1). He has fled to Midian after killing an Egyptian slave-master; and although we can understand what drove him to murder the man (2:11, 12), even his fellow Hebrews fear that Moses might do the same to them (2:14). A shepherd who is a fugitive from the law, Moses does not appear to be promising material for the role he is called to fill.

Of course, Moses was raised in Pharaoh's court, so he might have the advantage of knowing the ruler's weaknesses. But that was a long time ago, and the Pharaoh under whom he had grown up was now dead (2:23).

From a purely human perspective, Moses does not hold great promise for the liberation of his people. But then the liberation of the slaves does not depend on Moses' professional dossier, it depends on God. This is the God who has proven faithful age after age, "the God of Abraham, the God of Isaac, and the God of Jacob" (3:6), the God too great for mortal eye to behold (3:6), the God who attends to the "misery" and "sufferings" of the oppressed (3:7, 8), the God who is to be worshiped (3:12), the God whose name we cannot fathom (3:14). Because this astounding God will be "with" him (3:12), Moses the fugitive shepherd will become Moses the leader of his people. Because this astounding God is with us, we will become what we are called to be.

JEREMIAH 15:15-21

Interpreting the Text

The prophet recounts how he initially welcomed the words that God called him to speak: "Your words became to me a joy and the delight of my heart" (15:16). But the burden of insistently announcing God's judgment against the people has made Jeremiah an outcast: "Under the weight of your hand I sat alone" (15:17). The ostracism wears the prophet down so that he brings a searing indictment against God. Using images of a weary traveler in the wilderness, Jeremiah charges: "Truly, you are to me like a deceitful brook, like waters that fail" (15:18).

In a few brief verses Jeremiah has laid out the sadness and estrangement that his unpopular role has brought him. Jeremiah has had enough of being a prophet. It has left him estranged from God as well as the community.

But God is not willing to let Jeremiah go. He calls for Jeremiah to return and promises that he will protect Jeremiah (15:20, 21). These words of assurance answer the prayer that the prophet offers at the beginning of his complaint (15:15).

Responding to the Text

While I was in seminary during the 1960s, African American students took over the school's classroom and administration building, effectively shutting down all academic programs. The students were protesting institutional racism and demanding the hiring of more African American faculty.

The president, Gene Bartlett, prayerfully considered the truth of their judgment and the rightness of their cause, and entered negotiations with them in good faith. In the midst of those negotiations he periodically met with the other students and faculty in the basement of a school dormitory.

When someone asked why the state police were not summoned to throw the students out, he responded that these were our brothers and sisters in Christ; and the world may deal with conflict by the use of force, but it is not the way of the savior.

When the confrontation was finally settled to the satisfaction of the African American students and the administration, someone suggested there was no need to keep the agreement since it was reached under duress. But Gene Bartlett responded simply: "We gave our word."

Twenty years later, I had the privilege of reviewing these events with Gene Bartlett. By now the black church studies program that had resulted from the confrontation had made an invaluable contribution to the life of both black and white churches. As I listened to Gene Bartlett speak, I realized how lonely it had been to stand for what he believed was the word of God in that situation. He had known then what Jeremiah knew: "Under the weight of your hand I sat alone" (15:17). And twenty years later he realized that God had been with him "to save" and "deliver" (15:20).

RESPONSIVE READING
PSALM 105:1-6, 23-26, 45c

Interpreting the Text

The later verses (105:23-26) make clear that the "deeds," "wonderful works," and "miracles" of the opening verses (105:1-6) refer specifically to the way God has faithfully acted to preserve Israel. The psalm presents a poetic version of the escape from Egypt (105:26-45), compressing into a brief liturgical form the story that fills twelve chapters in Exodus.

Responding to the Text

Communities repeat the stories of their origins again and again in order to reinforce their core values, to reaffirm their sense of worth, and to strengthen their sense of belonging. These stories usually take a variety of forms because subsequent generations keep re-telling them in ways that make sense to them. The exodus was for Israel the central formative story; and in this psalm we can sense how vital it was to their worship. It gives them their identity as a people whom God liberated and feeds their passion to praise God (105:1-6, 45c).

PSALM 26

Interpreting the Text

The text indicates that the psalm is more than a private supplication to God. Its recitation might be part of a ritual act of purification "in the great congregation" (26:12). There is a vivid description of the speaker's liturgical actions: "I wash my hands in innocence, and go around your altar, O Lord, singing aloud a song of thanksgiving" (26:6-7a).

Responding to the Text

Sometimes the tone of voice in which we read something will determine its meaning. If we read this psalm with a self-righteous inflection, then we may be put off by the claim, "I do not sit with the worthless, nor do I consort with hypocrites" (26:4). But if we read with the voice of one who has genuinely sought to live with "integrity" (26:1, 11), then the tenor of the psalm changes, and we find ourselves wanting to join with the psalmist in "telling all [God's] wondrous deeds" (26:7b).

SECOND READING
ROMANS 12:9-21

Interpreting the Text

One brief exhortation follows another with no immediately discernible pattern. However, the end of the reading, "Do not be overcome by evil, but overcome evil with good" (12:21), is a restatement of the opening, "Let love be genuine; hate what is evil, hold fast to what is good" (12:9). The two verses are like the major theme that opens a symphonic movement and returns at the conclusion, helping to organize what we have heard in between. Paul's seemingly disparate injunctions are variations on his theme. They flesh out in detail what it takes for love to be "genuine," "to hold fast to what is good," and "not be overcome by evil."

An analysis of the various exhortations reveals that they fall into three categories: One, exhortations about the communal life of the church, "love one another with mutual affection" (12:10) and "Contribute to the needs of the saints" (12:13); two, exhortations about the need for maintaining a vital spiritual life, "be ardent in spirit" (12:11) and "persevere in prayer" (12:12); three, exhortations about relating to the world, "Bless those who persecute you" (12:14) and "live peaceably with all" (12:18).

Those rapid-fire exhortations, which at first reading seem so unrelated, in fact gather to a revelation: "genuine" love involves something greater than the efforts of our individual hearts. It requires a healthy community life, spiritual vitality, and living in peace with all persons.

Responding to the Text

I invite you to listen to an oratorio that you cannot purchase on a compact disc but that plays again and again in the human heart. The libretto comes from Romans 12:9-21. The dramatic narrative of the oratorio is the story of our lives that Paul's libretto awakens.

A thrilling opening chorus carries the title of the whole work: "Let love be genuine" (12:9). But soon after the beautiful theme has sounded, the music turns dark and brooding: "Hate what is evil, hold fast to what is good" (12:9). The chorus divides into parts that fight against each other, creating sharp dissonance and irreconcilable counterrhythms. We see life as it really is: neither purely good nor purely evil, but a struggle between them.

The opening chorus then ends on an unresolved chord, suggesting the tension that fills the rest of the oratorio, the rest of our lives. There are arias and choruses that keep oscillating between genuine love and love's distortions: manipulation, inappropriate intimacy, hiding issues of justice under a facile appeal to unity.

We hear a lively soprano aria to a gigue like tune telling us to "rejoice in hope," followed by a subdued contralto lament with English horn, "be patient in suffering, persevere in prayer" (12:12). And our memory supplies scenes we will never forget: the coffin of a beloved friend being rolled down the church aisle, someone's hand holding ours while we prayed.

As aria follows aria, we compare Paul's libretto to the life that we live and wonder: How can we ever embody the ideals singing in our hearts? But then we hear the solo, "Bless those who persecute you" (12:14), and we recognize in it the voice of one whose teaching Paul seldom quotes directly, the voice of Jesus (Luke 6:28). And now we know why we can live the faith that sings in our hearts: Because Christ has embodied genuine love, and Christ now pours into us the grace to join in the final chorus and to live its truth: "Do not be overcome by evil, but overcome evil with good" (12:21).

MATTHEW 16:21-28

Interpreting the Text

The opening phrase, "From that time on" (16:21), refers to Peter's confession of faith (16:16) and Jesus' affirmation of Peter's central role in the church (16:18, 19). The implications of Jesus' messiahship were not self-evident. Jesus had to teach the disciples the full meaning of Peter's confession, and this was not something easily learned: "Jesus *began to show* his disciples that he must go to Jerusalem and undergo great suffering . . . " (16:21). The emphasized phrase suggests that it took time for the disciples to absorb the hard and upsetting truth of what Jesus faced.

Peter is for Matthew a useful heuristic figure: The disciple who first acknowledged Jesus as the Christ failed to understand the full import of what he believed (16:22). And if Peter, the rock on whom the church is founded, had to grow into the knowledge of the meaning of Jesus' messiahship, then Matthew's community ought not to be surprised that the same is required of them.

Jesus' messiahship involves suffering, death, and resurrection. It is difficult for Peter and for Matthew's church to accept this because they have set their minds "not on divine things but on human things" (16:23).

The distinction between divine and human things leads to the need for a clear decision: "If any want to become my followers, let them deny themselves and take up their cross and follow me" (16:24). The pattern of Jesus life, "great suffering . . . be killed . . . raised" (16:21), is recapitulated in those who "deny themselves and take up their cross and follow me" (16:24). These are the disciples whose minds are "on divine things." Like the crucified and risen Christ, they will find their lives. But they whose minds are "on human things" may "gain the whole world but forfeit their life" (16:25).

Matthew's community was not eager for this sermon, especially in the face of growing persecution and their ever-increasing frustration at the delay of the parousia. Responsive to his listeners' exhausted patience, Matthew reassures them that they will not have to wait forever, that "there are some standing here who will not taste death before they see the Son of Man coming in his kingdom" (16:28). Then at long last their courage and faithfulness in following Jesus will be rewarded (16:27).

Responding to the Text

Today's Gospel can either enslave us or liberate us. It will enslave us if we distort the meaning of the cross as it has often been distorted in the history of the church. There are two major forms of distortion.

The first is to turn the cross into a symbol of violence: the burning cross of the Ku Klux Klan, the cross stamped on brochures urging hatred toward a particular group, the cross that rallies people to holy war. These distorted crosses awaken a profound sadness in those of us who find the cross of Christ a sign of God's love and grace. Surely Christ weeps when any of us, passionately convinced that our cause is divinely inspired, use the cross to justify hatred and violence.

The other major distortion of the cross is perhaps even more insidious because it can appear in the guise of Christian devotion. It is the cross of passivity. We say of someone who endures an abusive marriage or a group that suffers injustice: "It is their cross to bear." The cross becomes a symbol that justifies passive acceptance of wrong. The cross debilitates our energies for rebelling against evil so that we fail to claim the justice and respect that God wills for all people.

The cross of hatred and the cross of passivity are enslaving crosses. And they are a complete distortion of what Christ teaches: "If any want to become my followers, let them deny themselves and take up their cross and follow me" (16:24).

The biblical text guards against the misuse of the cross in several ways. First of all, Jesus does not command us to bear the cross. He does not say, "Take up the cross." He says, "If any *want* to become my followers, *let* them . . . " There is an enormous stress on the freedom of the decision. Not only is it a matter of choice, but once people have indicated they are willing to shoulder this burden, the cross is not imposed by someone else. That is totally different from the cross of violence and the cross of passivity. The cross of violence is forced upon others. The cross of passivity is accepted as an inescapable fate. But neither Jesus nor Matthew preach such pathological behavior.

SURELY CHRIST WEEPS WHEN ANY OF US, PASSIONATELY CONVINCED THAT OUR CAUSE IS DIVINELY INSPIRED, USE THE CROSS TO JUSTIFY HATRED AND VIOLENCE.

Furthermore, once we take up the cross, if that is what we decide to do, then we are called to "follow" Jesus. We are not to stand or sit in a static position crushed by the weight of what we are holding up. We are to move forward following Jesus; and Jesus gives us the example of how to bear the cross. He does not enter into carrying the cross easily: He prays in Gethsemane for its removal (26:39), and he cries out his own sense of abandonment (27:46).

And finally, the ultimate outcome of carrying the cross is not suffering and death, but resurrection and life. Matthew makes this clear by prefacing Jesus' instructions about taking up the cross with what sounds like an early church creed or catechism: "undergo great suffering . . . be killed . . . and on the third day be raised" (16:21). Christ did not carry the cross only to be killed. Beyond Golgotha (27:33) is the "mountain" where the disciples "worshiped" the risen Christ (28:16, 17), and beyond that is the coming of the kingdom (16:27, 28).

If we take up the true cross, not the cross of violence and passivity, then we will not be enslaved but liberated. We will "find" our lives (16:25).

FIFTEENTH SUNDAY
AFTER PENTECOST

SEPTEMBER 5, 1999 / PROPER 18

REVISED COMMON	EPISCOPAL (BCP)	ROMAN CATHOLIC
Exod. 12:1–14	Ezek. 33:7–11	Ezek. 33:7–9
or Ezek. 33:7–11		
Pss. 149; 119:33–40	Ps. 119:33–48	Ps. 95:1–2, 6–7, 8–9
Rom. 13:8–14	Rom. 12:9–21	Rom. 13:8–10
Matt. 18:15–20	Matt. 18:15–20	Matt. 18:15–20

Each reading deals with life in the community of faith. "The whole con-gregation of Israel" receives instruction on keeping the Passover (Exod. 12:3). Ezekiel addresses his words of warning to "the house of Israel" (Ezek. 33:7, 10). Paul summarizes the law for the congregation at Rome and reminds them how the approaching day of the Lord is to influence their interpersonal relationships (Romans 13). The gospel describes a process for reconciliation that depends upon members of the community acting in concert (Matthew 18). Corporate worship, love, and discipline are central to the life of the community of faith in every age.

FIRST READING
EXODUS 12:1–14

Interpreting the Text

The passage reads more like the rubrics of a prayerbook than a piece of historical reporting. In light of the exodus story, the writer reinterprets rituals that were originally connected to an agricultural calendar and to practices common in the ancient near east, such as the slaying of a lamb to ward off any harm that might come to the whole flock (12:4–6). The sacrifice also protected those households whose entrances were marked by the animal's blood (12:7, 13; compare 12:23).

The passage stresses the importance of the entire community keeping the Passover. God tells Moses and Aaron: "Tell the *whole congregation* that on the tenth of this month they are to take a lamb for *each family*, a lamb for *each household*" (12:3). And this is immediately followed with detailed instructions on how to handle the situation "If a household is too small for a whole lamb" (12:4). Keeping Passover is so central to Israel's identity as a community of faith that no member is to be left out.

Responding to the Text

We possess two kinds of memory: short-term memory and long-term memory. Short-term memory often becomes less reliable as we age. We forget to pick up a quart of milk or mail a letter.

But our long-term memory usually persists even when our short-term memory becomes fallible. Pastors encounter this phenomenon when they lead worship services in nursing homes. People who otherwise seem to have wandered from reality will join in the Lord's Prayer or sing all the words of a hymn they have sung from childhood. I think of a woman who was 105 years old. Her short-term memory was gone, but she still could sing every verse of "Jesus, I Have Promised to Serve Thee to the End." Her long-term memory preserved her eternal identity.

What is ritualized and repeated again and again takes deep and enduring root. This is true for communities as well as individuals. Israel marked the beginning of every new year with a ritual meal that reenacted the escape from Egypt. There were thorough instructions about how the congregation was to keep the Passover: slaughtering the lamb at twilight, putting some of the blood on their doorposts, roasting the animal, burning up the leftovers, and eating the meal in clothes appropriate to travel.

> AND WHEN WE SING OUR HYMNS AND CELEBRATE OUR RITUALS, WE STRENGTHEN OUR LONG-TERM MEMORY OF GOD'S GRACIOUSNESS JUST AS THE ISRAELITES DID THROUGH THE PASSOVER.

All of these rubrics helped generation after generation to fix in their long-term memory the story of the Exodus (12:14), reinforcing their identity as a people liberated by God. And when we sing our hymns and celebrate our rituals, we strengthen our long-term memory of God's graciousness just as the Israelites did through the Passover.

EZEKIEL 33:7-11

Interpreting the Text

The reading describes the interlocking relationships among three different parties: the prophet, the house of Israel, and God. The prophet is described as "a sentinel for the house of Israel" (33:7). Ancient towns depended upon sentinels to warn them of attacking enemies. In this passage, however, the role is transformed: Ezekiel is to warn the house of Israel about the impending judgment of God, not for them to defend themselves, but to repent (33:11).

If the prophet fails in his duty, then the resultant destruction will rest as heavily upon him as upon the people he failed to warn (33:8). But if he speaks and the people fail to respond, then they will die and the prophet will live (33:9).

There is a burden on Ezekiel to fulfill his prophetic role, but the people must acknowledge for themselves their wrongdoing (33:10) and "turn back from [their] evil ways" (33:11). If they do, then they will be saved because God is gracious, not vengeful: "I have no pleasure in the death of the wicked" (33:11).

Responding to the Text

Codependence is a word for describing a relationship in which someone becomes dependent upon another person's needing them. There are, for example, parents who do not treat their grown children as adults because they depend upon their offspring depending upon them. They are codependent.

Caring for people in healthy ways enables them to claim as much responsibility for their lives as possible. Nurses encourage patients to do all they can to care for themselves. They do not become codependent on their patients but help them regain capacities that have been temporarily lost.

To avoid becoming codependent, we have to be clear about what we can do for others and what we cannot. Ezekiel and the house of Israel confronted this difficult truth. Ezekiel was obligated to warn the people of God's impending judgment; and if he failed in this responsibility, God would hold him responsible (33:8). But what Ezekiel could not do was take responsibility for the people's repentance. They had to do that for themselves, not blaming previous generations or the prophet or anyone else for their wrongdoing: "*Our* transgressions and *our* sins weigh upon *us*" (33:10). Only if they realized their moral culpability and repented would God be merciful, for God does not take "pleasure in the death of the wicked" (33:11).

People, prophet, and God depend upon one another, but they are not codependent. All have unique responsibilities that no one else can fulfill for them. This principle sustains healthy, morally responsible communities. Instead of looking to cast blame upon others, we acknowledge our own need for repentance and new life.

RESPONSIVE READING
PSALM 149
————————

Interpreting the Text

There seems to be a tension in the psalm between an act of praise that features singing, dancing, and instrumental music (149:1-5), and a call to arms, vengeance, and judgment (149:6-9). However, if the "new song" heralds the new age that follows the exile, then the concluding verses may symbolize the celebration of God's final victory over foreign countries.

Responding to the Text

Many pastors are familiar with the resistance to singing a new hymn during the Sunday worship service. People want the old favorites. Yet the Psalter is filled with references to singing "a new song" (149:1; compare Psalms 33:3; 40:3; 96:1). If today's psalm is postexilic, then it may be that the new circumstances of Israel's situation cannot be adequately expressed by its inherited hymns. "The assembly of the faithful" (149:1) needs a "new song" to welcome the new age that starts with their release from captivity.

PSALM 119:33-40

Interpreting the Text

The entire psalm is a meditation upon the law of God. It reads like a book of religious maxims without a cumulative development of thought or larger narrative structure. The one thing that holds the verses together is an unwavering love of the law, which in today's reading is described with various synonyms: statutes, commandments, decrees, ways, ordinances, and precepts.

Responding to the Text

"Spirituality" has become a buzzword in popular culture. Talk shows often feature people holding forth about new forms of spiritual practice. Students in the seminary where I teach sign up in droves for courses in spirituality. Amidst all this activity, it may be forgotten that one of the most enduring forms of spiritual practice that shaped the life of Israel was to meditate upon the law of God. The object was not simply personal insight, but selfless, moral behavior (119:33, 36), and the righteousness of God that gives "life" (119:40).

SECOND READING
ROMANS 13:8-14

Interpreting the Text

Just as the epistle for the Thirteenth Sunday after Pentecost (Rom. 12:1-8) exhorts us not to be "conformed to this world"—literally "age" in Greek (12:2)—so today's reading urges us to live according to the new age that is about to begin: "The night is far gone, the day is near" (13:12). We are not to postpone living by the gospel until the start of the new age, but we are to live in anticipation of its imminent arrival: "Lay aside the works of darkness and put on the armor of light" (13:12).

Paul summarizes the moral dimensions of the life that conforms to the coming age in statements about love that are resonant with the teaching of Jesus: "The one who loves another has fulfilled the law" and "Love your neighbor as yourself" (13:8, 9).

Paul quotes from the ten commandments, making it clear that the list he gives is not exhaustive (13:9). Paul's use of the law at this point is significant. Although he has argued that the law does not put right our relationship to God, he has affirmed that "the law is holy" (7:13). The law reminds us that love is more than the feeling of affection.

Paul uses the law not as a means of salvation, but as a way of guiding our behavior. Saved by grace, we still need directions for our life together as a community.

Responding to the Text

When I was a child I sometimes put on my father's clothes. Though folded in enormous cuffs, the trousers covered his shoes that flopped on my feet. My hands came down to the elbows in his shirt, his tie dragged on the ground, and his brimmed hat covered my eyes. My parents and I found this very funny, but I also used to say to myself: Some day I will fit in these clothes. I am going to grow up to be like my father.

There was more truth in my childhood playfulness than I could then comprehend. All our lives we try out different fashions and ways of being and acting. Our experimenting extends far beyond the clothes we wear to the kind of people we will be. Paul announces in his letter to Romans a fashion that may not be the most coveted style in the world, but that will never go out of favor in the new age that God is bringing in: "Put on the armor of light" (13:12), "Put on the Lord Jesus Christ" (13:14).

What would it mean to wear "the armor of light" in an age shadowed by racial and ethnic misunderstanding? What kind of actions would make clear that we have "put on the Lord Jesus Christ" in a culture that thrives on self-advancement and greed? The most obvious answer is that we would be loving people. Paul says exactly that, using the word "love" no fewer than five times in three verses (12:8-10).

The difficulty with appealing to love in our age, however, is that our ideas about love are often as sloppy as I was in my father's oversized garments. A former colleague, Jim Ashbrook, used to call it "sloppy agape." When we say we love or do not love somebody we are usually describing our emotional relationship. But for Paul, love is less a feeling than a way of behaving: "Love does no wrong to a neighbor" (13:10). When we act in ways that honor all people, then we grow into the armor of light, then we put on the Lord Jesus Christ.

Gospel

209

FIFTEENTH
SUNDAY
AFTER PENTECOST

SEPTEMBER 5

MATTHEW 18:15-20

Interpreting the Text

The three-stage process that leads to reconciliation or excommunication (18:15-19) is placed between the parable of the lost sheep and a verse that speaks of the presence of Christ (18:20). The parable works against any facile appeal to excommunication (18:17). The gospel is more about finding lost sheep than tossing sheep out (18:13).

The affirmation of Christ's presence is stated in words that echo a rabbinic maxim that claims that the glory of God is present when two or three are gathered to study the Torah. Matthew believes that Jesus has come to fulfill the law and the prophets (5:17), and hence the rabbinic phrasing of 18:20 suggests that praying and studying the teachings of Christ are the necessary conditions for exercising church discipline.

Still another feature built into the passage serves to guard against autocratic judgments. The "church" is mentioned twice (18:15, 17), reminding readers that they are not acting as isolated individuals, but as members of the community, and are therefore responsible to the community.

The process attempts to settle things before they become a major explosion. The first confrontation when someone "sins against you" is to bring it up "when the two of you are alone" (18:15). The church is not to be a gossip mill that airs everybody's faults. Some ancient manuscripts lack the phrase "against you" so that the text reads "If another member of the church sins" (18:15), which suggests that our interest in a fellow Christian's behavior extends beyond what merely has a personal impact on us.

The second stage is introduced by the phrase, "But if you are not listened to" (18:16). It does *not* say "But if the other member does not agree with you." It may be that you are wrong or that the other member's position contains some truth. She or he is not required to agree instantly with you but to listen to you.

The second stage is interesting for the option it offers, "Take one *or* two others along with you" (18:16). This requires considerable sensitivity on your part: Which is necessary in any particular case, one or two? You are not simply to plunge ahead in judgment.

Only after these patient, strenuous steps is the whole church to be involved (18:17), and a final judgment to be rendered.

Responding to the Text

Guilty or innocent? How quickly we answer that question when it is raised about some politician or celebrity. Even if subsequent reporting and a trial conclude that the person is not guilty, the initial report of possible wrongdoing will usually taint or even destroy the individual's reputation. In addition to the injustice to the individual, harm is done to family and associates. Many lives and relationships can be cruelly and unfairly demolished.

But before the church speaks against the media, it needs to look at its own behavior. Talking with hundreds of clergy and lay leaders over the last twenty years, I have heard story after story about "the church grapevine," the tangled network of gossip that spreads rumors about the pastor or the pastor's family or other members of the congregation. And once it starts, neither denial nor proof that things are not as reported can completely erase the suspicion that the accused has acted in some reprehensible manner.

Although the church needs to make discriminating judgments about behavior that is unworthy of Christians, all judgments are to be tempered with an awareness of Christ's love for the lost and are to be guided by the savior who is among us. The process of judgment is to proceed in ways that respect the reputation and humanity of every member, even those who may have acted wrongly.

Matthew's Gospel reveals that all of these issues were alive in his community. In today's reading he lays out a detailed process for dealing with grievances among church members. Consider what would happen to the quality of community life if we all honored his elemental principles, including that the first time a matter is brought up it ought to be only between the individuals involved and only when they are alone (18:15). If we cannot say it to someone's face, that may be a sign that our charge is shaky and not sustainable.

On the other hand, if we are the one who is being accused, then we need to be willing to listen. Not one of us does not do things, either intentionally or unintentionally, that are harmful to others. If someone has the decency to point out how we have been hurtful, let us have the decency to listen with care. We may not end up agreeing, but if we listen as carefully as possible we may be able to clear up the misunderstanding and even apologize if we come to see that we did wrong.

And that is to be the end of it. It is between us "alone." No one else needs to know. No gossip, no innuendo, no ruined reputation, but the regaining of relationship (18:15).

Of course, at times this does not work, and someone really does need to be called to account for behavior that is destructive and wrong. Matthew knows that; yet still he proceeds with caution: The next step is to take "one or two others along with you" (18:16). If that does not work, only then is the matter brought before the church, not via the grapevine, but out in the open: "Tell it to the church" (18:17).

A church that acts like this offers a credible witness to how the gospel transforms our life together. It becomes a sign to the world that there is a more just and compassionate way of making judgments than by rumor and innuendo. It makes clear that the Christian life is not merely a matter of how we live as individuals but as a community.

SIXTEENTH SUNDAY AFTER PENTECOST

SEPTEMBER 12, 1999 / PROPER 19

REVISED COMMON	EPISCOPAL (BCP)	ROMAN CATHOLIC
Exod. 14:19-31	Gen. 50:15-21	Sir. 27:30—28:7
or Gen. 50:15-21		
Ps. 114	Ps. 103	Ps. 103:1-2, 3-4, 9-10,
or Exod. 15:1b-11,		11-12
20-21,		
Ps. 103:(1-7), 8-13		
Rom. 14:1-12	Rom. 14:5-12	Rom. 14:7-9
Matt. 18:21-35	Matt. 18:21-35	Matt. 18:21-35

VERSES THAT PICTURE THE LORD as a furious war deity are balanced by verses about forgiveness and the vast span of God's mercy. Moses sings: "You sent out your fury, it consumed them like stubble" (Exod. 15:7). The Psalmist sings "The Lord is merciful and gracious, slow to anger and abounding in steadfast love" (Ps. 103:8). Furious and merciful, destructive and redemptive, a complex God emerges through these varied readings. How do we assemble from such different pictures our dominant image of God? And does that image empower us to forgive again and again? (Matt. 18:22).

FIRST READING

EXODUS 14:19-31

Interpreting the Text

The phrase "stretched out his hand" occurs three time in this passage (14:21, 26, 27). The word "hand" is often a synecdoche for the power of God as in the song of Moses that follows this scene: "Your right hand, O Lord, shattered the enemy" (Exod. 15:6).

Although Moses is not God, Moses' hand is an expression of God's power. It is the Lord who instructs him, "Stretch out your hand over the sea, so that the water may come back upon the Egyptians, upon their chariots and chariot drivers" (14:26). A dramatic confrontation occurs between the hand that God stretches out and the military hardware of the Egyptians. Pharaoh's hand is no match for the hand of God.

In a similar manner, when Moses stretches out his hand over the sea, it is the Lord who sends the wind to divide the sea (14:21). The action resonates with the story of creation (Gen. 1:2, 9) and underscores how great the power is that protects the escaping slaves and destroys their pursuers.

Responding to the Text

When preachers announce that the topic of their sermon is "Are you saved?" there is usually an assumption that they will be speaking about the need for a personal relationship to God through Jesus Christ. Although that is a vital topic for preachers to address, it is far from the only meaning of salvation in the Bible.

Long before it signified the character of an individual's relationship to God, being "saved" was a social, political reality. In today's reading, the escape of the Hebrew slaves from their masters is summarized by the phrase, "Thus the LORD saved Israel that day from the Egyptians" (14:30). To be no longer the object of forced labor, no longer held and abused by those with power over them, no longer threatened with genocide, to be at long last free, this is the first biblical meaning of being saved.

Therefore, when people ask preachers not to mix politics with salvation, they are in fact asking that preachers abandon one of the major biblical understandings of salvation. God is a God who "saves" people from bondage, that is the meaning of the word in this passage; and it is reinforced by the song of Moses that immediately follows, which is one of the alternative psalms for today (Exod. 15:1b–11). Moses sings how the politically liberating Lord "has become my salvation" because the Lord's "right hand . . . has shattered the enemy" (15:2, 6).

WHEN PEOPLE ASK PREACHERS NOT TO MIX POLITICS WITH SALVATION, THEY ARE IN FACT ASKING THAT PREACHERS ABANDON ONE OF THE MAJOR BIBLICAL UNDERSTANDINGS OF SALVATION.

When preachers speak for the liberation of people from economic and political oppression, they are giving witness to the God who "saved" the Hebrews from slavery.

GENESIS 50:15–21 (alt.)

Interpreting the Text

Joseph responds to his brothers' request for forgiveness with more than tears (50:17). He asks an incisive theological question: "Am I in the place of God?" (50:19). Although Joseph holds a position of authority over his brothers, he, like them, is under the greater authority of God. Joseph is forgiving because he understands that he and his brothers were involved in the work of God, who intended for good what they meant for evil (50:20).

Joseph's theology contrasts with the Egyptians who held their pharaohs to be gods. Joseph's wisdom, coming as it does at the conclusion of Genesis, is a reversal of what happens in the garden at the beginning of the book. There the serpent tempts humanity with the suggestion that eating from the forbidden tree will make us like God (3:5). Joseph does not fall for this temptation, and the result is that the grace of the providential God flows through his words and his actions: "So have no fear; I myself will provide for you and your little ones" (50:21).

Responding to the Text

Few things are more delicious to the human heart than the taste of revenge: to do in the people who did us in, to even the score, to make sure they receive their just deserts.

Surely Joseph must have sometimes felt that way. People who have been violently assaulted relive the terror repeatedly in their dreams. The initial physical reaction to the experience will sweep again through their bodies when something triggers the memory of what was done to them.

Joseph was stripped, thrown into a pit, sold into slavery, and hauled off to Egypt (Gen. 37:17-28). The misery did not end there. He later found himself in jail, unjustly accused (39:6-18). Through all of this, there had to be times when the terror of what his brothers had done returned to him: his robe being ripped from his body, the dark and smell of the pit, the clasp of fetters rubbing raw the skin at his ankles and wrists, the desperation of being torn from his homeland. Would any of us blame Joseph if he took revenge? He would be perfectly justified in saying: "Guards, take my brothers, strip them, put them in chains and lead them away."

That is how Hollywood would end the story. We would call it "wimpy" if the hero's final line before the credits rolled across the screen were: "Am I in the place of God? . . . I will provide for you and your little ones" (50:19, 21).

But that is Joseph's final line, and it comes from the heart of God.

RESPONSIVE READING
PSALM 114

Interpreting the Text

Past and present fuse together in the psalm. It opens as an account of what once happened (114:1). But by the middle of the psalm questions are addressed to the sea and the Jordan as if they are parting before our very eyes

(114:5). The psalmist relives the exodus and the entrance into the Promised Land in the present moment.

Responding to the Text

For many people it is not enough to recall the central events of their history as nothing more than incidents long past and finished. They want to see with their own eyes what happened, and so they reenact great events from the past, often making replicas and period costumes. Through their dramatic involvement they enter the spirit of the past. In a similar manner, the psalmist is not content to recall the exodus but becomes a participant in the drama by calling out to the fleeing waters. Exodus becomes a living reality.

EXODUS 15:1b–11, 20–21 (alt.)

Interpreting the Text

Probably one of the most ancient passages in the Bible, the reading incorporates two different songs: The Song of Moses (15:1b–18) and The Song of Miriam (15:21), which predates that of Moses. The opening words of Moses modify the imperative voice of Miriam's song, suggesting that the writer is expanding and personalizing the more concise ancient tradition.

Responding to the Text

The editors who assembled the book of Exodus picture both Moses and Miriam celebrating the escape from Egypt. A man and a woman sing the same words of divine victory (15:21; compare 15:1b). The editors could have left out the woman's song since it is subsumed in the man's, but they did not. In ways the editors never dreamed, the inclusion of both Miriam and Moses is for our time a reminder that when God liberates people, women and men alike celebrate. Both are called to lead the community's praise.

PSALM 103:(1-7), 8-13

Interpreting the Text

The psalm appears to be postexilic because it draws upon later portions of the book of Isaiah (compare 103:9 and Isa. 57:16; 103:11 and Isa. 55:9). The pain of feeling God's judgment through the exile must have given a special poignancy to the words, "He will not always accuse, nor will he keep his anger forever" (103:9).

Responding to the Text

I have seen over the years in church newsletters and local newspapers a small feature titled "Words to Live By." Today's psalm provides words to live by for Greek Christians who sing it each morning as the day's first prayer. When we feel the world is against us, how comforting it is to recall that God is "slow to anger and abounding in steadfast love" (103:8). And when we are pained by the wrong we have done, it is reassuring to recall how far God removes our transgressions from us (103:12).

SECOND READING
ROMANS 14:1-12

Interpreting the Text

Paul addresses the problem of differences in religious practice that range from what Christians eat (14:2, 3) to what holy days they observe (14:5).

The food issue is more complicated than vegetarians versus meat eaters (14:2). The meat and wine sold in ancient markets had usually been dedicated to pagan deities so that some devout Christians had scruples about consuming them. But others considered such reservations an indication of insufficient faith. Paul is fair-handed and does not come down on one side or the other. He has enough pastoral wisdom to see that Christian practice can take multiple forms and neither group ought to judge the other: "Those who eat must not despise those who abstain, and those who abstain must not pass judgment on those who eat" (14:3).

The essential issue is the integrity with which we practice our devotion to Christ, "Let all be fully convinced in their own minds" (14:5). We are not saved by the form of our tradition but by Christ our Lord, to whom we belong whether we eat meat or not, whether we keep this or that day sacred, whether we live or die.

Paul refuses to allow the intolerance of another's religious practice to obscure the gospel that brings Jew and Gentile together as equals before "the judgment seat of God" (14:10). The church needs to embody the grace of Christ in its community life.

Responding to the Text

I have often heard but have never been able to trace to print this old preacher's saying: "The church is like Noah's ark: if it were not for the storm outside, you couldn't stand the stink inside."

The stink is bad in today's reading from Romans. Church members are arguing over their conflicting religious practices, making judgments against those whose tradition differs from theirs.

At first it may seem a shame that Paul, after having explored the profoundest theological issues (Romans 1–12), is reduced to dealing with ecclesiastical trivia, pietistic minutiae. But upon further reflection, we see that Paul's pastoral admonishment to the groups in conflict is an extension of his theology. All of the sublime things he has said about the grace of Christ Jesus are more than theological hot air, more than the convolutions of an intellect divorced from the messiness of human beings getting on together. Paul's theological claims carry practical consequences for how the church lives as a community of faith. If the church stinks like Noah's ark because of its internal squabbling over devotional practices, then it is not going to be a credible witness to Christ who "died and lived again, so that he might be Lord of both the dead and the living" (14:9).

If people agree with Paul that they are saved by grace rather than law, but then make their religious practices the standard of true faith, they effectively replace grace with a law of their own making and end up where they started! They have gone in a circle: from law to grace to law.

I have encountered this circular process again and again. Christians, claiming to be saved by grace, judge as inadequate the heartfelt prayers and hymns of another. Paul has it right: "Why do you pass judgment on your brother or sister? . . . So then, each of us will be accountable to God" (14:10, 12). If we lived Paul's wisdom, the stink in the church would be much less, and many who are out in the storms of this brutal world might then be glad to enter and find shelter.

GOSPEL

MATTHEW 18:21-35

Interpreting the Text

The passage breaks into two clear sections: an exchange between Peter and Jesus about forgiveness (18:21, 22), and a parable (18:23–35). Matthew has provided a transitional phrase between the two: "For this reason the kingdom of heaven may be compared to a king who wished to settle accounts with his slaves" (18:23). Upon initial reading, Matthew's marriage of the two seems forced. The statement from Jesus to Peter stresses an endless capacity for forgiveness (18:22) while the parable ends with severe judgment (18:34, 35).

Peter opens the exchange with Jesus by asking how often he should forgive "another member of the church" (18:21). Matthew often employs the character of Peter to represent the concerns of the post-Easter church, and that appears to be what is happening here. Matthew wants to speak forcefully to the need for forgiveness, and so he uses his standard formula for stressing the authority of Jesus' teaching, "*I tell you,* seventy-seven times" (18:22; compare 5:18, 20, 26).

"Seventy-seven times" can also be rendered "seventy times seven." Whichever translation is chosen, the intent of the large number is to move beyond keeping track of every right and wrong and to show a forgiving spirit to one another.

The parable, like the exchange between Peter and Jesus, uses exaggeration to drive home its point. A "talent" was more than fifteen years of wages for a common laborer so ten thousand talents would represent over 150,000 years of wages! This is what the slave who is initially released from his debt owed to the king.

By contrast, his fellow slave owed him about a hundred days worth of wages. The exaggerated contrast between the two figures echoes the incomprehensible difference between the forgiveness that God has shown to us and the forgiveness that we are called upon to extend to one another.

Just in case we miss the point, Matthew adds what sounds like his own severe warning: "So my heavenly Father will also do to every one of you, if you do not forgive your brother or sister from your heart" (18:35). The verse rankles with the tone of parents at the end of their patience. Matthew is probably exhausted by church squabbles. But he still gets the gospel right: forgiveness is not a calculable reality but the extension of a gracious spirit to each other from our hearts.

> MATTHEW IS PROBABLY EXHAUSTED BY CHURCH SQUABBLES. BUT HE STILL GETS THE GOSPEL RIGHT: FORGIVENESS IS NOT A CALCULABLE REALITY BUT THE EXTENSION OF A GRACIOUS SPIRIT TO EACH OTHER FROM OUR HEARTS.

Responding to the Text

While I preach on this passage, I hold in my hand a calculator. I need one because I want to figure out precisely how many times I must forgive people who have wronged me. I am willing to follow Jesus' instructions, but I do not intend to offer forgiveness beyond the number of times required of me as a good Christian.

Like Peter in today's reading, I want a number, a limit, a boundary. I want to know what the bottom line is for forgiveness: when have people spent everything in their account with me so I do not have to forgive them any longer?

I begin my calculations with Peter's question: Should I forgive as often as seven times? Seven times! That sounds generous. We usually say, "Three strikes and you're out." There were rabbinical teachings that settled for three times. Peter, then, is being generous: seven is twice the usual allotment plus one extra.

Jesus responds, "Not seven times, but, I tell you, seventy times seven" (18:22 with the variant reading from NRSV). Let me crunch these numbers with my calculator: seven times seventy equals 490, and 490 divided by three equals

163.3333. So I am to forgive 163 times more than the old standard. Or if I start with Peter's generous figure, I am to be seventy times more forgiving than he was willing to be.

I'd better get an account book so I can keep track of these figures. They begin to boggle the mind. Maybe the parable that follows will straighten things out because it also is filled with some very precise calculations.

The parable says that the first servant owed the king ten thousand talents. Now a talent was about fifteen years worth of wages which means the slave owed 150,000 years worth of wages.

If we calculate this in modern terms and allow fifteen dollars per hour after deductions and a forty hour work week, we come up with $600 per week or $31,200 per year, which in 150,000 years would equal forty-six million dollars. Forty-six million dollars! The king forgave him a debt of forty-six million dollars!

What about the second slave? How much did he owe the slave who had just been forgiven a debt of forty-six million dollars? The text says that it was "a hundred denarii" (18:28), which would have been a hundred days in back wages. If once again we figure fifteen dollars per hour, then an eight hour day would be worth $120 or twelve thousand dollars for a hundred days.

The slave who is forgiven a debt of forty-six million dollars refuses to forgive a fellow worker a twelve-thousand dollar debt even after the man promises him, "I will pay you" (18:29). After walking away scot-free from the king, the first slave sends his fellow worker to debtor's prison.

If I could I would hand that slave the calculator and let him see how wretchedly ungrateful he is. But it would do him no good, because what he needs is not a calculator, but a heart opened by the generosity that the king showed to him.

It was wildly extravagant generosity, like the wildly extravagant generosity that God has shown to us in Christ Jesus. No calculator can register the sum of God's grace, no spreadsheet can record the treasure of divine forgiveness. And every one of us has drawn upon that infinite and eternal account. I wonder then why it is so difficult for us to spare the small change of forgiveness for one another.

SEVENTEENTH SUNDAY AFTER PENTECOST

SEPTEMBER 19, 1999 / PROPER 20

REVISED COMMON	EPISCOPAL (BCP)	ROMAN CATHOLIC
Exod. 16:2-15 or Jonah 3:10—4:11	Jonah 3:10—4:11	Isa. 55:6-9
Pss. 105:1-6, 37-45; 145:1-8	Ps. 145	Ps. 145:2-3, 8-9, 17-18
Phil. 1:21-30	Phil. 1:21-27	Phil. 1:20-24, 27
Matt. 20:1-16	Matt. 20:1-16	Matt. 20:1-16

WE DO NOT CONTROL HOW GOD ACTS, and God often surprises and some-times infuriates us. After the escaped slaves, hungering on their journey, complain that it would be better never to have left Egypt, God feeds them in the wilderness (Exodus 16). Jonah is angry that God would forgive a pagan people that the prophet considers to be outside the pale of divine mercy (Jonah 4). And workers who have labored all day grumble when their employer pays those who worked a shorter period the same amount as themselves (Matthew 20). God's mercy is not negotiable on our human terms.

FIRST READING

EXODUS 16:2-15

Interpreting the Text

The Israelites do not complain directly against the Lord, but aim their ire at Moses and Aaron (16:2). Throughout the passage, Moses, with Aaron as his helper, serves the role of an intermediary between God and the people. God never speaks directly to the escaped slaves but always to Moses, who then reports what he has heard. Moses is so essential to understanding God's actions that without him the people cannot even identify the food that God sends them. Upon seeing manna for the first time, they ask "What is it?" (16:15).

The people have been looking back regretfully at what they left behind. They may have been slaves, but at least in Egypt they ate their "fill of bread" (16:3). Moses' role is a priestly one: He is to refocus the direction of their hearts from their former slavery to God: "Draw near to the LORD, for he has heard your complaining" (16:9). It is when they "looked toward the wilderness," the opposite direction from Egypt, that "the glory of the LORD appeared in the cloud" (16:10).

Responding to the Text

When we start any great venture in life, we are often buoyed up by the excitement of escaping what has been burdensome and enslaving. We move to a new part of the country, we take up a new career, we leave behind a destructive addiction, we begin a course of study in a field we know nothing about. At first we feel a sense of release and a rush of energy as we undertake our new venture.

But then another reality asserts itself: the long hard haul through the wilderness. Customs and expectations are different in our new location, the career change brings demands we never foresaw, the body cries out for the substance it is now denied, the field of study challenges our most comfortable beliefs and opinions. We begin to look back with longing hearts at what we left behind. We never before realized how good we had it.

At that moment of regret and exhaustion we are close in spirit to the discouragement of the Israelites. Their stomachs grumbling with hunger, they look back to Egypt convinced it would have been better to die as well-fed slaves than to be killed by hunger in the wilderness (16:3).

God does not instantly feed them upon their first complaint. Two things happen before their hunger is satisfied. First they change direction from looking back toward Egypt to looking toward the wilderness where the glory of the Lord appears (16:10), and second, Moses interprets what manna is (16:15).

God's goodness is not always self-apparent, especially if we have spent our energies complaining about the wilderness.

GOD'S GOODNESS IS NOT ALWAYS SELF-APPARENT, ESPECIALLY IF WE HAVE SPENT OUR ENERGIES COMPLAINING ABOUT THE WILDERNESS.

JONAH 3:10—4:11 (BCP)

Interpreting the Text

Is God too gracious? The reading presents a theological debate on the question through a scene that pits Jonah, the recalcitrant prophet, against the merciful God. Whereas most of the biblical prophets faced audiences hostile to their message, Jonah is fabulously successful. He brings an entire city to repentance, including the animals (3:5-9)! But instead of celebrating, Jonah is in a foul mood and waits to see if the penitents will revert to their evil ways (4:5).

There was an actual Assyrian city by the name of Nineveh, but in this biblical parable the city becomes more a symbol than a site. It represents the enemies of Israel who have become a byword for evil and godlessness. Jonah never wanted to see them repent because he knew God was gracious (4:2). He resents God's using him for purposes that he does not consider worthy of the God of justice, and his resentment turns to petulance over the withering of a castor bean plant (4:6-8), which God then uses to demonstrate the narrowness of Jonah's faith (4:9-11).

Responding to the Text

It is a shame that our attentions are usually focused on Jonah's underwater taxi ride (1:17). I have often wondered whether our concentration on Jonah's being swallowed by a gigantic sea creature and the many debates I have heard whether it were a whale or a great fish are not our way of avoiding the painful conclusion of the book. It is painful because it reveals something smallhearted not only about postexilic Israel to whom the book was addressed, but also about ourselves and the worst of our religious bigotry.

The Israelites had been through a terrifying national experience, their sacred temple destroyed, their leading citizens exiled. Jonah in this parable gives expression to their bitterness and their desire for a God of justice and vengeance, a God who belongs exclusively to them and who does not waste divine energies seeking the repentance of enemies who are not worth one iota of mercy.

Jonah appears ridiculous in the final scene. He pouts over the death of a castor bean plant, and when God asks, "Is it right for you to be angry about the bush?" he answers like a petulant child who has blown everything out of proportion, "Yes, angry enough to die" (4:9). Even though the writer of the parable is using caricature, the tone of this strikes me as close to the bone: We religious people can become this ingrown and constricted, this upset with the gracious God.

By the end of the book we do not know if Jonah has been won over by God's argument (4:11). But why worry about Jonah, what about ourselves?

RESPONSIVE READING
PSALM 105:1-6, 37-45

Interpreting the Text

The opening call to worship (105:1-6) leads to a recital of the great deeds that God has done in the history of Israel (105:7-45). These "wonderful works" (105:2) include the way God provided food and water for the Israelites in the wilderness (105:40-41). The psalmist omits any mention of the people's grumbling and yearning for Egypt (compare Exod. 16:2-15).

Responding to the Text

Our view of history, including the central events of the Bible, depends upon whose account we read. If we turn to the book of Exodus, we learn that the people wished they had never left Egypt; but when we turn to the psalmist, we get an idealized version: "They asked, and he brought quails, and gave them food in abundance" (105:40). We need both versions: Exodus to remind us of our proclivity to grumble, the Psalm to remind us of the unqualified joy of what God did.

PSALM 145:1-8

Interpreting the Text

Words of adoration tumble out of the psalmist one after another, an impetuous flowing stream of worship that cannot be stopped or diverted: *extol, bless, praise, laud, declare, proclaimed, celebrate,* and *sing.* And the source and goal of these actions is God, who is characterized by *glorious splendor, wondrous works, awesome deeds, abundant goodness,* and *righteousness.*

Responding to the Text

I recall when I came through a life-saving operation and saw my wife for the first time after the surgery. My heart broke into a rhapsody of irrepressible thanksgiving and praise to God: "Thank you, God, thank you, God, thank you, God." Parents have told me of similar experiences upon looking at their first child. These times of boundless, unquestioning, ecstatic praise bring us as close to the core of existence as we ever get. This is what we were created for: "Every day I will bless you, and praise your name forever and ever" (145:2).

SECOND READING

PHILIPPIANS 1:21-30

Interpreting the Text

Paul claims that he would rather die than live so that he might "be with Christ, for that is far better" (1:23). We can partially explain Paul's statement by considering his imprisonment and struggle (1:12, 30). But whatever historical factors we use to understand Paul's desire for death, it remains an astonishing statement of faith. The apostle is convinced that when he dies he will be with Christ, and that assurance emboldens his vision of how the Philippians ought to keep the faith (1:27-30).

Paul sees no reason for the Philippians to be "intimidated" by opponents (1:28). If they live "in a manner worthy of the gospel of Christ," it will be the "destruction" of their opponents because it will then be apparent that there is no way of making the Philippians back down from their faith (1:27, 28).

Paul's statement about his own desire to be with Christ adds force to his admonition to the Philippians. For if they, like him, are convinced that death brings a better state, then they will not fold in the face of any hostile threat.

Paul is writing to people who live in a city with cults dedicated to a wide range of gods and goddesses. Paul's personal statement serves, then, not only to strengthen the courage of the Philippians but also to remind them that they belong forever to Christ and not to any of the other deities whose shrines fill the city.

Responding to the Text

The cruise ship plows through a placid sea, passing an island of pure white sand shaded with palm trees. The camera focuses in on the deck where people are sunning and swimming in the ship's outdoor pool. A rumba begins and the camera focuses on another deck where svelte women and muscular men are dancing and drinking from tall glasses decorated with miniature umbrellas. A beautiful woman walks to center camera and announces "Now this is living!" The toll-free number for the cruise line flashes over the scene and the commercial ends.

Only a curmudgeon would begrudge people the joy of their dream vacation. We all need fantasies of delight, but with them comes the temptation to believe, "Now *this* is living"? It is living of a very limited sort, a surfeit of pleasure that after a week begins to pale. "It is good to be home again," we say as, tanned and a little heavier, we put our bags down in the hallway.

What of the life to which we return? What is the secret of a day-to-day existence that would make us say, "Now *this* is living." There is no glitzy commercial that can give us that heart-deep vitality for which we yearn. It requires something profounder, including a willingness to put aside our fantasies of delight and to face the hard realities of this world, its brutality and intolerance, the kind of authoritarianism that landed Paul the apostle in prison, where he wrote his letter to the Philippians.

What Paul told them is astounding: "For to me living is Christ and dying is gain" (1:21). Christ is so real to Paul that death is no threat to him, and therefore, he is freed truly to live, to stand for what he believes, and to encourage the Philippians to do the same. When "living is Christ," our daily deeds and words become an expression of the confidence that Paul felt, even while he was incarcerated in a Roman prison. "Now *this* is living."

GOSPEL

MATTHEW 20:1-16

Interpreting the Text

Because the parable often strikes readers as blatantly unfair, it is helpful to consider its context before turning to the story itself.

Matthew frames the parable with nearly identical words, making clear that the story is about something greater than employment practices (19:30; compare 20:16). Using the exaggeration and surprise typical of Jesus' authentic parables, the story speaks to the concerns that immediately precede it and that are alive in Matthew's community (19:27-30). People have made enormous sacrifices to follow Jesus, and now there are newcomers, including the Gentiles, who appear in the eyes of the longtime disciples to be Johnny-come-latelies. Are they to have the same blessings, the same respect in the church, and the same status in the reign of God as those who have sacrificed so much for so long? It is this typical human concern to get one's fair share that drives Peter's question: "Look, we have left everything and followed you. What then will we have?" (19:27).

Matthew follows the parable with his third prediction of the passion (20:17-19). If church members are huffy about whether or not they will get their due, let them remember what Christ unjustly endured.

In addition to these contextual factors, the parable carries within itself many details vital to its interpretation. It is only with the first group of laborers that the landowner settles on a specific wage (20:2). Notice how this is put, "After agreeing with the laborers." It sounds as though they had their say before they worked.

In the case of all the other groups, the arrangements are completely different. The landowner promises no fixed sum but only "whatever is right," and the laborers do not negotiate but simply go: "So they went" (20:4).

These details become significant at the end of the parable because they back up the landowner's claim that he is cheating no one but only acting generously toward those lately hired (20:13-15). The landowner personally addresses the grumbling laborers as "Friend," suggesting a special relationship to them.

This is what "the kingdom of heaven is like" (20:1): God, without breaking agreements with the friends who came early to the cause, will be generous to all, including the latecomers. The reign of God transforms our ideas of "whatever is right" (20:4) with a graciousness that confounds our usual expectations.

Responding to the Text

The landowner pays the same amount to those who worked an hour as those who worked all day. How do you respond? I find it all depends on what role I take in the story.

For now, assume that you are among the workers hired at dawn. You have negotiated with the landowner for the standard full day's wage, and you are hard at work before the sun is far above the horizon. It will be a long day, but you have the satisfaction of knowing that you will be paid fairly at day's end.

A little after nine o'clock, more workers arrive. Then still more come at noon, and over lunch you hear that the landowner has promised to pay them "whatever is right." Since they came at noon and you started in the morning, you figure they will get a half-day's wage. Still more workers show up at three and then at five, just an hour before quitting time. Looking at those pitiful latecomers, you are glad that you got down to the marketplace early so you could earn a full day's wage. An hour's pay is not enough to cover tonight's supper let alone tomorrow's breakfast.

Finally, the blessed moment comes, the landowner's manager shows up at the edge of the vineyard and declares it is quitting time. All the workers get in line to receive their wages. At first it seems unfair that you, who have labored all day in the sun, should have to wait at the end of the pay queue while those who more recently arrived are immediately taken care of. But then you see the manager giving them a full day's wage. They are all smiles and laughter, slapping each other's shoulders while they shake their heads in disbelief. You find their happiness infectious because you figure: If they received a full day's wage for an hour's work, then maybe you will get a week's wage for a day's work.

As you come up to receive your pay, you picture yourself enjoying a fine bottle of wine and a choice cut of lamb for your supper with some extra wood in the stove to keep off the night's chill. You put out your hand and receive exactly one day's wage. You, along with all of the others who have labored since morning, are enraged. The manager cowers before you and explains he is only acting according to instructions and sends you to sort out things with the landowner, whose words of explanation leave you baffled and feeling unfairly treated. You came for justice, and he speaks of generosity.

Put the parable on stop action, and rewind the story line to five o'clock. Now take the role of one who is to be last hired.

You are in the marketplace dreading the coming of night because you have not one spare cent for bread or milk or a stick of wood for the stove. Just when you are ready to give up, you are hired, even though there is only an hour of working time left in the day. You go to the vineyard, figuring that an hour's pay may mean the difference between fainting from hunger and having enough energy to try again tomorrow. An hour later you are in line waiting for the meager sum you earned, when the manager gives you a full day's pay. Oh, that splendid landowner! How generous, how generous! Thank God, thank God!

If changing roles can make that much difference in understanding the parable, think of what it might mean for how you understand your life.

Recommended Works
Although I have not footnoted references, I am deeply indebted to the following books, which not only supplied exegetical details but also stimulated my imagination for the "Responding to the Text" sections.

Achtemeier, Paul J., editor. *Harper's Bible Dictionary.* San Francisco: HarperSanFrancisco, 1985. Useful for looking up the significance of terms, names, and characters. These often will supply preachers with ideas that are not covered by commentaries.

Apostolos-Cappadona, Diane. *Dictionary of Christian Art.* New York: Continuum, 1995. A resource for probing how biblical words and stories have inspired the imaginative and symbolic work of artists.

Bellah, Robert N. and company. *Habits of the Heart: Individualism and Commitment in American Life.* Berkeley: University of California Press, 1985. Provides an analysis of American individualism that alerts us to the dangers of losing the corporate dimensions of the biblical witness.

The Bible and Culture Collective. *The Postmodern Bible.* New Haven: Yale Univ. Press, 1995. Essays that summarize a wide spectrum of approaches to the interpretation of the Bible. Although not directed at preachers, the book may challenge them to fresh interpretations of scripture.

Brown, Raymond E. *The Community of the Beloved Disciple.* New York: Paulist Press, 1979. Crucial work on John that presents an ecclesial understanding of the fourth gospel.

Cross, F. L., and Livingston, E. A. *The Oxford Dictionary of the Christian Church, Second Edition, Revised.* Oxford: Oxford Univ. Press, 1985. Useful to tracing the post-biblical development of scriptural ideas, such as the concepts of Trinity, church, and liturgy.

The Jewish Museum. *Chagall and the Bible.* New York: Universe Books, 1987. A collection of etchings by one of the greatest artists of the twentieth century. Studying these haunting pictures may especially inspire preachers who want to work on the patriarchal sagas of Genesis.

Keel, Othmar. *The Symbolism of the Biblical World: Ancient Near Eastern Iconography and the Book of Psalms.* New York: Seabury, 1978. The line drawings, lifted from archeological findings, enable preachers to visualize the worldview of the psalmists.

Mays, James L., editor. *Harper's Bible Commentary.* San Francisco: HarperSanFrancisco, 1988. Outstanding one-volume commentary for preachers. The exegesis of Romans is particular useful for this season of lectionary readings.

Meeks, Wayne A. *The First Urban Christians: The Social World of the Apostle Paul.* New Haven: Yale Univ. Press, 1983. Places Paul's letters in a social context and opens a way of developing sermons that deal not with the text alone, but with the conversation between the text and Paul's audience.

Meeks, Wayne A., editor. *The Harper Collins Study Bible, NRSV.* New York: HarperCollins Publishers, 1993. The best study Bible I used. The introductions to each book and the footnotes provide a wealth of material for preachers. It is worth reading every note and cross-reference in the gospel of Matthew. They supply a wealth of preaching ideas.

Metz, Johann Baptist. *Faith in History & Society: Toward a Practical Fundamental Theology.* New York: Seabury, 1980. A work of theology that can make preachers more attentive to how they draw upon the past to deal with the present.

Newsom, Carol A., and Ringe, Sharon H., editors. *The Women's Bible Commentary.* Louisville: Westminster/John Knox Press, 1992. This book provides scriptural perspectives that for too long have gone ignored. Very helpful in avoiding the sexism in the pulpit.

Weems, Renita J. *Just a Sister Away.* San Diego: LuraMedia, 1988. Excellent for probing the deeper personal and interpersonal dimensions of biblical texts. I drew upon it in considering Mary and the Magnificat.

Winter, Miriam Therese. *WomanWord: A Feminist Lectionary and Psalter, Women of the New Testament.* New York: Crossroad, 1990. A work that expands our appreciation for the experience of women in the New Testament. It models for preachers new forms of prayer and proclamation.

EIGHTEENTH SUNDAY
AFTER PENTECOST

SEPTEMBER 26, 1999 / PROPER 21

REVISED COMMON	EPISCOPAL (BCP)	ROMAN CATHOLIC
Exod. 17:1-7	Ezek. 18:1-4, 25-32	Ezek. 18:25-28
or Ezek. 18:1-4, 25-32		
Pss. 78:1-4, 12-16;	Ps. 25:1-14	Ps. 125:4-5, 6-7, 8-9
25:1-9		
Phil. 2:1-13	Phil. 2:1-13	Phil. 2:1-11 or 2:1-5
Matt. 21:23-32	Matt. 21:28-32	Matt. 21:28-32

FIRST READING
EXODUS 17:1-7

Interpreting the Text

The story of Moses bringing water from the rock focuses more on Israel's lack of faith than on the power of Yahweh that is manifested through Moses. In v. 2 Moses interprets the people's quarrel with him as an action that also puts Yahweh under examination. When the people renewed their murmuring and accused Moses of bringing death through the Exodus, instead of liberation and life, Moses interceded with Yahweh. His prayer in v. 4 concentrates on his own safety ("they are ready to stone me!") and not on the people's thirst. Yahweh promises a miracle of water from the rock, and this will be accomplished by his own presence at the holy mountain Horeb and through the agency of Moses. In performing the miracle, Moses uses the same staff with which he had struck the Nile (7:20), and he is accompanied by representatives of the people's leadership, that is, the elders of Israel.

The miracle itself is reported very tersely: "Moses did so." But Moses underscores the people's quarrel with himself and their testing of God (v. 2) by naming the site of this miracle Massah (testing) and Meribah (quarreling). The pericope ends with the people's jarring question: Is the LORD among us or not?

Responding to the Text

God provides for our basic needs, such as thirst, and these providential actions come from the same hand that accomplished our salvation. There is continuity between the God of the Exodus and the God who gives a thirsty people water, and between the God of Calvary and the God who addresses the economic, physical, and social struggles of our lives. The gospel is God's good news for all of our bad situations. The little crises of our daily life are where we need and perceive the power of God. Good preaching needs to move beyond surface symptoms to deeper theological problems, and it needs to turn confessions of God's deeds in the past into sources of power relevant to individuals and the church today.

The writer of this pericope shows the deeper malady that lies behind human complaining. It is surprising that the Israelites seem to have lost confidence in Moses even before they came to Mount Sinai, only a few weeks into a forty-year journey. Once trust dissolves in human relationships, even good deeds are seen in the worst possible light. The people claimed that the result of the Exodus, if not its purpose, was to kill them. But their contending with Moses was in the final analysis a quarrel with God and God's leadership. Every sin, finally, is a violation of the first commandment. The people failed to draw the proper inferences from the liberation they had just experienced. St. Paul saw the action of God through Christ as directly relevant to the challenges faced by his followers and himself: "If God is for us, who is against us? He who did not withhold his own Son, but gave him up for all of us, will he not with him also give us everything else?" (Rom. 8:31-32).

The good news in Exodus 17 is that despite the arrogant question of the people, God indeed was standing there on the rock at Horeb. Real leadership—of Moses and the elders, and of preachers today—is the ability to see beyond the complaints to the divine solution, and the ability to affirm God's presence in our troubles in a convincing way.

EZEKIEL 18:1-4, 25-32 (alt.)

Interpreting the Text

Ezekiel 18 is not the beginning of the idea of individualism, as many believe. Rather, it asserts that people cannot justify their failure to repent by claiming that they are limited in their faith possibilities by the deeds of previous generations (vv. 5-20) or by their own previous history of sinning (vv. 21-29). The proverb uttered by the prophet's opponents in v. 2, on the other hand, argued that the events experienced by Judah in exile were the results of the sins of a previous generation. Yahweh asserts that sinners die because of their own sins.

The controversy in vv. 25-32 centers on "fairness." Ezekiel's opponents claimed that Yahweh was unfair, but the oracle of Yahweh reverses the charge. Past righteousness will not spare present sinners from punishment, nor does past sinfulness make repentance impossible. God's "fairness" is shown in the call for repentance delivered by Ezekiel. Yahweh calls and invites people to life, that is, to existence in his presence. When backsliding to death and repenting to life are the real alternatives, the house of Israel's failure to repent is hard to comprehend. Because repentance is the goal of this chapter, the new heart and spirit are described as human achievements. Elsewhere in Ezekiel, where the emphasis is more theocentric, the new heart and spirit are identified as gifts of Yahweh (11:19; 36:26).

Responding to the Text

Two common responses to sin are discussed by Ezekiel. One response is to deny our own sin and to blame our troubles on our parents or other forebears. "Don't blame me for racism or pollution of the environment!" A second response is to give up on any change of improvement and claim we are trapped by our own past. "We've developed bad habits and we cannot break them!" God's call for repentance also conveys the promise that repentance is possible.

Ezekiel argues that the people are unfair in their complaints and that God's "fairness" comes in the command/promise to get a new heart and a new spirit. "Fairness" has an ironic ring here. We usually speak in such contexts about God's righteousness or about God's grace triumphing over God's wrath. God's "fairness" is anything but fair. It goes way beyond what God owes us; it contradicts God's anger and sorrow over our sin. In understating God's kindness to us, Ezekiel manages to highlight it. The paradox between our seeking a new heart and God giving a new heart is echoed in Paul: "Work out your own salvation with fear and trembling; for it is God who is at work in you" (Phil. 2:12-13).

RESPONSIVE READING
PSALM 78:1-4, 12-16

Interpreting the Text

This psalm rehearses God's many benefactions, culminating in the choice of Jerusalem and David, and the people's repeated rebellions. In the first four verses, a wisdom teacher invites readers to reflect on the deeds of Yahweh and pass their significance on to the next generation. In the second paragraph excerpted from the psalm, the poet alludes to acts of providence for Israel: liberation through the plagues in Egypt (v. 12), the crossing of the Reed Sea (v. 13), God's guidance through a pillar of cloud and fire (v. 14), and his miraculous provision of water (vv. 15-16). The rebellion of the people follows in vv. 17-31.

Responding to the Text

These brief excerpts from a very long psalm might lead to a homiletical focus on v. 4, where those who recite the psalm pledge to tell the coming generation about the LORD's glorious deeds. Parents in particular and the church in general need to take much more seriously the task and challenge of Christian education.

But these excerpts from Psalm 78 are also disturbing because they leave out one of the central themes of the psalm—the people's rebellion, their sin, and their testing of God. Israel in the wilderness cut God no slack: "OK you provided water; can you also give bread?" The great recital of God's grace must be seen in the context of and as a response to Israel's repeated failure. God in the abstract is not God—for them or for us.

PSALM 25:1-14 (BCP) (RC alt.)

Interpreting the Text

This acrostic psalm is a lament of an individual, whose special concern is his or her sins. The psalmist provides reasons for God to forgive because of his or her own trust (vv. 1-2, 15, 20), because of God's pity for the psalmist (vv. 16-18), and because of God's characteristics (a saving God, v. 5; mercy and steadfast love, v. 6; goodness, v. 7; God's name, v. 11). The psalmist is beset by enemies (vv. 2 and 19) and, therefore, also prays for protection. By asking for instruction in God's ways or paths, the psalmist commits to an obedient life (vv. 4-5). The psalmist concludes these petitions with a prayer for the redemption of the entire community (v. 22; cf. 14:7; 28:9; 130:7; 131:3).

SECOND READING
PHILIPPIANS 2:1-13

Interpreting the Text

On the basis of qualities that characterize life in Christ (v. 1), Paul admonishes the Philippians to practice unity and to demonstrate selfless love toward one another (vv. 2-3). Fellowship among Christians is based on Christ's consoling love for them and a common participation in the eschatological gift of the Spirit (v. 1). The humility of the Philippians should primarily be toward one another, not so much toward all people. Verse 5 can mean that Christians are to model themselves after Christ's humble example, or, more likely, it means that humility is appropriate for Christians because of their existence *in* Christ Jesus.

The following hymn celebrates the drama of redemption and makes known to the Philippians how they came to be "in Christ."

Most scholars today believe that vv. 6-11 are a pre-Pauline hymn. Paul quotes the hymn to summon the Philippians to live the selfless attitude that should characterize them on the basis of their being "in Christ." Verses 6-8 describe Christ's abasement and vv. 9-11 his exaltation. Christ Jesus did not use his Godlike status—at the beginning he was at God's side, like wisdom in Proverbs 8—for purely selfish ends, but freely rendered himself powerless. The paradox is that the Godlike and, therefore, immortal one took on human existence and even human mortality. The mention of "death on a cross" (v. 8) may be Paul's specific addition to this hymn, but it is appropriate to the position of slave that Christ Jesus freely chose. Nevertheless, God vindicated the one who exemplified obedience by exalting him and giving him the name "Lord," a name that is above all names. Jesus now deserves to be honored as universal Lord, and the universality of this claim is emphasized by the mention of a three-story universe that offers acclaim—heaven, earth, and the region below the earth. The entire cosmos is brought under the Lordship of Christ. The confession "Jesus is Lord" is also attested elsewhere in Paul's letters (1 Cor. 12:3; Rom. 10:9).

Paul calls for unity and humility on the basis of the Philippians' previous obedience to himself, an obedience that was more clear when he was absent than even when he was present (v. 12). Their "salvation" in v. 12 refers to the restoration to wholeness of a church that was full of rivalries and divisions. God's presence with them compensates for Paul's absence, and God's gracious assistance (his good pleasure) enables the Philippians to desire and to actively seek unity and humility.

Responding to the Text

We live in a consumerist society, and we are plagued by a disease that has been described as "Affluenza: I shop, therefore, I am." A few years ago I visited a local megachurch whose message could be summed up in the words, "It's not over until I win." Our society and to a certain degree our churches are also racked by divisions and by balkanization into like-minded groups.

Paul's invitation to the Philippians invites them—and us!—to an entirely different lifestyle marked by unity, humility, and selfless love. It is not a lifestyle precipitated by a fear of getting caught. Rather, the obedience of the Philippians was better with Paul absent than with him present. Such transformed relationships are possible for those who are *in* Christ.

PAUL'S INVITATION TO THE PHILIPPIANS INVITES THEM—AND US!—TO AN ENTIRELY DIFFERENT LIFESTYLE MARKED BY UNITY, HUMILITY, AND SELFLESS LOVE.

We come to be *in* Christ through our baptism, but the power behind that sacrament lies in the radical obedience of Jesus who humbled himself to the point of death. This radical obedience was followed by God's equally radical exaltation of Jesus, just as the radical trust demonstrated in Jesus' death led the centurion to recognize him as God's Son (Mark 15:39). Good news accompanies this radical call for humility and unity: God is at work in you, enabling you both to will and to work for his good pleasure.

GOSPEL

MATTHEW 21:23-32

Interpreting the Text

Matthew 21:23 through 22:46 contains five controversy stories, and all are part of the lectionary for this season of the church year, except for 22:23-33. In vv. 23-27 Matthew follows Mark 11:27-33 closely (cf. also Luke 20:1-8). The religious and civil leaders of the day (the chief priests and elders of the people) challenged the authority of Jesus to do "these things." This may refer to his teaching, his entry into the city, his cleansing of the temple, his healing, or his receiving praise from the crowds. Jesus countered the leaders' question with a question of his own, a method often used in the Talmud.

"Authority" is an important word in Matthew. In 7:29 the evangelist notes that Jesus taught with authority, while the healing of the paralytic in 9:6 demonstrated that the Son of Man has authority on earth to forgive sins. In 10:1 Jesus gave his disciples authority over evil spirits. The authority given to the resurrected Jesus is the basis for his issuance of the Great Commission to make disciples of all nations and to baptize them (28:16-20). Authority, therefore, usually refers to helping or saving actions rather than to any kind of domination.

Jesus' question about the baptism of John and his prophetic authority put the leaders in a dilemma. The Old Testament had offered criteria for choosing between true and false prophets (Deut. 13:1-5), but these criteria often proved to be very difficult to apply in concrete cases (Jer. 29:21-31). If the leaders would say that John's baptism had a divine mandate, they could not explain why they had not believed John. If they would belittle his baptism by saying it came only from a human origin, they would stir up bitterness among the common people who considered John a prophet. By answering "We do not know" they exposed their own incapacity in religious matters. This controversy story assumes that because the leaders could not discern who John was, they were not able to discern who Jesus is. The refusal of Jesus to answer them leads the reader to conclude that Jesus did have authority to do "these things."

The parable in vv. 28-32, which is a midrashic commentary on vv. 23-27, also poses a dilemma. Who is more obedient: a son who says he will not work in a vineyard, but then does, or a son who says he will work, but then does not? Obedient faith in Matthew is the test for fidelity, and Luke's story of the prodigal son also describes a son who first rebels and then obeys (15:11-32). Tax collectors and prostitutes, though they were public sinners, acknowledged the justice of God and were baptized by John (Luke 7:29-30). They were rebellious children who later believed. Jesus was known as a friend of tax collectors and sinners and had table fellowship with them (9:10-11; 10:3; 11:19; 18:17). The religious leaders of the day publicly said yes to God, but denied that faith by their disobedience, which continued even after they saw the repentance of the tax collectors and prostitutes. John's way of righteousness (v. 32) was the way leading to true righteousness, that is, the kingdom.

Responding to the Text

Many people have problems with "authority figures," or they do not know how to handle the exercise of authority even when it is appropriate. Authority figures can easily abuse their status, but everyone knows that without proper authority the body politic—or the church for that matter—would dissolve into chaos. People with authority hang-ups may never have resolved the problem of growing up and the proper differentiation and independence children need to gain in regard to their parents. Sometimes people who protest most about misuse of authority do not have the foggiest idea of how to use authority when their turn to use authority comes.

Jesus poses a dilemma to the chief priests and elders so that he would not get caught in their trap about the source of his authority. There is no question in the evangelist's mind, however, that Jesus indeed had authority to do "these things," the great miracles that have punctuated the immediately preceding chapters. Authority for Jesus meant, among other things, authority to forgive sins or authority to send his followers out in a worldwide mission. One of the prayers of the church notes that God's almighty power—his authority!—is known chiefly in his showing mercy and pity.

The chief priests and elders came up with a quick response to the second puzzle Jesus posed (v. 31). Clearly those who refused to work but later changed their mind were more faithful than those who merely said they would work, but in fact did nothing. Obedient faith is the real litmus test for fidelity. John called for righteousness and repentance, and the public sinners of his day, the tax collectors and prostitutes, believed what he said about God's inbreaking kingdom and repented. The religious leaders did not believe John, nor were they impressed at his impact on the public sinners.

OBEDIENT FAITH IS THE REAL LITMUS TEST FOR FIDELITY.

Effective preaching on this text requires the preacher and the hearers to identify with both sides in this dilemma. The respectable people of the church may be more impressed with their own commitment than they are with God's generosity. Their relative "goodness" may deafen them to God's call to repentance. Our ability to play the role of repentant public sinners may be directly related to our openness to seeing repentance and fidelity in those who are not so easily classified as respectable, or whose lifestyle seems to make them inferior to us. Before we can understand ourselves as beggars before God we must be willing to extend God's generous welcome to all sorts and conditions of people. That is often easier to do in the abstract than in the concrete.

Larry R. was my advisee at the seminary twenty-five years ago. He quit after the first month, finding no meaning in the academic study of theology. At the time, I was also serving as an interim pastor at an inner-city congregation, where Larry and his spouse continued to attend. Each Sunday they would bring to church someone they had picked up at the bus station, or someone who had hopped a box car and happened to drop off in our city. Some of his guests were beggars; many of them smelled. Larry said no to seminary but yes to God's call. He and his spouse did not approach these strangers with criticism or defensiveness; somehow they both had a credibility with them I could never achieve. I was a religious leader; the guests of Larry were tax collectors and prostitutes—sometimes literally. The memory of Larry never lets me hear this text comfortably.

NINETEENTH SUNDAY AFTER PENTECOST

OCTOBER 3, 1999 / PROPER 22

REVISED COMMON	EPISCOPAL (BCP)	ROMAN CATHOLIC
Exod. 20:1-4, 7-9, 12-20;	Isa. 5:1-7	Isa. 5:1-7
or Isa. 5:1-7		
Pss. 19; 80:7-15	Ps. 80	Ps. 80:9, 12, 13-14, 15-16, 19-20
Phil. 3:4b-14	Phil. 3:14-21	Phil. 4:6-9
Matt. 21:33-46	Matt. 21:33-43	Matt. 21:33-43

FIRST READING
EXODUS 20:1-4, 7-9, 12-20

Interpreting the Text

What makes the Decalog unique is not the specific ethical principles it enunciates, many of which are supported by people of goodwill everywhere. Rather, these commandments are special because they are given by the one who delivered the people who are to keep them from slavery in Egypt and so created a special relationship with them. This relationship is exclusive and all comprehensive. Anything people fear, love, and trust above anything else is their God, their idol. Eight of the Ten Commandments prohibit specific misdeeds, but thereby leave most of life open for responsible freedom. The two positive commandments underscore issues that are central to Israel's identity. Keeping the Sabbath day was a way of saying yes to God in a countercultural fashion since many of Israel's neighbors did not keep the Sabbath. The command to honor parents, like all the rest of the commandments, is addressed primarily to adults. This commandment refers not only to children's obedience to parents, but much more to the obligation all of us have to honor and care for the elderly, especially those who are no longer of a financial benefit to us.

Responding to the Text

The battle over the role of the Ten Commandments in our public life is badly misplaced, not so much because of constitutional issues, but because these commandments are instructions addressed to insiders. They speak to Israelites who worship the God of the Exodus or to Christians who are already *in* Christ. They are not some kind of club to intimidate the unwashed public into obedience. Their unique blend of categorically ruling out certain far-out behaviors like murder and adultery while inviting those addressed to live all of life in fidelity to God and neighbor means that they should not be trivialized into the lowest common denominator of ethical behavior.

The words of Jesus go beyond the original intention of the Decalog, but they do so in helpful ways. A tiny percent of people ever commit murder, but almost all of us hate or intensely dislike someone. Jesus identifies the real and potential violence in such feelings and says that anyone who hates sister or brother is a murderer. Adultery is somewhat more common, unfortunately also among Christians, but Jesus warns that anyone who looks with lust at someone other than spouse, who treats someone else as a sexual object, has already committed adultery. Our parents' generation interpreted this commandment in a pietistic way—well and good, I suppose, but sometimes to the detriment of seeing the wholesomeness of our sexuality. The sin of our generation, perhaps, is to turn sex into a commodity and to seriously loosen its inevitable connection to fidelity. The words of Jesus help us identify what love of God and love of neighbor might mean in regard to both violence and sexuality.

SECOND READING
ISAIAH 5:1-7

Interpreting the Text

This song begins by describing a lover's unrequited love for a vineyard. The reference could be to the relationship between a man and a woman or between a farmer and one of his crops. Despite constant and thorough attention by the lover, the vineyard yielded only bad grapes. Beginning with v. 3, the lover, now clearly to be identified with Yahweh, addresses the vineyard, now identified as the house of Israel and the people of Judah. Verse 3 calls upon the people of Jerusalem and Judah to acknowledge God's faithful actions in v. 2 and thereby condemn their own behavior (cf. 2 Sam. 12:1-12). God announces punishments in vv. 5-6, still using metaphors appropriate to the parable, but also clearly referring to an enemy's military attack on the land. Rainfall will also cease because of divine command.

The vineyard's wild grapes are translated into ethical categories in v. 7. God expected his benefactions would lead to a passion for justice, but they resulted only in violence. He hoped for Israel's faithfulness to the relationship he had established for them (righteousness), but all he heard was the cry of the oppressed. In Hebrew, "justice" and "bloodshed," on the one hand, and "righteousness" and a "cry," on the other hand, have a similar pronunciation. In these puns is disclosed God's disappointment in his people's behavior.

Responding to the Text

We have read this passage so frequently that it no longer surprises us, but its punch line is just as dramatic and unexpected as Nathan's "You are the man!" was to David (2 Sam. 12:7). By recovering the original, unexpected outcome of this song, we may learn to examine and criticize our own behavior much more closely.

Second, this love song of God for his vineyard was meant to evoke and empower justice and righteousness. God's unconditional love is a hot topic in the church today. That is appropriate if we mean that it is inconceivable that any person's sins are too great for God to forgive, or that God does not ask questions about lifestyle and status in dispensing salvation. But these words of unconditional love are misleading if they neglect that God always loves us with the sole purpose of effecting radical transformation. Paradoxically, God loves us unconditionally *and* conditionally.

> THESE WORDS OF UNCONDITIONAL LOVE ARE MISLEADING IF THEY NEGLECT THAT GOD ALWAYS LOVES US WITH THE SOLE PURPOSE OF EFFECTING RADICAL TRANSFORMATION. PARADOXICALLY, GOD LOVES US UNCONDITIONALLY AND CONDITIONALLY.

Third, God's disappointment in the human response is a powerful motif in this song. God's plaintive cry, "What more was there to do for my vineyard?" reminds us of God's unfathomable generosity in Jesus Christ and the sometimes tepid character of our response.

RESPONSIVE READING

PSALM 19

Interpreting the Text

The psalmist marvels at the self-revelatory power of the sky, which witnesses to God with "voice" and "words" without ever making a sound. At the center of the sky is the sun, here compared to the vigor of a groom or a warrior (vv. 1-6). The second half of the psalm meditates on the power of God's law, with several echoes of the description of the sun. God's instruction is viewed positively, as a guide to the redeemed. The psalmist asks for deliverance from hidden or inadvertent sins and from the power of insolent people. Verse 13 may also allude to insolent sins, that is, to deliberate disobedience. The "great transgression" (v. 13) may refer to adultery, idolatry, or other open rebellion.

Responding to the Text

The relationship of nature and grace is controversial in Christian theology. While grace has often been the clear victor in these discussions, much more attention has been paid in recent decades to the revelatory capability of nature itself or to the cosmic nature of Christ. Psalm 19 is aware of this distinction, and it correlates nicely the two types of revelation. The heavens do—all by themselves—tell the glory of God, but the "law" of the Lord (v. 7) is also God's revelation. It includes what Christians call law, but goes much beyond it to include the story of God or the instruction of God. This instruction is both a guide to the redeemed and a constant judge of our behavior. "Redeemer" is the final word in the psalm. In describing God it connotes family metaphors, that is, the psalmist hails God as the best brother or sister one ever had. While much of the psalm is told by a "spectator," the psalmist finally exclaims in engaged trust, "Lord, you are *my* rock and *my* redeemer."

PSALM 80

Interpreting the Text

This lament of the community may have originated in the Northern Kingdom (vv. 1-2). The psalmists complain about the attitude and actions of their enemies (vv. 6, 12-13, 16) and pledge themselves to repentance and a new obedient life (v. 18). The exodus and conquest are presented under the metaphor of a vine that God planted in the land, but that is now being ravaged by Israel's enemies (vv. 8-13), who are agents of God himself (v. 12). The psalm is structured by a refrain that appears in vv. 3, 7, and 19 (cf. v. 14). God's shining face brings salvation to Israel, and the psalmists pray that God's frowning face will bring destruction to the enemies (v. 16).

Second Reading
PHILIPPIANS 3:4b-14

Interpreting the Text

Paul was upset by the presence of rival Jewish-Christian missionaries at Philippi, whom he dismisses as "dogs" (v. 2). He could, in fact, claim great confidence in his own Israelite credentials (here referred to as confidence in the flesh). He cites his circumcision and his membership in the people of Israel and, specifically, in the tribe of Benjamin. Benjamin was the only child of Jacob born in the Promised Land, and from this tribe came the first king, Saul, which was Paul's birth name. Paul and his family still spoke Hebrew. He had chosen to be part of the Pharisees, whose zeal for the law was well known, and his own zeal was shown in his persecution of the church. Paul did not have a bad conscience; he felt himself blameless under the law.

Yet all these "gains" he counted as rubbish because of his knowledge of Christ. The law is indeed holy, just, and good; but because of sin, which the law cannot remedy, it remains a flawed way to righteousness and leads to death. The real "gain" is in Christ. By accepting in faith God's offer of a renewed relationship, made possible through Christ, Paul knew that he would at the end be able to stand before God. Righteousness cannot be acquired on one's own; it comes only as God's gift. Paul wanted to experience the power of the risen Lord in human lives and to share in Christ's sufferings and death. This idea has baptismal overtones. Paul wanted to die to his old life and be raised to a whole new existence.

Paul was already raised with Christ, but still awaited achieving his final goal. "This" in v. 12 may refer to the resurrection or righteousness he still hoped to obtain. Paul is like an athlete who pushes on in the race, hoping for God's call at the end of the race to rise from the dead and join Christ in everlasting life. The present is no time for perfectionism or quietism, but for an earnest seeking of the righteousness from God.

Responding to the Text

Diversity is a key word in Christian thinking today. My own denomination in the United States has been largely northern European in background and has been slow to include the totality of the human family within its numbers. Inclusivity is the top priority in my denomination today. The present attention to diversity in gender, color, and ethnicity has also meant that each segment of the church has learned to appreciate what it brings to the table in terms of hymnody, piety, theology, and liturgical customs. Paul too appreciated where he had come from and what he had inherited from his Jewish roots.

Amid diversity our unity lies in Christ and in our rebirth through holy baptism. Our diversity is finally significant because of our common unity; unity and diversity reach their full potential when they are seen in dialectical tension. For Paul the righteousness of God was revealed through the cross, and, therefore, he desired above all to have that righteousness that comes through faith in Christ.

Paul considered his own heritage under the law to be rubbish in comparison with gaining Christ and being found in him. We take a different view of our heritage. All of us, who have been incorporated into the Body of Christ through God's righteousness, are freed to treasure our own heritage, to welcome the heritage of others, and also to recognize that "heritage" can sometimes get in the way of inclusivity or even become something idolatrous. We treasure our heritages and we transcend them.

Paul's pressing toward the goal in vv. 12-14 reminds me of the distinction between church membership and discipleship. "Church membership" stresses the voluntary character of our relationship to other Christians and in many cases has no particular moral energy connected with it. "Discipleship" recognizes that the relationship sealed through our baptism is the beginning of constant, even daily, transformation. Discipleship recognizes that Christianity is an eschatological religion, which believes that God's future will be better than our past, and that God's future entices us and encourages us toward ever-greater sanctification. Discipleship is often more a race than a pilgrimage.

PHILIPPIANS 4:6-9

See the Second Lesson for the Twentieth Sunday after Pentecost.

GOSPEL

MATTHEW 21:33-46

Interpreting the Text

In its present context, this parable is an allegory, with clear references to people and events within the history of salvation. The absentee landowner is God; the vineyard is Israel; the tenants are the Judean leaders; the first group of slaves is Israelite prophets and the second group represents later Israelite prophets or Christian prophets; the son is Jesus. The song of the unfruitful vineyard (Isa. 5:1-7) forms the background for this parable, and that song is paraphrased in v. 33. The parable of the wicked tenants also appears in Mark 12:1-12 and Luke 20:9-19.

A group of slaves has replaced the single slave in Mark's account, and in that version of the parable he was only beaten and sent away, not killed. Matthew reports a much more violent reception for the owner's slaves and even refers to the stoning of the prophets in 23:37. The "omniscient narrator" knows what the absentee landowner thought when he sent his son (v. 37) and what the tenants said to themselves (v. 38). The hope of the tenants to inherit the vineyard if they kill the son assumes (falsely) that the landowner is no longer alive. In Mark 12:8 the tenants killed the son and then threw him out of the vineyard; in Matthew 21 they put the son out of the vineyard before they killed him. This may be a reference to the tradition that Jesus was crucified outside Jerusalem (John 19:17; Heb. 13:12-13).

When Jesus asks what the owner will do to the tenants, the religious and civil leaders (see 21:23) write their own condemnation (v. 21). "Miserable death" might refer to God's final judgment or to the destruction of Jerusalem in 70 C.E. Matthew even implies that the Jewish nation has lost its elect status. Jesus quotes Ps. 118:22-23 in v. 42 as providing scriptural support for the exaltation of the rejected son (cf. 1 Peter 2:6-7). The kingdom of God in v. 43 refers primarily to the reign of God over Israel rather than to the eschatological kingdom. The "nation" that produces fruit is the church, made up of believing Jews and converted Gentiles. The judgment Jesus announces in v. 43, which is unique to Matthew, lacks the violence threatened in v. 41. Verse 44 may have been taken from Luke 20:18 since it is missing in the so-called Western text. It states that Jesus will be a cause of stumbling and offense for many people and uses a figure of speech taken from Isa. 8:14 (see also 1 Peter 2:8).

The chief priests and Pharisees (v. 45; contrast v. 23) were again put in a dilemma: They wanted to arrest Jesus, but they feared the crowds who considered him, like John the Baptist (v. 26), a prophet (cf. v. 11).

Responding to the Text

Those who read this text in church or preach on it need to be sensitive that it comes from a time when early Christians were engaged in a fierce and often personal argument with the Judaism of their day. The words of Jesus were shaped to fit that specific controversy and should not be construed as an indictment of Judaism that is valid for all time. Because of the long history of anti-Semitism in the church, Christian leaders need to take extraordinary steps to guard against perpetuating false stereotypes.

In fact, this text might almost be turned around and the violence done to the owner's servants and son could foreshadow that violence done to Jews by Christians throughout much of the history of Christianity. Historically, there was very little violence done to the Hebrew prophets, and those who did abuse them were kings, hardly the common people. A strategy for dealing more equitably with this text might be to help listeners think their way into the posture

> THIS TEXT MIGHT ALMOST BE TURNED AROUND AND THE VIOLENCE DONE TO THE OWNER'S SERVANTS AND SON COULD FORESHADOW THAT VIOLENCE DONE TO JEWS BY CHRISTIANS THROUGHOUT MUCH OF THE HISTORY OF CHRISTIANITY.

of the wicked tenants who squandered their inheritance because they did not recognize the generosity and fidelity of the owner and his right to receive the fruits of his vineyard. Specific examples could be given of ways in which members of the church have failed to give God, the owner of the vineyard, what was due to him. The repeated emissaries sent by the absentee owner could represent God's repeated efforts to reach his people with the call of the transformative gospel, a call to which the church unto this day seems quite resistant. Verse 41 provides opportunity for Christian readers of this text to accept their condemnation and confess their sins.

The quotation (Ps. 118:22-23) in v. 43 announces the divine vindication of Jesus despite his near universal rejection by the human family. In fact, instead of being a stone to be thrown out, he is given an even more lofty position as the head cornerstone. God's vindication of his suffering servants surpasses their wildest imagination (cf. Isaiah 53). Luke saw this rejection and vindication incarnated in the crucifixion and resurrection of Jesus (Acts 4:11; cf. 1 Peter 2:7). As v. 44 makes clear, Jesus is the point where an important decision must be made. Response to him determines one's destiny.

The goal of God's conditional/unconditional love is to empower a people who will produce the fruits of the kingdom (v. 43). Today it is not the chief priests and Pharisees who hear this parable; but people like you and me realize that Jesus is speaking about us (v. 45). Hence the surprise experienced by the readers of the Song of the Vineyard in Isaiah 5 may be repeated when this text is read and reflected on in the church today.

While Matthew's relationship to the Jews of his day was heated, his attitude toward them should not be presented as totally bleak. The late rabbi Samuel Sandmel wrote, "Matthew, partisan though he is of a Gentile mission, does not wish to discount the Jews but rather wants them in his movement inaugurated by the new law of a figure greater than Moses. . . .[For Matthew] the priests remain complete rascals. Matthew seems to be saying that were "the Jews" to recognize the moral delinquency of the Jewish leaders they could find reason to come into the movement, for Christianity in Matthew's view is the authentic Judaism."

TWENTIETH SUNDAY AFTER PENTECOST

OCTOBER 10, 1999 / PROPER 23

REVISED COMMON	EPISCOPAL (BCP)	ROMAN CATHOLIC
Exod. 32:1-14	Isa. 25:1-9	Isa. 25:6-10
or Isa. 25:1-9		
Pss. 106:1-6, 19-23;	Ps. 23	Ps. 23:1-3, 3-4, 5, 6
23		
Phil. 4:1-9	Phil. 4:4-13	Phil. 4:12-14, 19-20
Matt. 22:1-14	Matt. 22:1-14	Matt. 22:1-14

FIRST READING
EXODUS 32:1-14

Interpreting the Text

Shortly after the giving of the Ten Commandments, the Israelites grew impatient with Moses' absence and worked with Aaron to create a golden calf. Their idolatrous worship of this calf is made even worse by their proclaiming that this calf was responsible for the Exodus (v. 4). In vv. 7–10, the Lord remonstrates with Moses and tells him that the people he brought out of Egypt have acted perversely. God intends to obliterate them and make of Moses a great nation (see Gen. 12:2).

Moses' intercession in vv. 11-14 is a model prayer. He reminds God that it is he who brought Israel out of Egypt and asks him to stop his anger lest his act of judgment allow the Egyptians to claim that the Lord himself had acted with malice in the Exodus. In asking God to change his mind, Moses appeals to God's promise to the ancestors to make them numerous and to give them the Holy Land. Moses reminds God that this promise had been supported by a divine oath, guaranteed by God's own self. The Lord is convinced by this prayer and changes his mind.

Responding to the Text

In v. 7 God seems to disassociate himself from Israel when he chides Moses: "Your people, whom you brought up out of the land of Egypt, have acted perversely." As Moses responds in prayer, he turns these words around and asks

God about the legitimacy of his anger toward "your people, whom you brought out of the land of Egypt." Even when they sin and are under judgment, Israel—and we—are still God's very own people.

Second, Moses brings another argument to persuade God from judgment: "What would the neighbors think?" If Israel were to be destroyed by God, the Egyptians might conclude that Yahweh had malicious intentions when he brought about the Exodus in the first place. As far as Moses is concerned, God's very name is at stake in this crisis.

Third, he asks God to contradict Godself: "Change your mind and do not bring disaster on your people." Such divine self-contradiction is at the heart of the Christian gospel as well. God's wrath is trumped by God's anger; God, who remembers everything, chooses to forget our sins.

Fourth, Moses holds God to the promises made to the ancestors like Sarah and Abraham, just as we in our distresses appeal to the promises God made to us in our baptism.

At the conclusion of this powerful prayer of Moses, God changes his mind! The theological argument can be made that God never changes and that it is only our perception of God that changes. But from our human perspective—the only perspective we really have—prayer does convince God to change. In fact, sometimes the only way God is able to remain for us the same loving God is by changing.

ISAIAH 25:1-9 (alt.)

Interpreting the Text

Verses 1-5 are a psalm praising God for his special benefactions to the poor and the weak. God's ancient wondrous acts have been trumped by his more recent destruction of the enemy's city and by his serving as a refuge for the disadvantaged. When God's people were beset by an enemy attack, marked by heat and loud noise, God provided a cloud cover that cooled things off and silenced the enemy.

In vv. 6-9 the prophet describes an eschatological banquet, at which all peoples of the world will celebrate God's victories. Death is compared to a shroud or a sheet, and God himself promises to swallow up death forever. This is a punishment that fits death's crime: in ancient religion death was depicted as a monster that swallowed up all the living. According to Isaiah, death, disgrace, and sorrow will depart forever. People are invited to believe in these promises because they are based on the reliability of the divine word (v. 8). "Waiting on" God is the language of faith. Faithful waiting will be rewarded with celebrative joy.

Responding to the Text

This Old Testament text describes the messianic banquet. This banquet is a metaphor for God's final victory over everything that limits or reduces our life, things like death, disgrace, and every sorrow. Some marriage liturgies urge couples to continue in love and faithfulness until they participate in that final marriage feast that has no ending. One very important feature of our celebrations of the Lord's Supper is that it is a foretaste of the feast to come. The fellowship with one another and with God that we experience at the Eucharist is a clear, if partial, realization of what God plans for his people. In a sense we hear at the Table the distant triumph song, we get one more tasteable assurance that God is indeed for us, and then our hearts are brave again and our arms are strong.

RESPONSIVE READING

PSALM 106:1-6, 19-23

Interpreting the Text

The psalm begins with the word Hallelujah, and this theme of praise lasts through v. 3. In vv. 4-5 the psalmist prays for his or her own personal deliverance when God will act in behalf of the whole community. A second prayer for the deliverance of the whole people occurs in v. 47. The community confesses its sins and those of its ancestors in v. 6 and thereby justifies God's acts of judgment on them. We know that during Israel's exile some of the people blamed all their troubles on the sins of their parents: "The parents have eaten sour grapes, and the children's teeth are set on edge" (Jer. 31:29; Ezek. 18:2). The rest of this psalm repeats a pattern in which God's acts of deliverance are followed by Israel's rebellion. Verses 19-23 deal in particular with the incident of the golden calf. By forgetting God's deliverance of them in the Exodus the people called forth a threat by God to destroy them. Moses, however, stood in the breach through his act of intercession and was able to turn away God's anger.

Responding to the Text

This psalm offers a poetic version of the incident with the golden calf. Two images offer creative possibilities for proclamation. The prayer for the personal salvation of the psalmist in vv. 4-5 reminds us that deliverance for the whole people of God consists of salvation for many individuals who make up that whole. The individuals gathered in our congregations will not be content with a generic word of salvation, but they need a word that addresses their particular challenges or problems, their strengths and weaknesses. Each person needs to know that the gospel is also "for me."

The second preachable image is of Moses standing in the breach to turn away God's anger. This is a military figure and one that emphasizes each individual's role on behalf of the whole. We are all called to pray for one another and to be willing to lay down our life for our friends.

PSALM 23

Interpreting the Text

The psalmist speaks from the role of a sheep in praising the divine shepherd. While God's actions are described in the third person at first, the psalmist breaks through to the direct address of prayer in v. 4: "You are with me." "Darkest valley" in v. 4 includes the threat of death, but also other dangers. The image shifts from divine shepherd to divine host in v. 5. God provides asylum for the psalmist, who is pursued by enemies. In the final verse, the author expresses confidence that God's goodness and loyalty will pursue him or her, just as enemies had pursued the psalmist in the past, and that his or her entire life will take place in God's presence and in God's land ("the house of the LORD").

Responding to the Text

Even in urbanized America, when sheep and shepherding are seldom part of one's personal experience, the words of this psalm of trust connect with people and transcend cultural boundaries. This psalm is both an expression of trust in God ("You are with me") and a witness to others that the psalmist is convinced that God is her or his shepherd. It is good to pay attention to the enemies faced by this psalmist lest we conclude that this psalmist was leading an idyllic existence. The good news in this psalm fits the dangerous experience of the psalmist. God will pursue with goodness and loyalty one who feels put on by personal or national enemies.

SECOND READING
PHILIPPIANS 4:1-9

Interpreting the Text

Paul urges his readers not to be seduced away from the new existence they have in Christ. Two women (Euodia and Syntyche) had apparently quarreled, and so Paul urges them to have a meeting of minds in the Lord. Paul appeals to his loyal yoke-fellow (Timothy, Epaphroditus, Silas, or Luke have been suggested) to assist in this reconciliation. Other leading women are mentioned in Romans 16:1-15; 1 Corinthians 1:11; 16:19; and Philemon 2. Paul is confident that the names of all of his co-workers are inscribed in God's Book of Life (Exod. 32:32; Ps. 69:28; Dan. 12:1).

The apostle urges his readers to rejoice in the exalted Jesus when they face persecution. "Gentleness" (v. 5) might be defined as "fair-mindedness" to people in spite of their faults. The early return of Jesus was articulated in the ancient prayer *Maranatha* ("Our Lord, come"; 1 Cor. 16:22; Rev. 22:20).

Worry (v. 6) shows lack of confidence in God's promise to protect and care for his people. Prayer to God in time of need should also express thanksgiving for God's past benefits. God's peace transcends every human thought and it performs more than human plans can accomplish. Paul prays that this peace will stand guard over the hearts and minds of the Philippians.

The virtues Paul urges in v. 8 come from the Stoic tradition. "Keep on doing" (v. 9) is a fine rendition of the present tense in Greek. Many of the senses are involved in receiving the gospel: the mind, the ears, and the eyes.

Responding to the Text

Trouble in congregations often starts with misunderstandings or disagreements between two individuals. The presence of disruptive Euodias and Syntyches in our local parishes are an invitation for various "loyal companions" to seek reconciliation between them before general mistrust of others sets in. Joy is not just emotion; it is our defiant response to the troubles faced by individual Christians or by the church at large. Just telling someone not to worry usually does not help, and it only seems to invalidate that person's feelings. In these final exhortations, Paul is not trying to sweep troubles under the rug, but to encourage his readers to take their problems and concerns to the God whom they trust enough to believe he can in fact help. Our prayers, even our public prayers in church, are too often a list of requests, often for very worthy

PEACE IS MORE THAN THE ABSENCE OF CONFLICT; PEACE IS THE PRESENCE OF EVERYTHING GOOD. GOD'S PEACE IS RICHER THAN WE COULD EVER IMAGINE OR DREAM UP.

courses, but too frequently only for our needs and our emergencies. Paul urges the Philippians to accompany all such requests with thanks for the countless times God has already stood by their side.

Peace is more than the absence of conflict; peace is the presence of everything good. God's peace is richer than we could ever imagine or dream up. Peace, as Paul understands it, is a deeply ironic metaphor, that occasionally may not be irenic: God's peace stands guard over our hearts and minds, also, even especially, in times of trouble and persecution.

PHILIPPIANS 4:4-13 or 4:12-14, 19-20

Interpreting the Text

These lessons depart from the previous discussion by the addition of vv. 10-13 (BCP) or 12-14, 19-20 (RC). Earlier Paul referred to a gift he had received from the Philippians (1:5; 2:25), and he now acknowledges again his receipt of their gift (v. 10). Verses 11-13 are an excursus in which Paul demonstrates his independence (1 Thess. 2:5-9; 1 Cor. 9:4-18; 2 Cor. 11:7-10; 12:13-18). Paul's contentment with every circumstance in life reflects Stoic virtues. But independence and self-contentment pale in comparison with his indebtedness to his Lord and his reliance on him (v. 13). The "things" Paul does (v. 13) may be the responsibilities of his apostolic office, but this word may refer more generally to his ability to deal with the vicissitudes of life. The closest Paul comes to a "thank you" is in v. 14. The Philippians shared in Paul's "distress." Does this mean his imprisonment or his role as an eschatological apostle?

Paul promises (or wishes) that God will meet the needs of the Philippians (v. 19). What God has a lot of is glory, the sign of his power and presence. Through his power and presence God will transform the Philippians and all other believers into his likeness.

Responding to the Text

In our world of ambition and consumption, Paul's discussion of his contentment in vv. 11-13 is good news indeed. Even he admits he grew into this, that is, he has learned the secret of such living (v. 12). His independence of material things is in direct proportion to his dependence on the Lord (v. 13). In his imitation of Christ's suffering, he experiences also the power of his resurrection: "I want to know Christ and the power of his resurrection and the sharing of his sufferings by becoming like him in his death" (3:10).

GOSPEL

MATTHEW 22:1-14

Interpreting the Text

This pericope actually contains two parables, one dealing with the rejection of a wedding invitation and the other with proper attire for the wedding. Luke has his own version in 14:16-24, which is similar to a passage from the Gospel of Thomas 64.

"Once more" in v. 1 refers back to the two preceding parables that have been read on the last two Sundays. The king's invitation to a wedding feast may refer to God's invitation to the expected messianic banquet (Isa. 25:1-9). Because this parable in its present form deals with the Jews' rejection of Jesus, the slaves sent to issue the invitation (v. 3) stand for the Israelite prophets. The word "ready" in vv. 4 and 8 lends urgency to the invitation: "Come while the food is hot!" When the guests refused the invitation (see Matt. 21:34-36), the king sent other slaves, perhaps referring to early Christian emissaries. Their message refers both to the bounty of the banquet as well as the urgency of the invitation. Those invited by them, however, found "better things to do," and some even acted violently toward the slaves. Their fate may reflect the persecution experienced by the early church. The king's harsh response, especially his destruction of their city (v. 7), results from the parable in its present form relating to the Roman destruction of Jerusalem under Titus in 70 c.e., which is interpreted as punishment for the rejection of Jesus by the religious establishment.

The king's next invitation is all-inclusive: "all whom they found, both good and bad." "Good and bad" may mean everyone on whatever byway, or it may be an anticipation of the mixed character of the church, which requires appropriate discipline. The effective invitation to the new clientele is similar to the generosity toward those hired late in the day in the Parable of the Laborers in the Vineyard (Matt. 20:1-16).

The second episode, or parable, in vv. 11-13 indicates the need for discipline within the church. While entry into the church is by gracious invitation, a high ethical response, symbolized by the wedding garment, is expected (cf. Rev. 19:8; the necessity for high ethical conduct in the church is also attested in Matt. 7:21-23). Matthew ignores the complication that those invited at the last minute would not have time to secure an appropriate garment. "Friend" (v. 12) is sarcastic. Readers are warned not to in their calling self-righteously lest they are later proven not to belong to the elect because of their own conduct. A person's behavior indicates whether he or she is among the elect, and there is to be harsh punishment for those who lack righteousness or faithfulness (cf. Matt. 8:12).

Responding to the Text

The first two reasons given for refusing the king's invitation to a wedding banquet in v. 5 have a familiar, contemporary ring today. People who are too busy for God's call today may simply be too busy, but they also offer just as clear a refusal to God's invitation as those who act much more confrontationally and violently in saying no to God. Claiming to be too busy is often a rationalization or a subterfuge and not really an honest excuse. Preachers would be wise to use this text for diagnosing modern responses to the gospel rather than using its historical, polemical meaning within early Jewish-Christian recriminations.

The king's "Plan B" actually corresponds to what many see as *the* mission imperative today, namely, the call to reach out to outsiders and become a more inclusive church. The Gospel's invitation should go out to all, without preconditions, both to the good and the bad. The primary task of the church in the foreseeable future is not "chaplaincy" among those who are already insiders, but an earnest search for those who are not yet part of the Christian movement. Congregations must be in mission, and the primary task of clergy in the next years will be to "gather together a new group of the faithful" or to equip and empower laity to gather or invite them. "Good and bad" could be taken in the sense of a merism, that is, everyone, or it may hint that not all those within the church are loyal and true.

Church discipline, which is the subject matter of vv. 11-13, has fallen on hard times in many parts of Western Christianity for a variety of reasons; and there surely is no need for us to return to the tough old days when sinners were branded with a scarlet letter. Still Dietrich Bonhoeffer did write about the "cost" of discipleship and the indifference with which many hear God's invitation. The recent revival of the word "discipleship" in Christian circles prods us to remember that accepting God's gracious invitation means something more or deeper than "joining" a church. It means practicing righteousness, or taking up Christ's cross and following.

When Matthew writes earlier in his Gospel about disciplining members of the church (in 18:15-18), he should not be understood on a baseball analogy—three strikes and you're out. Individual admonition, taking others along to discuss with the erring brother or sister, and appealing to the whole church are serious strategies designed to help gain the sister or brother.

The final epigram in v. 14 ("Many are called, but few are chosen") fits both vv. 1-10 and vv. 11-13. Those who rejected the king's invitation made light of it and assumed that, come what may, they were in no danger. Jesus, in Matthew's Gospel, indicates that deeds, not just words, disclose whether a person is or is not among the elect. In vv. 11-13, Jesus criticizes those who have said yes to God's gracious invitation, at least with their lips, but their deeds do not back up their words. In the Gospel of Thomas, logion 23, Jesus also indicates that not all who hear the gospel will be among the elect: "I shall choose you, one out of a thousand, and two out of ten thousand." The doctrine of the "two ways" makes a similar distinction between the wider group that has been called and the narrower group that has been elected: "Enter through the narrow gate; for the gate is wide and the road is easy that leads to destruction, and there are many who take it. For the gate is narrow and the road is hard that leads to life, and there are few who find it" (Matt. 7:13-14).

TWENTY-FIRST SUNDAY AFTER PENTECOST

OCTOBER 17, 1999 / PROPER 24

REVISED COMMON	EPISCOPAL (BCP)	ROMAN CATHOLIC
Exod. 33:12-23	Isa. 45:1-7	Isa. 45:1, 4-6
or Isa. 45:1-7		
Pss. 99; 96:1-9(10-13)	Ps. 96:1-9(10-13)	Ps. 96:1,3,4-5, 7-8, 9-10
1 Thess. 1:1-10	1 Thess. 1:1-10	1 Thess. 1:1-5
Matt. 22:15-22	Matt. 22:15-22	Matt. 22:15-21

FIRST READING
EXODUS 33:12-23

Interpreting the Text

The intercession by Moses in these verses comes in the wake of the incident with the golden calf. In Exod. 33:1-6 God ordered Israel to resume its march toward the Promised Land, but threatened not to go with them lest he consume them. Since God has shown his approval of Moses personally (by knowing his name and by showing him favor), Moses asks to see God's "ways" (actions), and he reminds God that the group with whom he is angry is his own people.

God promises that his presence (literally, his "face") will be with Moses. Moses remarks that if God's presence would not go with them, it would be better if they not start for Canaan at all. God's presence is what makes Israel different from all the other peoples.

After God reiterates once more his promise to accompany the people because of his approval of Moses and the intimacy of their knowledge of one another (v. 17), Moses asks to see God's glory. What God is in himself is called "holiness" in the Old Testament; what we actually see of God is called his "glory" (see Isa. 6:3). God's self-revelation consists of his pronouncing his own name, Yahweh, and showing grace and mercy to whomever he chooses. God's transcendence is preserved by his refusal to let Moses see his face. God hides Moses in a hollow of a rock and puts his hand over the rock so that Moses cannot see God's glory directly when he passes by. When God lifts his hand, Moses sees God's back, but he is not allowed to see God's face.

Responding to the Text

Moses exemplifies great intercessory prayer in which he holds God to his promises. Every time he offers a reason for God to act he reminds readers of why they may expect God to act. Despite God's distancing himself from Israel in vv. 1–3, Moses reminds God (and the readers) that this disobedient group is still God's people. This relationship is often summed up in the covenant formula: "I am your God; you are my people."

In v. 3 God had threatened not to go up with Israel, but in v. 14 God reverses himself and promises to be with Israel. Moses underscores the importance of that promise in vv. 15–16 and witnesses to Israel that God's presence requires their being distinct from all other peoples precisely because of this presence.

God knows each of us by name (v. 17). This affirmation is followed by three additional words of assurance that respond to the request to see God's glory. Moses does not get to see God directly, but only in God's gracious condescension to human need. God pronounces his own name, the name that was first disclosed in the context of the Exodus from Egypt. God's central identity and reputation—his name—have everything to do with liberation and freedom. God's sovereign and benevolent freedom is affirmed in a tautological sentence: "I will be gracious to whom I will be gracious, and will show mercy on whom I will show mercy." Grace is not seen as caprice or threat, but as God's ability to break through the web of retribution and contradict anger with grace.

In a stirring metaphor, God affirms once more that his face dare not be seen directly, but we do get to see God's back as he passes by. Whether God appears in nature or through other people, he indeed is present with his people even if not always in the exact way in which we might demand or even expect the presence to occur. Moses knew the importance of God's presence; he and we must learn to accept the presence where it comes to us, often through weakness and from strangers. We may only get to see God's back, but it is always *God's* back.

ISAIAH 45:1–7 (alt.)

Interpreting the Text

The prophet known as Second Isaiah designates Cyrus, king of Persia, as the agent through whom God will liberate the Judahite exiles in Babylon and bring them home to Jerusalem. God even calls Cyrus "anointed" or "messiah." God promises to go before Cyrus and to give him hidden riches and treasures to support his liberation efforts. The prophet expects Cyrus to acknowledge the God of Israel, whose election of Cyrus is signified by his knowing the king's name. God's selection of Cyrus is for the sole benefit of his servant Jacob/Israel.

Yahweh is an incomparable God and he alone is the one to be worshiped. His arming of Cyrus will not finally effect a personal transformation in Cyrus, but God does expect that all peoples—those in the east and west—will acknowledge him. As the only God in the universe, God creates light and darkness, weal and woe, good and evil. Persian religion, by way of contrast, was dualistic, with separate deities responsible for light and darkness.

Responding to the Text

Verse 1 is one of the most astonishing texts in the whole Old Testament. Yahweh announces that his anointed agent (messiah) who will set Israel free and bring them home will be none other than Cyrus, king of Persia. It would almost be like saying that the Ayatollah would be our deliverer. We often have difficulty in accepting the way in which God's help reaches us—sometimes it seems to reach us at the wrong time and through the wrong people.

God chose Cyrus for two reasons: so that his servant Jacob or Israel might be helped and so that other peoples would recognize how truly incomparable Yahweh is. God's mission is both toward Israel and toward the world.

In certain contexts, v. 7 might present a problem. How can we explain evil if there are no evil deities to wreak havoc on earth, but only the one God, Yahweh, who is responsible for everything? Monotheism may not be able to explain the origin of evil, but it also guarantees that nothing is outside God's interest or responsibility. This passage affirms that salvation lies only in Yahweh and not in the gods of Babylon. Israel in exile was tempted follow "other" gods, who had won the most recent war, and to conform to the ethos of its captor society. God's almighty power is seen in his gracious choice to use an able Persian king to set Judah free and in God's emphatic and simultaneous testimony to himself throughout this passage.

RESPONSIVE READING
PSALM 99

Interpreting the Text

Psalms 96–99 celebrate the kingship of Yahweh. In Psalm 99, God's kingship is hailed because of his invisible enthronement above the cherubim (v. 1) and his exalted presence in Jerusalem (v. 2). His greatness evokes praise from all the peoples, who acknowledge his holiness. God's power manifests itself concretely in his pursuit of justice and equity. The first stanza closes with an exhortation for all peoples to praise Yahweh and with a confession of his holiness. God's "footstool" may be an indirect reference to the ark, even as the earth itself is hailed as God's footstool in Isa. 66:1. Moses, Aaron, and Samuel are identified by the psalmist as great intercessors. For Moses see Exod. 32:10-14; 33:12-23; and Deut. 9:26-29; for Aaron see Num. 6:26-29; and for Samuel see 1 Sam. 7:9; 12:19-25; Jer. 15:1. The psalmist hails the obedience of these intercessors (v. 7), and God's willingness to forgive them when they erred. A final call to praise is based on God's unique "holiness."

Responding to the Text

God as "king" has been a controversial topic in recent years because this term tends to emphasize "maleness" and even "hierarchy." God's kingship in Psalm 99, however, locates the significance of his rule in a love for justice and equity. Praising Yahweh for justice commits the one praying to a similar agenda.

The psalmist also lays out the characteristics of great human leadership in Moses, Aaron, and Samuel. They interceded with God, listened to his revelation, and followed his laws. But their leadership was also human-sized: they sinned, were punished, and forgiven.

The psalmist also alternates between referring to God in the third person when he calls on others to praise, but also addressing God directly as the psalmist expresses her own praise and commitment. God's holiness is affirmed in vv. 3, 5, and 9.

PSALM 96:1-9 (10-13)

Interpreting the Text

This psalm is the first of the series of psalms dedicated to the kingship of Yahweh. The newness of Yahweh's actions requires a new song of praise. God's deeds are designated as salvation (or victory), glory, and marvelous works. Yahweh is compared to all the gods of the foreign countries, who are dismissed as idols. Yahweh's unique power is known in his creation of the heavens. The psalmist identifies four attributes of God: honor, majesty, strength, and beauty. God's "sanctuary" (v. 6) may be a reference to his heavenly house, of which the Jerusalem temple was thought to be a copy.

Verses 6-9 are an appeal for all nations to praise Yahweh, and they are arranged in what has been called stair-like parallelism (see Ps. 29:1-2). Those who praise Yahweh are also expected to bring a sacrifice (v. 8). "Holy splendor" in v. 9 may refer to God's radiance or to the condition of the worshiper (traditionally, "the beauty of holiness"). Others would translate: "Worship the LORD when he appears in his holiness."

The optional verses (in parentheses) hail the present kingship of the Lord and anticipate his coming to judge the entire world.

Responding to the Text

The psalmist hails God as a deity who does things. God creates whereas all the gods of the peoples are dismissed as idols. Therefore, the psalmist also calls all peoples and, indeed, the entire natural world to praise God. Nature gives God a standing ovation as he comes to exercise his kingship as a judge, who follows the principles of righteousness, equity, and truth.

SECOND READING
1 THESSALONIANS 1:1-10

Interpreting the Text

This first chapter of this oldest book in the New Testament celebrates the way in which the Thessalonians had received the gospel. Paul was writing from Corinth in Achaia, and the other senders are Silvanus (cf. Silas in Acts 17:4) and Timothy, Paul's chief aide. Verses 2-5 and 6-8 are each one verse in length in the Greek text. Jesus' messianic identity is confirmed by the title Christ; he is called Lord because God raised him from the dead. Verse 3 contains Paul's first use of faith, hope, and love in one context. Hope is patient waiting for the return of the Lord Jesus despite the tribulations of the age. The term "brothers and sisters" (v. 4) is used nineteen times in 1 Thessalonians to show Paul's affection for the church in Thessalonica. The Thessalonians' reception of the gospel confirms their elect status. The proclamation of the gospel is a demonstration of God's power, just as miracles are (v. 5).

The Thessalonians became imitators of Paul and Jesus both by sharing in eschatological affliction and by proclaiming the gospel. Joy, which a person experiences in the presence of God (3:9), was inspired in them by the Holy Spirit. The Thessalonians became examples to believers in the province of Macedonia, in which Thessalonica was located, and in Achaia, where Corinth was located. Even people outside these provinces had heard about the success of Paul at Thessalonica. The people had shown him hospitality and they had truly repented, turning *from* idols and *toward* the living and true God. God lives in history and in nature, and God has been faithful to his covenantal promises (5:24).

By raising Jesus from the dead (v. 10) God identified Jesus as the one by whom God will bring about salvation. The use of the present participle in v. 10 ("rescues") indicates that deliverance has already begun though the final manifestation of God's saving work has not yet appeared. The "wrath that is coming" refers to God's final judgment.

Responding to the Text

Faith, hope, and love in this passage are depicted as active virtues, producing work, labor, and steadfastness. Paul affirms that his message to the church at Thessalonica came with words that were reinforced by miracles and by the power of the Holy Spirit. Paul recognizes that faith is engendered by God and cannot be sidetracked by minor things, such as persecution.

Paul and the Thessalonians lived with eschatological expectation. "Waiting for the Son" (v. 10) is one important way in which Paul calls for faith among his readers. Paul is absolutely convinced that God raised Jesus from the dead, and that this Jesus already is delivering the faithful from the "judgment day wrath" that is coming.

Paul does not fear judgment day since he knows that God is already delivering him from the end-time acts of judgment. This faith is already present also in the Thessalonians!

Everything at that point seems right among the Thessalonians. In 1993, my wife and I, who were on sabbatical in Berlin at the time, took a trip to Greece and Turkey to visit the locations associated with Paul. It only took me a few hours to realize that today there is virtually no trace of Christianity in Turkey at all, although Paul's and the Thessalonians' witness has been effective throughout the world. The absence of Christianity in Paul's original mission field reminds us that faith is always a fragile enterprise: it comes to us from the Holy Spirit, but it faces persecution, indifference, and apathy. This takes nothing away from Paul's accomplishments; but it reminds us all to treasure our election, to praise the ways in which God's faithfulness has been manifested in our lives, and to remember that the whole world is avidly watching us to see how we respond to the gospel.

GOSPEL

MATTHEW 22:15-22

Interpreting the Text

This is the first of four controversy stories in vv. 15–46, three of which will appear in the Gospel readings. Matthew displays antipathy toward the Pharisees throughout his Gospel because they posed a threat to the church of his day. The Pharisees disliked the Romans, but eschewed revolution since they thought it showed a lack of faith in God's power to save. The Herodians were pro-Roman. These two groups tried to entrap Jesus on a highly disputed political question, but began the conversation with words of flattery (v. 16). They said Jesus was sincere or faithful and that he showed no partiality, that is, he did not cater to people who were wealthy or powerful.

On the basis of this flattery, they posed a dilemma with regard to the payment of Roman taxes. If he would say they should not pay taxes, he could be accused of being treasonous toward Rome. If he endorsed the paying of taxes, he would become unpopular with the people, who thought paying taxes acknowledged as legitimate a foreign power that was exercising sovereignty over Israel.

Jesus saw through the flattery of his opponents, called them hypocrites, and accused them of trying to put him to the test. Thirteen of the seventeen uses of "hypocrites" in the New Testament are in Matthew. When Jesus asked them for a coin used for the payment of taxes, they gave him a denarius, which amounted to a day's wages and was the standard coin used for taxes (contrast 17:24-27). These coins often showed a glorified likeness of the Caesar and some kind of inscription with religious or cultic overtones. A coin of Tiberius, a contemporary of Jesus, read "Tiberius Caesar, son of the divine Augustus, great high priest."

Jesus told them to give the emperor the things that belonged to the emperor, that is, money, with the emperor's own image on it. Jesus thus appears to support the state, perhaps reckoning it as the lesser of two evils—anarchy would be even worse. His answer got him off the horns of the dilemma, without offending either the empire or the common people. Later, the political implications of what Jesus did and said were deemed revolutionary by the Romans, who sentenced him to death.

But Jesus also ordered his followers to give God what belongs to God. In the next chapter Jesus indicates that love of God and neighbor are the two greatest divine commandments (23:37-39). This may be "what belongs to God." Or one could argue that we, who are created in God's image and bear his image, ought to give ourselves back to God. The "things that are God's," however, are not identified specifically, and they may be interpreted in different ways by different interpreters. Jesus' opponents were amazed (cf. 8:27; 9:33; 15:31; 21:20; and 27:14) at his answer and left him alone.

Responding to the Text

Paying taxes in our society does not have the potentially bad connotations it had in the time of Jesus. Unlike those in Roman Palestine, we have chosen our government, and it has the full legal right to tax us. We often complain about the taxes we pay, and we rightly criticize waste in government or the excessive proportion of our taxes that goes toward the military-industrial complex. We need to be careful, however, lest we participate in the cheap and trivializing joking that goes on about taxes. Taxes are a part of the social contract that holds us together as a people, and they are a recognition that some social problems or public works are so immense that they can only be approached by all of us together working for the common good. We need to give to Caesar what belongs to Caesar.

Jesus also urges us to give to God the things that are God's. All that we are and have comes from God and is entrusted to our stewardship. Our intellect, our energy, our compassion, our artistic abilities, and our money are gifts bestowed by God to enable us to use them for the greater good of all. Genesis 1 affirms that we are created in God's image, that we are in some crucial ways like God. According to Genesis, our stewardship of these gifts is demonstrated particularly by the way we exercise God's rule, in his stead, over the entirety of creation. Ancient Assyrian emperors often erected statues, also in Palestine, to remind captured peoples who was in charge. We human beings, therefore, are signs and agents of God's rule on earth. The way we conduct ourselves as human beings, as church members, and as citizens should demonstrate the passion of God for justice and righteousness throughout creation. We give ourselves to God as we serve our fellow human beings and as we attend to the protection of the entire created order that has been entrusted to our care. We give ourselves to God as we use our minds and our talents to think new thoughts, raise holistic families, witness to Christ in our daily life, and enjoy that which is beautiful and true in God's creation.

WE GIVE OURSELVES TO GOD AS WE USE OUR MINDS AND OUR TALENTS TO THINK NEW THOUGHTS, RAISE HOLISTIC FAMILIES, WITNESS TO CHRIST IN OUR DAILY LIFE, AND ENJOY THAT WHICH IS BEAUTIFUL AND TRUE IN GOD'S CREATION.

Using wisely and well the gifts God has given us is one way of returning these gifts to God. Another is to dedicate these gifts and ourselves directly to God. Financial support of the church in its global, national, and local expressions and contributing to benevolences and social ministries responds to Jesus' command. Committing one's whole being to ministry in daily life or to one of the church's rostered ministries is to heed the call to give to God what is God's.

We are God's because of God's creation of the universe and because of God's gift of life to each one of us. We are born anew to a living hope by Christ's death and his rising from the grave. Each morning as we remember our baptism we remind ourselves who we are and whose we are. Whenever I went out as a teenager, my parents would always say, "Remember whose son you are." I resented that then, thinking that in some ways they were criticizing or restricting me, excessively concerned about what other people might think of me and our family. As I have grown older, I have come to treasure their admonition, which was also full of love and promise. Yes, I am the son of George and Pauline Klein, but I am also God's child by creation and rebirth. I am created in God's image with the awesome assignment of exercising God's rule. Since I am God's, why not live for God?

TWENTY-SECOND SUNDAY AFTER PENTECOST

OCTOBER 24, 1999 / PROPER 25

REVISED COMMON	EPISCOPAL (BCP)	ROMAN CATHOLIC
Deut. 34:1-12	Exod. 22:21-27	Exod. 22:20-26
or Lev. 19:1-2, 15-18		
Ps. 90:1-6, 13-17;	Ps. 1	Ps. 18:2-3, 3-4, 47, 51
or Ps. 1		
1 Thess. 2:1-8	1 Thess. 2:1-8	1 Thess. 1:1-5
Matt. 22:34-46	Matt. 22:34-46	Matt. 22:34-40

FIRST READING
DEUTERONOMY 34:1-12

Interpreting the Text

Surprisingly, Moses died in Trans-Jordan and did not enter Canaan. The reason for this was said to be his lack of trust (Num. 20:12) or God's anger with the whole people of Israel that required the punishment of Moses (Deut. 1:37; 3:25-26; 4:21). God did, however, show him the whole Promised Land, from north to south, and indicated that this was the land promised to Israel's ancestors and their descendants. A second surprise is that Moses was placed in an unknown grave site. Whatever the historical reason for this, the "founder" of Israel's religion lies buried somewhere in obscurity. Despite his age, Moses still had good eyesight and (sexual?) vigor at his death (v. 7). Israel mourned for him for thirty days (see Num. 20:29). Joshua succeeded Moses. He had a wise spirit because Moses had placed his hands on him, and Joshua kept Israel obedient during his entire lifetime (see Judg. 2:7, 11-15).

The writer hails Moses as an incomparable prophet because of his intimate knowledge of God (v. 10). While such "face to face" knowledge is recorded in Exod. 33:11, the following pericope says that Moses only saw God's back, but could not see his face (Exod. 33:23). Verse 10 is a modification of Deut. 18:15-18 where the Lord promised that he would raise up again and again a prophet like Moses, who would receive a word from Yahweh and deliver it to the people. While Deuteronomy 18 sees the whole line of prophets as a continuation of the charisma once granted to Moses, the writer of Deut. 34:10 believed that no subsequent prophet was the equal of Moses, and he therefore expected an eschatological prophet to come. This expectation of an end-time prophet was seen as fulfilled in Jesus by some in the New Testament period (John 6:14; Acts 2:30-32). God's power had manifested itself through Moses in the plagues and the Exodus itself (vv. 11-12; cf. Deut. 4:34, 37; 26:8).

Responding to the Text

Moses saw the promised land, but never entered it himself. All of us remember how Martin Luther King, Jr., on the night before his assassination, saw himself in this Mosaic role. It is a very provocative image and one that typifies Christian hope. We know, and have even seen, what God promises his children, but we never get there in this life even if we are energized and strengthened by the sight itself.

Verse 10 is a good example of how the word of God sometimes has to change to remain the same. God's promise in Deut. 18:15 to raise up a long line of prophets, who would be like Moses, gave credibility to people like Jeremiah and Ezekiel. Deuteronomy suggested that their controversial messages were what Moses would have said if he were still alive. The implication of this promise is that people ought to listen to the prophets.

And yet, none of these prophets—Amos, Isaiah, Jeremiah or any other—was quite the equal of Moses. A later writer noted this in Deut. 34:10, and later believers drew the appropriate consequence. If God had promised that there would be a prophet like Moses, and that prophet had not yet appeared, then that prophet was still to be expected. God's future fulfillment of his promise would be better than anything he had accomplished so far. What had originally been a promise of a long line of prophets became the promise of one, final, climactic prophet.

The last verses in the book of Deuteronomy heap lavish praise on Moses, but only because he was the channel of the God whose unfulfilled promise of a prophet like Moses was still to be cashed in. We are all like Moses, catching a vision of the Promised Land, but also placed in positions of expectant hope, trusting that the God who finally took Israel into the land will fulfill all of his promises to us. Sometimes the fulfillment turns out to be better than the promise itself, for Jesus, who gives us the bread of life, was the promised prophet, and God raised him up, not just as a prophet, but from the dark grave itself (Acts 2:24).

LEVITICUS 19:1-2, 15-18 (alt.)

Interpreting the Text

This passage from the Holiness Code contains the saying that gives this code its name: "You shall be holy, for I the LORD your God am holy." The Holiness Code probably reached its present form no earlier than the sixth century B.C.E. Verse 15 advocates evenhanded justice: neither yielding to the poor out of sympathy nor favoring the rich because of their influence. People are not to profit by or ignore the violence done to their neighbors. A person is supposed to correct his neighbor when he errs, and to love one's neighbor as oneself (v. 18). Jesus links this passage with a citation from Deut. 6:5 ("You shall love the LORD your God") as the two greatest commandments in the law (Matt. 22:37-39).

Responding to the Text

God is holy; what we see of God is God's glory. This text commands and invites us to be like God in his holiness. Avoidance of sin is a part of holiness, but surely does not comprehend its total meaning. We can always ask ourselves, "What would God do in these challenging circumstances that we face?"

Verses 15-18 give some concrete examples of holiness. Justice in the courts is a proper exercise of holiness, but so is refusal to slander our neighbor or refusing to stand by idly when the neighbor is harmed (v. 16). Hate and vengeance are the opposite of loving one's neighbor as oneself (vv. 17-18). People do not seek to harm themselves or their best interests unless they are emotionally or mentally ill. God asserts that he is Yahweh, the one who made his name known in the context of the Exodus from Egypt. That identity is his authority for calling us to justice; that identity is also the power that makes it possible for us to be just—and holy.

EXODUS 22:21-27 or 20-26

Interpreting the Text

These lessons are from the Covenant Code or Book of the Covenant (Exod. 20:22—23:33), generally held to be the oldest legislation in the Bible. Verse 20 indicates that public worship of other gods was a capital crime. Israel was to treat foreigners kindly since that was what it was itself in Egypt. Widows and orphans were *the* poor people in the Bible, and mistreatment of them exposes the perpetrator to capital punishment, which would make a widow and orphans out of his own family. The prohibition against interest stems from the fact that loans were seen as a means of offering relief to the poor. In our society they have become the way one "gets ahead." The gist of this law is that one is to help the poor. Finally, a person was not to take a neighbor's cloak as a guarantee for repayment of a loan, especially if the neighbor owned only one cloak. God indeed has a preferential option for the weak, the poor, and the oppressed.

Responding to the Text

It is interesting to note that all of these legal injunctions are apodictic or categorical. Extenuating circumstances are not considered since the lawgiver has the needs of the neighbor in mind. Israel's attitude toward those less well off was motivated by memory of their liberation from their own slavery in Egypt, which would make them refrain from imposing such hardship on others. But it was also motivated by pity for those in harsh circumstances (v. 27).

The words about God in this passage note God's swift and sure judgment against those who mistreat the weak and the poor. God also promises to hear—and thus to help—all those who cry out in need. God is "compassionate," or as the Hebrew might more literally be translated "gracious."

RESPONSIVE READING
PSALM 90:1-6, 13-17

Interpreting the Text

The first two verses begin with the word "LORD" and end with the word "God." This envelope surrounds other words that affirm that God was God long before there was a world and that he will still be God into the endless future. Human beings on the other hand are mortal (vv. 3-6); they flourish like grass in the morning and wither like grass by the evening. A long human lifetime may be seventy or eighty years; a thousand years for God are inconsequential.

In vv. 13-17 the psalmists pray for God to have compassion on them and make their days of happiness at least as long as their days of affliction. God is seen as the source of both conditions. They pray that God's work, or power, will be known to them. By identifying themselves as God's servants (v. 16), they are pledging themselves to do God's will. God's favor can make whatever they undertake successful.

Responding to the Text

I was a graduate student at Harvard in November 1963. When John F. Kennedy was assassinated, my fellow students and I found our way, numbly, to Memorial Chapel, where the chaplain tried to put our shock and grief into perspective. I still remember singing, "O God, Our Help in Ages Past," on that day, accompanied by the mighty roar of the organ. That hymn is based on the first five verses of Psalm 90. The psalm assures us that God has been God even before creation, before any of the tangible things all around us ever came into existence. Recent studies have pointed out what a fitting sequel Psalm 90 is to Psalm 89, where those who prayed lamented the fact that their king, the descendant of David, was being taunted by the enemies. At a time of national disaster, one needs to cling to the old truths about God's faithfulness, reported by no one less than Moses himself.

One of those old truths is the word "work" in v. 16. Many of us have résumés that sum up our education and our various accomplishments. God's work is often expressed in the Bible as singular; there is only one thing that God is really up to—loving people, helping people, serving people, comforting and challenging people. People in trouble need this work, power, and favor.

PSALM 1

Interpreting the Text

This first psalm introduces the whole Psalter. Those who meditate on God's law or instruction (v. 2) may be those who study the Pentateuch or reflect on God's commandments. But God's instruction is also the 149 psalms that follow, and this psalmist invites the reader to meditate on these day and night.

The writer compares the righteous to a tree that flourishes by a river bank while the wicked are like the dried chaff on the threshing floor, and he asks implicitly, "Which would you rather be, a lively tree or dead chaff?" Progressive yielding to temptation is graphically described in v. 1: the righteous are those who do not walk (follow) in the advice of the wicked, stand in (take) the path of the sinners, or sit in the seat of scoffers.

In v. 6 the righteous are depicted as dependent, as objects of God's gaze. The autonomy of the wicked is not all it is cracked up to be; they perish.

Responding to the Text

Psalm 1 provides wonderful educational guidance. It shows that God rewards the righteous, and that one of the real choices in life is that of being like a tree rather than like chaff. It makes the faithful life attractive and alluring. God knows the way of the righteous. Why would one not want to be righteous?

But a person also needs to be careful in reading Psalm 1. The choices between right and wrong are usually not so clear or easy as this psalm implies, nor is the fate of the believer always superior to the faithless person. Success does not necessarily reflect a life of faithfulness; bad fortune is surely not always a consequence of infidelity.

> THE CHOICES BETWEEN RIGHT AND WRONG ARE USUALLY NOT SO CLEAR OR EASY AS THIS PSALM IMPLIES, NOR IS THE FATE OF THE BELIEVER ALWAYS SUPERIOR TO THE FAITHLESS PERSON.

Both interpretations of this psalm need to be conveyed to God's people: the invitation to be righteous and the fact that not all faithful people are materially blessed. People might be asked to reflect on these two ways of viewing this psalm to discover when this psalm is useful and under what circumstances.

PSALM 18:2-3, 3-4, 47, 51

This royal psalm of thanksgiving also appears in 2 Samuel 22. The psalm begins with several natural and military images that convey God's strength and give the psalmist reason to believe in his ultimate deliverance from the threat of death. God appeared as a divine warrior to deliver the king (vv. 7-19), who portrays himself as a model of moral virtue (vv. 20-24). The king praises God for enabling him to defeat his enemies (vv. 30-45). The psalm ends with praise for the living Lord, who delivers the king (v. 46), and in general shows great loyalty to him and to the whole royal line (v. 50).

SECOND READING

1 THESSALONIANS 2:1-8

Interpreting the Text

Paul offers in these verses an autobiographical confession, somewhat like the confessions in the book of Jeremiah, and defends himself against criticisms from outside the church. His visit to Thessalonica had not been in vain, and it had lacked neither power nor substance. In v. 2 he refers to trying events in Philippi, when he and Silas had been beaten and imprisoned despite the fact that they were Roman citizens. In the wake of these reverses, Paul had shown prophetic boldness when there had been efforts in Thessalonica to keep him from preaching or the readers from accepting the gospel (v. 2).

Paul defends himself against the charge of basing his message on error or compromising it by moral impurity, and he affirms that he had not used dishonest methods to trick people into believing his message. Just as his credentials have been based on divine approval, so it has been his duty and goal to please his divine master (v. 4). He also disavows the use of flattery and denies that he was a missionary for the sake of money or praise from other human beings. He and Silas (Timothy is not to be considered an apostle) had also not used their status as apostles to make extraordinary demands. Rather, their ministry was gentle, much like a mother who takes care of her own children rather than entrusting them to others.

Verse 8 demonstrates the deep affection of Paul and his companions for the Thessalonians. Their first goal was to share the gospel of God, but they also were willing to give their very lives in an act of self-giving for the sake of the congregation at Thessalonica.

Responding to the Text   265

TWENTY-SECOND
SUNDAY
AFTER PENTECOST
─────────────
OCTOBER 24

Ministry means responding to the context appropriately. Occasionally one hears about the "alligators" that are out there in the church. I know firsthand that church people can be cruel and unloving, but the term "alligators" seems to write off such opponents as beyond hope and surely beyond respect. Paul reacted to such a potentially hostile context by being gentle among the Thessalonians, like a nurse tenderly caring for her own children. She would never call these children "brats" or "alligators." Paul notes how deeply he cared for the Thessalonians and how dear they are to him.

Paul and his companions were determined to share the gospel amidst the conflicts of Thessalonica. Each of us has his or her shorthand for the gospel; but all of these expressions somehow circle back to the confession that God has acted decisively for us through the life, death, and resurrection of Jesus. God has said "yes" to us when he could have more justifiably said "no." God is free to contradict his own anger over human evil: to forgive, to trust people, to raise the lowly and put down the haughty.

And Paul and his companions also gave of themselves for the sake of the gospel and for the sake of the Thessalonians. Paul did not manipulate people with his words nor did he pull rank as an apostle. Rather, like his Lord, he was willing to lay down his life for the sake of his Thessalonian friends. Paul rings the changes on traits that might damage ministry. He has avoided deceit, impure motives, trickery, flattery, greed, or even praise for himself. Clearly, he was in ministry for the sake of others.

With such high standards Paul's ministry was not, and our ministry dare not be, in vain (v. 1).

1 THESSALONIANS 1:1-5

Interpreting the Text

These verses were discussed for the Twenty-first Sunday after Pentecost.

GOSPEL

MATTHEW 22:34-46

Interpreting the Text

The Pharisees were satisfied with the way Jesus had bested the Sadducees with regard to the resurrection (Matt. 22:23-33, omitted in the lectionary). In the next controversy saying (vv. 34-40; cf. Mark 12:28-34 and Luke 10:25-28), a person skilled in the law of Moses (a lawyer) asks Jesus which commandment in the law is the greatest. That is, what is the center or summary of the law? Jesus quotes Deut. 6:5 in v. 37, part of the ancient Shema or creed of Judaism that is contained in Deut 6:4-9. But he linked to this commandment a second commandment from Lev. 19:18, and put love of neighbor on the same plane as love for God. The bringing together of these two passages is also found in the pseudepigraphic Jewish book called the "Testament of Issachar" (5:2), and the lawyer himself, presumably reflecting Jewish tradition, put these two commandments together in Luke 10:27. Jesus insists that the essence of the divine demand lies in these two commandments. They are the center of the Pentateuch and the Prophets (Joshua—2 Kings, Isaiah, Jeremiah, Ezekiel, and the Twelve). This pericope may imply that the Pharisaic concentration on the development of minor laws might lead them to miss the law's true center.

In the next saying (vv. 41-46; cf. Mark 12:35-37 and Luke 20:41-44), Jesus takes the initiative and poses a question to the Pharisees about the messiah. They respond that the messiah is the son of David. This answer would be expected from the data in the Old Testament and even the book of Matthew itself (Isa. 11:1; Jer. 23:5; and Matt. 1:1). Perhaps the best contemporary explication of what this son of David might do is in *Psalms of Solomon* 17. But Jesus throws the adequacy of this response into doubt by posing a question about the interpretation of Ps. 110:1: "The Lord said to my Lord, 'Sit at my right hand, until I put your enemies under your feet.'" Jesus assumes that the author of this psalm was David himself and that he was gifted by the Spirit with prophetic insight. In this reading, David would mean: The Lord (= God) said to my Lord (= the messiah). Since a father (superior) does not call his son (an inferior) "Lord," Jesus is raising a question about the appropriateness or sufficiency of calling the messiah the son of David. Modern exegetical understanding of the psalm in its original context assumes that the speaker is a court theologian whose thought might be summarized in this way: "The Lord (= Yahweh) said to my Lord (= the current king)." The psalm, therefore, is talking about the power or prestige given to the king by God at his coronation. The author of the book of Matthew may have preferred titles like Son of God, Son of Man, or Lord for Jesus rather than the title Son of David. In any case, this argument of Jesus effectively ended his discussion with the Pharisees.

Responding to the Text

While neither of the issues discussed in these two controversy stories is debated in the church today, the central saying of Jesus in each case is most useful for the life of Christians today.

"Love" of God is a rather late development in Old Testament theology. Hosea, in fact, in the eighth century, was the first canonical writer to use "love" to describe God's attitude toward human beings; but even he did not dare to talk about human love for God. The biblical writers do not discuss why they avoided the term love, but it may have had something to do with the way in which fertility rites were common among their neighbors; and so "love" for (or by) God might be easily misconstrued. "Love" has its own dangers in our culture where it can be easily sentimentalized, or where it can add to our already rampant individualism.

In the Old Testament world, "love" had legal or political connotations. When the Bible says Hiram, king of Tyre, was a lover of David (1 Kings 5:1; NRSV reads "friend"), it meant that these two neighboring kings were loyal allies or trading partners. The Deuteronomist, in the seventh century, was the first writer to use "love" to describe the human attitude toward God; and he clearly implied loyalty, faithfulness, and obedience by this verb. Hence he called on his readers to love the Lord with all their heart, soul, and mind.

Jesus was probably not the first Jew (and certainly not the last) to link love of God with selfless love of neighbor. This linkage is central to Jewish and Christian ethics. Most biblical ethical injunctions rule out certain behaviors or, occasionally, urge people to follow certain courses of actions. But there could never be enough laws to fit all the ethical decisions you and I need to make every day of our lives. In our freedom we are called to love. Christian freedom is not Christian license. Rather, those who love God and the neighbor possess the basis for making appropriate ethical decisions. Augustine once said, "Love God, and then do whatever you want." This double-barreled love ethic preserves freedom and flexibility, but it is always an invitation to move beyond mere legal compliance to the deepest possible ethics.

The term "Christ" (that is, messiah) has become central in Christian self-understanding. But how is the one we proclaim as Lord and Savior related to the ideal royal person Israel expected? How is Jesus the son of David? How is he the messiah?

Christians believe that the fulfillment of the messianic promise in Jesus goes well beyond the original promise. We confess that God sent not only an ideal son of David, but actually God's own dear son. Christians also confess that the most important thing about this messiah is his atoning death on the cross. This is a dramatic shift from earlier thinking. Before the time of Jesus, Jews did not believe in the salvific nature of the messiah's death and even his death is nowhere expected in the Old Testament. Even Paul said that the confession of Christ (messiah) crucified would be a stumbling block to the Jews (1 Cor. 1:23).

But Christians also need to concede that their messiah, or at least their activities in the messiah's name, have not lived up to the transforming power that was expected with the messiah's advent. The Christian era has not seen a wave of egalitarian prosperity or even of unmitigated peace. On the contrary, the Christian church has often retarded the quest for justice, become a divisive power itself, and contributed as individuals and as a corporate entity to anti-Semitism and racial bigotry.

When we ask, therefore, how Christ is the son of David it should cause us to ponder how God often fulfills his promises beyond all expectations and how our bearing the name of Christ (as in our naming ourselves "Christian") frequently calls us to repentance and renewal.

TWENTY-THIRD SUNDAY AFTER PENTECOST

October 31, 1999 / Proper 26

Revised Common	Episcopal (BCP)	Roman Catholic
Josh. 3:7-17	Micah 3:5-12	Mal. 1:14—2:2, 8-10
or Micah 3:5-12		
Pss. 107:1-7, 33-37; 43	Ps. 43	Ps. 131:1, 2, 3
1 Thess. 2:9-13	1 Thess. 2:9-13, 17-20	1 Thess. 2:7-9, 13
Matt. 23:1-12	Matt. 23:1-12	Matt. 23:1-12

First Reading
JOSHUA 3:7-17

Interpreting the Text

Crossing the Jordan River mirrors crossing the Sea of Reeds in Exodus 14–15; both events bracket Israel's formative phase in the wilderness (cf. Josh. 4:23). The Canaanite God Baal defeated an enemy called Prince Sea and Judge River, and his reputation is now outdone by Yahweh, who "defeats" the Reed Sea and the Jordan River. Yahweh promises to use the crossing of the Jordan as a way to underscore the authority of Joshua and to indicate that God is also with him. God is referred to as the "living God" whose promises were made manifest in his gift of the land. The groups in Canaan that preceded Israel in v. 10 come from a conventional list that appears twenty-eight times in the Bible. The ark contained the Ten Commandments and therefore was called the ark of the covenant by some writers. The ark also signified God's presence, especially in holy war (cf. Num. 10:35-36). The long divine title connected with the ark in v. 11 indicates in this context Yahweh's power over the realm of nature. When the feet of the priests carrying the ark touched the waters, the river piled up in a heap upstream at Adam, 16 miles north of the ford near Jericho. Zarethan is an additional eleven miles north of Adam. The remaining part of the river drained off into the Dead Sea. In the world of the text (not the same as the world of history), the priests remained standing in the river bottom until all two million Israelites had crossed over.

The twelve men selected in v. 12 gathered twelve stones from the river bottom in chapter 4 and set them up as a memorial to help instruct children of a future generation about Israel's miraculous crossing of the Jordan on dry ground.

Responding to the Text

It is hard to imagine a more reassuring word from God than "I am with you," or "I will be with you." In two short Hebrew words Joshua is told that God accepts him and that God empowers him. At the time of his own call, Moses was filled with self-doubt and said: "Who am I that I should go to Pharaoh, and bring the Israelites out of Egypt?" God's good news for this bad situation was, "I will be with you" (Exod. 3:11-12). When Moses protested that he was not a good speaker, God once more reassured him, "I will be with your mouth" (Exod. 4:10-12). The reader of the biblical story knows the glorious outcome of God's acceptance and empowerment of Moses—the successful battle with Pharaoh in the story of the plagues, the Exodus from Egypt, the giving of the law on Sinai and Moses' steady, if somewhat flawed, leadership of the people during their forty years in the wilderness. Who would want to contest that God had been with Moses? Just as God had been with Moses, so he would be with Joshua in the great new adventure in the land.

The ark also plays an important symbolic role in this story. The ark in the Old Testament sometimes represented God's presence in holy war. But it could also be the place where God was invisibly enthroned, and its lid was the place where the central rite at the Day of Atonements was performed. The Ten Commandments were kept in the ark and so here it is fittingly called the ark of the covenant. The ark in the middle of the Jordan might convey any one of these connotations to different people or groups as they observed it, but the writer argued that it showed above all that God was alive and would carry through on his promise to give Israel the land. The twelve men who carried the ark represented all of Israel, that is, one man for each of the tribes. While each of us is called to bear witness to our faith, this story reminds us that the church as a whole also bears witness. That witness is often clouded by the foibles of the church, and by its divisions. This story calls the church to reflect on how it as a body can bear witness to the living God, and to the God who died and lives anew.

MICAH 3:5-12 (alt.)

Interpreting the Text

The "peace prophets" were those who assured the people everything was going to be all right and there was no need to repent. Micah accuses them of selling their services and putting those who refused to pay them under a curse. On the other hand, Micah feels himself empowered to tell Jacob and Israel about their sins. The prophet's indictment of the political and religious leaders is particularly strong. After selling their services to the highest bidder, they outwardly lean on (= have faith in) the Lord and trust that God's presence will protect them from all danger. Because of their infidelity Micah foresees the imminent destruction of Jerusalem and the temple.

Responding to the Text

None of us in church leadership would be so craven as to sell out to the highest bidder; but every church leader stands in danger of setting sails to match prevailing congregational or community winds. It is especially difficult to call individuals away from their sins. Micah's fourfold endowment—with power, spirit, justice, and might—made him bold to tell Jacob and Israel their transgressions and sins. Such courage in the abstract or at the distance of many centuries is easier than when dealing with people who know and love you, and who pay one's salary.

Verse 11 demonstrates how the slogan "I am with you" (see the discussion of Josh. 3:7-17) can be perverted into complacency and false security. The corrupt leadership of Judah brazenly shouted, "Surely the Lord is with us! No harm shall come upon us." The corruption of the community's leadership is the very reason Micah thought Jerusalem had to be destroyed. Leaders are persons to whom much has been given, and from whom much is expected.

MALACHI 1:14—2:2, 8-10

Interpreting the Text

Malachi lived sometime after the dedication of the second Jerusalem temple in 515 B.C.E. and before the work of Nehemiah in the second half of the fifth century. The prophet criticizes the people for lack of piety and announces the coming of a messenger, who will purify Judah prior to the day of the Lord (3:1-4).

In the verses selected from Malachi for the First Lesson, the prophet chastises those who sacrifice blemished animals to Yahweh (1:14). The priests were especially culpable in this regard (1:6-13), and God promises to turn their blessings of the people into curses (2:1-2). The priests are also criticized for the way they give instruction (= Torah, vv. 8-9), and contrasts are drawn between them and their ancestor Levi (vv. 4-6) and with the reputation of priests in general, who are called the "messenger of the Lord of hosts" (v. 7). Verse 10 considers Judahites as an extended family with God as divine parent. Verse 11, not included in the lesson, criticizes some of the people of Judah for marrying outside this family to a "daughter of a foreign god."

Responding to the Text

Many of the issues discussed by Malachi are unique to his day and are no longer concerns in the church. Since many congregations have stewardship emphases in late fall, the words of this text may serve to remind us how miserly we often are in our gifts to God. The indictment of the priests may cause contemporary members of the clergy to reflect on ways they might be accused of corruption or of giving instruction that is not faithful to the church's tradition.

Verse 10 is one of the few references to God as father in the Old Testament. While that idea has become increasingly problematic in our time, this verse does provide occasion to reflect on the oneness of the human, created family, and to reflect on the need to be much more loyal to fellow members of the Christian community.

RESPONSIVE READING
PSALM 107:1-7, 33-37

Interpreting the Text

The initial call to give thanks in this psalm names Yahweh's goodness and his everlasting loyalty to his people. The word "redeem" in the Bible refers to faithful or saving actions taken by a person on behalf of members of the family. When used of God's actions, therefore, this word has an especially warm and intimate connotation. The actions referred to in vv. 2-3 may allude to the return from the Babylonian exile. God's actions came in response to the people's prayer. The psalm also thanks God for deliverance from prison (vv. 10-16), from illness (vv. 17-22), and from the perils of the sea (vv. 23-32).

God's judgment on the wicked dries up water supplies and makes good land unprofitable (vv. 33-34), but he blesses the righteous by giving them water, establishing them in a town, and increasing the yield of their agriculture. The final verse of the psalm (v. 43) calls for wise reflection. Those who read this psalm need to ponder the implications of God's loyalty or steadfast love for their own life of discipleship.

Responding to the Text

The first verse of this psalm has been a common table prayer in my tradition, "O, give thanks unto the Lord for he is good, for his mercy endureth forever." It really is a beautiful prayer even if frequent use has robbed it of its original power. The one addressed as Lord is the one who disclosed his own name, Yahweh, to his people as he led them from slavery to freedom (Exodus 3 and 6). This Lord is "good." This adjective is an understatement; but it allows the one praying to bring to divine attention the four crises listed in this psalm or whatever other needs have been experienced. During my lifetime, translators have moved from "mercy" to "steadfast love" and, most recently, to "loyalty" as the preferred rendition for that attribute of God that lasts forever. God's loyalty to his human children invites and empowers them to similar loyalty to the covenantal relationship God has established with them. God's loyalty has shown itself in God's being the best father or mother we could ever know. That's why those who pray this psalm name themselves "the redeemed."

PSALM 43

Interpreting the Text

It is generally agreed that Psalms 42–43 are really a single psalm of lament. There is no superscription for Psalm 43, and a similar refrain appears in 42:5, 11, and 43:5. The psalmist is beset by wicked enemies and seeks refuge in God even though God himself seems to reject the psalmist. Despite depression over present circumstances, the psalmist urges his or her innermost being to hope in God. The psalmist confidently expects to praise God for help (salvation) received. Whatever the present circumstances, God is still "my God." He or she prays that God would send out light and truth to lead the psalmist to the sanctuary where the psalmist will praise God with music and the offering of sacrifices for deliverance received. The psalmist remembers fondly such joyful celebrations in God's house in the past.

Responding to the Text

A local congregation is handing out bumper stickers that say, "I'm too blessed to be depressed." The refrain in 42:5, 11, and 43:5 flows from similar theology, which has dared to ask harder questions, such as, "Why have you cast me off?" (43:2). The psalmist questions herself on the reasons for her discouragement and then preaches to herself: "Hope in God." Good preaching always begins at home. The defiant confession at the end of the refrain remains the psalmist of our only refuge. The one who helps is—one says with confident astonishment—my God.

PSALM 131

In this brief psalm of trust, the psalmist rejects an attitude of arrogance and compares his or her own contentment with that of a weaned child lying on the bosom of its mother. The psalm concludes with an exhortation for all Israel to hope in the Lord. (Cf. Ps. 25:22 on the Eighteenth Sunday after Pentecost.)

SECOND READING

1 THESSALONIANS 2:9-13

Interpreting the Text

Paul reminds the Thessalonians that he was not a burden to them financially, but worked to provide his own income, untiringly and with some pain, presumably as a leather worker or tent maker (Acts 18:3). The gospel he preached came from God and proclaimed what God had done. Paul believed that the good conduct of the apostles could be attested not only by the experience of the Thessalonians with them, but also by God, who cannot be deceived. His righteous conduct met the standards of justice, and he could not be accused of falling short of that standard. Paul compares his role as an ethical instructor to that of a father (v. 11), just as he claimed to be a nurse (v. 7) in his role as nourisher. The purpose of his preaching and his ethical conduct was to encourage and even demand that the Thessalonians themselves lead lives worthy of God. God's holiness requires corresponding human holiness: "You shall be holy, for I am holy" (Lev. 11:45). God's kingdom (v. 12) is the future realm in which God's full salvation will be manifest. "Glory" has a similar, eschatological meaning. The word spoken by the mouth of Paul and heard by Thessalonian ears was in fact the very word of God. This word also operated powerfully in the lives of the believers in Thessalonica.

Responding to the Text

What Paul did for the Thessalonians made him an ideal father; but there is no gender stereotyping here. Urging, encouraging, and pleading are what parents of any sex would do if they could help their spiritual—or physical—children to lead a life worthy of God. To urge is to command or exhort, to call people to transcend what they would naturally do. To encourage is to help, to show gentleness like a nurse (v. 7), to call attention to God's promises to help, to recognize the difficulty faced by the other, to stand with and for the other person. To plead might at first seem to be excessive, but not when we reflect on the goal of it all: to lead a life worthy of God.

Paul had proclaimed the gospel of God (v. 9). This might be taken as the good news that comes from God (subjective genitive), with all the connotations that might mean in terms of reinforcing Paul's urging, encouraging, and pleading. Or it could also be taken as good news about God (objective genitive), telling the Thessalonians and all who would hear of God's saving and reconciling work in Jesus Christ.

Verse 13 describes the miracle of preaching. After a week of study, participation in pericope groups, living our own lives, and participating in the lives of our

congregations and communities, we finally sit down to draft a speech for Sunday
275

TWENTY-THIRD
SUNDAY
AFTER PENTECOST
———
OCTOBER 31

morning. And, more often than not, the listeners look expectantly to us to hear
our exposition of God's word. What's more, they accept our preaching as the
word of God. They are right in this conclusion, Paul says, and this word accom-
plishes much among them.

GOSPEL
MATTHEW 23:1-12

Interpreting the Text

This chapter begins the fifth discourse in Matthew and is directed primarily to the public (v. 1), while chaps. 24–25 are addressed to the disciples or
the church of Matthew's day. There are parallels to this pericope in Mark 12:38-
40, and Luke 11:37-52 and 20:45-47. "Moses' seat" (v. 2) was a place in the contemporary synagogue where authorized teachers sat. Jesus does not contest the
teaching or doctrine of the Pharisees, but he accuses them of hypocrisy. By the
time of the *Didache* (8.1), "hypocrites" had become interchangeable with "Jews"
in polemical speech. The religious duties they imposed on others would be difficult to practice by people in the trades or other forms of business, but were not
a particular burden for themselves (v. 4). The Dead Sea Scrolls describe the Pharisees as "expounders of smooth things." Phylacteries were small leather cases that
contained specific biblical passages (Deut. 11:13-22; 6:4-9; Exod. 13:11-16;
13:2-10) and could be attached to the hand and forehead. Fringes were attached
to the corners of Jewish garments in accordance with Num. 15:38-39 and Deut.
22:12. Jesus also wore them (Matt. 9:20; 14:36). In addition to such showy use
of religious symbols, the leaders also coveted the best and most honorable seats at
banquets and in the synagogues. In vv. 8-10 Jesus expresses criticism of a number of religious titles that may have only become current in the Judaism of
Matthew's time. These verses are addressed to the disciples, that is, the Matthean
church, and they fit an ethos of humility in the church. Christian leaders are not
to call themselves "rabbi" because Jesus alone is their teacher and they are all equal
brothers and sisters (NRSV: "students"). Jesus also forbids the use of the title
"father" for a religious leader and reserves that title for the heavenly Father. Saul
ben Batnith (80–120 C.E.) is the first known Jewish sage to bear the title "father."
Paul describes his own role as father in 1 Thess. 2:11. Some scholars interpret v.
10 as a duplicate of v. 8, but others contend that to call Jesus/the Messiah
"instructor" may have contrasted him as the Teacher with the Teacher of Righteousness in the Qumran community. Verse 11 has a parallel in Matt. 20:20-28,
where Jesus describes the role of the Son of Man as that of a servant who gives

his life as a ransom for many. Verse 12, a passage taken from Q (Luke 14:11), advocates service more than self-negation.

Responding to the Text

Practice what you preach! That has always been a sobering sentence for pastors to hear since it is one thing to preach about forgiveness and quite another to forgive, or to advocate trust in God and to be able to express that trust oneself. Pastors are people just like everyone else in the congregation; but in the ordination rite in my church they are called to adorn the gospel with a godly life. Since the clergy are the primary preachers, they are often the primary practitioners. The command to practice what one preaches can be excessive; but in this era of widespread clergy sexual misconduct it is a commandment whose importance can hardly be overestimated.

Jesus criticizes his opponents for loading burdens on others and not lifting a finger themselves, for a religiosity that is all for show, and for their claiming titles of honor in the community. Titles themselves are not so much a problem today. Everyone at the seminary calls me, my colleagues, and even our president by our first names. If anything, I have the feeling we have overdone avoidance of titles. Whether we call ourselves Ralph or Dr. Klein, however, it is still all too easy for us to bask in any attention paid to us and to consider those around us beneath us. We compare ourselves to others in the number of friends or church members we have, in our publications, in our earned degrees, in our cars or computers, and in hundreds of other categories. Clerical vestments were once intended to downplay the role of the individual; but stoles, albs, chasubles, and clerical collars—very good in and of themselves!—have a way of drawing lines between laity and clergy, to the disadvantage of the former.

Verse 9 was not problematic for most of my ministry. Clergy in my denomination are rarely called "father," and it seemed so natural to address God as Father. In the last generation a number of women have told us how God as Father tends to emphasize the maleness of God and the hierarchical structures in the church and in the family. I am not at all sure that "Creator, Redeemer, and Sanctifier" is altogether adequate as a Trinitarian formula; but is it not ironic that a word from Jesus meant to undercut all hierarchy in the community now seems to reinforce it? The preacher's task is to undercut all hierarchies in the present community with new words and images.

BUT IS IT NOT IRONIC THAT A WORD FROM JESUS MEANT TO UNDERCUT ALL HIERARCHY IN THE COMMUNITY NOW SEEMS TO REINFORCE IT?

The greatest among you will be your servant. This is the topsy-turvy economy of God, who brings down the powerful from their thrones and lifts up the lowly. The one called the Messiah did not hesitate to go all the way to the depths of the cross for us and therefore is hailed as Lord. Of course, even this word can be misunderstood today if it is used to perpetuate the role of men over women or of white people over people of color. We need to practice the greatness of being servants in our own lives before we dare ask anyone to follow us.

The final verse in this pericope offers eschatological judgment or eschatological exaltation to the proud and the humble respectively. To the proud this verse offers an urgent invitation to repent before it is too late; to the humble it offers grace appropriate to the situation. That is the wonder of the task of preaching. How can we make the gospel as liberating today as it was in the first century? We err in focusing on the scribes and Pharisees. Rather, we need to hear Jesus calling the religious leaders of every generation to seek the greatness of servanthood.

ALL SAINTS' DAY

November 1, 1999

Revised Common	Episcopal (BCP)	Roman Catholic
Rev. 7:9-17	Sir. 44:1-10, 13-14 or Sir. 2:(1-6) 7-11	Rev. 7:2-4, 9-14
Ps. 34:1-10, 22	Ps. 149	Ps. 24:1-2, 3-4, 5-6
1 John 3:1-3	Rev. 7:2-4, 9-17 or Eph. 1:(11-14) 15-23	1 John 3:1-3
Matt. 5:1-12	Matt. 5:1-12 or Luke 6:20-26 (27-36)	Matt. 5:1-12

First Reading

REVELATION 7:9-17

Interpreting the Text

Chapter 7 consists of two visions inserted between the opening of the sixth and seventh seals. The multitude of saints in vv. 9-17 is innumerable, while the group in vv. 1-8 numbered 144,000—12,000 from each of the twelve tribes. This second group represents all the faithful who remained loyal to the end. The expression "palm branches" in v. 9 connotes victory. "Victory" is probably also a better translation for the first word of their song in v. 10. Victory belongs to God and the Lamb. One of the twenty-four elders assumes the role of the interpreting angel and strikes up a conversation with John in vv. 13-17. He interprets the innumerable group as those who have survived the persecution at the endtime. Since garments symbolize the inner state of the people involved, we learn that these faithful have been inwardly cleansed through the blood of the Lamb. Behind the symbolism lie the actions of repentance, conversion, and baptism. These faithful will enjoy life in God's presence. All their physical needs will be met (no hunger or thirst), and they will be freed from every kind of sorrow. The Lamb becomes the shepherd (cf. Psalm 23), who gives them water and protects them.

Responding to the Text

All Saints' Day allows us to look behind the veil of death and gaze on the victory celebration of those who have gone before us. The one who said at the beginning that everything that he had made was "very good" (Gen. 1:31) promises to restore human life to its pristine condition at the end. No more hunger, thirst, sunburn and, above all, no more tears. Some of the dead in Revelation are survivors of "the great ordeal," the time of tribulation that was expected before the end of the world. But all who die are products of ordeals of some sort—disappointments, pain, aging, separation, and terminal illness. On All Saints' Day, we the living listen in on the sevenfold cheer of those who offer God blessing, glory, wisdom, thanksgiving, honor, power, and might.

The saints wear white garments and wave victory palms. The Lamb's shedding of blood on the cross is the detergent that turns all their garments sparkling white. Strange alchemy. Blood normally stains and makes things ritually impure. Christ's sacrifice, on the other hand, cleanses, purifies, and transforms. Saint Paul writes, "God proves his love for us in that while we still were sinners Christ died for us" (Rom. 5:8).

> ALL SAINTS' DAY ALLOWS US TO LOOK BEHIND THE VEIL OF DEATH AND GAZE ON THE VICTORY CELEBRATION OF THOSE WHO HAVE GONE BEFORE US.

In our urbanized, North-American setting people may understand a sacrificial lamb; but this lamb—in God's topsy-turvy economy—is at the same time a shepherd who makes us lie down in green pastures and leads us beside still waters. All Saints' Day is a time for all saints to shout defiantly, "I shall dwell in the house of the Lord forever" (Ps. 23:6).

SIRACH (ECCLESIASTICUS) 44:1-10, 13-14

Interpreting the Text

God gave recognition to great people in the past (v. 2) who achieved success in a variety of tasks (vv. 3-6). While all were honored in their lifetime, the reputation of some of them has endured, but others have been completely forgotten. The writer hails the righteousness of these former leaders, noting that their descendants will always continue. Though their bodies have died, their name, or reputation, will endure forever. The list of the great heroes of the past begins at v. 16 and continues through chapter 51.

Responding to the Text

I enjoy walking through cemeteries and studying the names, dates, pictures, and Bible verses on the tombstones, especially the older ones. Occasionally I'll see an old grave that is quite neatly kept. A grandson or granddaughter cares enough to come by and plant a few flowers or pull a few weeds. When I visited Germany some years ago, I learned that people only rented their burial space for thirty years. It is legal for your descendants to buy you another term, but I understand that few do. After thirty years, there's better use for the money.

All Saints' Day gives us a chance to remember those mothers and fathers who kept the faith going, by teaching their children, participating in the congregation and the community, caring for the sick, sitting in a back pew, praying unannounced for all members of the congregation, and living out their lives in obscure faithfulness. They perished as if they never existed (v. 9).

These people live in their descendants, in God who remembers their righteous deeds, and by our congregations who declare their (anonymous) wisdom and proclaim their (anonymous) praise.

SIRACH (ECCLESIASTICUS) 2:(1-6) 7-11

Interpreting the Text

God's merciful compassion is a theme spelled out in Exod. 34:6-7. On the basis of this divine characteristic, the author calls on readers to withstand the trials they must inevitably go through, knowing that God will help them and that in the end their piety will be rewarded. To the rhetorical questions in v. 10, one is tempted to ask, "What about Job?" The author of Psalm 22 also felt that he had been abandoned by God, at least for a time.

Responding to the Text

The wisdom writers knew that not every exception can be explained. In general, God stands by the righteous—Job and the author of Psalm 22 are exceptions that prove the rule. We remind ourselves as we worship together that the Lord is compassionate and merciful, that he forgives sins and saves in time of distress. All Saints' Day can get the whole people of God ready for the great ordeal. When Cardinal Bernadin announced to the press that he had terminal cancer, the Chicago reporters wanted to know if he was afraid. "I have been helping people die for forty years," he replied. "Now it's my turn to believe what I preached."

RESPONSIVE READING
PSALM 34:1-10, 22

Interpreting the Text

This psalm is an acrostic, with each verse beginning with a different letter of the Hebrew alphabet. It blends thanksgiving and wisdom. On the basis of his own experience (vv. 4, 6), the psalmist knows that God delivers those who call upon him in time of trouble. He therefore praises God, urges other worshipers to do the same (v. 3) and then offers advice to his fellow believers, who will no doubt experience many trials in life (vv. 11-22). The psalmist recognizes that peace never comes easily (v. 14). We must seek peace *and* pursue it. The "angel of the LORD" (v. 7) is an expression often used to talk about God's own actions (cf. Josh. 5:13-15). This angel, or God himself, watches over all who have faith in him (v. 7). Early Christians understood v. 8a eucharistically ("O taste and see that the Lord is good"). I would translate v. 8b as follows: "How to be emulated are those who take refuge in him." In addition to this admonition, the psalmist also affirms that none of those taking refuge in God will ever be condemned (v. 22). Those who fear the Lord may have the wherewithal to undergo adversity, but it does not mean that they will escape being brokenhearted or crushed in spirit.

Responding to the Text

All of us like to tell our story—how we enjoyed our grandchild or relaxed on vacation. The psalmist tells about another story: He had prayed in a time of trouble and God answered him by delivering him. "Fear" in the Old Testament usually means trust rather than terror. The angel of the Lord is like a whole army protecting those who trust in God. At the Eucharist we taste the Lord's goodness in the past and in the present.

The term "holy ones" in v. 9 reminds us that God's people alive today are as much his saints as those who have gone before us. The psalmist reassures us that we will lack nothing good, and he invites us to emulate others who trust in God. In our society victory often goes to the strong, young, and powerful. But while these self-reliant people can suffer want and hunger, we know, as the psalmist knew, that the Lord is our shepherd and therefore we will not want.

PSALM 149

Interpreting the Text

The psalmist urges Israel to offer a new song (v. 1) in recognition of the newness of Yahweh's impending actions for his people. This praise is to be rendered in the public assembly and with accompanying musical instruments and dancing. The parallelism of the Hebrew poetry is especially instructive in v. 4: The Lord's taking pleasure in his people is balanced by his adorning them with victory (salvation). God's people are placed in juxtaposition with the "humble" or with the "oppressed." The service of praise turns into a military liturgy in v. 6. Symbolically the people execute punishment on the nations and their kings, who have mistreated Israel. Their ritual actions anticipate God's final deliverance. God's judgment will mean honor for all those who remain loyal to God. This psalm has an eschatological overtone—people are called to praise God for his judgment against the foreign peoples, judgment that still lies in the future. This psalm begins and ends with the word "Hallelujah!" "Praise the LORD!"

Responding to the Text

Worship of God is always surrounded by a "Hallelujah" at its beginning and at its end. We saints gather together to remember how God made us, rules us, and takes pleasure in us. The psalmist knows that those who have experienced God's goodness cannot sit still—they need to dance and sing and play musical instruments. Verse 6 announces a strange (to us) liturgy. The same people who praise God march around with weapons in their hands. They know that God usually works mediately, that is, through people. They also know that our small victories now are but a foretaste of the great victory to come. The preacher may want to translate the enemy countries into those present and persistent habits and predilections that keep us from trusting God. Armed with praise for God's ultimate victory over those powers, we use every means at our disposal to put them behind us now.

PSALM 24:1-6

Interpreting the Text

This psalm is an entrance liturgy to the temple, pledging the psalmists to an obedient life (cf. Psalm 15). The creation themes in vv. 1-2 echo the divine conquest of chaos in the religion of Israel's neighbors. A priest asks a question about who may enter the sanctuary in v. 3. The response in vv. 4-6 by those seeking admittance to the sanctuary rejects idolatry and false oaths. Verse 6 expresses acceptance of these conditions by those desiring to enter the temple area. Verses 7-11 describe the entrance of the Lord of hosts (armies) to the sanctuary.

SECOND READING
1 JOHN 3:1-3

Interpreting the Text

First John was written about 100 C.E., probably from Ephesus. The author criticizes those who had departed from the community's traditional beliefs about Jesus. The opponents held a docetic Christology, believing that Jesus was a spirit and not fully human. The author, however, affirmed the identity of the human Jesus with the divine Son of God and believed in the saving value of his death. He urged his readers to love one another and to obey Christ's commandments. One cannot believe in Jesus without loving other believers.

The verses from the Second Lesson affirm that we are already children of God but recognize that we will be transformed further after the return of Christ. In the Old Testament, "children of God" is a term used to refer to the members of God's council, often called angels. In Job 1:6, for example, the "children of God" (NRSV "heavenly beings") came together to present themselves before the Lord. Hosea promised that in the future Israel would be called "children of the living God" (1:10). In 1 John, identity as God's (adopted) children is a central part of the community's confession. God is love (4:8), and God shows this love to us by designating us as his children. Those who do not recognize us as God's children also do not recognize him (the Father? Christ?).

The author's hope is clear and simple: We shall be like him. He believes this because he is assured we will see Christ face to face. The consequence of our present identity as God's children is a desire to purify oneself, just as Christ is pure. In the following verses (vv. 4-10) the author urges readers to seek sinlessness in practice, and he warns against persisting in sin.

Responding to the Text

We do not know much about the life to come: what happens between our death and our resurrection, how we will relate, if at all, to former family and friends. Streets of gold and gates of pearl are metaphors; even the prospect of harp music does not particularly thrill me. Would someone with a glorified body really be me?

There's a story about an old theologian who had written a two-volume work on the resurrection. When his children gathered at his deathbed, they asked: "Is there anything else you wish you had said about the resurrection?" "I know I will be safe," he replied.

The reason we all know we will be safe is because God designates us his children right now. In our baptism, in God's daily assurance of forgiveness, and in the gathering together on Sundays of all of God's children, God reinforces the message and so we confess: "God's children—that is what we already are!"

In some ways we will be like God because in some way we will see God. In this time and space no one can see God and live. Even Moses only got to see God's "back parts." How can we see one who is immortal, invisible, and all the rest? Faith is enough for now; sight can wait until then. Even saints do not comprehend what it means to be like God although they all can understand being "safe."

Saints of God with this hope are called to respond and to purify themselves, just as God is pure. In v. 10 the author identifies two impurities: people who do not do what is right (I'll let you fill in the details) and—here's the concrete hard part—those who do not love their brothers and sisters.

EPHESIANS 1:(11–14) 15–23

See the Last Sunday after Pentecost.

GOSPEL

MATTHEW 5:1–12

Interpreting the Text

There are nine beatitudes in Matthew, but only four in Luke (6:20b–23), where they are cast in the second person and followed by a series of woes (6:24–26). The beatitude form is based on precedents in the psalms and the wisdom literature of the Old Testament (e.g., Psalm 1). In the Old Testament it might best be translated as "Oh, how to be emulated is the person who. . . ." Some scholars detect a connotation of congratulations addressed to the recipients of the beatitudes since those presently suffering will experience eschatological reversal. Note the exhortation to rejoice and be glad in v. 12. We might speak of the "theological passives" in vv. 4, 6, and 9 since they imply that God himself will comfort the mourners, fill the hungry, and call the peacemakers children of God. The beatitudes reinforce the promises of the kingdom and at the same time call for deeper ethical behavior.

The "poor in spirit" (v. 3; Luke 6:20 reads "poor") are those who have confidence only in God because of their long social and economic distress. The "poor" designated a special piety in Judaism, marked by humility, detachment from wealth, and even voluntary poverty. God shows special care for them. The mourners (v. 4) may be lamenting the condition of humiliated Israel (cf. Luke 2:25). The meek (v. 5) are humble or powerless people who will inherit the new promised land of the kingdom (cf. Ps. 37:11). Whereas Luke included the physically hungry in his beatitudes (6:21), Matthew reapplied this term to those who hunger and thirst after righteousness (v. 6). These hungry and thirsty people could denote those who desire to conform themselves to God's will, while "righteousness" itself might refer to the coming vindication of God's people, which would be eagerly anticipated by the disciples. The pure in heart (v. 8) are told they will see God (cf. Ps. 17:15; 42:3). Such sight is a synonym for the final bliss of the kingdom (cf. Rev. 22:4).

Jesus refers to the nonmilitant character of true disciples when he urges them to be peacemakers (v. 9). He also offers specific rewards for those who have undergone persecution (v. 10; note the perfect tense of the verb). Suffering for righteousness' sake refers to faithfulness to God's law. No doubt some in Matthew's audience were presently being persecuted (cf. 23:34). Oral abuse (v. 11: revile; utter all kinds of evil against you) can be as serious as physical harm. The promise of reward (v. 12) occurs fairly frequently in Matthew (5:19, 46; 6:1; 19:29; 20:8). The reward here is not identified with a share in the kingdom, but a more specific reward for those who have undergone persecution. Persecution of the prophets is not attested within the Old Testament canon, but it is a tradition from early Judaism that is assumed in the New Testament (cf. Matt. 23:30). Jesus may refer to some of his early disciples as prophets. If so, they would be the predecessors of the audience of Matthew.

Responding to the Text

The beatitudes call the living saints to new obedience and promise them what they will become in God's new age. This might be expressed by the following alternate translations. "How to be emulated are the poor in spirit" puts the emphasis on ethics. "Congratulations to those who are poor in spirit" would suggest the ultimate role reversal that awaits people blessed in the beatitudes.

Each person preaching on the beatitudes will need to make some kind of selection among the nine. The following comments refer to vv. 3, 6, and 9.

The blessing spoken to the poor in spirit calls the listener to an attitude of dependence on God. It is a piety expressed in thanksgiving for what God has given and in prayer for daily needs. The publican's prayer, "God, be merciful to me a sinner," provides an appropriate role model. This salutary emphasis might well be contrasted with the similar beatitude in Luke (6:20) where the (economically) poor are made the special object of God's care. Whether or not the economic poor are in the worshiping congregation, they are the concern of contemporary Christians, who will be generous to them and support those societal changes that work for the eradication of poverty. Luke's emphasis on economic poverty prevents discussion of the "poor in spirit" from romanticizing poverty by focusing too much on the piety expressed by the poor. Real poverty kills, or, at least, it makes life meaner and harder than God wants it to be.

The blessing spoken on those who hunger and thirst for righteousness urges the saints today to show passion for the doing of God's will. The proper ethical question is not what can we get away with or what is permitted, but rather how can we in each and every situation maximize love for God and for the neighbor. Throughout the Sermon on the Mount Jesus calls for a higher righteousness. "Do not think that I have come to abolish the law or the prophets; I have come not to abolish but to fulfill" (5:17). Specific examples of "righteousness" might be gleaned by a reading of the entire Sermon on the Mount. If hungering and thirsting for righteousness means a strong desire for God's righteousness to become real, for God to vindicate his people, this beatitude might be related to "Your kingdom come" from the Lord's prayer. A comparison with Luke 6:21 might prevent any easy acceptance of or rationalization of physical hunger.

The blessing spoken on the peacemakers recalls the famous speech to Congress by President Jimmy Carter after the Camp David accords. Carter, a Christian, referred to the Muslim Anwar Sadat and the Jewish Menahem Begin as peacemaking children of God for the courage they exhibited in reaching that historic accord. How those three ought to be emulated! As the leading power in the world, the United States has the opportunity to be a great peacemaker. Reflecting on this beatitude might sort out the differences between enforcing our self-interest and truly seeking peace and justice (or peace through justice) throughout the world. The preacher may want to address a particular current international issue with Christian reflections. Finally, this beatitude calls all in our violence-obsessed society, where domestic violence and abuse are prevalent, to remember that peace and nonviolence begin at home. Peacemaking in the home might prevent family breakups. And parents who refrain from violence toward their children exhibit a profound role model for children who will have to face the many conflicts in an adult world.

The power to emulate these virtues, as well as the power to effect eschatological reversals, comes from one whose power or authority was exercised in the forgiveness of sins, the healing of the paralytic, or the sending of his followers into the world to make disciples of all nations.

TWENTY-FOURTH SUNDAY AFTER PENTECOST

NOVEMBER 7, 1999 / PROPER 27

REVISED COMMON	EPISCOPAL (BCP)	ROMAN CATHOLIC

Josh. 24:1-3a, 14-25;
  or Wis. 6:12-16
  or Amos 5:18-24
	Amos 5:18-24	Wis. 6:12-16

Ps. 78:1-7,
  or Wis. 6:17-20;
  or Ps. 70
	Ps. 70	Ps. 63:2, 3-4, 5-6, 7-8

1 Thess. 4:13-18	1 Thess. 4:13-18	1 Thess. 4:13-18 or 1 Thess. 4:13-14
Matt. 25:1-13	Matt. 25:1-13	Matt. 25:1-13

FIRST READING
JOSHUA 24:1-3a, 14-25

Interpreting the Text

In this second farewell address (cf. Josh. 23), Joshua begins by reciting the call of Sarah and Abraham. After a rehearsal of God's saving acts through the time of the conquest (omitted in the lectionary), Joshua poses an either-or challenge to the people: either worship the gods whom your ancestors served in Mesopotamia or worship Yahweh. Joshua, with whom the reader is expected to identify, pledges his whole household to the worship of Yahweh. Clearly the writer who recorded these words saw the principal threat in his time to be idolatry. The people eagerly chose Yahweh because of his track record in the Exodus from Egypt, his care in the wilderness, and his gift of the land in the conquest of Canaan.

Joshua did not immediately accept the people's choice and reminded them of Yahweh's character as a holy and jealous God, who would brook no disobedience or hesitate to enter into acts of judgment, even if he had shown great favor in the past. This challenge evoked an even stronger pledge to serve Yahweh. Joshua then transformed the scene to a courtroom and identified the people as witnesses against themselves that they had made this pledge. As a result the people gladly accepted their new identity. In a subsequent speech, Joshua made clear that the sin of idolatry is indeed a present reality, demanding repentance of present, and not just former, sins. The covenant he struck with them indicated that the faithful are to live in obedience.

Responding to the Text

"As for me and my household, we will serve the Lord" (v. 15). Joshua presupposes a social system in which the father of the family could commit the whole family to a specific religious action. While we no longer live in such a society, it is incumbent upon parents to help their children know the gospel and to urge them to accept it. "Serving" can connote obedience, but it also can refer to worship. This ambivalence in the Hebrew verb "serve" might suggest both a greater devotion to obedience and a deeper resolve to worship the Lord.

Our choice is not between the Lord and the gods our ancestors served beyond the River, but between the Lord and the idols of our own devising—anything that we fear, love, and trust more than we fear, love, and trust the Lord. In making this choice, the people reminded themselves of what God had done in the Exodus, the wilderness wanderings, and the entrance into the land. That is, they preached the gospel to themselves for it is the good news of God's actions that enables people to make such a choice. In helping contemporary people to make this choice, we need to tell them how God proved himself to be their God in the life, death, and resurrection of Jesus, how God made them his own in holy baptism, and how God has cared for then in a variety of ways throughout their life. "Therefore we also will serve the Lord, for he is our God." We do not believe in God in general or in the abstract, but in the God who has come very near to each one of us.

Joshua reminded the people that this is no idle choice. God is holy (entirely other) and he is jealous; that is, God brooks no rivals, no divided loyalties. Choosing God is much more than opting for church membership. Deciding for God has consequences in the way we serve, that is, in the way we worship and the way we live. Jesus calls us to discipleship. While Joshua makes a stone serve as a witness against the people in v. 27, in v. 22 he calls the people themselves to be witnesses against themselves that they have chosen the Lord. To choose the God made known to us through Jesus Christ involves a real decision, which puts our whole life at stake.

WISDOM OF SOLOMON 6:12-16 (alt.)

Interpreting the Text

The Wisdom of Solomon was composed in Egypt shortly before the turn of the era. "Wisdom," which has many meanings in the Bible, is related to creation; and wisdom can stand for the "order" that is inherent in the entire created world. Wisdom is gained by experience, and those who love wisdom can easily find her. Wise people are carefree. Because wisdom is omnipresent and available outside strictly religious realms (graciously appearing to people in their paths, v. 16), it formed an important element in early Christology.

Responding to the Text

This lesson from Wisdom invites us to reflect on the relationship between nature and grace, and on how God can be known through or in the realm of creation. What is it that makes sense in life, that reveals its true meaning? Is it not natural to worship God? Do not our highest ethical principles often echo those of other people of good will? Wisdom is as hospitable as Jesus himself, seeking us out where we are, not being distant from our cares or troubles. Wisdom meets us in our every thought. Christianity demands no sacrifice of the intellect. A faith worth believing is a faith worth thinking about and exploring.

> CHRISTIANITY DEMANDS NO SACRIFICE OF THE INTELLECT. A FAITH WORTH BELIEVING IS A FAITH WORTH THINKING ABOUT AND EXPLORING.

AMOS 5:18-24 (alt.)

Interpreting the Text

Amos warns that God's presence can mean judgment as well as grace. Those who desire God to be present need to recognize that he can be present in anger as well as in love, and that God's leadership in holy war can as easily be against Israel as it can be against foreign countries. In vv. 21-24, Amos rings the changes on the public worship of his day, not because he was against liturgy or worship, but because he recognized that religious words can be contradicted by unjust deeds. "Righteousness" in v. 24 connotes fidelity to the relationships in which one stands, whether those relationships are with God or with fellow human beings. "Justice" denotes those concrete actions done by those who live in a faithful relationship with God.

Responding to the Text

God wants more than lip service. To say that we want God to have his "day" may mask real indifference on our part. If our lives are not lived in God's presence and in obedience to God, God's day will bring terror and not joy. Our worship is or can be the greatest service we offer God. But it can also mean going through the motions or repeating pious talk that shuts out the realities of the world. The God who is not anti-intellectual is also not anti-liturgical. It is not "smells and bells" and sacraments that turn God off, but worship that does not promote faithful living or worship that does not celebrate, or plead for, God's justice. Justice and righteousness are to be as constant as the water in a waterfall.

RESPONSIVE READING

PSALM 78:1-7

Interpreting the Text

The psalmist is a wisdom teacher who calls the reader to pay attention to his words. The basic premise of the faith in this psalm is that wisdom is validated by the test of time and needs to be shared or passed on. Verse 7 outlines three foci in this tradition. We are to urge our children to hope in God or to exhort them to trust God's promises. Second, we are not to forget God's works. Those works in this psalm range from the liberation experience in the Exodus through the choice of David as king. Third, we remember God's works best by keeping his commandments and living a life of obedience.

Responding to the Text

The remaining portions of Psalm 78 recall ways in which Israel did in fact forget God in spite of his works. This culminated in the rejection of the Northern Kingdom and the choosing of Mount Zion, where the temple was, and of David (vv. 67-72). The clear implication is that Jerusalem and the king are vulnerable if the people repeat the mistakes of their ancestors by forgetting the works of God and not keeping God's commandments.

This Sunday's lessons from Joshua and Amos also urge us not to presume upon the generosity of God by honoring him only with our mouth and by thinking God will always be on our side. I well remember a seminary chapel sermon of thirty years ago that addressed the text of Isaiah 14, the account of the downfall of Babylon. The average reader on hearing this passage might nod in silent agreement with the decision that Babylon will be punished; but that creative chapel sermon reminded us that, for most people in the world today, the United States is Babylon. Seeing ourselves addressed in Isaiah 14 reminds us that God will not always give us perpetual victories over all our enemies, especially when we are a significant part of the problem. When we as a people oppress others, use an unfair portion of the world's resources, or act violently, Psalm 78 would ask us to repent and change before it is too late. We are not to forget the works of God, but keep his commandments.

WISDOM 6:17-20 (alt.)

This pericope describes an ascending chain of actions: Wisdom begins by seeking instruction; concern for instruction means love of wisdom; love of wisdom leads to keeping God's laws; keeping God's laws results in immortality; and immortality ushers one into God's presence. Hence the desire for wisdom leads to the kingdom.

PSALM 70 (alt.)

This psalm, a duplicate of Ps. 40:13-17, is an individual lament, seeking relief from personal enemies. The psalmist identifies God as "my help" and "my deliverer" and invites other believers to confess that God is great (v. 4). In asking for the defeat of the enemies, the psalmist expresses urgency and even impatience.

PSALM 63:2-8

This beautiful psalm of trust confesses that the steadfast or loyal love of God is better than life itself (v. 3). The final verses of the psalm, not included in the lectionary, indicate that the royal psalmist is threatened by enemies. The king confidently hopes in their defeat and praises God for his presence in the sanctuary and during the king's insomnia (v. 6). Among the many rich images of God in this psalm is that of a bird under whose wings the psalmist seeks refuge (v. 7).

SECOND READING
1 THESSALONIANS 4:13-18

Interpreting the Text

The second lesson for the third to last Sunday in the church year deals appropriately with issues of death and resurrection. Paul contrasts his readers with those who have no hope, that is, those who do not believe in the resurrection. Jesus' own death and resurrection are the pattern and the promise for all those who believe (v. 14).

In v. 15 Paul claims to have experienced a special revelation ("by the word of the Lord") that those who are still alive when Christ returns will have no advantage over those who have died in the meantime. He clearly expected Christ's imminent return since he included himself among those who would still be alive on the last day. Elsewhere Paul considers the possibility of his own death before the return of Christ (2 Cor. 5:1-5; Phil. 1:20-23). The word "coming" in v. 15 is a translation for the word *parousia,* which was the technical term in the Greco-Roman world for a ruler's state visit.

The Lord will come as a triumphant warrior, announced by the archangel's call and the blast of the trumpet (v. 16). All who are still living will be "caught up" (the source of the notion of a "rapture") in the clouds (cf. Dan. 7:13, where the son of man comes with the clouds of heaven). Paul does not describe the afterlife in this passage. Rather, it is enough to say that we will be with the Lord forever. He exhorts the Thessalonians to keep on encouraging one another (present imperative) with the message of death and resurrection he has just shared with them.

Responding to the Text

Hopelessness has many forms. People find themselves caught in loveless marriages or relationships and see no way to extricate themselves without serious consequences and harm to all who are involved. Others suffer extreme financial loss, through their own mistakes or through no fault of their own, and are brought to the brink of despair. Death itself, or the process of dying, leads some people to give up all hope. When hope is gone, everything is gone.

Paul uses a specific issue at Thessalonica as an occasion to bear witness to his own hope in the resurrection. I suspect that there are not many worries among contemporary Christians about whether the advantage at the resurrection will lie with those who have already died or those who are still alive at the time of Christ's return. But many in our time live with no hope either because of the problems like those outlined above or because in general they have no faith in God that transcends this life. Hopeless people make too much of this life or too little. They either act as if the pursuit of this world's goods is the only aim and purpose of life or they find life meaningless because it finally goes nowhere.

Paul had the advantage of a direct revelation from God about resurrection (v. 15). But we have the advantage of sisters and brothers in the faith assuring us of their own confidence in the resurrection and the advantage of hearing Paul's own words in 1 Corinthians 15 that in Jesus resurrection has started to happen.

"Keep on encouraging one another with these words," Paul advises. Other words, such as "Keep a stiff upper lip," or "Keep your chin up," or "Things will get better sooner or later," do not have the power of faith in the resurrection. That is a word that gives life a goal and a destiny and that suggests that God's final word to each of us will be yes and not no. The command to "keep on" recognizes the spiritual health of the people in our congregations and it acknowledges the constant need to tell the old story one more time.

MATTHEW 25:1-13

Interpreting the Text

The parable of the ten bridesmaids in its present form has a number of allegorical details, and some scholars attempt to reconstruct an earlier form of the parable lacking these allegorical overtones. As an allegory, the groom represents Christ, the ten bridesmaids stand for the expectant Christian community, the delay of the groom points to the postponement of the *parousia,* the shout in v. 6 expresses the church's longing for the consummation of the kingdom, the wedding dinner alludes to the messianic banquet, and the rejection of the foolish maidens foreshadows the final judgment. The extra flasks of oil probably show the wise bridesmaids' preparation for unexpected circumstances. It seems unlikely that the extra oil represents allegorically the amount of good works done by the bridesmaids. The last verses in Matthew 24 are parallel in thought to this parable and describe a man who also foolishly miscalculated the significance of the delay of Christ's return (24:45-51).

While most parables of the kingdom compare it to some present reality (e.g., Matt. 13:24), the word "then" in v. 1 and the future tense relate this parable to eschatological events. The bridesmaids were supposed to welcome the bride and groom into their new household; but the bride goes unmentioned in this parable. Already in v. 2 the bridesmaids are categorized in advance as foolish and wise, and the wise show their intelligence by doing careful planning for the groom's homecoming. Since all ten fall asleep, the lesson of the parable has more to do with readiness than absolute vigilance. The wise bridesmaids could sleep securely knowing that they were ready for every eventuality. The delay of the *parousia* is also alluded to in Matt. 24:36-51 and 25:19.

When the groom approaches unexpectedly at midnight, the bridesmaids start to prepare their lamps to greet him. The wise bridesmaids refuse to share their extra oil with the foolish women, who then scurry to the nearest shops in a desperate attempt to find additional oil. In their absence the groom arrived, and he and the five wise bridesmaids went to the wedding banquet and locked the door (cf. Luke 13:25; Matt. 7:22-23, where there are other harsh sayings about foolish latecomers). The groom's sharp rejection of the foolish bridesmaids indicates the seriousness of the command to be prepared for the coming kingdom (Matt. 22:11-14). The admonition to keep awake in v. 13, echoing 24:36, 42, 44, and 50, implies in this context the need for readiness and not necessarily for absolute, unsleeping vigilance.

Responding to the Text

Philipp Nicolai saw in this parable a positive encouragement for the faithful and built his hymn, "Wake, Awake for Night is Flying," around it:

> Midnight hears the welcome voices,
> And at the thrilling cry rejoices:
> "Come forth, you maidens! Night is past.
> The bridegroom comes! Awake;
> Your lamps with gladness take!"
>
> . . .
>
> Prepare yourselves to meet the Lord,
> Whose light has stirred the waiting guard.

Nicolai adds two ideas to the parable. First, he mentions the gracious invitation of the Lord for the maidens to come forth and the good news that the night is past. This world may not seem so nightlike to us, but in comparison to God's future the point is well taken. Whatever its good parts, life is also a place for tears, pain, separation, grief, and disappointment. Though we are often tempted to hold onto it with all our might, its importance pales and fades in comparison with the life that is to come.

Second, Nicolai also adds that the Lord's light—and not just the shouts or the trumpets—has stirred the waiting guard. Jesus is the light of the world who shines into the darkness of our lives. The people walking in darkness will indeed see great light (Isa. 9:2). We love light rather than darkness and therefore our Lord's return holds little terror for us. Light, dazzling light, is one metaphorical way of signaling God's presence.

How are we, almost two thousand years after Matthew, to assess the importance of the delay of the *parousia*? We might begin by noting the importance of this world as the arena for carrying out our Christian calling. We must use this world and the gifts God has given us as part of our responsibility as people created by God. But we also need to remind ourselves that even if the world were to last for thousands of years, God's impending advent calls all our assumptions into question and urges us to take with renewed seriousness how we live our lives in readiness. For whether our end comes by parousia or car wreck or heart attack, we may soon be ushered into God's presence to give account of how we lived our lives. How will it be with our "lamps"? How will we be "ready"? Luther's catechism reminds us that people are ready for communion and, I would add, for the life to come, who have faith in these words: "[Christ's body and blood] are given

> WHATEVER ITS GOOD PARTS, LIFE IS ALSO A PLACE FOR TEARS, PAIN, SEPARATION, GRIEF, AND DISAPPOINTMENT.

to you for the forgiveness of sins." We face the end of the world with confidence because Jesus has promised to be with us until the end of the age.

Nicolai threw all care to the wind in his final stanza:

> Now let all the heav'ns adore you,
> And saints and angels sing before you.
> The harps and cymbals all unite.
> Of one pearl each shining portal,
> Where, dwelling with the choir immortal,
> We gather round your dazzling light.
> No eye has seen, no ear
> Has yet been trained to hear.
> What joy is ours!
> Crescendos rise;
> Your halls resound;
> Hosannas blend in cosmic sound.

TWENTY-FIFTH SUNDAY AFTER PENTECOST

NOVEMBER 14, 1999 / PROPER 28

REVISED COMMON	EPISCOPAL (BCP)	ROMAN CATHOLIC
Judg. 4:1-7	Zeph. 1:7, 12-18	Prov. 31:10-13, 19-20,
or Zeph. 1:7, 12-18		30-31
Ps. 123;	Ps. 90 or 90:1-8, 12	Ps. 128:1-2, 3, 4-5
or 90:1-8 (9-11), 12		
1 Thess. 5:1-11	1 Thess. 5:1-10	1 Thess. 5:1-6
Matt. 25:14-30	Matt. 25:14-15, 19-29	Matt. 25:14-30
		or 25:14-15, 19-20

FIRST READING

JUDGES 4:1-7

Interpreting the Text

Most of the book of Judges, including this pericope, is dominated by a recurring pattern: the people sinned, God judged them by handing them over to an enemy, they prayed to the Lord, and the Lord delivered them. This sequence shows not only the consequences of sin, but the ever-urgent need for repentance. Jabin was a king who ruled Hazor, a very large city in north Canaan; his commander Sisera would meet a violent and dramatic death through the hands of a heroic woman named Jael (vv. 17-22). Early Israel lived during the Iron Age, and Jabin's army made use of the latest technology in lording it over the Israelites.

The hero of this account, in addition to Jael, is Deborah, who is hailed as both a prophetess and a judge. The poem in Judges 5 is generally known as the Song of Deborah. She was famous enough to have a palm tree named after her, and the Israelites came to her for help in resolving disputes. As a prophetess, Deborah received divine revelation, and she gave orders to Barak to marshal troops against Jabin and Sisera. More important than even Deborah and Barak in this crisis is God's promise to lure Sisera into an indefensible position and turn him over to Israel's control.

Responding to the Text

The pattern in the book of Judges—sin, punishment, cry to the Lord, deliverance—is characteristic also of the Christian life, both individually and collectively. The end of the church year provides an opportunity for taking assessment of our own lives and acting appropriately, through contrition and repentance, to amend our way of life. The pattern should lead to the expectation that God answers repentant sinners, repeatedly and with power. While we should never presume upon the goodness of God, the demonstration of his commitment to the human family through Christ reinforces the expectation of his readiness to save.

The texts of Judges 4 and 5 also provide strong women as role models for the community of faith. Deboráh is a prophetess who passes on the word of God that had been revealed to her (4:6-7). She served as an agent of justice in her office as judge. Deborah's song (chap. 5) is one of the oldest poems in the entire Bible. Jael, too, is an assertive woman in her courageous action to deliver Israel from the threats of Sisera (4:21-22). The church does well to point out exemplary actions of women on the contemporary scene as well as in antiquity.

All human actions, however, male or female, depend for their effectiveness on God's own intervention. His promise to give Sisera into the hands of the Israelites reminds us that we have no power or authority except that given to us by God. The threatening power of our enemies, whether they are today's nuclear nations or the iron chariots of Sisera, have not power against God.

ZEPHANIAH 1:7, 12-18

Interpreting the Text

The day of the Lord announced by Zephaniah in the reign of Josiah consists of a holy war directed *against* Judah. God's devastating judgment is described as a ruthless divine search of Jerusalem, looking for those who think that faith and discipleship make no difference. For them God has become irrelevant. Those who are rich and complacent are sentenced with frustration oracles: They will build houses and plant vineyards in vain.

Verse 14 is a clear reminder that God's future moves toward us and not we toward it. God's day is closer than anyone could imagine and the prophet exhausts himself in seeking nouns to define it: wrath, distress, anguish, ruin, devastation, darkness, gloom, clouds, thick darkness, trumpet blast, and battle cry (vv. 15-16). No amount of military protection offers safety on Yahweh's day. Sin is identified as the cause of these catastrophes in v. 17, and the coming judgment becomes comprehensive, covering all the earth, in v. 18.

Responding to the Text

The "day of the Lord" in Christianity refers to the day when Jesus will return in final victory. That day picks up the notion of the Lord's day from the

Old Testament, which was either his day of victory for Israel or his day of judgment against Israel.

God's expected coming/return calls for each of us to examine our sins of commission or indifference. Our secular age cannot be frightened into the faith. Many have discounted the possibility of God to act: "The Lord will not do good, nor will God do harm." The only effective counterproposal is to report what God has done and still continues to do in our own lives.

Even Christians have perhaps denied the coming of Christ in the very near future. Verse 14 highlights what is meant by Advent: "The great day of the LORD is near, near and hastening fast."

PROVERBS 31:10-13, 19-20, 30-31

Interpreting the Text

The Ode to a Capable Wife in vv. 10-31 gives high praise to a woman who is at once energetic and resourceful, and who has notable managerial and entrepreneurial gifts. The poem is an acrostic, that is, every verse begins with a different letter of the Hebrew alphabet.

Verses 19-20 focus on her hands. They are great assets in weaving; but the hands of this capable woman set an example for all people of good will by demonstrating generosity to the poor and the needy.

The poet may demonstrate his own chauvinism by referring to the deceitful charms and vain beauty of women; but he also acknowledges that for women as well as men the fear of the Lord is the beginning of wisdom (v. 30). Women deserve to participate in the wealth their labor generates and their personified accomplishments build their reputation in public places (v. 31).

Responding to the Text

1. The church needs to take every opportunity to recognize and acknowledge the gifts of women, especially because of its long defective record in this regard.

2. The piecemeal way in which this passage is included in the lectionary may need to be remedied by reading and reflecting on the entire passage.

3. While this is one of the best passages on women in the Old Testament, it also values this ideal woman primarily for the benefits she brings her husband. Any contemporary reflection will need to value women for their own sake.

4. What gives a person worth, whether male or female, finally transcends issues of gender. God's goal for all is to create fear/trust in all members of the human family.

RESPONSIVE READING

299

TWENTY-FIFTH
SUNDAY
AFTER PENTECOST

NOVEMBER 14

PSALM 123

Interpreting the Text

In this communal lament, verse 1 is spoken by an individual on behalf of the whole community. "Eyes" form the central image in vv. 1–3, eyes that look longingly from positions of weakness to the person in power, eyes that give God no peace until he relents and has mercy. The metaphorical use of the imagery of servant and master, mistress and maid in v. 2 is echoed ironically in the second half of the psalm where such class distinctions are the cause of the psalmists' distress. The needy people who cry to God in this psalm envision a God with cosmic power, enthroned in the heavens and not just on the cherubim. Only a God with power enough to save will do.

Verses 3–4 seek to motivate God's mercy out of compassion for the wretched state of those who pray. Their suffering stems directly from the arrogance of those who are in power. The psalmists expect God to find this situation unfair and intolerable.

Responding to the Text

This psalm graphically describes the intensity of prayer by comparing the people's prayer to the way servants look at the "hand" of their master or mistress. Do they look at the hand as the means of punishment, or do they think of it as the source of pay and food? Or do they expect that hand to deliver them from all those who mistreat or harass them? The psalmist may be calling on those who pray to endure to the end and even to importune God. Those who hold God to his promises remind themselves of the promises God has made to them. The psalmist knows that sooner or later God will have to relent from inactivity and come to save.

The community of the faithful needs to become sensitive to the fact that there are people in each of our locations who are as desperate as those described in vv. 3–4 and then develop plans to offer relief to the poor and weak or to change the oppressive system. Perhaps the sermon can highlight local injustices that are perceived by those lacking power as outrageous scorn and contempt by their enemies. Do the "truly desperate," whether in the Two-Thirds World or in our own towns, consider the church and/or its members as those who scorn and offer contempt? Can worship publicly process such pain?

PSALM 90:1-8 (9-11),12

See the discussion under the Twenty-second Sunday after Pentecost.

PSALM 128

Interpreting the Text

This wisdom psalm presents an idyllic picture of home life and has a number of parallels with Ps. 127. The first verse might be translated: "How to be emulated is everyone who fears. . . ." Faith and obedience are followed by success in one's occupation and a happy family life. The final blessings come from Jerusalem and redound to Jerusalem. Here, as in Ps. 125:5, the psalmist concludes with a benediction of peace for all Israel.

SECOND READING

1 THESSALONIANS 5:1-11

Interpreting the Text

Paul refuses to indulge in speculation about signs of the endtime lest that lead the Thessalonians to let down their guard. The "day of the Lord" may once have referred to Yahweh's victory in battle for Israel; but by the time of Amos (5:18-20) that day might also mean impending judgment for God's people. While the wicked might comfort themselves and become complacent because of the relative tranquility of their lives, their final destruction could also come as suddenly as a woman's labor pains.

In Paul's view the Thessalonians were children of the light and of the day and, therefore, they should live like daytime people. The contrast between the faithful children of light and the unfaithful children of darkness is also known in the Dead Sea Scrolls. Two metaphors are used for lack of preparation: getting drunk and falling asleep. These activities are what is expected of children of the night. Children of the day, however, will show their preparedness by putting on military garments: faith, love, and hope. Paul uses this metaphor of the well-armed/dressed soldier elsewhere (Rom. 13:12; 2 Cor. 6:7; 10:4; Eph. 6:13-17; Phil. 1:27-30). It is used of God in Isa. 59:17.

God's choice of the Thessalonians (cf. 1:4) should lead them to live in a way appropriate to their future salvation (v. 9). Salvation, not condemnation, at the final judgment, however, depends on the atoning death of Jesus Christ (Rom. 3:24-26; 2 Cor. 5:19-21). Just as in 4:13, Paul insists in v. 10 that there is no difference in regard to salvation whether one is dead (asleep) or alive (awake). He urges his Thessalonian readers to keep on encouraging one another to live like people of the day. Believers can be built up by the encouragement of other believers.

Responding to the Text

Why is it that we consider ourselves "people of the day"? The first reason is that God has in Christ called us from darkness into God's own marvelous light. Light stands for God's presence and help; darkness connotes the nefarious behavior of those who cowardly use the cover of darkness to deprive fellow beings of their property, their rights, or even their safety. Hence, counting oneself a person of the day also requires a commitment to God's agenda and to all that is good, true, just, and beautiful. The difference between night and day is the difference between drunkenness and sobriety.

Commitment to the "agenda of the day-time" involves believers in full-scale warfare against evil. Yet their uniforms consist of breastplates of faith and love and helmets of the hope of salvation. The best offense, in short, is a good defense. Radical faith, Paul reminds readers in 1 Corinthians 13, may be able to move mountains with God's help, but without love the person of faith is worth absolutely nothing. Lavish generosity and willingness for martyrdom are contradicted by the absence of love. Faith can and must be active in love.

The best defense against sliding (back) into darkness is to set one's attention on God's coming vindication of his people, on eschatological salvation. Hope for such deliverance becomes available through the ministry and mediation of Jesus. Faith, love, and hope are no abstractions or bars over which the individual must jump. They are the daily pulse of the faithful and are nurtured by individuals' support of one another in the community. That's why Paul admonishes the community to mutual encouragement and congratulates the community for already practicing it. In radical discontinuity to the ethos of the western world, the Christian community rejoices in the success of others and goes out of its way to support the development in others of faith, love, and hope.

GOSPEL

MATTHEW 25:14-30

Interpreting the Text

In this parable of the talents, Jesus offers instruction for the Christian life and urges preparedness for the *parousia*. The parallel passage in Luke 19:11-27 refutes any expectation that the kingdom of God would appear immediately (v. 11). The master, about to leave on a journey, assigns a certain amount of money to each servant and appropriate, corresponding responsibilities (v. 15). Each of the servants was given a substantial amount of money since a talent was the equivalent of 15 years of wages (see note m in NRSV). The slave with five talents "worked" with them in trading or investing and earned an additional five. The slave with two talents acted similarly; but the person with only one talent settled for hiding his master's money in a hole in the ground.

Verse 19 notes that a long time had passed during the master's absence, perhaps referring to the delay of the *parousia;* "settling accounts" denotes the final judgment. When the first two slaves make their reports, the master calls them good and trustworthy, promises to put them in charge of many things, and invites them to enter their master's joy. Their faithfulness consisted in their acting in a trustworthy way that included some risk-taking. St. Paul notes that the kingdom of God is not food and drink but righteousness and peace and joy in the Holy Spirit (Rom. 14:17).

The person entrusted with one talent admitted he had acted out of fear since his master was a harsh man, reaping where he had not sown. The master actually confirms that the slave had accurately understood his master's character—he was the kind of person who could turn a profit out of nothing—although he significantly omits the slave's use of the adjective *harsh*. He scolds the slave for his inaction and laziness. The least the slave could have done was to turn the investment over to the bankers, who could have brought him a profit without any effort on his own part. The passive construction in v. 29 suggests that it is God who will give more to those who have something and will take away what little they have from those who have nothing. Jesus makes the same point in 13:12. If a person is open to God's plan of salvation (the secrets of the kingdom), he or she will make great progress in understanding it; but if one closes oneself to this plan, one can lose the offer itself (cf. Mark 4:25; Luke 8:16). There may be a criticism of contemporary Judean leaders in this proverbial saying. The inaction of the slave, in any case, earns him damnation, where people will weep and gnash their teeth (cf. Matt. 8:12, 13:42, 13:50; 22:13, and 24:51).

Responding to the Text

The Gospel for this Sunday follows and builds on the parable of the ten bridesmaids from the previous Sunday. The parable explicates Matt. 25:13: "Keep awake therefore for you know neither the day nor the hour." How does one keep awake? How does one become like the wise bridesmaids?

At the end of the church year we often speak of the nearness of Christ's return, but this parable presupposes his delay and provides guidance on how to live responsibly in Christ's absence. The fear of the slave with one talent led him to excessive caution: he did not keep awake. Verse 29 comments more generally on God's retribution. All those who have [talents or whatever], such as the disciples, will receive even more; those who do not have much or do not understand the significance of what they have will lose even their small possessions. Jesus seems to be referring to the scribes or others among the religious leaders of his day.

Clearly, this is not a lesson on investing nor even necessarily about money. The translation "talents" may tempt us to concentrate too closely on individual abilities. What are we to do with everything God has given us? One way to focus a sermon would be to ask how the picture of God's rule in the Scriptures might be translated into a day-to-day lifestyle. When we read that God favors the poor, desires to offer forgiveness, or seeks to transform lives, how might we implement this as Christians in our families, our workplace, or our communities?

Another way to organize a sermon would be to ask about the responsibility of those who have heard, understood, and accepted the good news about Jesus. Are we not to tell that story to those who have never heard the gospel or who have misheard it as something judging and legalistic? Both of these proposals put more stress on the faithful servants, who were entrusted with ten and five talents respectively.

How might the attitude of the rich master be translated into Christian proclamation? He was a person who reaped where he did not sow, and gathered where he had not scattered seed. Is the only response to inactivity terror? Or might one try to emulate this master by loving where there was little thought of return or forgiving when the other party would continue in hostility? Might we learn to see in others God's creation when the culture would despise such persons as ignorant, poor, handicapped, and of no economic worth? These questions are not asking so much what Jesus or Matthew might have meant, but what sort of response does a modern reader have to this most unique image? And cannot this characterization be used fruitfully to understand the significance of Jesus? He did not go to the rich and powerful and pious. He called a ragtag group of disciples and made them the basis of his church. He takes sinners and makes them saints.

> MIGHT WE LEARN TO SEE IN OTHERS GOD'S CREATION WHEN THE CULTURE WOULD DESPISE SUCH PERSONS AS IGNORANT, POOR, HANDICAPPED, AND OF NO ECONOMIC WORTH?

Keeping awake is "as if" (v. 14). Jesus offers a comparison that may have been understood first of all as encouragement to his disciples and as criticism of the scribes. Twin dangers attend the preparation of a sermon on this text: Either we too quickly identify ourselves or other prominent people in the church as the persons with ten or five talents, or we congratulate ourselves on our own achievement without recognizing that we are what we are because Jesus made something out of our nothingness.

LAST SUNDAY
AFTER PENTECOST

REVISED COMMON	EPISCOPAL (BCP)	ROMAN CATHOLIC
Ezek. 34:11-16, 20-24	Ezek. 34:11-17	Ezek. 34:11-12, 15-17
Ps. 100	Ps. 95:1-7	Ps. 23:1-2, 2-3, 5-6
Eph. 1:15-23	1 Cor. 15:20-28	1 Cor. 15:20-26, 28
Matt. 25:31-46	Matt. 25:31-46	Matt. 25:31-46

FIRST READING
EZEKIEL 34:11-16, 20-24

Interpreting the Text

The first part of this chapter indicts the shepherds (the kings of Israel) for aggrandizing themselves at the expense of their sheep (the people of Israel). In vv. 11-16, Yahweh, the good shepherd, promises to seek out those sheep who have been scattered or exiled on the Lord's day against Israel (a day of clouds and thick darkness v. 12). The new Exodus announced by Ezekiel will have many starting points in different countries, but one destination, the land of Israel. In that land God will feed the people, give them rest and security, and provide special protection and help to all who are weak or injured.

Verses 17-19 indict bad sheep (people), who make it difficult for other sheep (people) to get decent food and drinking water. Yahweh particularly indicts the fat sheep (rich and powerful people) who throw their weight around to the great disadvantage of the weak. In saving the flock, Yahweh will also sort out the bad sheep from the good (vv. 20-22; cf. Ezek. 20:35-38).

In the final two verses of this pericope, Yahweh promises to set up a shepherd-messiah, a new David, who will provide food for the people and serve as their shepherd in God's stead. In addition to citing the first part of the so-called covenant formula, "I will be their God" (often followed by "you shall be my people"), Ezekiel's God promises that the new David will serve as "prince" among the people. Ezekiel has very little use for his contemporary Judahite kings and has great difficulty identifying the messiah as a king in the line of David. Instead, picking up an old word from Israelite traditions, he calls this future heir of David a "prince," that is, a "king" in quotation marks, a monarch with built-in checks and balances. The messiah will have a role as the prime worshiper in Israel (46:11-12); but he also will be effectively blocked from the schemes his predecessors used to exploit people financially and in other ways.

305

LAST SUNDAY
AFTER PENTECOST

NOVEMBER 21

Responding to the Text

In the midst of Israel's exile, Ezekiel focuses on the kingship of Yahweh. Yahweh's royal role is not one of domination, but of protecting all the weak and injured sheep who have suffered in Israel's wars. As king, Yahweh will also bring about a new Exodus (cf. Exod. 15:18) and will provide food for all the people. This royal Yahweh is the exact opposite of all the earthly kings who ruled over Judah and who used their power only to exploit the people.

God's rule over the world often takes place mediately, through human agents. At the end of Genesis 1 God establishes men and women as the vice presidents of his earthly estate, created in his image, and charged with ruling the world wisely. Yahweh had promised to serve as father to David, and designated him as God's son. Ezekiel's Davidic and messianic prince will reign in God's name and in God's stead. He is the sign of the covenant that continues to exist between God and Israel.

God's word is the guarantee of this future according to Ezekiel ("I the Lord, have spoken," v. 24). According to Christian belief, Jesus plays the role of Davidic king. He fed people through his many miraculous feedings, and he was present with the people not as a prince, but as a servant. Not only did his word demonstrate God's promise, but he himself was that word of God that took up its presence in our midst. This king-crowned-with-thorns also takes care of all the spiritual and physical needs of his people. Just like king Yahweh in Ezekiel, Jesus brought back those who had gone astray, bound up the injured, and strengthened the weak; but he also brought down the strong (v. 16).

Responsive Reading

PSALM 100

Interpreting the Text

This hymn of praise and thanksgiving adds to the shepherd/sheep imagery that is abundant in the lessons for this Sunday. In v. 3 the psalmist asserts an interesting doctrine of creation: God has made us and therefore we belong to him. We are God's people, or the sheep of his own pasture. Using a creation theology, the psalmist includes all people and all things in an invitation to praise (v. 1). God's goodness (v. 5) is defined or made clear by two other characteristics. God's loyalty to his people and the reliability of his promises can be counted on, now and forever.

Responding to the Text

The king hailed in this psalm rules over all peoples, and the whole earth is invited to worship and fall down before him. While the term "king" itself is not used of Yahweh in this psalm, the people identify themselves as God's sheep and therefore God is the divine shepherd-king. It is often stated that the word translated "thanks" in the Psalter should usually be translated "praise." I can thank a person by just saying, "Thank you." But when I praise someone I have to say it in a whole sentence and a third party is almost always involved. Praise of Yahweh takes place because of his steadfast love and faithfulness, and that testimony is given to all of us readers so that we can both believe and join the praise.

PSALM 95:1-7

Interpreting the Text

The familiar words of the Venite (vv. 1-7) are followed by words of admonition (vv. 8-11). God's kingship puts everything under divine control: depths and heights, sea and dry ground. Verse 6 hails God as creator. The metaphor in v. 7 is curiously ambivalent about seeing ourselves as people and as sheep. While one would expect sheep to be associated with pastures and people with God's hand, the poet mixes the metaphor and therefore provides new opportunities for reflection.

Responding to the Text

As king, Yahweh is greater than any of the other gods. As preserver of the world, he literally has the whole world in his hands, and his ownership is certified by his creation of the totality of this cosmos, both its sea and its dry land. Bowing and kneeling before Yahweh the king, the psalmists confess God as *our* maker.

This psalm is used in Morning Prayer and elsewhere without vv. 7b-11. The remaining psalm makes eminent sense by itself, but the church in singing a truncated version tends to deemphasize the transformative power that God intends to exert on his people. The very ones who shout Yahweh's praises need to be warned about the consequences of having one's heart go astray and of not paying attention to God's ethical ways. The first Exodus generation did not get to enter the land of rest (v. 11); but the Book of Hebrews, in commenting on this psalm, affirms that there still remains a Sabbath rest for the people of God (4:9). Through the kingship of Jesus, the way into Yahweh's promised rest has been reopened.

See Twentieth Sunday after Pentecost.

Second Reading
EPHESIANS 1:15–23

Interpreting the Text

The writer of the second lesson gives thanks for the two great virtues of the Ephesians: their faith in the Lord Jesus and their love for one another. He prays that God will give them in addition a spirit of wisdom, that is, a humble knowledge of God and a sense of how to live appropriately. Such knowledge will enlighten the readers and raise their sights by the glorious expectation of things to come. These expectations include the hope to which they have been called, the riches of his glorious inheritance among the saints, and the greatness of God's power for us. The inheritance among the "saints" probably refers in this verse to life among the angels, whereas the writer uses "saints" elsewhere to refer to members of the earthly congregation in (1:1, 15).

God's power was demonstrated when God raised Jesus from the dead and exalted him to his present seat at God's right hand (Ps. 110:1). Whereas Paul refers to the church as Christ's body made up of diverse members, here the writer exalts Christ as the *head* of the church, a concept that is never mentioned in unquestionably authentic Pauline letters. The last clause in v. 23—"the fullness of him who fills all in all"—is highly debated. It may mean that Christ is incomplete until the church provides for him that which is lacking. Or it may mean that Christ is the source and goal of the body's growth.

Responding to the Text

It would be hard to give someone a better compliment than the one the author extends to the Ephesians. He has heard of their faith in the Lord Jesus and their love toward one another. But he prays in addition that they may come to know the hope to which Christ has called them.

Faith, love, and hope (cf. 1 Corinthians 13)! Hope includes the knowledge that Christ now enjoys a glorious inheritance among the angels (v. 18). Life is sometimes meaningless or humdrum, going nowhere. But the present exaltation of Christ is at the same time a promise for what we shall all become. In 4:1 the author begs his readers to lead a life worthy of the calling to which they have been called. He could have added that they—and we—should lead a life worthy of the hope to which we have been called. That would include dissatisfaction with the many compromises of life and a joy in doing the good works which God prepared beforehand to be our way of life (2:10). We are all called to equip the saints for their work of ministry until we all come to the unity of faith and to maturity in Christ (4:12-13).

Hope also means that we know God has put great power into action *for us,* just as he demonstrated great power in raising Christ from the dead. Many people feel powerless because of their social location in life, their work, their family, or their lack of success. Hope recognizes that God has used great power for us so that we indeed can view ourselves as power-filled.

Christ's lordship over all things is for the sake of the church. The whole cosmos, therefore, works efficiently for the benefit of the church, and the church needs to see that it is also responsible for the care of the whole cosmos. Power is not an end in itself, but power is used for the sake of God's people. Later the author concludes: "I pray that you may have the power to comprehend . . . what is the breadth

> THE WHOLE COSMOS, THEREFORE, WORKS EFFICIENTLY FOR THE BENEFIT OF THE CHURCH, AND THE CHURCH NEEDS TO SEE THAT IT IS ALSO RESPONSIBLE FOR THE CARE OF THE WHOLE COSMOS.

and length and height and depth, and to know the love of Christ that surpasses knowledge, so that you may be filled with all the fullness of God" (3:18-19).

SECOND READING
1 CORINTHIANS 15:20-28

Interpreting the Text

All the Judeans at the time of Jesus believed in the resurrection, with the notable exception of the Sadducees. What was new about Christ is that he was the first human being who was in fact raised, and with his resurrection the new age has begun to dawn. Paul's Adam-Christ typology means that through Adam death came to all just as through Christ resurrection and life will come to all. We humans must wait for our time of resurrection until the second coming of Christ when he will have accomplished all of his remaining tasks, including especially his defeat of death itself. The personification of death is well known in the Old Testament (Ps. 33:19; Jer. 9:21). By putting all things under his feet, Christ will implicitly fulfill the words of Pss. 8:7 and 110:1. Only one thing is not included in the word "all," namely God himself. Once Christ has subjected everything else to his rule, he will subject himself to God who then will be "all in all."

While the Gospel reading for this day stresses human accountability at the second coming of Christ, this second reading from 1 Corinthians stresses the great hope that is part of the expectation of Christ's coming. The return of Christ will mean resurrection for all who have died, and the guarantee of that is Christ's own resurrection and subsequent rule, a rule that will lead to victory over death itself.

Because the resurrection of the dead is one of the signs of the new age, and since in Christ such resurrection has already started to happen, we Christians should expect and welcome other signs of the new age: the gift of the spirit, the inclusion of the nations, and even some signs of eschatological peace. The resurrection of Christ, therefore, fills believers with zeal for trying to implement these signs of God's future in our present lives.

At Christ's coming, the saving rule of Christ will be complete. Once again he will be able to say, "It is finished." Until then Christ and we believers, too, struggle against "rulers and authorities and powers" that are allied against Christ and the church (v. 24).

Gospel

MATTHEW 25:31-46

Interpreting the Text

In this description of the judgment of the nations, discipleship is characterized by care for the needy. This not a denial of the need for faith, but it shows that real faith is always active in love. The pericope deals with the behavior of disciples who are already in the church. It shows them how to live as they wait for Christ's return.

All the nations, including Israel, will be gathered before the enthroned Son of Man, who will separate them into two groups like a shepherd, who divides a flock between sheep and goats. The background for this motif lies in Ezek. 34:17-22, where God makes a distinction between good and bad sheep, that is, between good and bad members of the house of Israel. Those on the right-hand side of the king are invited to enter the kingdom, while those on the left are ordered to go to the place of eternal punishment, prepared for the devil and his angels. According to the book of Revelation, the devil, the beast, and the false prophet will all be thrown into a lake of fire (Rev. 20:10).

Six acts of mercy toward the needy are identified as marks of love for Christ. Too much emphasis should not be placed on the apparent surprise of the righteous. Rather, their questions allow the Son of Man to reinforce the point that service to the needy equals love for Christ. In his earlier reply to John the Baptist, John identified his own similar miraculous acts of mercy as signs that he in fact was the one who was to come (Matt. 11:2-6).

The NRSV's inclusive translation "who are members of my family" in v. 40 is not a completely satisfactory rendering for the Greek "brothers." A brother or sister in Matthew may be a member of the Christian community (12:48-50; 18:15); but the term can also refer to *any* human being who is a potential object of our ethical duty to help the lowly (cf. Matt. 5:22-24; 7:3-5). The wider referent of the term brother/sister seems to be intended in this pericope. Note that the word "brothers" ("members of my family" is not used at all in the Son of Man's response to the wicked in v. 45). The two camps into which all people will be divided is characteristic of other (proto-) apocalyptic passages in the Bible (Isa. 66:24; Dan. 12:2). The passage as a whole shows how seriously Jesus considered the ethical behavior of the disciples.

Responding to the Text

This text is very familiar, perhaps even in this age of relative biblical illiteracy. Such familiarity can prevent us from hearing it afresh, or we can succumb to the moralism and even self-righteousness that have so often accompanied its reading. Here are a few pointers on the way to a sermon that seeks fresh understandings.

1. This pericope is a call to life now rather than a clear picture of what Judgment day will be like. The social ministry of the church as a whole is also to characterize the ministry of individuals in their daily lives and citizenship. While support for the church as institution is important, we must never forget that the church exists primarily for the world and its welfare and transformation. The vivid concreteness of the text needs to be matched by concrete diagnosis of the ministerial settings in which we find ourselves.

2. Service to Christ takes place indirectly through care for the least of his sisters and brothers. They are the members of Christ's family only insofar as all human beings are members of that family. That is, human need is the focus, not just helping "our own kind." Generous use of time and money for the most marginal in society must be balanced by attention to those social changes that will eliminate or reduce the causes of hunger, thirst, and imprisonment.

3. Jesus himself serves as the model of such ministry throughout the Gospel of Matthew, as well as the other Gospels. His miracles of healing and feeding are signs of God's preferential option for the dispossessed. His message to the disciples of John showed that his ministry was a fulfillment of Isaiah's prophetic expectations (Matt. 11:2-6).

4. A church that takes the Great Commission as its marching orders knows that evangelistic outreach must be balanced by a teaching ministry (Matt. 28:19-

20). We are to create disciples, not just members. Teaching "everything that I have commanded you" would include prominently the words of Jesus in Matt. 25:31-46. All nations are the goal of the Christian mission, and the weak and disadvantaged of those nations need to be central in the church's concern. North American Christians need to take more seriously the ways in which our lifestyle choices often have adverse effects on the rest of the people in the world.

5. As with many other texts in Matthew, this pericope on the last judgment could prove to be overwhelming, just as the Sermon on the Mount enunciates an ethic seemingly beyond our powers to realize it. But Jesus adds an important reminder at the end of the Great Commission that provides strength and empowerment for all disciples along the way: "I am always with you." Jesus was "with" the disciples as he walked the streets of Palestine, as he dined with them at the last supper, as he hung on the cross, and as he rose triumphantly from the tomb. In being with them, he demonstrated that he did not let their failings alienate him. Jesus promised to remain as an abiding presence even after his earthly departure. Being with someone is often a way to empower that person. In Christ's presence the church finds its resource to demonstrate a faith that is active in love and that hopes for—rather than fears—the final day of judgment.